BERNARD NESFIELD-COO̶ fessional life as a businessman, school teacher, ~~~ writer. Most recently he was principal of Hawkwood College, an independent centre for adult education. His publications include *Rudolf Steiner's Vision of Love* and *The Mystery of the Two Jesus Children.*

By the same author:
The Mystery of the Two Jesus Children
Rudolf Steiner's Vision of Love
William Blake: Prophet of Universal Brotherhood

MICHAEL AND THE TWO-HORNED BEAST

*The Challenge of Evil Today in the Light
of Rudolf Steiner's Science of the Spirit*

Bernard Nesfield-Cookson

TEMPLE LODGE

Dedicated—in deep affection—to the memory of Herta Bredendiek (20 January 1909–20 April 1995) who, during her entire adult life, cared for and taught boys and girls who were in need of special care—first at Lauenstein in Germany and then, for over 50 years, at Mikaelgården in Sweden. 'Liebt das Böse—gut'* was written as a motto and goal in one of her diaries.

* From Christian Morgenstern's poem 'Brüder' ('Brothers'). 'Liebt das Böse—gut' could be translated into English somewhat as follows: 'Through the Power of Love transform Evil so that it becomes Good'.

Contents

Amid the storm of the world,
In which our souls share,
We seek the fiery leader of the Angel-host,
Michael, Lord of true human thinking.
His sword of iron drives away fear
Which would entangle and ensnare man's will,
His radiant purposes can fill our souls
With Light Divine when autumn darkens earth.
He leads to Christ, and fights for Christ, for ever;
So may we follow him, and fight beside him
With our whole being's love, and thought, and fire.

*Adam Bittleston**

* In: *Meditative Prayers for Today* (Christian Community Press, London, 1953).

Acknowledgements

I owe a special debt to Peter Tradowsky and Wolfgang Weirauch and F. Herbert Hillringhaus. Their various books and essays touching on the main theme discussed in the following pages have rendered me helpful guidance.

In particular, I wish to record my fraternal gratitude to Stephen Roberts. His many editorial suggestions have been incorporated into the text to its considerable improvement.

I also wish to thank Eileen Lloyd for her careful copy-editing, and the librarian at Rudolf Steiner House, Margaret Jonas, for her willing assistance on numerous occasions.

My gratitude is also extended to Sevak Gulbekian of Temple Lodge for bringing *Michael and the Two-horned Beast* to publication.

As on previous occasions I also have to thank my wife, Ruth, for her understanding, patience and encouragement.

Prologue

In traditional angelologies Michael—whose name means 'like unto God'—is described as an Archangel, one among seven such spiritual beings who have a certain influence on humankind, the earth, its seasons and its evolution. Traditionally, Michael's period of maximum influence is the autumn, culminating in a festival named after him on 29 September. He is commemorated for his deed of slaying the Dragon. Usually depicted with sword and shield, Michael is the standard bearer and preparer of the way for Christ.

In Rudolf Steiner's spiritual science Michael's function is accorded far greater significance. The spiritual being known as Michael is, in fact, pivotal to Rudolf Steiner's conception of the life and evolution of both mankind and the cosmos. He is the Guardian of Cosmic Intelligence. Steiner speaks of him as being the 'fiery Prince of Thought in the Universe' (GA 26,* 17/08/24). Michael, Rudolf Steiner states, has always worked so 'that which works as intelligence throughout the whole cosmos should ultimately become concentrated within the human individuality' (GA 137, 08/08/24).

Michael conveys thoughts and ideas through which we can comprehend the spiritual and gain intellectual understanding of the physical world. He conveys to the human intellect the original thought forces of the Gods, 'full of soul and inwardly warm' (GA 26, 23/11/24).

Rudolf Steiner speaks of Michael maintaining the balance between a world-picture, which is too much disembodied fantasy (i.e. dominated by Lucifer), and world-intellect, which is too literal and materialized (i.e. dominated by Ahriman) (cf. GA 26, 30/11/24). Christ, too, 'holds' the balance between these two extremes. We shall see in the following pages that Christ and Michael are closely 'intertwined', for Michael is the Countenance of the Christ.

* See Bibliography on p. 353ff.

* * *

At the core of Rudolf Steiner's spiritual science lies the concept that it was Christ who brought to human beings the power which makes them individualized ego-beings, capable of developing love out of their own strength; that it was Christ who brought the power of self-generated creative thought to mankind.

Also at the core of Steiner's spiritual science is the recognition that it was Christ's ministry of three years, His suffering, Crucifixion and Ascension—Steiner usually speaks of this as being the 'Mystery of Golgotha'—which has given meaning and purpose to both human and cosmic life and evolution.[1]

* * *

In our materialistic and sceptical age it is difficult for the majority of people to take seriously the notion of the existence of real spiritual beings who are evil. The materialist and sceptic believes that the New Testament's account of Christ's experiences of the Devil and Satan in the wilderness can mean nothing other than that the temptation must have been, at most, in His own soul, certainly not spoken by any Devil or Satan. However, that there are Beings of Light such as Angels and Archangels in the spiritual worlds has been the direct personal experience not only of past founders of religions but also of, say, those who have gone through near-death experiences in the present age. And likewise there are 'evil' beings, spirits of darkness, who 'tempt' human beings today, just as they once tempted Christ in the wilderness.

These beings are neither hallucinations nor human inventions, but are clearly perceived by those with spiritual 'sight' as realities.

Rudolf Steiner characterizes two categories of evil beings in particular, and to their leaders he gave the time-honoured names of Lucifer and Ahriman. They are evil in the sense that they both strive to hinder the human being's spiritual development. The former says, 'You shall be as gods'; the latter, 'You are essentially no different from animals, and you have neither soul nor spirit. The world in which you spend your days is nothing but a machine.'

This is all that needs to be said of the spiritual beings at this point. But they are an essential element in Rudolf Steiner's world outlook and they will be referred to again in the following pages by the names given to them here.

1. Michael

In the revelations of St John the Divine we are given an archetypal picture of Michael's battle with evil, with the Dragon (12:1–9 and 13–17).

This picture of the battle between Michael and the Dragon is not to be seen as a description of a single conflict which took place in the distant past in the spiritual world, but as a symbol of many such confrontations during the course of world and human evolution.

Rudolf Steiner draws our attention to the fact that the image of the conquest of Michael over the Dragon has been understood in different ways during the process of human evolution. Consistent throughout, however, has been the recognition that Michael is the spiritual being who has cast the adversarial Spirit, the Dragon, down to earth.

The Michael–Dragon battle, described in John's Revelation as taking place in heaven, was transferred to the human soul. In answer to the question as to the whereabouts of the Dragon after his expulsion from heaven, from the spiritual world, Rudolf Steiner on one occasion gave the following answer:

> Anywhere wherever there were human beings on earth. That's where he was. Michael must henceforth continue the struggle within human nature... The outer cosmic conflict of Michael and the Dragon was transferred to the inner human being, because only in human nature could the Dragon now find his sphere of action. [GA 223, 27/09/23]

In regard to the presence of the Dragon, of evil, we might ask: 'Is it not unwise on the part of Providence to allow human beings to be subjected, exposed to the power of such a force? Would it not have been wiser to have averted such a frightful fate from the outset?'

In one of his lectures on St John's Revelation Rudolf

Steiner answers this question in the following simple, yet profound, terms:

> If it were impossible for human beings to sink into the abyss of evil, they would not have been able to attain what on the one hand we call love and on the other freedom; since to the spiritual scientist freedom is inseparably connected with the idea of love... Those unable, of their own free decision, to choose good or evil would be beings who would only be led on the leading-string to a good which must be attained of necessity and who had no power to choose the good of their own fully purified will, by the love which springs from freedom. If it were impossible for men and women to follow in the trail of the monster with two horns, it would also be impossible for them to follow God out of their own individual love. [GA 104, 30/06/08]

The Dragon is not a being who should be blindly resisted, nor is he a force we should contemplate banishing from our souls. For it is through his activity—or rather through the interactivity between evil and good—that something of vital importance for human development, namely, freedom, is brought into being. We shall consider this matter in greater detail in due course; for the moment we may say that without the presence of the Dragon—confining ourselves here to Johns' imagery—neither independence of thought nor freedom of will would be possible. Without the conflict between Michael and the Dragon within the soul the human being would have become an automaton.

* * *

Rudolf Steiner has given us, in a form relevant to our time, what had previously been taught by, for instance, Hermes Trismegistus, Dionysius the Areopagite,[1] the great teachers of the School of Chartres, and by the Rosicrucians, namely, the reality of the ninefold order of spiritual, hierarchical beings—from Angels, Archangels, Archai, through the Exusiai, Dynamis and Kyriotetes, to the Thrones, Cherubim and Seraphim. Each nation is guided by a spiritual being of the rank of an Archangel (Folk Spirit). Humanity as a whole, however, receives impulses in its evolution from a spiritual

being of a higher rank than that of the Archangels, namely,
from the rank of the Archai.

The instreaming of new impulses into human evolution
during each period of about 350 years is fostered successively
by seven guiding Archangels who, during their respective
'reigns', act as Time Spirits (Archai). Each such Time Spirit
has particular missions to fulfil. Early in the sixteenth century
Gabriel, who directs the forces of the Moon, became the
ruling Archangel. In 1879 the rulership was assumed by
Michael, the Archangel of the Sun. Just as the planet Moon
and Sun differ radically from each other, so also do these two
archangelic Ages manifest fundamentally different features.
Some basic difference may be indicated as follows:

Gabriel Age (1510–1879)	*Michael Age* (1879–*c.*2233)
Emphasis on heredity, blood relationships	Emphasis on spiritual relationships
Nationalism	Cosmopolitanism
Materialistic science	Spiritual science
Earth-bound, brain-bound intelligence	Brain-free intelligence
Analysis, fragmentation	Synthesis, holism
Christ peripheral; made human or ignored.	Christ central; cosmic.

The impulses issuing from these two Archangels are
characterized by Steiner:

Gabriel rules over the whole realm of the physical forces of
heredity within humanity. He is the supersensible Spirit who is
connected essentially with the sequence of the generations...
Michael is the Archangel who in his rulership has paramountly
to do with the power of the intelligence in mankind, with
everything, therefore, that concerns the intellectual, the spiritual
evolution and culture of mankind.

Steiner then goes on to say:

In any study of the earthly circumstances of humanity it is
extremely important to realize that the Gabriel rulership,

which in the spiritual sphere has an effect upon what is most deeply *physical*, is always followed by the regency of Michael, who has to do with the *spiritual* element in culture [GA 240, 19/07/24].

As we have just noted, it was Gabriel who, as the Time Spirit from 1510 to 1879, guided mankind ever more closely into materialism. This guidance into materialism should not be regarded as being either a negative or a retrogressive influence. As Rudolf Steiner repeatedly emphasized, it was necessary that human beings should lose their atavistic clairvoyance altogether and, as a consequence, cease to see into the spiritual world, cease to have an instinctive relationship with the spiritual world. As long as human beings could see spiritual beings without making any conscious effort, they could do no other than believe in their existence and activity. But the possibility of disbelief was—and is—an essential part of human freedom.

It was also a part of Gabriel's mission to infuse a strengthened sense of nationhood into the various peoples of the earth and to foster in them a sense of patriotism.

We could ask ourselves: why is it that such strong nationalistic feeling is so blatantly obvious today when it is Michael who is the Time Spirit? On one occasion Steiner answers this question in the following few words: 'It is only by degrees that the impulse of Michael can make its way into what is, to a great extent, a legacy from the past reign of Gabriel' (GA 240, 19/07/24).

Steiner then goes on to say that when a Michael Age dawns a longing begins to grow among men and women to overcome racial distinctions. A further characteristic of the Michael-impulse is the striving to foster and spread throughout the nations of the earth the most spiritual form of culture. 'Michael's rulership is always characterized by the growth of cosmopolitanism [and] by the spread of a spiritual impulse among peoples who are ready to receive it, no matter what language they speak' (ibid.).

* * *

Michael's task as Time Spirit is of quite a different nature than Gabriel's nationalistic one. First and foremost, he has a special relationship with the Christ. From him flows the impulse which we, in freedom, can take into ourselves and thereby create a personal relationship with the living Christ as He is now—in the etheric.[2] This is quite a different relationship from that prevailing before Michael's ascendency in the latter half of the nineteenth century, when, certainly for the vast majority of men and women, the approach to Christ was made through the mediation and under the authority of the Church. Today, in ever-increasing numbers, men and women seek the path towards Christ through their own initiative in spiritual development.

Through the Michael-impulse the opportunity is given to us to come together as free individuals so that we recognize not only our common humanity but also the Christ who lives within each one of us—no matter to which nation or race each one of us as individuals may belong. Under the regency of Michael the principle of nationality has ceased to be in harmony with the spirit of the time. However, whenever a new impulse in the evolutionary process begins to make itself felt, hindering forces—luciferic and ahrimanic—also begin to become more active. It is these forces which transform a healthy patriotism into the 'evil' of adamant nationalism and, in many quarters, opposing religious fanaticisms.

Something of the quality of the Michael-impulse may be perceived in a lecture Rudolf Steiner gave a few weeks after the cessation of the First World War. Here he stresses the need to cultivate genuine human brotherhood, to cultivate elective affinity instead of remaining confined to mere blood affinity. Expressed differently: we need to move out of the 'remnants' of the Gabriel Age and enter fully into the Michael Age.

Such an elective affinity—a realized consequence of the power of the Michael-impulse—does not, of course, deny the reality of blood affinity; it does, however, cross the boundaries of both family and nation (GA 186, 07/12/18).

As described above, seven Archangels 'take turns' as

rulers during a period from 300 to 400 years each. Michael, however, is the spiritual being who rises from the Hierarchy of the Archangels to that of the Archai. This is an evolutionary process which is taking place in our time:

> ... evolution embraces all beings. Beings are in an ascending evolution, and we live in the era when Michael, the chief of those of the nature of the Archangels, passes over into the nature of the Archai. He will gradually pass over into a Guiding Being, he will become the Spirit of the Time, the being who leads and guides the whole of humanity. It is of the utmost importance that we should understand this. It means that something which in all previous epochs was not there for the whole of mankind now can and *must* [author's italics] become a possession of all mankind. What formerly appeared among certain people here and there—spiritual deepening—can now be something for the whole of mankind. [GA 152, 18/05/19]

The last time Michael assumed the spiritual responsibility of rulership he was still of the Hierarchy of the Archangels. This was during the centuries leading up to the Incarnation of Christ. At that time Michael was a messenger of Yahveh (the Hebrew word for God). He was the countenance of Yahveh (GA 194, 22/11/19). Part of his task at that time was to prepare, with the Hebrews, the right conditions for the Incarnation of Christ in Jesus. From the time of the Incarnation he is no longer the messenger, the countenance, of Yahveh, but has that role in respect of Christ.

In a lecture dealing with some aspects of the Michael Impulse and the Mystery of Golgotha Rudolf Steiner makes the following statement:

> If one wants to understand the evolution of mankind, one must understand that Michael too has evolved: one must understand that it is the same being who paved the way for the preparation of the Mystery of Golgotha, and who now in our day paves the way for the understanding of the Mystery of Golgotha. Then, however, he was a Folk Spirit, now he is a Time Spirit; then he was the Messenger of Yahveh, now he is the Messenger of Christ. We speak of the Christ in the right way when we speak of Michael and his mission, knowing that Michael, who was for-

merly the bearer of the Jehovah-mission, is now the bearer of the
Mission of the Christ. [GA 152, 20/05/19]

Spiritual beings are not static, they are involved in a constant process of evolution. Michael is a spiritual being whose
task is constantly changing too. For example, in earlier times
he was experienced as an active conqueror of the Dragon.
Today, however, he assumes a 'waiting and watching' stance
in his relation to human beings. He does not exert any form
of coercion. So, for instance, as we shall see later, he leaves us
free as to whether we follow the path towards the experience
of the Etheric Christ or not.

> We are presently living in the age of the Michael-Revelation.
> This revelation exists in the same way that earlier revelations
> did. But it does not force itself upon us, because humanity has
> entered the evolutionary phase of developing freedom. [GA 194
> 23/11/19]

Out of our own free will we must approach the Michael
Revelation. We must so prepare ourselves that Michael may
imbue us with the strongest forces so that we may become
aware not only of the reality of the spiritual world but also of
the supersensible in our immediate earthly surroundings.

Michael is a spiritual being who concerns himself most of
all with that which human beings create out of the spirit. He
differs greatly from the other ruling Archangels, for they live
more with the causes of what human beings create, whereas
he lives with the consequences. Whereas the other Archangels 'prompt' human beings as to what they should do, how
they should act, Michael 'wants to be the spiritual hero of
Freedom; he lets us do' (GA 233, 13/01/24).

Other beings of the Hierarchy of Archangels give us the
impression that, to a greater or lesser degree, the impulses to
do this or that come to us from them. Of Michael Rudolf
Steiner says that he 'is the Spirit from whom no impulses
come, to begin with; for his characteristic period of rulership
is that which is now coming, when things are to arise out of
human freedom' (ibid.).

An aspect of Michael's mission and function which will

engage our attention in greater detail in this book is that of his relation to intelligence (see Chapter 8). Here it may suffice to remind ourselves that though the word 'intelligence' is now used mostly in an abstract sense, up to the Middle Ages the spiritual beings who were thought to govern the multifarious workings of the natural world were called 'Intelligences' (GA 240, 21/08/24). Rudolf Steiner speaks of 'Cosmic Intelligence' as a spiritual substance produced by the life of the Gods as they go about their work of creating the world. The Archangel Michael had assumed the task of guarding this spiritual substance so that men and women could one day avail themselves of it when they had been created 'in the image of God'.

Referring to the epoch during which Michael was the ruling Archangel prior to his resumption of this role in 1879 (i.e. to the period 550–200 BC) Rudolf Steiner makes the following observation:

> Think of the Michael Age at the time of Alexander [356–323 BC]. As I have often said, human beings in our day are extremely clever—that is to say, they form concepts, they have ideas; they are intellectual, possessing, as it were, a self-made intellectuality. People were clever, too, in the days of Alexander. Only if in those times they had been asked: Whence do you derive your concepts, your ideas?—they would not have said: We have produced them out of ourselves...No, they received into themselves the spiritual revelations, and together with these revelations, the ideas. They did not regard the ideas as something which human beings evolve out of themselves, but as something revealed to them in their spiritual nature. The task of Michael at that time was to administer this *heavenly* intellectuality—in contrast to earthly intellectuality. Michael was the greatest of the Archangels who had their abode on the sun. He was the Spirit who sent down from thence to the earth not only the sun's physical-etheric rays but, within them, the inspired intellectuality. And in those past days people knew: the power of intelligence on earth is a gift of the heavens, of the sun; it is sent down from the sun. And the one who actually sends the spiritual intellectuality down to the earth is Michael...This Cosmic Intelligence, inspired in human beings, is a gift of Michael.

> Then came the epoch when human beings were to be made
> ready to unfold intellect out of their own, individual forces of
> soul; they were not merely to receive the Cosmic Intelligence
> through revelation but to evolve intelligence out of their inner
> forces. Preparation for this was made by Aristotelianism ... By
> means of Aristotelianism earthly intelligence emerged as though
> from the shell of the Cosmic Intelligence. [GA 240, 19/07/24]

Elsewhere Steiner says:

> It is Michael's task to administer a power that is essentially
> *spiritual*, reaching its zenith in the human faculty of *intellectual
> understanding*. Michael is not the Spirit who, if I may put it so,
> cultivates intellectuality *per se*; the spirituality he bestows strives
> to bring enlightenment to humankind in the form of ideas and
> thoughts—but ideas and thoughts that grasp the spiritual. [Ibid.]

In the last eleven hundred years or so the Cosmic Intelligence has passed out of the 'hands' of Michael and, since the
eighth century, human beings have more and more regarded
their thoughts as arising out of their own souls instead of
being received by way of inspiration.

We have made tremendous use of intelligence in developing, in particular, science and technology. However, we
also need to be fully conscious of the fact that ahrimanic
beings have also made use of it, in increasing measure since
the fifteenth century, to seduce humankind to plunge into
ever greater depths of materialistic thinking.

'What Michael desires,' Rudolf Steiner writes, 'is to keep
the intelligence, which is developing within humanity, per-
manently in connection with the divine-spiritual beings. But
in this he is meeting with opposition' (GA 26, 26/10/24).

He is opposed by Ahriman, by ahrimanic beings. It is the
nature of such spiritual beings to absorb into themselves 'the
sum-total of all intellectuality and thus they become the
greatest, the most comprehensive and penetrating intelligences in the cosmos. Michael foresees how human beings, in
progressing more and more towards their own individual use
of intelligence, must meet with these ahrimanic beings, and
how by uniting with them he may then succumb to them. For

this reason Michael brings the ahrimanic powers under his feet; he continually thrusts them into a deeper region than the one in which human beings are evolving. Michael thrusting the Dragon at his feet into the abyss: that is the mighty picture which lives in human consciousness of the supersensible fact...' (Ibid.)

Through the ages Michael has been portrayed as the Archangel who overcomes the Dragon. The connotation of the Dragon has changed with changing consciousness. The idea that persisted into the late eighteenth century was that the lower instincts in men and women had to be overcome by the higher soul-forces. In the present Michael Age it is incumbent upon us to recognize that the Dragon forces are those which would fetter us to the materialistic conceptions which, in the Gabriel Age, had their rightful place, but which threaten humanity with destruction if prolonged into the future. Instead of picturing a celestial being clad in armour slaying the Dragon, today we need to show, and recognize, a shining sunlike Michael from whose penetrating light the dark, desiccated figure of Ahriman retreats. It is Ahriman's power which blinds men and women to the spirit, causes them to deny the very existence of the spiritual world rationalized by the belief that world evolution is a materialistic-chemical process. It is through his influence that humanity is dragged down to the subhuman level, unfree and machine-like.

As we shall discuss in greater detail later, it is Ahriman and his hosts who lead us to feed on abstractions, on educational, social and political programmes devoid of any true moral value; it is Ahriman, too, who engenders fragmentation, fear, hatred—leading to race riots, genocide, and so forth. It is Ahriman and his hosts, the Spirits of Darkness, who inspire the 'I'm all right, Jack' attitude—the very antithesis of the Michael-impulse to serve one's neighbours selflessly.

In our present age we need to recognize the Dragon as that influence which seeks to drive us into earthly hardness, coldness and rigidity. It is this influence with which Michael is seen as doing battle.

This chilling process of hardening and rigidification which has taken place during the course of evolution—and against which Michael seeks to guard humanity—is due to the fact that the world around us is no longer experienced as being permeated with creative spiritual forces. More and more, since the fifteenth/sixteenth century, the divine-spiritual beings have withdrawn—as far as human consciousness is concerned—from the sense-perceptible world. The generally accepted view today is that the world in which we live is 'god-forsaken', that is, devoid of spirit. And that, in fact, such a 'god-forsaken' world is the only reality.

It could be argued with some justification that there are definite signs, as we approach the end of the century, of an increasing awareness of the activity of spiritual beings in the world.

To fail to recognize and, at least to some small degree, to experience the activity of spiritual beings in ourselves and in the world around us is to fall victim to the hardening (ahrimanic) process of which mention has been made.

Michael is the spiritual being who has always 'kept a watchful eye' on us human beings. He regards it as one of his tasks to show us the way to free ourselves from the entanglement of matter and to offer to guide our capacity for knowledge in such a way that we become fully aware of, gain conscious knowledge of, the spiritual world.

Just as Christ, the Spirit of the Sun, united Himself with the earth through the Mystery of Golgotha[3] in order that He might offer the earth the possibility of a future spiritualized existence, so it is the mission of Michael to bring to human knowledge the warmth-filled light of the Spiritual Sun and thus render it possible for human beings to understand the deed of Christ.

It is Michael's aim to show us the way to a true knowledge of Christ, to a knowledge which, finding expression in moral action, leads the individual to freedom, and humanity in its totality to harmony.[4]

As the Archangel of the sun-forces, Michael is most profoundly connected with the Christ, the sublime Being of the

Sun who, since the Mystery of Golgotha, has united Himself with the Earth evolution.

But as intimated already, Michael does not use any form of compulsion upon us. His task is a passive one. He merely 'points the way' towards the Christ and leaves the choice to us. But by his presence he ensures it is an informed choice.

Characteristic of the second half of the twentieth century, and unlike any former ages, is the prevailing urge to free oneself from the fetters of dogma and tradition. With the growing range of freedom there is inevitably also, on the one hand, the danger of being exposed in greater measure than in earlier ages to the one-sided influences of either Lucifer or Ahriman (or both), and, on the other hand, the need for a deeper and wider sense of responsibility. The tasks performed in earlier times under the guidance of the Godhead now have to be undertaken by human beings on their own responsibility. At each fresh step on the path towards freedom authoritarian divine guidance is withdrawn from us in increasing measure. A free being must have unrestricted possibilities of choice. It would be a contradiction to speak of freedom unless there were at least two principles to choose from. Freedom without choice is meaningless. The presence of evil impulses is the very touchstone for freedom. For every step towards freedom we take the closer do we come in contact and conflict with those powers, Lucifer and Ahriman, whose very existence gives freedom its full value.

The twentieth century has seen a growth of the 'area' of freedom and concomitant confrontation with the two categories of spiritual beings which, led by Lucifer and Ahriman, strive to hinder human beings from following the path towards which Michael points, the path which ultimately leads to the experience of 'Not I, but Christ in me'.

Among the numerous phenomena indicative of the widening measure of freedom and responsibility, on the one hand, and of the power of the forces of seduction and darkness, on the other, is the discovery of atomic energy, which can either bring considerable benefit to us in our daily lives or, in the blackest of scenarios, bring about the total anni-hilation of life on earth.

We could speak in similar terms of the emerging genetic engineering (see Appendix Eleven). It could certainly be regarded as having beneficial consequences, but we also have to recognize that interference in the moral, soul and spiritual foundations of human life is a real possibility.

Again, the area of freedom has been much enlarged through the awe-inspiring successes of space exploration. Here too, however, there is the possibility of misuse for destructive military purposes.

These few examples—many more could be mentioned—may serve to illustrate the conception that an increase in human faculties often brings with it the risk that dangers have to be run. Each new danger, each new temptation, brings with it the possibility of a strengthening of the human soul. Such a strengthening of the soul is assured if, as students of spirit-knowledge, we heed Michael's wise sign (GA 238, 28/09/24).

2. Evil

No attempt will be made here to give a comprehensive picture of the origin and multifarious manifestations of evil. However, our theme, 'Michael's Battle with Evil', does require that some of the more important aspects of evil should be discussed.

Rudolf Steiner repeatedly draws our attention to the fact that it is erroneous to think of good and evil in terms of a duality. It is a matter of trinity, not of duality. Evil is split within itself. We can, in fact, speak of duality in respect of evil, that it is split into opposing tendencies. We could even say, using a biblical term, that evil is split into two opposing temptations. These temptations, aberrations, issue from luciferic spiritual beings on the one side and from ahrimanic spiritual beings on the other. Expressing a fundamental aspect of these two temptations we may say: the luciferic tempter inspires the human soul with the desire to be detached from earthly responsibilities and duties and to live in an egotistical yearning for heavenly bliss; the ahrimanic tempter strives to fasten our attention solely upon earthly matters and to regard the spiritual as no more that illusion. The ahrimanic tempter would have us totally bound to material existence and sever us from the spiritual.

Lucifer would make us caricatures of the Angels and would imbue us with egotistical arrogance, conceit and self-deification. Ahriman would drag us down so that we become no more than 'animal-men' and solely content with the pursuit and satisfaction of physical needs (GA 147, 25/08/13).

Time and again Rudolf Steiner warns us not to commit the naïve error that we should, at all costs, avoid the influence of these two opposing forces (if such avoidance were indeed in reality possible), for they compose an all-essential element in both cosmic and human spiritual development. 'The good would not be so great a good if it were not to grow through the conquest of evil. Love would not be so intense if it had not to become love so great as to be able even to overcome the wickedness in the countenance of evil men' (GA 104, 25/06/08).

What we need to heed, however, is the danger of falling prey to the extremes of one-sidedness emanating from the Adversaries.

Here, as already mentioned, we can only give a few indications in regard to the nature and role of these opposing forces.

They belonged, as we can learn from Rudolf Steiner, in the long distant past—before, in fact, our earth as we know it today had come into being—to the ranks of what, for want of a better name, we may call 'good' spiritual beings. Steiner describes how, during the Ancient Sun embodiment[1] of the Earth (GA 13), certain high-ranking spiritual beings among the Cherubim renounced sacrifices offered to them by spiritual beings of a lower rank, the Thrones. The consequence of this renunciation on the part of certain Cherubim was that the Thrones, whose offering was not accepted, began to be active 'outside' the harmonious working together of the other spiritual beings. 'Independent experiences now arose—states of rebellion, as it were' (GA 13, Ch. 4). These rebellious spiritual beings, luciferic beings, 'remained behind', and no longer formed an integral element in the progressive evolution taking place in the spiritual world (see GA 13 and GA 132). These luciferic beings and, later, also ahrimanic beings evolved into one-sided adversarial forces which, once the earth had come into being, began to influence human beings.

Without the influence of Lucifer our consciousness could have been harmonized with the 'great universe, and made into a faithful image of it... We would have become beings with a consciousness whose content mirrored back the universe in the pictures of the life of knowledge, as by natural necessity, not by our own free intention' (GA 13, Ch. 4). Through the influence of Lucifer human consciousness was divested of the character of a mere mirror of the universe, for there was kindled in the human soul the power to regulate and control the pictures in consciousness. The human being became the possessor of an individual—a personal—faculty of cognition (GA 13, Ch. 4).

We might easily suppose that the spiritual beings—luciferic and ahrimanic—who 'remained behind' would be actually injurious to the evolution of the world. That their activity has had 'hindering' effects can hardly be disputed. However, Rudolf Steiner draws our attention to the fact that we also need to recognize the positive influence these spiritual beings have had on human evolution. For instance, human beings would never have attained their freedom, or the capacity for individual initiative, had not the luciferic beings 'remained behind'.

The influence of both Lucifer and Ahriman is of a negative and a positive nature.

For example, on the one hand it is owing to the luciferic spiritual beings that human beings have, in their astral bodies, in their souls, certain passions, emotions and desires which, to a greater or lesser degree, deprive them of their true human dignity. On the other hand, however, if we were unable to err from the good, if we were bound to the good, we would not be able to act out of our own free will; we would not have freedom of choice.

Expressed in simple terms: we owe our freedom to Lucifer.

To claim that Lucifer and Ahriman can do no other than lead human beings astray is not valid. Without the presence of the influence of these spiritual beings men and women would never be able to acquire true human dignity.[2]

Referring back to what was outlined above we can now say that human beings could not have attained self-consciousness without the activities of those spiritual beings who 'remained behind'. Furthermore these beings would not have 'remained behind' if the Cherubim had accepted their offering.

To make it possible for beings to become thus independent, renunciation previously took place. Thus, in cosmic evolution it is the case that the Gods themselves have called their opponents into being. If the Gods [i.e. Cherubim] had not renounced the sacrifice, beings would not have been able to oppose them. Put into simple words, we may suppose the Gods had foreseen as follows: 'If we merely go on creating as we have done [up to now] ... there would never be any free beings, capable of acting from their own initiative. In order that beings of this nature might come into existence, the possibility must be given for opponents to arise against us in the universe ... If we ourselves ordain everything we shall meet with no such resistance. We could make everything very easy for ourselves by accepting the sacrifice offered to us; then would the whole of evolution be subject unto us. But this will not do, we want beings which are able to resist us. We will therefore not accept the sacrifice; so that through our resignation they become our opponents!'

So we see that we must not look for the origin of evil in the so-called 'evil' beings, but in the 'good'. Beings, who, through their resignation first brought evil about through those beings who were able to bring it into the world. [GA 132, 14/11/11]

Steiner helps us to come closer to an understanding of this immense picture of cosmic renunciation and sacrifice by reminding us of Christ's sacrifice for the sake of humankind, and of the fact that He could have summoned a host of Angels to His aid if He had wished 'to avoid the death of sacrifice':

That which Christ might have accepted ... He rejected in resignation and renunciation. And the greatest renunciation made by Christ confronts us when, by having made it, He allows the opponent himself—Judas—to enter His sphere. If we are able to see in Christ Jesus all that is to be seen, we must see in Him an image of those beings with whom, at a certain stage of evolution, we have just become acquainted, those who must renounce the proffered sacrifice, those whose very nature was resignation. Christ renounced that which would have occurred if He had not allowed Judas to appear as His opponent just as once upon a time ... the Gods themselves called forth their opponents by the renunciation they made. So we see a repetition of this event in a picture here on earth, that of the Christ seated among the twelve, and Judas, the betrayer, in the centre. In order that that which makes humankind of such immeasurable value might enter into evolution, Christ Himself had to place His opponent in opposition to Him... When we recall the words, 'He who dips his bread into the bowl with me, he it is who shall betray me,' we see an earthly reflection of the opponent of the Gods, placed in opposition to them by the Gods themselves. [Ibid.]

3. Lucifer

Lucifer lays hold of human consciousness in such a way that super-consciousness intermingles with consciousness. Ahriman, the ahrimanic element, on the other hand, exerts an influence mainly in the subconscious.[1]

Rudolf Steiner characterized Lucifer and Ahriman from many different viewpoints. On one occasion he said: 'Lucifer is a proud spirit and likes to soar away into the heights where lofty visions open out. Ahriman is a morally lonely spirit who does not readily make his presence known; he sets his nature to work in people's subconscious, works upon their subconscious, conjures judgements out of it.' *People then believe that their alert consciousness underpins their judgements, whereas they often form an opinion from subconscious impulses.* Or, according to Rudolf Steiner, 'they often allow it to be conjured forth by the ahrimanic forces themselves'.

Steiner then goes on to say: 'Peter was not far wrong in calling Ahriman a "prowling lion seeking whom he might devour". For Ahriman really does prowl in the hidden parts of man's nature, in his subconscious' (GA 184, 04/10/18).

Mention was made in the previous chapter of a certain group of Thrones who 'remained behind' as luciferic beings. However, it is clear from numerous statements made by Steiner that in *all* ranks of the three Hierarchies there are such beings—right up to the highest members of the First Hierarchy, the Seraphim, the Spirits of Love. Most frequently, Steiner speaks of luciferic beings as being Exusiai, Spirits of Form, who have 'remained behind' (e.g. GA 141, 14/01/13). On one occasion we hear Steiner saying: 'Above the Spirits of Form stand the Spirits of Motion, above these the Spirits of Wisdom, above these the Spirits of Will, above them the Cherubim, the Seraphim. In all ranks of these spiritual beings there are those who can be likened to what we have described as luciferic spirits' (GA 136, 08/04/12).

Elsewhere Steiner states: 'In our present cycle of time

there are luciferic spirits in every category of the Hierarchies' (GA 136, 13/04/12).

Speaking of Lucifer himself—as distinct from luciferic beings—Steiner makes it clear that during a very early incarnation of our earth, during the Ancient Sun (see GA 13), the being of Lucifer was quite different from what it is today. In that far-off time Lucifer was the ruler of Venus: 'We find the sun still as a planet among the seven planets, we find Venus with Lucifer as her ruler, and these two, the Sun Spirit and the Venus Spirit—in other words, Christ and Lucifer—appear at first sight like brothers' (GA 137, 12/06/12).

Rudolf Steiner is extremely careful here to stress that it is extraordinarily difficult to differentiate between Lucifer and Christ in the time of the Ancient Sun. 'Please,' he asks, 'take what I am now going to say as no more than an attempt to characterize, as well as may be, the difference that clair-voyant consciousness can perceive between Christ and Lucifer in the time of the Ancient Sun.' Steiner then goes on to say:

> Lucifer, the ruler of Venus, appears in a form that is extra-ordinarily full of light—I mean, of course, spiritual light... But then we notice, when we begin to perceive his *intentions* ... that Lucifer is a spirit endowed in his very nature with infinite pride, so great a pride that it can prove a temptation to human beings... And how does the Christ figure look beside Lucifer? The Christ figure in the time of the Old Sun—the Lord and Ruler of the Sun—is a picture of utmost devotion, entire devo-tion to all that is around Him in the world. Whereas Lucifer looks like one who thinks only of himself—we are obliged to clothe it all in human words, notwithstanding the fact that these are quite inadequate—Christ appears as wholly dedicated, in devotion, to all that is around Him in the great wide world. [GA 137, 12/06/12][2]

As indicated earlier, Steiner represents this pride as a powerful force which, in its heroic greatness, acted as temp-tation. We can also recognize, however, that this majestic pride was none other than an innate burgeoning desire for self-reliance and independence which saturated Lucifer's nature. It was upon this craving that his activity in cosmic events was founded. It was this urge towards self-reliance which gave birth, as it were, to the impulse of freedom. Spiritual freedom forms the very basis for the goal of humankind's mission on earth—the attainment of the pure selfless power of love.

This majestic pride, this unconquerable craving for independence, became the tempter of other spiritual beings throughout the ranks of the three Hierarchies. It gradually 'descended' right 'down' to the realm of humanity where it manifests itself as iniquity—sin. Here, through the choice of either good or evil, through the soul-spiritual conflict undergone, freedom is born.

Most of Steiner's descriptions of Lucifer are concerned to give us a picture of him at much later periods in the process of world-evolution than that of Old Sun. For instance, it is to the light of Lucifer that we owe our gradually maturing thinking through the ages. Steiner also speaks of Lucifer as being the Spirit of Egoism—also the Spirit of Beauty, or Art, and of Wisdom-filled Light. We may also recognize in Lucifer an instigator of creative spiritual life in human beings. Hence we may also recognize the validity of Rudolf Steiner's statement that to gain a true understanding of the Christ, the Light from Lucifer's realm must increasingly illumine our souls. We shall return to this seemingly paradoxical assertion in due course. Let us first return to the time in which Lucifer, as Regent of Venus (cf. Isa. 14:12), 'stood' beside Christ, the Ruler of the Sun.

As we have already seen, Steiner describes Lucifer as living for himself, for his own pride alone. As a consequence the rulership of Venus fell from him. From then on he has suffered an infinite longing for his own domain, Venus. He suffers a cosmic homesickness. 'That is the salient feature of the luciferic nature seen from the cosmic aspect. Clairvoyant consciousness comes to know just what the star of Venus is by entering into the soul of Lucifer, thus experiencing from the earth Lucifer's tragic longing, like a wonderful cosmic nostalgia, for the star Phosphorus, Lucifer or Venus' (GA 129,

21/08/11). Lucifer, who did not receive the Word of the Worlds, 'went downward, he had to remain behind in his evolution ... Christ went forward' (GA 137, 12/06/12). The Christ Spirit, the Sun Spirit, evolved ever 'forward' until at length He was to appear on earth at the Baptism in the River Jordan. Through His having received—and identified Himself with—the divinely creative, inexpressible Word, through His having rejected pride, the contrast between Him and Lucifer is clear to see. Lucifer became the opponent of Christ and it was, above all, Michael, the Countenance of Christ, who repulsed Lucifer in victorious battle whenever he stepped beyond his rightful domain.

What is Lucifer's rightful domain? What is the role he can play, which is not against but in accord with the universal cosmic order? His task is, in a certain respect, 'to tear the human being and everything in the world pertaining to the soul away from living and being absorbed in the physical-sensory alone. If there were no luciferic power in the world, we would dream along in the perceptions streaming into us from the external world and in what comes to us from the world through the intellect' (GA 147, 25/08/13). If it were not for Lucifer's influence we would dedicate our lives to nothing other than the attainment of ever-increasing sensual comfort. Indeed, is this not an ideal put before us by Ahriman with ever greater persuasion in our present age, an age in which astounding discoveries in the field of technology serve almost exclusively our physical comfort, our love of ease? Lucifer constantly strives to tear us away from just this comfort of the physical and sense-accessible. He is concerned to awaken in us everything of the spirit:

> Wherever the human being creates something through his imagination and his soul life of feeling, no longer clinging dully to the sense-world but rising above it, Lucifer is the power that tears us out of that world. A large part of what is uplifting and liberating in the artistic development of humankind is inspired by Lucifer. We can designate something else as the inspiration of Lucifer: human beings have the chance through luciferic powers to free their thinking from a mere photograph-like copying of

the sense-world; they can raise themselves above this in freedom. This they do, for instance, in their philosophy. From this
point of view all philosophizing is the inspiration of Lucifer. One
could even write a history of the philosophical development of
humankind, in so far as this is not pure Positivism—that is, does
not keep to the external materialistic (ahrimanic)—and could
say: the history of the development of philosophy is a continual
testimony to the inspiration of Lucifer. All creative work, in fact,
that rises above the sense-world we owe to Lucifer's rightful
activities and powers. [GA 147, 25/08/13][3]

Lucifer strives to raise human beings out of their earthly
evolution and make spirit-beings of them, beings who would
populate his, Lucifer's, own kingdom—a kingdom which he,
in his proud rejection of the World Word, desires to create.

Lucifer has the tendency continually to overstep his
'rightful domain' by contaminating the feeling life of the
human soul. Whereas Ahriman in our present age has more
to do with our thinking, Lucifer pays greater attention to our
life of the emotions, passions, impulses and desires. Whereas
Ahriman strives to confine our thinking to the physical sense-
world, Lucifer, as we have seen, does the opposite. He has the
tendency to detach this feeling life of the soul from the
physical world, to spiritualize it, to move it, as it were, to a
special luciferic kingdom set up in opposition to the general
cosmic order. (See GA 147, 25/08/13.) Here we see Ahriman
and Lucifer working in opposition to each other.

Rudolf Steiner describes how, in response to the actions of
luciferic spirits in the Atlantean period (see GA 13, Ch. 4),
ahrimanic spirits mingled with the process of perception
exerted by human beings, so that we today only see the
external world in the form in which our physical senses show
it to us; that is, not as it is in reality.

Beings we term luciferic gained access to the human being's
astral body. As a consequence the expulsion from Paradise took
place sooner than originally intended; and the consequence of
this luciferic activity was the interference of the ahrimanic spirits
in the human being's perception of the outer world ... the belief
was induced in the human being that the outer world is nothing

but a material existence, that there is no such thing as spirit
underlying and permeating all material substance. [GA 112, 28/
06/09][4]

What the senses can perceive is no more than the external
appearance. Behind all 'external' happenings we have to look
for spiritual forces. Steiner gives us many examples of the
presence and activity of such forces. One such example is that
of our need for and taking in of material nourishment. We
need to be clear, Steiner says,

> that the very thing that materialism often sees as the whole
> human being, the very thing that for most people is the princi-
> pal concern and care of life—to receive nourishment—has
> only come into existence through the ... luciferic influence.
> For human beings were not destined to receive material nour-
> ishment, they were originally intended to have a kind of exis-
> tence that did not require it. This fact brings to expression in a
> marvellous way how through the temptation of Lucifer there
> has come about what we may call the 'expulsion from Para-
> dise'. For to be in Paradise means nothing else than to be a
> spiritual being and to have no need of physical nourishment.
> [GA 134, 29/12/11]

Through Lucifer's 'interference' human beings have come
into close contact with the material world. And as a consequence, Ahriman, whose realm is the mineral earth, has
won influence over humankind.

From what has been stated already it is clear that Ahriman
strives to destroy everything that Lucifer endeavours to
create. While Lucifer desires to draw us upwards, away from
the world of the senses, and to spiritualize us, Ahriman
strives to 'harden' us more and more, to mummify us.

When Lucifer inspires a person with noble ideals and
endows him or her with enthusiasm, Ahriman creeps in, so to
speak, to mix perverse motives with the spiritual endeavour.

Rudolf Steiner describes how Lucifer looks back upon his
activities and has to acknowledge that ever and again Ahriman has destroyed what he has sought to achieve.

Let us now summarize, in Rudolf Steiner's own words,

some of the major aspects of Lucifer's activity we have been considering:

> The powers that are developing normally could have brought it about that human beings ... would be filled more and more with the gifts of the spiritual world, and finally, when the earth had reached its goal, it stands to reason that we would be imbued with everything given to us by the spiritual worlds. However, one thing would not be possible: we should not have been able to develop that original and ardent power of striving, that devotion and fiery enthusiasm for all that is created in one age of civilization after another. The same grounds which bring forth every single aspiration, every desire, equally bring forth the aspiration for the great ideals of humanity, the desire to ennoble and beautify human existence, to create art in the successive periods of human civilization. The same grounds which bring forth injurious desires leading to evil also bring forth the striving after the highest that can be accomplished upon earth. And this capacity of the human soul to be enkindled for the highest ideals would not exist if it was not possible on the other hand for this same ardent desire to sink into vice and evil. That this is possible in the evolution of mankind is the work of the luciferic spirits. We must not fail to recognize that together with the possibility of evil the luciferic spirits have brought us freedom, so that we may freely receive what would otherwise simply flow into our souls.
>
> ... Lucifer challenges Ahriman and as the former develops his activity in the successive periods, Ahriman joins in and destroys bit by bit what Lucifer has brought on earth. The cosmic evolution of humanity is a continuous interplay between Ahriman and Lucifer. Without Lucifer's work in human development there would be no passion, no enthusiasm for the progressive stream of human evolution; without Ahriman, who destroys in culture after culture whatever arose from Lucifer's influence and is not part of the progressive stream, Lucifer would simply perpetuate individual cultures *ad infinitum.* [GA 120, 28/05/10]

Steiner then speaks of the 'I', the ego in the human being in relation to the attainment of freedom (see also Appendix One):

> If we reached all our goals at the end of the earth's development because they were given to us, our 'I' could not be free; for from

the beginning it was predestined that all the good of the earth's evolution should flow into the human being. The human being could only become free by adding to this 'I' another which is capable of error... The lower 'I' had to be given us by Lucifer in order that our striving towards the higher 'I' should be our own original deed.

This is what gave us the possibility of free will. Free will is something which we may acquire bit by bit in the course of time ... this possibility of free will is a constant ideal before our minds. [Ibid.]

In the absolute sense we can recognize that our will is never free, because, *inter alia*, at any moment in life it may succumb to the luciferic and ahrimanic elements.

With reference to our life on earth we may say that we are approaching nearer to free will to the same degree as we succeed in mastering the influences of Lucifer and Ahriman. This mastery we can obtain over the luciferic and ahrimanic influences only by means of knowledge—self-knowledge and knowledge of the world in which we live. 'The two must work together. Self-knowledge and knowledge of the outer world must become part of our being; then we shall be able to be clear about our relationship to Lucifer' (ibid.), and, we may add, also about our relationship to Ahriman.

4. Lucifer and Christ

We noted earlier that Lucifer could not look back upon his activity and claim that what he had done was good. All that he does is doomed to be destroyed. This, Rudolf Steiner states, is Lucifer's continual disappointment and his ever-recurring pain. (Cf. GA 120, 28/05/10.)

Lucifer would look into a future of eternal torment were it not that other majestic spiritual forces are active in world– and human evolution.

He had inoculated human beings with his grandiose pride and he had endowed them with the craving for independence and self-reliance. But, in doing this and thus rendering the human being a rebel against the 'good', progressive Gods (in whose womb men and women had up till then reposed without a will of their own), Lucifer also gave human beings the possibility to rebel against him himself. After the Fall from Paradise the germ of freedom took root in the human soul; the human being could choose between good and evil.

At the beginning of the evolutionary process on earth the temptations issuing from Lucifer still held sway over the fledgling will. As individual will it was weak, but it was gradually being strengthened, for, from the cosmic distances, the Christ Force was streaming 'down' and gradually nearing the earth.

The forces of the Christ Spirit approaching the earth increasingly intervened in human evolution. Here we cannot go into any detail in respect of such a profound and vast subject, but simply mention that the attacks of Lucifer—and later also of Ahriman—were threefold: against the sense-organs, against the life-organs, and (from the Atlantean period onwards) against the soul-organs of thinking, feeling and willing. And each time, that soul-spiritual being who later incarnated as the 'Nathan' Jesus brought harmony into the threatened human organism.[1] (See also Appendix Two.)

Christ's Sacrifice—begun already in the Ancient Sun

epoch—was completed upon Golgotha. 'When the Mystery of Golgotha took place the earthly body of Jesus of Nazareth was given over to the elements of the earth. From that time onwards Christ has been united with the spiritual sphere of the earth—and He lives "within" it' (GA 152, 02/05/13). The earth's aura is imbued with the Christ-substance. We move, so to speak, in this substance. Whether we receive it into our souls or whether we reject it depends entirely upon us, upon our will. It is with us that the future destiny of Lucifer lies, for he is so intimately bound up with us that all our soul-experiences are shared, experienced by him too. Because of his intimacy with the human soul, Lucifer also feels all the greatness—and beauty—that the human soul can experience through receiving the Christ.

In what form this will come to pass we cannot conceive. Yet from a picture of the future drawn for us by Rudolf Steiner, we have an inkling of how the great change in Lucifer can become a reality through the efforts of men and women on earth:

> Let us take a human being who has voluntarily received the Christ—Christianity is only at its beginning, but let us take an ideal situation—a human ego has with complete free will allowed the Christ Power to flow into it. When the ego has progressed so far as to be permeated by the Christ, then the Christ Power also irradiates the astral body. The Christ Power rays out from within the astral body where previously the luciferic beings had injected their influences. But now what will happen in the future? Because with the help of Christ, and with His help only, we can extinguish those qualities in us that stem from Lucifer; we gradually release the luciferic powers too. A time will come when the luciferic powers, which had to sink to a lower stage of evolution for the sake of the freedom of human beings and therefore were unable to experience the Christ Power on earth, will eventually experience the Christ Power through us and thus be redeemed. We shall be able to redeem Lucifer if we receive the Christ Power in the appropriate way and, as a result, we shall grow stronger than we would otherwise have been. For imagine, if the human race had not received the luciferic forces, the Christ Power would have rayed out but

would not have encountered any luciferic obstacles. It would have been impossible for human beings to progress in goodness, truth and wisdom as far as they now can without first having to overcome the powers of hindrance. [GA 110, 18/04/09]

It belongs to the lofty task of human beings to bring freedom into the world—and, together with freedom, love. Without freedom there can be no real love. Freedom and love, Steiner asserts, form a polarity, form two poles which belong together. If love is to enter our cosmos as a force of purification and redemption, it can only come into being through freedom, that is, through Lucifer and Christ, through the sacrifices made by both Lucifer and Christ (cf. GA 110, 18/04/09).

Infinite love, of which we at present can form no more than a faint image, this completely selfless love which will increasingly permeate the human soul till it has, some day, become entirely one with the irradiating Christ Power, this true and deep experience of 'Not I, but Christ in me', is what ultimately will imbue and transform Lucifer's being. Lucifer, who has given us knowledge, will himself be possessed of this knowledge of the Christ Power we have gained. Lucifer will know again that Christ is not his enemy, that He enfolds him in selfless Divine Love as He once did upon the Ancient Sun. The transformed Lucifer regains his true nature—the Light-bearer will 'walk' before Christ.

Through human beings' experience of the Christ-impulse Lucifer will be cleansed and purified in the fire of Christianity, and the wrong done by him and his hosts will be transformed into powers of blessing.

Through Christ's infinite love, brought to Lucifer by those human beings who experience Christ's living presence, Lucifer's pride will change to deep humility and he will devote his majestic power to serving Him.

When we know the Christ, when we absorb the wisdom which gives rise to insight into what Christ truly is, truly signifies, not only for human evolution but also for that of the cosmos itself, then we redeem ourselves *and* Lucifer and his hosts through this knowledge of Christ.

'Lucifer who has brought us freedom also makes it possible for us, if we so will, to turn it to account in order to understand Christ' (GA 107, 22/03/09). It is then that Lucifer is cleansed and purified in the fire of Christianity; it is then that Lucifer serves Christ.

Rudolf Steiner gives us a picture of the Lucifer of the future, Lucifer 'conquered' by Christ through infinite love. Transformed, Lucifer will return to his true nature. The Bearer of Light will walk before Christ; he will become the Holy Spirit of the future:

> This was foretold by Christ Himself to those around Him, when He said: 'You should be illumined by the New Spirit, by the Holy Spirit' [see John 14:26]. This Holy Spirit is none other than He through whom will be grasped what Christ really accomplished. This Holy Spirit is none other than the resurrected Lucifer, resurrected now into a new and higher glory. He is the spirit of self-radiant, wisdom-filled knowledge. The resurrected Lucifer carries the torch before Christ. Christ *is* the Light, Lucifer the Light-*bearer*. [GA 107, 22/03/09]

*   *   *

Legends speak of Lucifer as a 'fallen' Angel. Indeed, the decisive act of Lucifer was a Fall—a fall from his place alongside the Christ Spirit. Legends also tell of Lucifer's original greatness and majesty, for they tell that when Lucifer was hurled down from heaven to earth a precious stone fell from his crown. Out of this precious stone the vessel was formed which Christ used at the Last Supper—the vessel into which Christ's blood flowed from His wounds on the Cross. Out of this jewel was formed the Holy Grail (see GA 113, 23/08/09; also Appendix Three).

It was Michael who, with his flaming sword, struck a precious stone, one spirit, out of the corona of spirits. This one spirit, we are given to understand, need not have fallen down to earth with the other spirits but did so voluntarily. He gave up his heavenly home, sacrificed himself, in order to prepare the way for the Sun Spirit, the Christ, who followed him. For He, the Christ, took the same path down to the earth

as the falling spirits after their defeat by Michael. Spirits of
Wisdom were they all who fell from the heights into the
depths. Out of his own free will the brightest spirit of them all
became the Vessel of Love.

René Querido, in his book on the Mystery of the Holy
Grail, gives us a significant clue as to the identity of 'the
brightest spirit of them all'. He reminds us of the question
Parzival poses in Wagner's version of the Grail legend.
Instead of asking '*What* is the Grail?' Parzival's question is
'*Who* is the Grail?' '[This] question,' Querido points out, 'is
not as foolish as it might appear. In early Christian writings
before the fifth century, we find an answer in a sermon by St
John Chrysostomos. He describes the Jesus-child as being
like a crescent moon who received the sun when he grew up
and was baptized at the age of 30. It was only for a period of
less than three years that the divine Christ Being dwelt within
the body of Jesus of Nazareth. It was as if the moonlike
temple of the body of Jesus received the divine content of the
Sun Being. The grail cup was likened to the body or temple
and the blood contained in it to the spirit "I am" substance
that fills the vessel.'

We may now say: The 'brightest spirit of them all' who
came to earth voluntarily was that of the Nathan Jesus-child
(see Appendix Two).

The Grail was filled with the blood of Christ who redeems
Lucifer himself. This is the Grail Mystery. Through yielding
to Lucifer's temptation in the Garden of Eden the human
being 'fell' to earth. Through partaking of the Grail we are
raised again. 'That,' says W.J. Stein, 'is the real meaning of
the Lord's Supper.'[2]

We see here the weaving of cosmic, spiritual destiny:
Michael, the Countenance of Christ, casts Lucifer and his
hosts down to earth, but, in striking, a precious stone is freed
from Lucifer's crown, which sows the seed, as it were, for the
redemption not only of mankind but also of Lucifer himself.
We may see this 'stone' as forming the vehicle, the receptive
foundation for a new spiritual wisdom imbued with Christ's
love and compassion. Indeed, Christ spoke of Himself as 'the

stone which the builders rejected' which then became 'the head of the corner' (Matt. 21:42; cf. Eph. 2:20).

Lucifer, the Spirit of Egoism, works in the human astral body. The astral body may be described as an egoist (cf. GA 145, 26/03/13).

Rudolf Steiner reminds us that there are occasions in life in which egoism 'expands' as a necessary factor of life. One example of this is the fundamental characteristic of maternal love. Here egoism extends from the mother to the child. Her child is an 'extension' of herself. An attack upon her child she feels to be an attack upon herself. 'It is a fortunate provision of nature that egoism can be transferred in this way from one person to another; that one can regard a neighbour as a part of oneself and is able to "extend" one's egoism to others. Thus we see that egoism loses its negative aspect when we transfer our feelings and thinking to another and consider a neighbour to be a part of our own being' (ibid.).

The interests of our astral body must embrace the whole earth and the whole of mankind. 'When, in our astral body, we are interested in all terrestrial affairs, when all the affairs of the earth become our own concern, then we may entrust ourselves to the egoity of our astral body. But it is necessary that the interests of mankind should become our interest' (ibid.).

We may recognize that, through the particular mode of egoism activity we are looking at here, Lucifer, the Spirit of Egoism, may be regarded, paradoxically, as being a 'servant' of the Countenance of Christ, Michael.

To help us gain a clearer understanding of the point he is making Rudolf Steiner refers us to two legends: the Paradise legend and the Grail legend (see Appendix Three). Both, he says, were imparted to mankind with the intention of raising us above our purely personal interests in order to devote ourselves to the interests of others.

While the Paradise legend takes us back to the initial stage of Earth evolution and is given in order to enlarge our horizon to embrace all of mankind, the Grail legend is given in order that it may permeate the inmost depths of the astral body, 'into the fundamental interest of the astral body because, if left to itself, it becomes an egoist and takes into consideration only its egoistic interests.

> When it is a question of the interests of the astral body one can err in two directions only: that of Amfortas and, before Amfortas is fully redeemed, that of Parzival. The true development of the human being lies between these two in so far as the astral body is concerned. This astral body tries to develop within itself the forces of egoism. But if it introduces personal interests into this egoism, it is undermined; while it ought to extend its interests to embrace the whole earth, these interests are limited to the single, isolated personality. But that must not be, for if it happens, then through the influence of the personality whose ego is expressed in the blood, the whole human personality is wounded: we fall into the error of Amfortas... The moment we introduce personal interests into the sphere where the astral body ought to overcome personal interests it is fatal, we become the wounded Amfortas. [GA 145, 26/03/13]

At first Parzival is not sufficiently awake inwardly to be able to ask the question: What is the meaning and purpose of the Grail? What does it ask of us? In the case of Amfortas it asks that he should overcome his self-centred personal interest and expand his interest to embrace that of all mankind in accordance with the example set by Christ Himself. In the case of Parzival it asks that he should raise his interest above that of a mere innocent spectator so that he reaches an inner understanding of what is common to the whole of mankind—the gift of the life-giving force of the Holy Grail. Thus, in a wonderful way, Rudolf Steiner says, the ideal of the Mystery of Golgotha manifests itself between the wounded Amfortas and the innocent Parzival. 'If the astral body follows its innate, original interest it will raise itself to the ideal of universal humanity which is attained when these words become truth: "Where two or three are gathered together in my name, there am I in the midst of them" (Matt. 18:20), no matter where these two may be found in the course of terrestrial evolution' (GA 145, 26/03/13).

Before Parzival could find the Grail again he had to go

through the inner experience of Easter Friday and learn of the love of Christ who gave His life for mankind. Parzival had to go through the experience of doubt, doubt which brought with it intense suffering, before he could attain blessedness.

As we have seen already, Lucifer, too, undergoes suffering. He, too, made a sacrifice. Rudolf Steiner gives us many descriptions of how Lucifer and his hosts have forwarded human evolution through their sacrificial deeds. For instance, he states that to enable 'the Christ to intervene in *Earth* evolution at the right moment, certain *Moon* spirits [luciferic spirits] had to sacrifice their *Moon* mission and prepare for Him. This shows us that Lucifer's retardation on the *Moon* [i.e. Ancient Moon] can also be regarded in the light of a sacrifice' (GA 112, 28/06/09). In a cycle of lectures entitled *The East in the Light of the West* we find a confirmation of this statement:

> It is possible for us to experience the Christ as soul substance when we direct our gaze to that figure of the Christ which meets us in the Gospels. But to describe and understand Him in the way that other phenomena and events in the world are understood, thereby to gain an insight into His greatness, His significance and His causative connection with world evolution, is only possible when the Christian initiate advances to knowledge of the Luciferic realms.
>
> Thus in Rosicrucian science it is Lucifer who gives us the faculty for describing and understanding the Christ. [GA 113, 28/08/09][3]

Further on in this same lecture Steiner says: 'The interpretation of the Christ by spiritual faculties illuminated by Lucifer is the inner and essential kernel of the spiritual stream which must flow through the western channel. And what I have said represents the mission of Rosicrucianism in the future' (ibid.).

Shortly after this statement Steiner sets forth the thought that when, in the future, human beings desire to ascend to the spiritual world concealed by the veil of the sense-perceptual world they must penetrate through the sense-world into the spiritual world and must allow themselves to be borne to the Light by Lucifer. We would be 'drowned' in the sea of materialism if we did not 'ascend to inspiration through the luciferic principle. Just as the Christ-principle exists to strengthen our inner being, so the luciferic principle intensifies and develops those faculties by means of which we have to penetrate into the spiritual world fully and completely. Lucifer will intensify our understanding and comprehension of the world; the Christ will strengthen us perpetually within' (ibid.).

We saw earlier that, through the intervention of Lucifer and his hosts, the human being was exposed to the possibility of straying from the right path, exposed to both good *and* evil. Without their intervention mankind would never have been exposed to such possibilities; nor would men and women have had the possibility of developing free will.

If evolution had proceeded without Lucifer's intervention human beings would have attained a certain spiritual maturity by the middle of the Atlantean epoch (cf. GA 13), but without the possibility of freedom. If human beings had reached the middle of that epoch merely by a 'higher spiritual instinct', without freedom and, therefore, without any merit on their part, they would not have been mature enough for the descent of the Christ-principle to earth. However, freedom had been given to human beings, and they had thereby 'been pushed down below the stage of instinctive normal development. As a consequence they had to mature by themselves so that they might later be able to receive the Christ-principle'. 'We must clearly understand,' Steiner continues, 'that the descent of Christ and His work was delayed by the intervention of Lucifer and his hosts, but through this intervention mankind was more mature when, ultimately, Christ did descend' (GA 105, 10/08/08).

Luciferic beings prepared mankind for the descent of the Christ-principle.

The luciferic beings might have said: If we leave human beings in such a condition that they only live instinctively ... they will receive the Christ-principle also instinctively; they will not be

free, not mature in freedom. We will, therefore, sacrifice ourselves; we will develop in them certain capacities and qualities,
thus delaying the moment when they can see the Christ. [Ibid.]

In pre-Christian times there were two principles at work
which we may characterize as follows: there was a binding
principle which worked through blood relationship, and
there was a principle which sought to tear men and woman
away from such a relationship and centre them in their own
personality. It was the Jehovah principle which worked in the
forces of blood relationship. Order and harmony were produced through this relationship. One's relationship to one's
fellow human beings—to love for instance—was implanted
by the laws of nature. Opposed to Jehovah was Lucifer, who
directed relentless attacks against the principle of blood
relationship and sought to centre each and every individual
within his or her own personality, thus preparing the way for
the Christ who then 'appears and centres human beings
entirely within their own personality by giving them their
inward power, thereby making wisdom and grace the most
inward impulses of their being' (GA 105, 10/08/08).

We learn from Rudolf Steiner that the leaders of the old
Hebrew nation rebuked their people for reaching a state in
which each individual stressed the personal ego in him/her-
self. They were told that development would be furthered
only by subduing the personal ego and strengthening those
forces that guide them to the consciousness of being all-
connected, of being members of a great, single organism
reaching back to Abraham. The struggle against the luciferic
influence was carried on longest by the Hebrew people; they
preserved longer than any other nation what Steiner calls an
echo of the old Atlantean initiate teaching.

With the coming of Christ this teaching of the old initiates
was transmuted. Human beings need not obey the physical
bonds of blood relationship alone; each individual can look
into his or her own ego and there find the divine. 'The Christ-
impulse bears within it the force which, if we unite with it,
offers us the possibility of establishing a spiritual bond of

brother- and sisterhood among human beings, in spite of the individuality of the ego' (GA 112, 28/06/09).

If love had continued to be restricted to blood ties, mankind would have eventually been herded together into one community without enjoying full consciousness; men and women would never have risen to a complete awareness of their independence and freedom. But, as we have seen already, that is just what the luciferic spirits implanted in the human astral body before the coming of Christ. These spirits, infused with the being of Lucifer, worked to make human beings independent of each other, to segregate them. Now, if this influence had prevailed for too long, mankind would have lost its capacity for love altogether. But Christ turned to good the evil that would have resulted had Lucifer's influence become extreme. Lucifer endowed the human being with independence and freedom; Christ transmuted this freedom into love. 'The transformation of Lucifer's influence into good—that was the deed of Christ... And the bond Christ brought to mankind is what will lead us to spiritual love' (ibid.).

This point of view, Steiner says, 'throws a different light on the deeds of the luciferic spirits':

> Are we still justified in thinking of their once having lagged behind as due to indolence and laziness? No indeed, for it was done in order to fulfil a definite mission in *Earth* evolution: to prevent human beings from becoming fused into a mere mass through purely natural ties, as well as to prepare the way to Christ... This is one of the examples that show how an ostensible evil, a seeming error, can turn out for the best in the whole context of world events. *To enable the Christ to intervene in Earth evolution at the right moment, certain Moon spirits had to sacrifice their Moon mission and prepare for Him* [author's italics]. This shows us that Lucifer's retardation on the Moon can also be regarded in the light of a sacrifice. [GA 112, 28/06/09; see also GA 105, 10/08/08]

Steiner asks us to consider the following question: Can that which the backward spirits, luciferic spirits, did to mankind be termed 'bad in the trivial sense?' Our answer to this must surely be 'no'.

If we consider the facts which clairvoyant vision is able to test we find that in reality they have accelerated human evolution. Mankind would have had to wait until the very last point of time for the development of certain capacities, whereas through the action of these beings we gained them earlier... This was not wrong, but, wonderful as it may seem, something which in a higher sense indicates an infinitely wise guidance in the progressive evolution of humanity. [GA 105, 10/08/08]

The deeds of spiritual beings are intimately interwoven with the destiny of human beings on earth; our deeds are likewise interwoven with the karma of spiritual beings. In the future we shall need to create with love what hitherto has been created under the influence of Lucifer. We shall need to develop a love that does not concern mankind only, but penetrates right into the cosmos. Through developing what Rudolf Steiner terms 'a superabundance of love' (GA 120, 28/05/10) we repay Lucifer, consciously, for the services he has rendered us and through this repayment we contribute to his redemption.

Speaking of the task that lies before us Rudolf Steiner says:

We shall be able to channel this love into beings higher than ourselves, and they will accept this as our offering. It will be a soul sacrifice. This sacrifice in soul will rise up to those who once poured their gifts upon us like the smoke of incense rose up to the spirits in times when human beings still possessed the gifts of the spirit. In those days human beings were only able to send up the symbolic smoke of sacrifice to the gods. In times to come human beings will send up streams of love to the spirits and out of this offering of love higher forces will pour down to humankind which will work, with ever-increasing power, in our physical world, directed by the spiritual world. [GA 120, 28/05/08]

*   *   *

In a series of lectures entitled *Initiation, Eternity and the Passing Moment* (GA 138), Rudolf Steiner gives us a glimpse of Lucifer in relation to the temporal and eternal and also of our experience of him in the spiritual world. Steiner expresses himself very precisely in regard to this profound matter and it is therefore apposite to quote him at some length:

> When, in the world of the higher Hierarchies, we feel influenced to draw away from eternity to a state of independent concentration in the world, then it is that we feel the working of Lucifer... In sensory existence it is quite natural for us to be placed into the temporal, whereas in the spiritual world that lies—so to speak from a transitory point of view—above the astral world, it is natural for us no longer to perceive what is temporal, but only what is eternal. This devachanic experience that appears there as a longing for temporal life is echoed in the longing for eternity. The interplay of actually experienced time—time experienced in the passing moment—with the longing for eternity, arises because of the penetration of our world of the senses by the devachanic world, the world of spiritland. Just as for ordinary sense perception the spiritland is hidden behind our physical world, so the eternal is hidden behind the passing moment. Just as there is no point where we can say, 'Here ends the world of the senses, and here begins the spiritual world,' but everywhere the spiritual world permeates sensory existence, so each passing moment, in accordance with its quality, is permeated by eternity. We do not experience eternity by coming out of time, but by being able to experience it clairvoyantly in the moment itself... When speaking from the standpoint of clairvoyant consciousness, you can never say of beings that one is temporal and another eternal. To say that here is a temporal being or there an eternal being has no meaning for spiritual consciousness. Real meaning lies in something quite different. What underlies existence—the passing moment and eternity—is everywhere and forever, and the only way to put the question is, 'How comes it that eternity sometimes appears as the passing moment, that the eternal sometimes appears temporal, and that a being in the world assumes a form that is temporal?' It simply comes from this—that sensory existence, wherever it occurs, is interspersed with luciferic beings, and to the extent that these beings play into sensory existence eternity is rendered temporal. It must be said, 'A being appearing anywhere in time is eternal in so far as it has power to liberate itself from the luciferic existence, but in so far as it is subject to it, it remains temporal.' [GA 138, 29/08/12]

Steiner then goes on to make it clear that when we describe things in a spiritual way we can no longer use expressions of ordinary life. For instance, in ordinary life we should say: 'The human being has a body as an outer sheath and within it there is a soul and spirit being. The body is mortal, but the being of soul and spirit is immortal and eternal.' However, from the standpoint of the spiritual world, such a description would not be correct. 'Then,' says Steiner, 'it must be put in this way: "The human being is a being in whose nature as a whole, progressive, divine beings must work together with luciferic beings; to the extent that progressive, divine beings are in him, part of his being wrests itself away from all that is luciferic, and so comes to participate in the eternal. In so far as divine [progressive] beings work in us, we share in the eternal; in so far as the luciferic world works in us, all that is bound up with the temporal and transitory becomes part of our very being."

'The temporal and eternal thus appear as the working together of diverse beings. In the higher worlds there is no longer any sense in speaking of abstract opposites such as the temporal and the eternal because there they cease to have any meaning. There we have to speak of beings' (ibid.).

We see then that the concepts 'transitory' and 'temporal' are bound up with the luciferic principle, whereas, as Steiner illustrates in these lectures (GA 138), the Christ-principle is bound up with such concepts as 'eternity' and 'immortality'. We might be tempted to undervalue the luciferic principle and reject it in all circumstances because by it we perceive the temporal, the more transitory. However, Steiner stressed on numerous occasions that it is not right to look upon the Light-bearer as one of whom we should be afraid.

> Nor is it right to think that we must turn our back on Lucifer as from one from whom we must always escape. If one does that it is to forget the teaching of true occultism, namely, that here in the world of the senses there is a feeling analogous to that in the supersensible world. In sensory life one feels, 'I live in the temporal and yearn after the eternal; I live in the passing moment and crave for eternity.' In spiritual life there is the

feeling, 'I live in the eternal and long for the passing moment.' [Ibid.]

The more we learn from Rudolf Steiner about Lucifer and, as we shall see, Ahriman, the more it becomes apparent that we cannot form rigid or one-sided opinions about them; nor should we shun them indiscriminately.

Continuing his discussion on the 'transitory' and 'immortal', the 'moment' and 'eternity', Steiner describes the experience of someone who has become clairvoyant by his or her own efforts to open the 'eyes of the soul' and who meets Lucifer in supersensible worlds.

He [Lucifer] comes before the soul as a being forever striving to make the eternal, which otherwise is in constant movement and change, into the stable, temporal momentary, so that as something individual it can rejoice in its power to grow individually great... He appears [in supersensible worlds] as the great Light-bearer who leads, really leads, to bringing down into sensory existence all the treasures that pertain to real being in the spiritual world, and to the creation of its reflection and revelation in the world of the senses. If you follow Lucifer in this striving of his in supersensible worlds, then you are working for the fulfilment of the primordial task of the universe; that is, *to reveal the unrevealed* [author's italics], to commit to the moment all that is eternal and to make it possible that all that flows away into limitless eternity should be held fast in the inward greatness of the individual moment.

Now a desire exists in every human soul as an echo from the spiritual worlds to bring to fulfilment this striving to make manifest the unrevealed, to fix the external in the passing moment. Hence it is that when we enter supersensible worlds, either by way of initiation or by death, it is really Lucifer who acts as our Light-bearer. The dangers to which we are exposed when face to face with Lucifer in higher worlds are really only present when we take with us into these worlds too great a measure of what in sensory existence constitutes our right relation to Lucifer. Lucifer is only dangerous for our life in higher worlds if we take with us too much of the nature and essential being of our physical being...

The self-seeking strivings of every human soul that we regard as human and egoistic play into the life of the senses, and we know that the development of every soul must start from egoism. That is natural. We also know that human beings can work their way out from egoism. Into all that souls have been able to do on earth through egoism, there comes what we may call the manifestation of the eternal in the passing moment. Luciferic forces are forever playing into what is fixed in the individual soul and also into all that the individual human being can do for the whole world-order and existence through being an egoist and having the power to develop within an inward greatness that wells forth from his or her inner being. For what is individual greatness in the individual soul but the seed of all the greatness in the whole world evolution of the human being? What gave Homer, Shakespeare, Dante, Goethe their power to affect mankind? It was their egohood, and because within them there were whole worlds, worlds that issued forth from their inner being alone, out of their egohood. In this indirect way, through egohood, the impulses of spiritual life are introduced which are, from epoch to epoch, the mediators of the greatest spiritual deeds of mankind. In this we find Lucifer again. It is he who is Light-bearer, impulse and power behind all the greatness that radiates into human evolution from the mighty forces of eternity that, at a certain point in time, surge up from the individual human soul.

The human soul is placed between two poles that are simply the impression and reflection of all the worlds in which the soul actually stands. At the one pole the human soul hardens within itself, winds itself into the cocoon of its selfhood, and only desires what is of service to itself, what is for its self-gratification. At the other pole the human soul draws forces from its own depths that are able to radiate into the whole life of humanity. When does this egohood of the human being become light? This happens the moment we think how necessary it is for each one of us to sacrifice for others what ... belongs most deeply to our individual egohoods. But in all that we can do for our fellow human beings out of our individual egohoods lives Lucifer, the other pole of Lucifer; in all that each one of us can thus achieve for humanity under the influence of the Light-bearer lies a reflection of what Lucifer really is in higher worlds, a reflection of his creative activity, which is the revealing of the unrevealed.

Can we then say that Lucifer is evil, or can we say that Lucifer is good? One can only say that if we maintain that Lucifer is evil, and that we must flee from him, then it must also be said that we must avoid fire, because in certain circumstances it destroys life. On the path of initiation we find that the words 'good' and 'evil' cannot be used in this way for the description of any being of the supersensible world order. Fire is good when it acts in good conditions, evil when it works in evil ones; in itself it is neither the one nor the other. So it is with Lucifer . . . Lucifer becomes an evil being—rather, what he does becomes evil—when he arouses impulses leading only to self-gratification in the human soul . . . The acts of supersensible beings can be described as good or bad; the beings themselves, never! [GA 138, 30/08/12]

5. Ahriman

Through Lucifer's intervention humankind has been thrust down deeper into material, sensory existence than would have otherwise been the case and has thus come under the influence of Ahriman, whose realm is the mineral earth.

Whereas luciferic forces have imprinted themselves upon the inner being of the human being, Ahriman exerts his power from without (GA 121, 15/06/10).

Ahriman can be best characterized by saying: he is the Lord of Death; he is

> far and wide the ruler of all the powers that have to bring about in the physical sense-world what this world has to have, i.e. the annihilation and death of its entities [*Wesenheiten*]. Death in the sense-world is a necessary part of its organization, for otherwise the beings in it would accumulate to excess, if destruction of life were not at hand. The task of regulating this in a lawful way fell to Ahriman from the spiritual world... [GA 147, 25/08/13]

Ahriman's sovereign domain is the mineral world, a world that is dead. Now, because the earth world is constituted as it is, the mineral world and its laws pervade all the kingdoms of nature. All these kingdoms absorb mineral substances and are therefore subject to all the forces and laws that prevail in the mineral kingdom.

In whatever surrounds us as external, sensory nature, Ahriman is the rightful Lord of Death and, in this respect, should clearly not be regarded as being an evil power. Steiner states:

> We will enter into a right relationship with the sense-world only when we bring a creditable interest to bear upon it, when our interest in the sense-world is so reasonable that we can see everything in it without greedily demanding eternal life for any of its physical forms; on the contrary, that we can do without them when they meet their natural death. To be able to rejoice rightly in the things of the sense-world but not to be so depen-

dent on them as to contradict the laws of death and decay—this is the right relationship of the human being to the sense-world. To bring about this right relationship to growth and decay, human beings have the impulses of Ahriman within themselves; for this reason they pulsate in them. [GA 147, 25/08/13]

Ahriman, however, can (and does) overstep his legitimate bounds. Above all he can so far overstep them that he sets to work on human thinking. Those who do not see into the spiritual world and have no understanding of it will, of course, not lend credence to the fact that Ahriman can approach and influence our thinking. In so far as human thinking 'lives' in the sense-perceptual world, it is bound to the physical brain, which, according to the law of the mineral world previously mentioned, is subject to decay, to death. It is Ahriman's task to regulate the path of the human brain towards decay, but when he oversteps his territory Ahriman has the tendency to snatch our thinking out of the current of decay.

Because Ahriman is active in this way in human thinking and because, bound to the sense-world, people naturally perceive only the effects of the spiritual beings, those who are thus in the clutches of Ahriman feel the impulse to wrench their thinking out of its place in the great cosmic order. *The result is the materialistic frame of mind* [author's italics]; this is the reason people want to apply their thinking only to the sense-world, and those who refuse to believe in a spiritual world are those who are particularly obsessed by Ahriman—it is he who enters their thinking and prevails upon its remaining in the sense-world. [GA 147, 25/08/13]

A crass example of the way in which Ahriman manifests his power can be seen in spiritualistic seances during which fragments of etheric and astral bodies of those who have died are called into being. We may understand what is happening here when we consider that if we do not think spiritual thoughts, but only have thoughts that are oriented solely in accordance with a material content, then the way is open for Ahriman to tear phantoms and shadows out of such thinking which then roam through the sensory world. In quite a different context, but relevant to the thought just expressed, Steiner says:

> If people have not become practical occultists, the result of their inner attitude will be that they become rank, coarse-grained materialists who want to know nothing about spiritual matters. It is Ahriman who has enticed them into this, only they do not notice it. For Ahriman, however, the process is the following: when he succeeds in severing the physical thinking from its brain-bound foundation, he throws shadows and phantoms out into the world which then swarm through the physical world; with these, Ahriman is continually trying to establish a special ahrimanic kingdom.
>
> Unremittingly he lies in wait when people's thinking is about to pass into the stream wherein they themselves will journey through the gate of death; there Ahriman lurks, on the watch to snatch away and hold back as much of this thinking as possible, and to form out of it, to tear from its mother-soil, shadows and phantoms that will populate the physical world. Occultly observed, these phantoms drift around in the physical world disturbing the universal order. [GA 147, 25/08/13]

Elsewhere Rudolf Steiner gives us a clear picture of Ahriman's striving to establish a kingdom which Steiner designated the Eighth Sphere (see Appendix Four). One can say of Ahriman and his hosts that they want to wipe out the entire past; they want to do away with the 'balloon' of Saturn, Sun, Moon. None of that is to have any meaning for mankind. Ahriman wants to leave human beings with no more than what they have gained directly on the earth. In particular Ahriman and his hosts would like to destroy everything that the earth has brought over from the Old Moon. They would like the animal world to disappear, the plant world to disappear, and of the mineral world only the physical laws to remain. Above all they would like human beings to be removed from the earth and to form a new Saturn out of machines, a new world purely of machines. In this way the world should go on; that is actually their ideal. In the domain of external science it is their ideal to reduce everything to matter, to mechanize everything (GA 203, 11/03/21).

Clearly Ahriman has had a field day since Rudolf Steiner spoke in this manner over 70 years ago!

People who are treading the path of spiritual development, the development of the Self and the astral body, reach a point where they approach things in quite a different way from that to which they were accustomed before they undertook such a development. For instance, they learn to recognize that desire which comes from without (not that which comes from within, for that is luciferic), which attracts them to the objects and beings around them, is ahrimanic. 'In short, everything from without that tempts us to indulgence, this we recognize as the mark of Ahriman' (GA 145, 28/03/13).

We also learn to recognize as the hallmark of Ahriman everything from without that instils, inspires, fear in us—fear, in particular, of the spiritual world.

'The two poles are enjoyment and fear.' Steiner then goes on to say:

> Around us are the so-called material world and the so-called spiritual world; both these worlds appear to waking consciousness as *maya* or illusion. The sensible world appears as *maya*, for people do not realize that wherever external objects and entities stimulate the pleasures of the senses Ahriman is lurking, and it is he who excites desires in the soul. The fact that everywhere matter is imbued with spirit—which materialists deny—engenders fear; and when the materialists perceive that fear is welling up from within, from the astral domain, they stupefy themselves by inventing materialistic theories. And the words of the poet are profoundly true: 'The naïve never notice the Devil, that is Ahriman, even when he has them by the throat.' What is the purpose of monistic [i.e. materialistic] meetings? To conjure up the Devil. This is literally true, but people do not know it. Whenever meetings of materialistic monists are held today, proclaiming in neatly rounded theories that matter alone exists, Ahriman has them by the throat. There is no better opportunity for studying the Devil today than to attend the gatherings of materialists or monists. Thus when people have undergone a certain development in their astral body and Self, Ahriman accompanies them at every step. When we begin to see him, we can protect ourselves against him, for we are aware that behind

the allurements of sensual pleasure and the emotions of fear lurks Ahriman ... Wherever we dream of matter, there in reality is Ahriman. And the atomic theory of physics is grossly misleading, for the material atoms are simply the forces of Ahriman. [GA 145, 28/03/13]

Rudolf Steiner points out that in the ancient Mystery Schools it was taken for granted that those who sought and acquired knowledge would treat it with reverence. Only those who swore that they would regard the knowledge acquired as holy and would use it in the service of the Gods were admitted to the Mystery Schools. Such a reverential attitude was also engendered by atavistic feelings. Today it is essential for mankind to adopt this attitude again, but now in full waking consciousness. Humanity has passed through— indeed, is still passing through—an age of materialism. It needs to heal itself of materialism. This will only come about when mankind is once again imbued with the feeling, with the inner experience, of divine service which was once at the core of knowing.

But in the future this will have to be brought about consciously, and will only be possible if spiritual science spreads to more and more of humanity. Knowledge should not be like the seed that rots on the ground. Everything that is used for external convenience and arranging things mechanically is like the seed that rots. What is not placed in the service of the Gods is lost ... But Ahriman is able to do something with knowledge that is not acquired in the context of the service of the Gods. This knowledge is taken over into the service of Ahriman and establishes his power. His 'servants' introduce it into the world process and thereby create more obstacles for the world process than rightfully ought to be there or would otherwise have to be there. For, after all, Ahriman is the god of hindrance. [GA 170, 12/08/16]

From Rudolf Steiner we understand that, in 1879, Michael gained a victory over certain ahrimanic powers. He speaks in some detail about this victory and the preceding decades of battle between Michael and these ahrimanic powers in a series of lectures entitled *The Fall of the Spirits of Darkness*

(GA 177). Among other matters Steiner discusses in these lectures is that of education. For well over a century now we may say that whether at school, technical college or university it is particularly scientific attitudes and thinking 'patterns' which are imbibed by both child and adult. Their philosophy of life is then inevitably founded in a materialistic, scientific approach and they can but regard only those things to be real which can be perceived with their physical senses, only those things to be real which can be seen, heard, touched, smelt and tasted with physical sense-organs. Everything else is regarded as being no more than imaginary. When people think like this, Ahriman has the upper hand. It need hardly be mentioned that ahrimanic powers are finding abundant nourishment in our highly technological age. 'Who,' asks Steiner, 'are these ahrimanic powers which have established their fortresses in human minds since 1879?

> They are certainly not human. They are Angels, but they are backward Angels, Angels who are not following their proper course of evolution [see GA 13] and therefore no longer know how to perform their proper function in the spiritual world that is next to our own. If they still knew how to do it, they would not have been cast down [by Michael] in 1879. They now want to perform their function with the aid of human brains... 'Monistic' thinking is not really done by humans... We cannot stand up to this by putting our heads in the sand like ostriches, but only by consciously entering into the experience. We cannot deal with this by not knowing what monists think, for example, but only by knowing it. [GA 177, 20/10/17]

What is called for today is the building of bridges between ahrimanic science and spiritual science:

> It is indeed true, and initiates have always said so: 'When human beings are filled with spiritual wisdom, these are great horrors of darkness for the ahrimanic powers and a consuming fire. It feels good to the ahrimanic Angels to dwell in heads filled with ahrimanic science; but heads filled with spiritual wisdom are like a consuming fire and the horrors of darkness to them.' If we consider this in all seriousness we can feel: filled with spiritual wisdom we go through the world in a way which allows us to

establish the right relationship with the ahrimanic powers; doing the things we do in the light of this, we build a place for the consuming fire of sacrifice for the salvation of the world, the place where the terror of darkness radiates out over the harmful ahrimanic element. [GA 177, 20/10/17]

To Ahriman a free spiritual life (i.e. not entangled in the economic or political life) would mean a kind of darkness, and man's interest in it a burning fire. It is essential to establish a free spiritual life so that the right relationship may be adopted to the ahrimanic powers—and to the incarnation of Ahriman in the West in the future (GA 191, 01/11/19; GA 193, 04/11/19. See also Chapter 17).

Whereas through the millennia directly preceding Christianity, pagan wisdom was inspired by Lucifer who incarnated in the Far East (GA 191, 01/11/19; GA 193, 27/10/19 and 04/11/19), in the third millennium before Christ, since the middle of the fifteenth century—since the impulse for the development of individuality has been active—other forces have been at work whereby preparations are being made for the incarnation of Ahriman before only a part of the third millennium of the Christian era has elapsed. It is, Steiner states, of paramount importance that mankind shall find the right attitude towards the event of Ahriman's incarnation. His incarnation is being prepared for well in advance. He is, in fact, guiding certain trends and forces in evolution in such a way that they may be of the greatest possible advantage to him. 'Evil would result were people to live on in a state of drowsy unawareness, unable to recognize certain phenomena in life as preparations for Ahriman's incarnation' (GA 191, 01/11/19). The right stand to take is for us to begin to recognize certain phenomena in life that constitute preparations for Ahriman's incarnation.

One of these is evident in the generally accepted contention that what happens in the cosmos can be fully explained by means of mechanistic, mathematical conceptions (inaugurated by Galileo, Copernicus, Newton and others in the sixteenth and seventeenth centuries).

That is why anthroposophical spiritual science lays such stress upon the fact that *spirit* and *soul* must be discerned in the cosmos, not merely mathematical, mechanistic laws ... as if the cosmos were some huge machine. It would augur success for Ahriman's temptings if scientists were to persist in merely calculating the revolutions of the heavenly bodies, in studying astrophysics for the sole purpose of ascertaining the material composition of the planets—an achievement of which the modern world is so proud. [Ibid.]

These words, spoken over 70 years ago, are clearly just as valid today.

Another phenomenon connected with Ahriman's incarnation manifests itself in his endeavour to preserve and deepen the already widely accepted view that in regard to public welfare it suffices to provide for the economic and material needs of people. In the face of this view it is heartening to recognize that there is a growing number of people, particularly among the young, who—in recent times—realize that there is much more to life, to a happy and fulfilling life, than monetary wealth and material possessions. Nevertheless, by far the greater majority of people regard any striving along a path leading to the spiritual as superfluous. Such striving is regarded as useless as it does not help anyone to acquire a good position in life; it does not put money in people's pockets nor does it put food in their mouths.

'To the extent to which people can be roused into conducting their affairs not for material ends alone and into regarding a free and independent spiritual life, equally with economic life, as an integral part of the social organism—to that same extent Ahriman's incarnation will be awaited with an attitude worthy of humanity' (GA 191, 01/11/19).

Another tendency of benefit to Ahriman in preparing his incarnation—which we shall consider more closely later—is nationalism. Here we shall merely state that whatever drives wedges between groups of people and thus alienates them from mutual understanding strengthens Ahriman's hand.

Again, what will be of particular advantage to Ahriman is the narrow and simplistic conception of the Gospels which is

growing apace as we approach the third millennium. To go
into any detail in regard to a spiritual scientific understanding
of the New Testament, upon which Rudolf Steiner has
expounded in his many lectures on the four Gospels, the
Apocalypse, the Mystery of Golgotha, and so forth, would
however go beyond the framework of this book. Here we can
do no more than note that to swear by the literal content of
the Gospels is an illusory conception arising from what
Steiner calls a 'dimming of consciousness'. 'With the dimming of consciousness that inevitably occurs when the deeper
content of the Gospels is not revealed, people would fall
wholly into Ahriman's service, helping in a most effective
way to prepare his incarnation, and adopting towards him the
very attitude he desires' (ibid.).

                    *   *   *

Rudolf Steiner gives many more examples illustrating how
we may be led astray in a direction favourable to Ahriman for
his future incarnation in the third millennium AD, an event
also described in a later chapter.

Enough has been indicated here to give us a glimpse as to
how this event is being prepared. Some indication has also
been given as to how it should be understood and confronted.
In this connection a statement made by Steiner on numerous
occasions and in a variety of contexts regarding the relationship between Lucifer and Ahriman is of particular significance:

> It should be realized that just as external science becomes
> ahrimanic, the higher development of one's inner nature
> becomes luciferic if one gives oneself up to mystical experiences.
> The luciferic tendency wakens and becomes especially powerful
> in everyone who, without the self-training described in the book
> *Knowledge of the Higher Worlds and its Attainment* [GA 10], sets
> about any mystical deepening of the impulses already inherent in
> his or her nature. [GA 191, 02/11/19][1]

Rudolf Steiner continues:

> It all amounts to this, that in our time one only speaks truly of

oneself when one says that one hovers perpetually between two extremes: between the ahrimanic on the one side, where one is presented with an outer delusion, a *fata Morgana*, and, on the other, the luciferic element within one which induces the tendency to illusions, hallucinations and the like.[2] The ahrimanic tendencies in human beings today live themselves out in science, the luciferic tendencies in religion, while in art they swing between the one extreme and the other[3]... And then there are those who want to be neither the one nor the other, who do not rightly assess either the luciferic or the ahrimanic but want to avoid both... They want to be virtuous, avoiding both the ahrimanic and the luciferic.

But the truth of the matter is that Lucifer and Ahriman must be regarded as two scales of a balance and it is *we* who must hold the beam in equipoise.

And how can we train ourselves to do this?—By permeating what takes ahrimanic form within us with a strongly luciferic element. What is it that arises in people today in an ahrimanic form? It is their knowledge of the outer world. There is nothing more ahrimanic than this knowledge of the material world, for it is sheer illusion. Nevertheless, if the *fata Morgana* that arises out of the various branches of natural science can fill us with fiery enthusiasm and interest, then through our interest—which is itself luciferic—we can wrest from Ahriman what is his own.

That, however, is just what human beings have no desire to do; they find it irksome. And many people who flee from external, materialistic knowledge are misconceiving their task and preparing the best possible incarnation for Ahriman in earth-existence. Again, what wells up in people's inmost being today is very strongly luciferic.[4] How can we train ourselves rightly in this direction?—By diving into it with our ahrimanic nature, that is to say, by trying to avoid all illusions about our own inner life and impulses and observing *ourselves* just as we observe the outer world. [GA 191, 02/11/19]

Objective self-knowledge is fraught with 'many pitfalls and hazards', but to enter into this complex matter here is not our present task. Those who are earnestly striving after true self-knowledge may find considerable help in a number of lectures Steiner gave on this particular theme (e.g. GA 176, 10/07/17; GA 154, 26/05/14; also GA 16 and GA 10).

According to Rudolf Steiner the essential thing is that people should approach their own inner nature with 'ahrimanic cold-bloodedness and dispassion. Their inner nature is still fiery enough even when cooled down in this way! There is no need to fear that it will be over-cooled'.

> If the right stand is to be taken to Ahriman's future incarnation, we must become more objective where our own impulses are concerned, and far, far more subjective where the external world is concerned—not by introducing pictures of fantasy but by bringing interest, alert attention and devotion to the things of immediate, everyday life.

Nothing does more to prepare the path for Ahriman's incarnation than to find this or that tedious, boring:

> When people find one thing or another in everyday life tedious, boring ... the path which Ahriman wants to take for the benefit of his incarnation is greatly smoothed. Tedium is so widespread nowadays! I have known numbers of people who find it irksome to acquaint themselves, for example, with banking procedures, or the Stock Exchange, or single or double entry in bookkeeping. But that is never the right attitude. It simply means that the point has not been discovered where a thing burns with interest. Once this point is reached, even a dry cash-book can be just as interesting as ... Shakespeare's *Hamlet*. It is only a question of finding the point at which every single thing in life becomes interesting. [GA 191, 02/11/19]

What we need to realize—and a growing number of people are beginning to do so today—is that it is not the world but *we* who are at fault. Nothing, Steiner states, is more amenable to Ahriman than our failure to find interest in whatever meets us in life. In this connection, incidentally, Steiner makes the following relevant point: 'To be interested in something does not mean that one considers it justifiable. It means simply that one develops an inner energy to get to grips with it and steer it into the right channel' (ibid.).

One one occasion Rudolf Steiner described ahrimanic beings as 'beings of pain' who are striving to achieve the upright, the earth-sun oriented form of the human being. In this striving they undergo intense suffering: 'It is as though an animal were dimly to feel that it must stand upright, that it must be a man and that this tears its very being to pieces' (GA 208, 23/10/21). Their suffering can only be alleviated when they 'seize hold' of the human intellect. They strive again and again to fetter the human intellect in such a way that the human being is prevented from rising to higher levels of consciousness (Imagination, Inspiration, Intuition—see Appendix Five).[5] The outcome of this ahrimanic striving is, as we mentioned earlier, everything that has come into being—particularly since the fifteenth and sixteenth centuries—in the form of materialistic science. When materialism holds the reins in science Ahriman is able to unite himself with the human being. Ahriman's influence, manifest in everything that is mechanical, technical, is at work too in everything that tends to rob human beings of their true intelligence and make them into machines, robots. As just indicated, since the Renaissance the whole trend of life is towards mechanization, towards an ahrimanic science devoid of the spiritual.

To reiterate: the scientific view of the world is almost entirely if not totally ahrimanic. Rudolf Steiner makes the point that if we are to hold our own against the power of Ahriman then we must make every effort to understand and be fully conscious of his activity and purpose. 'We can do no better service for Ahriman,' Steiner claims, 'than to ignore the scientific view or to fight it out of ignorance. Uninformed criticism of scientific views does not combat Ahriman but helps him to spread illusion and confusion in a field that should really be shown in a clear light' (GA 177, 20/10/17).

What is now essential for mankind to develop is a real understanding of the nature of the Christ Being, otherwise materialistic science and the mechanized, computerized industrial and commercial life of today 'will inevitably send us into the jaws of earthly death, that is to say, a world of human beings living in a state of petrification will be created for the edification of the ahrimanic beings unless a spiritual understanding of the Christ can be introduced into our materialistic civilization' (GA 208, 23/10/21). It would mean a victory for Ahriman if we were unable to unfold a really spiritual conception of Christ free of theological abstraction. Such a spiritual understanding is not only a necessity in regard to the salvation of mankind but, Rudolf Steiner states, 'if we can bring Imagination, Inspiration, Intuition into what is now knowledge of the outer world, we shall be able to redeem the ahrimanic beings' (ibid.).[6] Ahriman will be victorious if mankind proves unable to unfold a living spiritual conception of Christ, free of theological abstraction.

Materialism—finding expression in materialistic monism and mechanized industrialism—can do no other than lead us into a world in which human beings exist (it can hardly be said that they live) in a state of petrification. Ahriman would succeed in bringing into being a world of lifeless and spiritless ice-bound rigidity[7] should we fail to introduce a spiritual comprehension of the Christ into a civilization which Ahriman currently dominates to a very large extent.

We need to remind ourselves that without Ahriman there would be no death, hence the necessity for his presence and activity in evolution. Without Ahriman there would be no pain and no sorrow (there is no joy in Ahriman's kingdom). But without pain or sorrow human beings would not be able to progress towards spiritual knowledge.

We can recognize here how true are the words spoken by Mephistopheles in answer to Faust's question, 'Who art thou then?' For Mephisto answers: 'Part of that Power, not understood, which always wills the Bad, and always works the Good.'

However, it is clear that Ahriman is totally against spiritual activity. His plan is to reduce everything to a formula, to a rigid form which allows of no change, no metamorphosis, no life to manifest itself. Ahriman can see no reason for architects to create beautiful buildings, of varying artistic beauty, when it is much simpler to manufacture a standard size and shape. Buildings should be constructed, Ahriman would contend, not, for instance, taking into account the aesthetic pleasure of the occupants but solely with utilitarian ends in mind. We can see that Ahriman would turn us away from the creation of original handicrafts and would have us confine production to models of which millions of copies can be mass-produced by computerized machinery. Ahriman, Rudolf Steiner points out, is able to manifest himself in an endless number of copies through the secret of number. Steiner gives us a telling example of this in the eighth scene of his Mystery Play *The Guardian of the Threshold*. There we are made cognizant of the fact that Ahriman is the ruler over those forces which, on earth, are active, at work, in the laws of measure and number (GA 14).[8]

Ahriman has no interest in human beings as individualities. He counts human beings only as far as number is concerned. They are no more than ciphers. It is his intention to bring them into his power; in particular he strives to do this by preventing them from taking the path towards spiritual science.

We may say that science as we know it today is concerned, basically, with 'counting' and 'measuring'. What can be counted and measured is accepted by science. For instance, the power needed to take a manned rocket to the moon has to be calculated—a well-nigh infinite number of extremely complex 'measurements' and 'quantities' have to be undertaken in order to make such an awe-inspiring journey to the moon and back. In Ahriman's kingdom the *qualitative* element is lacking entirely, for quality can be neither weighed nor measured; it is left out of account. For that very reason, all knowledge that is based solely on the quantitative and can touch no more than the surface of things is, in this sense, superficial. It is one-sided, not dealing with 'the innermost *being* of things' (GA 191, 02/11/19). Knowledge derived solely from the principles of weight and measure is, in short, illusion. 'Yes, with my intelligence I can apprehend the external world in the way that is the ideal of natural science. But the vista thus presented to me is wholly ahrimanic. This does not mean,' Rudolf Steiner emphasizes, 'that natural science is to be ignored or put aside; it is a matter of realizing that this natural science leads only to the ahrimanic illusion' (ibid.).

In his foreword to Rudolf Steiner's series of lectures entitled *The Boundaries of Natural Science* (GA 322), Saul Bellow draws our attention to an important fact that should never be lost sight of: 'To conclude ... that Steiner is "anti-science" would be a great mistake. To him science is a necessary, indeed indispensable stage in the development of the human spirit. The scientific examination of the external world awakens consciousness to clear concepts and it is by means of clear conceptual thinking that we become truly human.'

What things signify in space and time is their external aspect only. This temporal and spatial world is a world that is nothing but a *fata Morgana* if we take it to be reality. To 'surrender' to the external aspects of things is to allow ourselves to be enslaved by Ahriman. However, to give ourselves up entirely to our own inner life also leads to illusion, to dominance by Lucifer. All kinds of hallucinatory tendencies, 'all kinds of faculties fraught with illusion come into play' (GA 191, 02/11/19).

On many occasions we find Rudolf Steiner demonstrating the principles and potentialities of a spiritual science born out of an exact western type of knowledge. He often found it necessary to speak on this theme to those people who were striving to find an escape from the fetters of materialism and, in doing so, were falling victim to Lucifer's influence by perpetuating forms of medieval mysticism, or a theosophy with an oriental direction.

> Modern humanity has no business becoming rickety in soul by following a nebulous, imperfect mysticism. What is required today is to penetrate into our true inner nature with strength of spirit, with the same strength we have achieved in a much more disciplined way for the external world by pursuing natural science. And it is not in vain that we have achieved this. Natural science must not be undervalued! Indeed, we must seek to acquire the disciplined and methodical side of natural science. And it is precisely when one has assimilated this scientific method that one values the achievements of a nebulous mysticism at their true worth, but one also knows that this nebulous

mysticism is not what spiritual science must foster. On the contrary, the task of spiritual science is to seek clear comprehension of the human being's own inner being, whereby a clear, spiritual understanding of the external world is made possible in turn. [GA 322, 03/10/20][9]

* * *

Whereas before the Mystery of Golgotha mankind was exposed essentially to the influence of Lucifer, since that Mystery the human intellect is particularly exposed to the influence of Ahriman. As we have noted already, Ahriman's main objective is to stifle people's consciousness of their connection with the spiritual world. All the tendencies to materialism that we develop in our life of thought stem from this relationship between our intellect and the influence, the 'attacks', of Ahriman. The materialistic tendencies which predominate in our time originate in the confusion which Ahriman strives to promote in the human intellect (cf. GA 176, 14/08/17).

In ancient times there were people who knew, through their gift of clairvoyance, that Christ was present in the spiritual world and that He would incarnate on earth in a physical body. Paradoxically, people knew of the Christ who has to come, but once He had come they could no longer know of Him in the same way. Thus it was inevitable that from early on in the development of Christianity *faith* rather than *knowledge* was emphasized.

> Yet the Mystery of Golgotha is meant to illumine our world of concepts, for ideas born of faith are also concepts, are also our mental pictures. Furthermore, that is the realm in which the impulse from the Mystery of Golgotha meets all the attacks of Ahriman. Our intellect is the arena where the impulse of Christ fights the impulse of Ahriman. [Ibid.]

The stronger the power of Ahriman becomes the greater the need human beings will have of a force with which, over and above faith, they will be able to establish the Christ-impulse in their earthly consciousness. This force, Steiner states, is spiritual knowledge through which we should make the impulse of Christ our own. Spiritual knowledge will enable us to find within ourselves the spiritual power with which to protect and sustain the Christ-impulse in our consciousness against the assaults mounted by Ahriman.

Since the Mystery of Golgotha the Christ-impulse has been present in the world, and it is beyond Ahriman's power to eradicate it. Ahriman cannot change the fact that Christ, at the Baptism in the River Jordan, came into the world. But what he can do is so to transform the concept of Christ in the human intellect that a false picture of Him is created. 'Ahriman clouds and confuses the human intellect in many ways in order to attain his goal, not least in those places where people are apt to seek religious counsel' (ibid.). There we find that the cosmic-spiritual is seen completely in terms of the earthly. Indeed, the cosmic aspect is increasingly disappearing through the influence of Ahriman. Through his influence there is very little, if any, inclination today to recognize Christ as the 'Great Cosmic Spirit' who descended from cosmic heights to incarnate in the human body of Jesus of Nazareth. Ahriman's whole interest lies in diverting humankind away from the spiritual. Ahriman uses every possible trick to prevent us from seeing any cosmic aspect in the personality of Christ. Many are the descriptions of Christ which are strikingly ahrimanic: He is made to appear purely human, bereft of everything supersensible; everything possible is done to eliminate every suggestion of a cosmic quality.

One of the moves in this direction to humanize, and thus diminish, the importance of Christ is to make him into the 'Simple Man of Nazareth'. A recent example of this is in a serious study of evil by the author Brian Masters, whose previous books have included in-depth enquiries into the minds of serial murders. Masters's 1996 work, *The Evil that Men Do*, contains some very important observations on the subject, yet in the same book he also posits a very superficial view of Jesus Christ. For instance, he writes: 'I say Jesus is almost unique [i.e. in his wisdom] because to make him without parallel of any kind *would be to fall into the trap of god-creation* [author's emphasis]. Francis of Assisi surpassed him in compassion and humility (Jesus could be quite proud at times); Dr Johnson surpassed him in creative wisdom; Theresa of Avila was more humorous, less solemn, and Aelred of Rievaulx more friendly. Grand Duchess Ella had more courage, and even Audrey Hepburn more spunk.' Masters clearly endorses A.N. Wilson's conception of Christ, for Wilson writes: 'To suggest that he was an incarnate divinity threatens to deprive the central figure in the Gospels of his moral seriousness' (A.N. Wilson, *Jesus*, Sinclair-Stevenson 1992, p. 158).

An equally materialistic and even more irreligious view of Christ is promulgated by the increasing number of published books dealing with the 'mystery' of the French village of Rennes le Château, a niche 'industry' sparked off by the publication of *The Holy Blood and the Holy Grail* in 1982. This book and many of the titles that have followed in its wake stress Jesus as a mere human who never underwent the Crucifixion and Resurrection (some titles deny that these events occurred) and who, through a subsequent relationship with Mary Magdalene, fathered a blood-line that became the Merovingian kings of France. The Knights Templar feature greatly in a number of these books, often in a denigratory or misleading way, while other titles claim secret information on the origin of Freemasonry and on the Hermetic tradition. The various titles are written in a very plausible pseudo-academic and authoritative style, quoting 'original' research mixed in with verifiable facts, the combination of which a gullible reader will trustingly assume is completely true and objectively presented.

Speaking 90 years ago, Rudolf Steiner says in the first lecture of the cycle *The Gospel of St John* (Hamburg, 18–31 May 1908):

> This expression 'the Simple Man of Nazareth' ... has a very close connection with the materialistic tendency of mankind which has been in process of development now for centuries... But in

those periods of human evolution in which humanity could still
lift its perceptions to the unseen world, it was possible to say: Of
course this or that historical personality outwardly, in external
appearance, may be compared with the 'Simple Man of Nazareth', but in what is spiritual and invisible in His personality, Jesus
of Nazareth stands before us as a unique figure ... Let us have no
illusions! Materialism first forced its way into the religious life.
Materialism in its relation to the facts of outer natural science is
very, very much less dangerous for the spiritual development of
mankind than it is in its relation to the interpretation of religious
mysteries. [GA 103]

The true Christ-impulse can, in our time, only be perceived, presented and experienced by spiritual science. What
we can find in spiritual science we cannot find in any natural
scientific or historical account to be a description of Christ in
His spiritual form. Spiritual science is concerned with spiritual perception.

Just as spiritual science can describe a faculty of sight which is on
a higher level than that of the [physical] eye, so it can describe
the Christ-impulse through which the spiritual world becomes
visible. It is therefore possible to attain insight into the Christ-
impulse, but insight does not prevent attacks from Ahriman.
They must be met with courage. The reason people do not want
to know about the concept of Christ attained through spiritual
science is because of a subconscious fear that as soon as the
Christ-impulse is understood it will arouse Ahriman's opposition. [Ibid.]

On one occasion, answering the question so many people
ask—Why does a good God allow evil and pain to exist?—
Rudolf Steiner, referring specifically to pain, answers:
'Nothing in the way of joy, happiness, blessedness has come
about except through pain. To refuse pain and opposition is
to refuse beauty, greatness and goodness' (ibid.).
The Christ-impulse cannot be attained without pain. It
cannot be attained through painless, sensuous feelings of
well-being such as those conveyed by, for example, Ralph
Waldo Trine in his book *In Tune with the Infinite.*
Rudolf Steiner reminds us again and again that Lucifer acts

in partnership with Ahriman. They both have great interest in deluding us concerning the necessity of our entering courageously into the conflict between Christ and Ahriman. They conjure up such mental pictures in us as 'in tune with the Infinite' and thus divert us from facing the conflict. Lucifer–Ahriman's joint invention, 'harmony with the Infinite', is so much more comfortable and pleasant. 'However, it is an attitude that is the equivalent of going through life blindfolded, seeking only appeasement. In modern times people shrink from the many-sided battle to attain spiritual insight; this attitude is bound to call up opposing forces just as appear when something right, which ought to be furthered, is left neglected' (ibid.).

The Christ-impulse can only be reached by courageously undergoing the suffering and pain that is involved in facing the conflict that takes place in our intellect—or in our consciousness in general—between the Christ-impulse and ahrimanic impulse.

From Rudolf Steiner we learn that it is only when reason is permeated by Ahriman that it leads into untruth. Similarly, when Lucifer permeates faith it leads away from truth. 'But neither faith nor reason as such lead to untruth or error. In the religious sense they are gifts of God' (GA 176, 21/08/17). It is when Ahriman insinuates himself into reason that confusion is brought about. Such insight, Rudolf Steiner states, can only be obtained by penetrating into the actual spiritual world. 'To do this requires one to make the effort to grasp the ideas, the descriptions which depict the spiritual world. If one persists in living in arid abstractions one sins against reason and remains ignorant of the fact that through the development of reason in the fifth post-Atlantean epoch the human "I" is to enter the consciousness soul' (ibid.).

It is only since the fifteenth century that it has 'become most thoroughly possible for the human being to take hold of the Intelligence. For since that time the spiritual soul/consciousness soul [see Appendix Six] is present in us, and the spiritual soul is the human being's very own, therefore it can make the intelligence its very own' (GA 237, 03/08/24). Since the onset of the age of the spiritual soul materialism has become more and more predominant and, therewith, also the influence of Ahriman (cf. GA 238, 12/09/24). The possibilities for Ahriman to interfere in the life of human beings have clearly become ever greater since the fifteenth century.

In our modern age both Ahriman and Lucifer can exert a particularly strong influence upon human beings when a diminution, a dimming of consciousness occurs. Any loss of the power of reasoning gives splendid opportunity for Ahriman to instil into the human soul all kinds of suggestions.

> Ahriman uses such methods to bring his influence to bear...
> When we are fully conscious [he has] no real access to our soul.
> But when our spirit, i.e. our consciousness, is suppressed then ahrimanic beings have immediate access. Dimmed consciousness is for ahrimanic and luciferic beings the window or door through which they can enter the world and carry out their intentions. They attack people when they are in a state of dimmed consciousness and take possession of them. [GA 176, 04/09/17][10]

We shall return to this theme in a later chapter.

Ahriman's ceaseless endeavour is to appropriate our intelligence and not allow us to realize what we can achieve by means of our own thinking. To this end, he also has powerful allies, the Asuras [see Appendix Seven]. We must constantly be on the alert to Ahriman's encroachment. In particular, Ahriman takes full advantage of moments when we fall into a kind of twilight consciousness, 'when we feel not quite securely anchored in the physical world and begin to yield ourselves to the whirl of the universe, when we do not stand firmly and steadily on our own feet as individualities. These are the moments when it behoves us to be on our guard' (GA 254, 25/10/15). The best protection against Ahriman's insinuation is to develop clear, exact thinking. 'We should go even further,' says Steiner, 'and try to avoid colloquialisms and current catchwords, for directly we use such words which come not from thought but from habits of speech we are not exercising thinking—even if only for a very short time. These are particularly dangerous moments because they are not heeded. We should really be careful to avoid using words behind which there is not sufficient reflection' (ibid.).

Ahriman finds easy access to us whenever our consciousness is limited to the purely material aspects of things, or (as already intimated) dimmed down below normal, as can happen through organic causes (e.g. the use of a drug such as cocaine), agitation, rage or other forms of uncontrolled behaviour (cf. GA 176, 04/09/17). At such times our Double also comes into its own [see Appendix Eight].

Nothing, Rudolf Steiner maintains, can effectively be done in any sphere of life unless wide-awake consciousness is developed and nurtured. Life-situations—whether individual or global—need to be approached with concepts and ideas gained from spiritual knowledge, spiritual science. Spiritual knowledge can stir us to wide-awake participation, whereas a solely materialistic view of life-events allows us to 'sleep' through, be unaware of, things which demand a clear and proper judgement (ibid.).

Here the point needs to be made again that Rudolf Steiner is not suggesting that materialistic science should be ignored and that one should dedicate oneself solely to spiritual science in order to approach life-events fruitfully: 'Contrary to the belief of many, it is not a question of adhering solely to one or the other science, nor can one be substituted for the other. Rather could they be compared with the right and left ear; both are necessary for proper hearing' (GA 176, 14/08/17).[11]

It may be said that today human beings are in the very throes of the struggle to attain a condition of balance between Lucifer and Ahriman. 'Deep reflection upon the powers which can grow in us as a gift from the Christ, upon spiritual knowledge and upon a spiritual view of the world suited to the time—this and this alone will enable us to find our way to a condition of balance between the luciferic influence on the one side and the ahrimanic influence on the other' (GA 208, 23/10/21).

Of the two powers, Lucifer and Ahriman, it is the latter which in the present age is the more influential, the more powerful. We are 'obliged' to carry on the struggle just mentioned within an Ahriman-dominated world. It is in this world that we need to be wide awake and aware of Ahriman's influence; lack of such alert awareness would—indeed, frequently does—see us succumb to an utterly mechanical order of things. Lucifer strives to restrain us from action and make us into dreamers, mystics, who sooner or later lose all interest in earthly existence. The aim of Ahriman, on the other hand, is to fetter us to earthly existence. That is why Ahriman wants to mechanize everything, to 'press everything down to the level of mineral existence' (GA 208, 23/10/21).[12] In contrast to Lucifer, it is not Ahriman's aim that we should be inactive; we can act and work as much as we find possible, *but* everything must be stereotyped, carried out according to a rigid, pedantic routine. Ahriman is the great inspirer of routine. 'He is the inspiring genius behind the everlasting drawing-up of statutes. Ahriman is in his element when he sees a committee drawing up statutes! Statute I provides for such and such a procedure; Statute II provides for something else; Statute III deals with the privileges of Members; under Statute IV the Members must do this or they must do that. And so it goes on, *ad infinitum*' (ibid.). Ahriman stimulates us to action—only, of course, everything must be done in accordance with a prescribed pattern and schedule. Every-thing must be compressed into so and so many paragraphs, as it were. Ahriman would have everyone slavishly follow a programme of what he or she has to do during the day—and then carry it out 'mechanically', without any consideration to the prevailing circumstances. 'Thinking with his or her legs, as it were, and not with the head' (ibid.). Whereas Lucifer tries to make us think only with our head, Ahriman's aim is to make us think with our legs.[13] On the one side there are people whose ideal is to dwell in a state of exaltation with their legs crossed under them like a statue of the Buddha; on the other side we find the typical Westerners whose 'legs' rush them from one event to another—often giving the impression that they are not really conscious of what they are doing. The only way of salvation from these two extremes is, according to Steiner, to nurture spiritual knowledge, to permeate everyday life—in both thought and action—with spiritual knowledge. Thought must be spiritualized in order that the spirit may lay hold of the whole human being, not only of the head. When the spirit lays hold of the whole human being, the world of Ahriman can be conquered, and when the world of Ahriman is conquered by the spirit it is redeemed.

On a number of occasions Rudolf Steiner makes a point of stressing that there can be no question of censuring Ahriman's influence nor of denegrating that which is useful and justified in, for instance, the drawing-up of statutes and programmes. The point he repeatedly makes in this connection is that such things must be spiritualized. In our modern age we can hardly do otherwise than avail ourselves of ahrimanic devices. For instance, in a lecture entitled 'Technology and Art' we can hear:

> It can easily happen that people imagine they must take great care not to expose themselves to these destructive forces; that they must protect themselves from all the influences of modern life; that they must closet themselves in a room containing the right surroundings, with walls of the colour indicated by theosophy [sic], to make sure that modern life cannot reach them in any way that would be harmful to their bodily organization.
>
> I really do not want my lectures to have this effect. Everything of the nature of withdrawing and protecting oneself from the influences of all that we necessarily have to encounter as world karma arises out of weakness. But anthroposophy can only strengthen the human soul [Gemüt], and should develop those forces that inwardly strengthen and arm us against these influences. Therefore, never within the compass of our spiritual movement could any kind of recommendation be given to cut oneself off from modern life, or *to turn spiritual life into a kind of hothouse culture* [author's emphasis]. [GA 275, 28/12/14]

Elsewhere Steiner is even more 'down-to-earth':

> If anthroposophy were to adopt a fanatic attitude, if anthroposophy were ascetic, it would thunder against the modern

civilization based on electricity. Of course this would be non-sense, for only world-conceptions that do not reckon with reality can speak in this way. They may say: 'Oh, this is ahrimanic, let us avoid it!' But this can only be done in an abstract way. For the very people who thunder against Ahriman, and tell us to beware of him, go downstairs after their sectarian meeting and enter an electric tramcar! So that all their thundering against Ahriman, no matter how holy it may sound, is (excuse the trivial expression) simply rubbish. *We cannot shut our eyes to the fact that we must live with Ahriman, but we must live with him in the right way, that is to say, we must not allow him to have the upper hand* [author's italics].

After giving some important explanations as to how our thinking must be changed, Steiner concludes this lecture concerning electricity with the words:

We must have the courage to use moral concepts against these anti-moral concepts, when speaking of electricity. This is what modern men and women find uncanny and sinister. They find it uncomfortable to admit to themselves that when they get into the electric tramcar they are sitting on the seat of Ahriman. So they become all mystical and form sectarian meetings in which they say: 'One has to beware of Ahriman,' but that is not what matters. What matters is that we know: from now on the development of the earth will be such that the nature forces, which enter into our cultural lives, must themselves come under the influence of Ahriman. And only if one is conscious of this can one find the right way. To develop this consciousness is one of the duties of anthroposophists. Anthroposophy cannot just be taken as a kind of substitute for what was formerly given in the various religious doctrines. [GA 220, 28/01/23][14]

Clearly today Steiner could give an illustrative example of greater relevance than that of the electric tramcar. For instance, he would, no doubt, speak in similar terms about the use or non-use of the computer or telephone.

If we succeed in spiritualizing all the various branches of our modern civilization, even the use of such an ahrimanic invention as the computer 'can be raised to a level where the ahrimanic element is redeemed. Conscious realization of spiritual life and spiritual reality alone can make this possible. Those who are materialists and use ... machines today are very deeply involved in the world of Ahriman. These words are not intended to be a censure of the demonology that has made its way into our modern civilization; the point is that the demons themselves must be redeemed... When it is a matter of spiritual science, of course means must be used to ensure that its accuracy is preserved'—by accurate mechanical recording, for instance. 'In this sense the ahrimanic element can be made to render genuine service to the spiritual life' (ibid.).

One of the main characteristics of Ahriman is that he neither knows, nor is concerned with, an impartial relation to truth. He knows nothing about striving for truth by simply trying to arrive at ideas which accord with objective reality. It is a matter of complete indifference to him whether an idea he formulates is in accordance with reality. What he says is said *not* because it is in accord with facts, but only in order to achieve, produce, an *effect*. 'It would be ahrimanic,' Rudolf Steiner says, 'if I were to tell someone something about our building [i.e. the First Goetheanum] in order to get the person in question to undertake a certain task—saying things that I know will influence the person to undertake the task without any regard for whether or not what I say is true' (GA 170, 28/08/16). When Ahriman 'speaks' he is interested in the effects of what he says, not with the truth in the human sense. It is not difficult to recognize his influence in much of the commercial advertising and political propaganda perpetrated today.

Steiner gives us many examples of Ahriman's 'legitimate' tasks in the spiritual world and—as paradoxical as it may seem—also in human affairs. Mention has just been made of an example of the latter, namely, where Ahriman creates a disharmony between facts and the ideas we form and express about such facts. If Ahriman were not active in this way, there would be no lying in the world. If he were not exerting his influence we should all be like innocent lambs, for the impulse would always be present *never* to form concepts which did not tally with the facts. We should only express what we have actually observed as fact, but we should do this of *necessity*. It would be impossible for us to do anything else and there would, therefore, be no question of human beings being capable of free spiritual activity. In order to be able to speak the truth as *free* beings, the possibility to lie must be in us. Without the intervention of Ahriman in the evolutionary process, we should have no possibility of attaining such freedom.

> If we are to be able to speak the truth as free beings it must be possible for us to lie, and we are therefore obliged to develop within ourselves the power to conquer Ahriman every time we speak. He has to be there, 'provocative and active, doing his devil's work'. Those words should give you a picture of Ahriman's presence and of how error only occurs when we follow him directly instead of remembering that he is the one to be overcome as, provocative and active, he goes about his devil's work. Some people speak about flight. They say, pulling long faces: 'But is this not perhaps something ahrimanic? Oh, I must not have anything to do with this!' In many cases, the only thing all this signifies is that the person in question is moving towards the comforts of Lucifer and leaving freedom behind. [GA 170, 26/08/16]

Both forces, those of Lucifer and of Ahriman, play an essential role in the liberation of the individual human being. Without them we would not—and could not—attain to love- and wisdom-filled freedom of spiritual activity. Through the luciferic temptation in the Garden of Eden the separation from the divine world (heaven) took place without which human beings would not have been given the opportunity to achieve selfless love in full consciousness. It is just through the activity of Lucifer that a seed was sown that can grow and blossom into our attainment of spiritual freedom.

As we have just noted, Ahriman, the Spirit of Lies, and of soulless material abundance and ease, also places us in a situation where we have freedom—freedom of choice. For instance, through his activity we are given the possibility of either succumbing to a robot existence or of availing ourselves of the technological and scientific achievements he has inspired in us in order to lead a life more free from the restraints, limits, of natural law and necessity than it otherwise could be. We have also noted already that it is to Ahriman that we owe our technological ingenuity.

It is to Lucifer that we owe our artistic gifts. Rightly approached luciferic forces can free us from Ahriman, who would direct our attention solely to the prosaic, factual circumstances of the physical world. Through this liberation we can gain the faculty of creative, imaginative thinking, by means of which the first steps towards a conscious experience of the reality of the spiritual world are taken and the barriers to supersensible knowledge, erected by our sense-bound intellect, are broken through.

Similarly, consciously faced and understood, the ahrimanic forces can help us lead responsible lives in the world into which we have incarnated. They can assist us to remain consciously aware of every step we take in our spiritual striving and prevent us creating a luciferic fanciful world permeated by illusion.

Held in balance by the Christ-imbued heart, both Lucifer and Ahriman are the 'servants' we need to fulfil our mission on earth as the one and only being who, in full consciousness and freedom, can assist the Michaelic forces to redeem, spiritualize, the earth and bring into being the New Jerusalem.

In short, with Rudolf Steiner, we may say: 'The task of evil is to promote the ascent of the human being' (GA 95, 29/08/06).

A few days before he died, Rudolf Steiner wrote of the dangers of falling victim to 'sub-nature'. He points out that by far the greater part of that which is active in modern civilization through technology and industry is not nature at all, but sub-nature. 'It is a world which emancipates itself from nature—emancipates itself in a downward direction... Technical science and industry become sub-nature' (GA 26, 12/03/25). We must find the inner strength of knowledge so that we do not become Ahriman's slaves in our technical civilization. We need to understand sub-nature for what it really is. It is we, under the dazzling influence of Ahriman, who have created a new world, a world of sub-nature. We are—in this creation—the 'handmaidens' of the Lord of this World, Ahriman. He is the originator of our ideas, but we are responsible for their manifestation in the world in which we live. It is only now—during the last few decades of the twentieth century—that our scientists and inventors are beginning to realize that our world of technology is not a creation of nature but a creation of ourselves. In short, we must take the responsibility for what is invented.

Steiner goes further than this. We need to find, in conscious experience, a knowledge of the spirit, 'wherein human beings will rise as high above nature as in their sub-natural technical activities they sink beneath her. They will thus create within themselves the inner strength *not to go under*' (ibid.). Steiner himself, in 1925, refers to electricity in this connection. Today, over seven decades later, we could speak of nuclear energy as a particularly powerful force which leads down from nature to sub-nature.

Needless to say—Rudolf Steiner stresses this point time and again—there can be no question of advocating a return to earlier states of civilization. We need this relation to sub-nature for the development of the consciousness soul, the spiritual soul. What is now required of us is that we acquire a right relation to the ahrimanic. This implies, *inter alia*, that we can no longer say that, as scientists, we are not concerned with morality; we can no longer say that science is amoral. The attitude that so many technologists and scientists of today take is: 'I am only concerned with objective facts. It is not my task to be involved with their goodness or badness.' Such an attitude plays right into the hands of Ahriman.

In the mechanical-material sphere the purely ahrimanic is dominant. In spiritual science, on the other hand, another sphere is created in which there is no ahrimanic element: 'It is just by receiving in knowledge this spirituality to which the ahrimanic powers have no access that man is strengthened to confront Ahriman *within the world*' (ibid.).[15]

6. The Fall of Lucifer and the Human Astral Body

It has already been indicated that more than one battle with the Dragon has taken place. It should also be noted that it has not always been Michael, either alone or together with other spiritual beings, who has opposed and conquered the Dragon. The battles between progressive spiritual beings and adversarial, hindering spiritual beings began in the long-distant past—well before the earth, as we know it today, came into being. It is beyond the scope of these pages to follow Rudolf Steiner's descriptions of all these confrontations. We shall confine ourselves, in this chapter, to a consideration of the War between Angels on the Old Moon, and, in the following chapter, to Michael's battles against Ahriman in the past with particular reference to the nineteenth century.

Before looking at the fall of Lucifer here, it is appropriate to include a few supplementary words regarding the significance of evil for the evolution of the earth and of mankind.

On one occasion, to help us approach an understanding of the need for the presence of evil, Steiner says the following:

In order that the evolution of the world might progress, something quite extraordinary had to intervene ... In the ancient Mysteries one attempted to make it comprehensible in the following manner. At a certain stage of initiation into the ancient Mysteries, the neophytes were led into the presence of hostile powers who had a cruel and horrible appearance and who performed the most dreadful deeds in the sight of the neophytes. But, in reality, the performers were none other than masked priests, masked sages. In order to bring about the necessary temptation, priests had disguised themselves in ghastly demonic forms, as dreadful beings, performing the most terrible deeds that one could possibly imagine. [GA 110, 18/04/09]

This performance was done in order to show the neophytes how far they, in their development, could stray from the right path. They were given the illusion that they stood face to face with evil. It was only when the unmasking took place that they could see the truth. In order to strengthen the neophytes and arm them against it, evil was enacted by the priests. This, Rudolf Steiner states, 'was only a reflection of something that actually took place in cosmic development' (ibid.).

Rudolf Steiner gives us a picture of this development in the lecture from which has just been quoted. He shows us how, at an early stage of cosmic development—and for the good of mankind's future development—certain spiritual beings of the Second Hierarchy, the Mights (Dynamis), had to receive what he calls 'adverse orders'. These Mights may be termed the 'Gods of Hindrance', of impediment in the widest sense of the word. These 'detached' Mights were not evil in themselves; on the contrary, by throwing obstacles across the path of evolution they were the greatest promoters of evolution. Mankind would certainly have continued to develop without these obstacles. However, humanity could be made stronger by having obstacles put in its path. Steiner gives us a simple picture to illustrate what he means: 'Suppose you have to push a cart. You develop your strength in pushing it. If it were more heavily loaded, you would have to push harder but as a result you would also develop greater strength' (GA 110, 18/04/09).

The adversarial Mights (Dynamis), though one need not regard them as being evil, were, nevertheless, the originators of evil because, out of the conflicts that arose between them and the 'good Gods', evil gradually arose. Their course of development took quite a different turn from that of those Mights who had not received 'adverse orders'. The adversely commanded Mights acted quite differently and as a result they became the tempters of the beings we know as Angels. During the Old Moon development the Angels were passing through their 'human' stage (cf. GA 13, Ch. 4). These Angel-human beings, as Steiner calls them, witnessed the effect of the obstacles on the course of evolution. Some of them

remained with the good Gods, others chose to join the
adversely commanded Mights. When the Old Moon evolution passed over into that of the Earth the whole process was
repeated. In consequence both advanced Angel-human
beings (those who did not attach themselves to the stream of
adversarial Mights) and retrograde Angel-human beings
appeared during Earth evolution. The former approached
the human beings during Lemuria when they became mature
enough to receive the seed of the ego. 'They gave them the
choice, as it were, of ascending then and there into the
spiritual world, thus having nothing to do with what had
mingled with the course of world evolution since the Old
Moon' (GA 110, 18/04/09). The retrograde Angel-human
beings—luciferic beings—approached the human astral body
(they were unable to reach the human ego) and 'injected'
into the human astral body the results of the conflicts
between advanced and retrograde spiritual beings, the results
of the War in Heaven. Mights (Dynamis), who had been
'adversely commanded' and became Spirits of Hindrance,
slipped the consequence of their deeds into the human astral
body. But here, when the Old Moon evolution passed over
into that of the Earth, these deeds signified something quite
different. They became the possibility of error and evil.
'Human beings had now been given the possibility of error
and evil, but at the same time they also received the capacity
to rise above error and evil through their own strength'
(ibid.).

We need to realize here that such exalted spiritual beings as
the Mights could not have the power to become evil of their
own free volition. They had to be 'adversely commanded'.
Only the Angels, the spiritual beings closest to us human
beings, had the possibility, during the Old Moon evolution, to
either follow or not to follow the Powers of Hindrance, the
adversarial Mights. 'Those who did not succumb are represented in pictures depicting the victories fought out in the
heavens. They express what came to pass during the Moon
evolution when the human being had progressed to the stage
of the incarnation of the astral body, that is, to the human-

animal stage (cf. GA 13, Ch. 4). Those Angel beings who remained pure, as it were, tore themselves away from the course of the Moon development and escaped from what was taking place below on the Moon' (GA 110, 18/04/09). This happening is represented in many different ways. Originally it was depicted in the fight between the Archangel Michael and the Dragon. We also find it particularly clearly expressed in illustrations of Mithras and the Bull. The purpose of such illustrations was not to suggest that these Angel beings had forsaken their duty by tearing themselves away from the course of the Moon development. They were meant, Rudolf Steiner advises us, to depict an ideal for the future. ' "These beings," it was said, "preferred to ascend into spiritual worlds. You, on the other hand, descended and so have many other beings with you who follow the Powers of Hindrance. It is now up to you to transform what you have absorbed through your descent, and carry it upwards into the spiritual world. On the upward path you are called upon to become a Michael, a conqueror of the Bull," for symbols of this kind may be interpreted in two such different ways' (ibid.).

* * *

We have already considered some aspects of the luciferic influence. We have seen that, during the Lemurian stage of Earth evolution, it was the human astral body that was 'penetrated' by this influence and that as a consequence the human 'I' was drawn into the sphere of luciferic forces and thus contains an egoistic component.

Contrasting the activities and 'natures' of the Spirits of Hindrance—luciferic and ahrimanic beings—with those of the Progressive Spirits, the good Gods, Steiner speaks of the latter as Spirits of Light and the former as Spirits of Darkness. In spite of his name and function as Light-bearer, Lucifer may rightly be seen as a great Spirit of Darkness when brought into relation to the Progressive Spirits.

Luciferic beings were in league with ahrimanic beings from Atlantean times onwards (cf. GA 13 and GA 177). The aims of these spirits gave rise to counter-aims of 'Good Spirits',

Spirits of Light. As Steiner repeatedly stresses (we have noted this fact already), the Spirits of Darkness wanted, fundamentally, the best for humanity in those early times. They wanted human beings to have the capacity for absolute freedom—but humanity was not mature enough for this at the time. The Spirits of Darkness wanted to provide humanity with impulses that would enable every human being to be an independent individual. However, as humanity was not yet ready for such a development a counter-force had to be set up, brought into action, by the Spirits of Light. A brake had to be put on the aims of the Spirits of Darkness. This was done by 'moving' human beings from the spiritual heights and 'placing' them on the earth— symbolically described in the expulsion from the Garden of Eden. This means, in reality, that human beings were being placed in the stream of heredity. If the power of the Spirits of Darkness had not been countered by the Spirits of Light, not only would every human being have become an independent individuality but it would also have meant that everyone would have become spiritual very quickly, effortlessly, while still immature. But this was not to be. Human beings were to come to full development through undergoing education on earth, through confronting and working with the forces of the earth. This was achieved by the Spirits of Light by placing mankind in the stream of hereditary traits. Human beings were connected with the earth through everything connected with procreation, with love in the earthly sense, and with the process and experience of physical death. (See Appendix Nine.) This, says Steiner, is the reason why there are so many symbols of procreation and heredity in the ancient religions. People had to learn to live together in nations and tribes, 'with blood relationships as the signature for the way affairs were ordered on earth' (GA 177, 16/10/17). Such was the expression of the counter-forces exercised by the Spirits of Light right up to, roughly, the beginning of the fifteenth century. Then the situation began to change; by the last third of the nineteenth century it was completely reversed. We shall be considering this change later. (See p. 87.)

From the Lemurian to the Atlantean time the human being was drawn more and more forcefully into dense matter by the luciferic influence. In this way it became possible for Lucifer to take possession of the human astral body to such an extent that men and women inevitably descended ever deeper into a dense physical body. Rudolf Steiner describes how, during the same period, spiritual beings who had formerly been Lucifer's companions rose ever higher and refused to have anything to do with the retarded beings. A battle took place between Michael and his hosts against Lucifer and his followers. While the luciferic beings invaded the human astral body, the higher spiritual beings cast them down.

> One of these higher beings is represented in Michael, who cast the luciferic beings into the abyss and assigned the earth to them as their sphere of action; and it was within the astral body of the human being that they sought to exercise their influence. 'Heaven' was no longer the habitation of these beings. They had been cast down to earth by the beings whose scene of action was now found in heaven. All evil, all harm, however, has its good side and its place in cosmic wisdom. Thus it was inevitable that these beings had to remain behind in evolution in order to draw the human beings down into physical matter, where alone one could learn to address oneself as 'I', to develop self-consciousness. Without being enmeshed in *maya* this could never have been learnt. [GA 112, 07/07/08]

Self-consciousness could only be developed in the 'darkness'. The human being had to descend out of the light of the divine creator beings into the 'darkness' of existence on earth in a material, physical body. One could never have 'seen' one's own divine spark of ego, divine spark of ego-consciousness, in the brilliance of the light of the Gods.

In a lecture dealing with the mission of the Archangel Michael, Rudolf Steiner speaks of the human intelligence as being the consequence of a battle between Michael and the Dragon—in this instance with luciferic beings at the beginning of Earth evolution:

> We have asked about the origin of human intelligence, about the origin of human intelligent behaviour which, stating it simply,

has its instrument in our head organism. And we have seen that this intelligent constitution of our soul stems from that deed of the Archangel Michael which is commonly presented in the symbol of the Fall, the casting down of the Dragon. This is actually a very trivial symbol. For if we really conceive of Michael and the Dragon, we have to visualize first the Michael Being and secondly the Dragon who, in reality, consists of all that which enters into our so-called reason, into our intelligence. Not into a hell does Michael cast his opposing hosts, but into the human heads; there this luciferic impulse continues to live... I have characterized human intelligence as an actual luciferic impulse. Thus we may say: if we look back into the evolution of the *Earth*, we find the *Michael-deed*, and to this Michael-deed is joined the illumination of human beings by their reason. [GA 194, 19/11/19]

7. The Battles Between Michael and the Dragon

Rudolf Steiner mentions on several occasions that a number of battles have taken place between Michael and ahrimanic powers during the course of *Earth* evolution. On each occasion the consequences of such a battle have a specific character. Every battle between Michael and his followers against certain ahrimanic powers in the spiritual world is similar to the great battle that took place in modern times—from the early 1840s until the autumn of 1879 (this is discussed in greater detail later in this book).

Battles have recurred over and over again, but always on different issues. For example, in the distant past, after one of these battles, the crowd of ahrimanic spirits that were cast down from the spiritual worlds into the earthly realm populated the earth with the earthly life-forms we today know as bacilli. 'Everything which has the power to act as a bacillus, everything in which bacilli are involved, is the result of crowds of ahrimanic spirits being cast down from heaven to earth at a time when the Dragon had been overcome' (GA 177, 14/10/17).

In quite another context Rudolf Steiner speaks about bacilli, germs and mankind in the following way:

> Germs flourish most intensively when we take nothing but materialistic thoughts into sleep with us. There is no better way to encourage them to flourish than to enter sleep with only materialistic ideas ... The only other method that is just as good is to live in the centre of an epidemic or endemic illness and to think of nothing but the sickness all around, filled with a fear of getting sick. [GA 154, 05/05/14]

Steiner then points out that if we wish to understand the existence of bacilli correctly we must realize that they express spiritual facts, namely, the relationship between human beings and Ahriman. 'This relationship is established through a *materialistic* attitude and purely egotistical states of *fear* [author's italics]. We see the conditions allowing the existence of such parasite beings correctly if we realize that they are a symptom of Ahriman intervening in the world' (ibid.).

Another battle between Michael and the ahrimanic powers resulted in certain moon influences taking effect on earth.

> The moon was once part of the earth; it was cast out from the earth [cf. GA 13, Ch. 4; GA 11, Ch. 3]. As a result, then, certain moon influences took effect on earth, and this, too, followed a victory won by Michael over the Dragon. We are therefore also able to say that everything connected with certain effects relating to the phases of the moon, and all impulses which reach the earth from the moon, have their origin in a similar battle between Michael and the Dragon. [GA 177, 14/10/17]

Steiner does not go into any detail in the lecture from which we have just quoted regarding the nature of the influence exerted by the conquered ahrimanic powers, but from a later lecture (GA 177, 26/10/17) we may understand that these fallen ahrimanic powers were concerned to counteract everything connected with procreation and heredity, for it was not only Lucifer but also Ahriman, the ahrimanic powers, who wanted every human being to be an independent individual. The ahrimanic powers we have just been considering, together with certain luciferic powers, made it their concern to work against anything connected with heredity through blood relationships. In other words, these Spirits of Darkness were the source of all rebellion against the Spirits of Light who, as we have seen earlier, placed human beings in the stream of heredity. These Spirits of Darkness have been among human beings from Lemurian and Atlantean times (cf. GA 177, 26/10/17).

Through the whole of this time Spirits of Darkness were active on earth, while certain other Spirits of Darkness, ahrimanic spirits, related to those down on earth among mankind, were still in the spiritual world (cf. GA 177, 21/10/17 and 26/10/17). The year 1841 saw the beginning of the mighty battle between Michael and these Spirits of Darkness still in the spiritual world—a battle which ended in the autumn of 1879 when these Spirits of Darkness were cast out of the spiritual world and had to join their kindred spirits on earth. Those beings who rebelled and waged war (from 1841 to 1879) against Michael and his hosts had, prior to this battle, been in the service of the wise progressive powers. From 1841 on, however, the aims of these rebellious spirits ran counter to the beings superior to them. Since the autumn of 1879, when these Spirits of Darkness, ahrimanic spirits, were cast down from the spiritual world to the earth, they have been active among human beings, infiltrating their impulses of will, their motives, their ideas—in fact, into all human affairs. Since 1879 'their fortress, their field of activity, is in the thinking, the inner responses and the will impulses of human beings, and this is specifically the case in the epoch in which we now are' (GA 177, 20/10/17). Eighty years after these words were spoken we can say that, if anything, 'their field of activity' is even more entrenched. Elsewhere Rudolf Steiner describes the aims of these fallen ahrimanic spirits in the following terms: 'They wanted to be able to prevent the spiritual wisdom, which will be revealed from the twentieth century onwards, from flowing into the souls of human beings on earth' (GA 178, 13/11/17). This was their aim while still in the spiritual world and was the cause of the 'War in Heaven'. Michael and his followers saw it as their task to remove the hindering Spirits of Darkness from the spiritual realm, for it was only by their removal from the spiritual realm that the minds and hearts of human beings could be opened to receive, from the twentieth century onwards, the spiritual knowledge destined for them. 'Wandering' as they now do among us, these ahrimanic Spirits of Darkness make every effort to confuse our minds and hearts and will. 'They want to prevent the establishment of the right attitude *vis-à-vis* spiritual truths, they want to withhold from human beings the blessings which it is the purpose of spiritual truths to bring to humankind' (GA 178, 13/11/17).

Clear knowledge of the activities of these Spirits of

Darkness is the only means, says Steiner, whereby their aims may be counteracted (cf. GA 178, 13/11/17). The fact that in 1879 those Spirits of Darkness just mentioned were cast into the human kingdom has had significant consequences, one of which is that since that time clear thinking has become more important than ever before. 'For if our thinking lacks clarity in the age in which we are actually living and in the time to come, we will not be able to see in their right light the ripened truths which are to fall from the spiritual world' (ibid.). Nor will we be able to recognize the machinations of the ahrimanic spirits to confine our thinking to material concerns only. Above all, Steiner states, we will fail to realize the profound significance of the Mystery of Golgotha and of the coming of Christ in the etheric for the whole evolution of humankind.

Previous ages were still in possession of a heritage from the days when spirituality pervaded the atavistic inner life of human beings. Now, for the first time—'actually only from the year 1879 onwards' [GA 178, 13/11/17]—we must strive for spirituality, if we desire it. We have the freedom to do so.

Thought, Rudolf Steiner emphasizes again and again, will have to 'be known as a concretely real power of the soul, not merely as the miserable abstraction produced so proudly by the modern age' (ibid.). The time has come when everything that 'is *conscious* must become a real power—hence the Spirits of Darkness strive to counter really effective thoughts by abstract thoughts in the form of all kinds of programmes for the world'. (Ibid.)

*   *   *

Earlier we saw that the Spirits of Darkness, which were cast out of the spiritual world during the Lemurian and Atlantean times, worked against the Spirits of Light, who had placed human beings in the stream of hereditary traits in order to bring about the greatest possible differentiation among human beings. But the power of these Spirits of Darkness began to wane in the fifteenth century (Rudolf Steiner speaks of the year AD 1413 as seeing the 'beginning' of the development of the consciousness soul). By then mankind had progressed so far in its development of consciousness that the free individuality could come into being in increasing measure. At the same time a change began to take place in regard to the tasks of the Spirits of Light. By the end of the 1870s the situation had been completely reversed. For, by then, enough had been done to establish what needed to be established through blood, tribal, racial and similar bonds. In more recent times, we learn from Steiner, the Spirits of Light have changed their function. They now inspire human beings to develop their individuality; to develop independent ideas, feelings and will impulses; to free themselves from age-old traditions which bind them to ties of blood.

The function that belonged to the sphere of the good Spirits of Light, which, we may say, was right in the past, was handed over to the Spirits of Darkness, ahrimanic spirits, during the last third of the nineteenth century. We might be tempted here to assume that the Spirits of Light are doing no other that perpetuating the endeavours of the Spirits of Darkness. However, we need to realize that their reason for emphasizing independence, individuality, and so on, are entirely different from those of the Spirits of Darkness. Similarly, the reason for placing the human being in the stream of heredity which had previously been the task of the Spirits of Light is entirely different from the endeavours of the Spirits of Darkness to perpetuate that trend. Rudolf Steiner suggests that a person of the fourteenth century, for example, when speaking of the ideals of race and nation would have been speaking in terms of the progressive tendencies of human evolution, whereas someone who speaks of the ideal of race and nation and of tribal membership today is speaking of impulses that are part of the decline of humanity. 'Nothing is more designed to take humanity into its decline than the propagation of ideas of race, nation and blood. Nothing is more likely to prevent human progress than proclamations of national ideals belonging to earlier centuries which continue to be preserved by the luciferic and ahrimanic powers' (GA 177, 26/10/17). The twentieth century has witnessed an extreme case of reactionary nationalism in the form of Adolf Hitler's National Socialism, with its insane ideal of the pure blond and blue-eyed Aryan race and its 'final solution'—the obliteration of the Jewish race. 'The true ideal must arise from what we find in the world of the spirit, not in the blood' (ibid.).

Steiner was highly critical of Woodrow Wilson's world programmes.[1] On one occasion we hear Steiner saying: 'It would be equally unintelligent for people in the future to speak of a social structure for the whole world based on the blood bonds of nations. It is Wilsonianism, of course, but also ahrimanism—of the Spirits of Darkness' (ibid.). It is not on the foundation of 'Blood and Soil' (*Blut und Boden*—a telling Nazi slogan) that a social structure for the whole of humanity will be found, but on the recognition of the power of Michael whose 'gaze' is showing us the path towards the inner cosmic life of the Christ-impulse.

Now, we need to bear in mind that what has been indicated is not meant to suggest that we should turn away from the earth. Indeed, it was through descending to earth that, for instance, mankind was given the opportunity to develop selfless love out of free will. Humanity had to unite with the earth in order to be able to attain this goal.[2] Humanity was able to unite with the earth because, when the descent from heaven to earth took place, certain Spirits of Darkness descended too and it was they, as we have seen already, who laid an adequate foundation for human independence during the time the laws of heredity, nationality and race prevailed. What the Spirits of Darkness, Lucifer and Ahriman, had done became a good thing in so far as humanity, through them, was enabled to unite with the earth. If we turn our inner gaze back to the time before humanity descended to earth, before, in short, Lucifer took action, we see that humanity was united with the whole cosmos; human beings lost this union with the total cosmos after their separation from, in biblical terms, the Garden of Eden, and became united with the earth because hereditary traits (original sin in biblical terms) were implanted into them. This made us part of the earth. 'You see, therefore,' Rudolf Steiner says, 'that Lucifer and Ahriman are servants of the Progressive Powers' (GA 177, 26/10/17).

* * *

The years beginning with the early forties of the nineteenth century were of paramount significance for the evolution of mankind, for the time had then arrived when the old differentiations had to be overcome. The divided human race had to be formed into a unity. We can recognize trends towards such a unity in the cosmopolitan views which came to the fore during the first half of that century.[3] These views are 'reflections' of what occurred in the spiritual world. There, from the beginning of the 1840s, the Archangel Michael gradually rose from the rank of an Archangel—a folk, nation spirit—to that of the Archai, a Time Spirit (Spirit of Personality).

Rudolf Steiner broadens our view of the momentous event which took place in the spiritual world in the 1870s in a lecture he gave in Arnhem, 19 July 1924 (GA 240). There he refers to the change of rulership from the Archangel Gabriel to that of Michael. Gabriel, we recollect, was the ruling Spirit from AD 1550 to 1879 (see pp. 6–8). Gabriel, we learn, rules over the whole realm of the physical forces of heredity. The forces of Gabriel are active in the *spiritual* processes underlying the physical processes involved in propagation. Michael's rulership is altogether different in character from that of Gabriel. Whereas the latter's rulership comes to expression in spiritual impulses active in the physical, Michael has paramountly to do with the intelligence in mankind. Steiner describes each Gabriel reign as being preparatory to an age when the various peoples on the earth become more widely separated from one another and more differentiated.

In the age following his [Gabriel's] dominion the nationalistic tendency also becomes accentuated. So, if you ask yourself why it is that such strong nationalistic feeling is asserting itself today[4] under the leadership of Michael ... the answer is that preparation took place spiritually a long time ago; the influence worked on and then began to decline, but the after-effects—often worse than the event itself—continue. It is only by degrees that the impulse of Michael can make its way into what is, to a great extent, a legacy from the past reign of Gabriel. But always when an age of Michael dawns, a longing begins to arise in mankind to overcome racial distinctions and to spread through all the peoples living on the earth the highest and most spiritual form of culture produced by that particular age. [GA 240, 19/07/24]

Michael's rulership is always characterized by the growth of cosmopolitanism.

* * *

We have previously seen how humanity was able to unite with the earth. We are now at a time when human beings are not merely united with the earth but, through the presence of the ahrimanic spirits cast down onto earth by Michael in the battle with the Dragon between 1841 and 1879, an influence 'dwells' within our thinking, feeling and willing with such power that, today, it is not difficult to recognize that the general attitude of men and women is to regard life on earth in a physical material body as being the only reality. We need to be constantly alert in our endeavour to rectify this one-sided materialistic attitude of soul.

> Humanity must develop awareness of not being primarily of this earth, and this awareness must grow stronger and stronger. In future, human beings must walk on this earth who say to themselves: 'Yes, at birth I enter into a physical body, but this is a transitional stage. I really remain in the spiritual world. I am conscious that only part of my essential nature is united with the earth, and that I do not leave the world where I am between death and rebirth with the whole of my essential nature.' A feeling of belonging to the spiritual world must develop in us. [GA 177, 26/10/17]

This feeling needs to prevail alongside an understanding of physical life as well as an understanding of the activities of both Lucifer and Ahriman. In earlier times, those who sought to lead a life of the spirit often felt the compulsion to with-draw from daily life and to mortify the physical body, to practise various forms of asceticism.

Let us look at asceticism as it was practised in earlier times in a few of its details. Asceticism, as then practised, was essentially a matter of certain exercises. They consisted in training the body by means of pain and suffering, by morti-fication. Mortification and enhanced endurance (self-flagellation, near-starvation, and so forth) were pursued until the ascetics could bear physical suffering without losing the balance of their minds. Now (and Rudolf Steiner confirms this), it is a matter of experience that spirit becomes per-ceptible when the activity of the physical body is suppressed. However, such medieval methods are not relevant to modern times. In earlier ages it was recognized that if one sought enlightenment in regard to the spiritual world, one should go to hermits, to those who had withdrawn from ordinary life. Such solitude and mortification, which former ages (up to, say, the fourteenth/fifteenth century) regarded as the prerequisite of spiritual knowledge, has no place in modern life. Life today needs men and women to be active. They need to enter fully into life, not to retire from it—not, we may also say, to fall victim to Lucifer's seductive power. To attempt to acquire the state of mind of the ascetic in relation to spiritual knowledge is, indeed, contrary to the reality of life today. We need, therefore, to gain knowledge of the spiritual world without damaging the health of our physical body by ascetic practices. This we can do because, through the development of natural science during the past few cen-turies, we have been able to acquire exact concepts. 'We can discipline our thinking by means of this natural-scientific development.' Intellectuality—nurtured, one could say, by Ahriman—'must be at the basis of it all, there must be a foundation of clear thinking. But upon the basis of this intellectuality, of this clear thought, there must be built what can lead into the spiritual world' (GA 305, 18/08/22). What the ascetic attained by mortification and suppression of the physical body, by external means, we today need to attain by taking in hand our own soul's development. Then, says Steiner:

> We shall achieve inwardly what the ascetic of old achieved by external means. The ascetic rendered the body weak so that will and cognition should arise out of the weakened body, and the body should be translucent to the spiritual world. We [today] must make our will strong, and make strong our powers of thought, so that they may be stronger than the body ... and thus we shall constrain the body to be transparent to the world of spirit. We do the precise opposite of the ascetics of old. [Ibid.][5]

Since 1879 there are, essentially, two possibilities in regard to human development open to us: we can either strive to 'open' our souls to the rulership of the Time Spirit Michael and thus acquire spiritualized concepts, a spiritualized intellectual life, or we can submit to the power of the counter-striving spirits—the ahrimanic spirits who were cast down from the spiritual world by Michael into human souls on earth in 1879. It is these spirits who deceive us into denying the existence of the spiritual world.

> If we fight against the materialism of our time, we should be constantly aware of the fact that we must not fight against what is good in our age but against the lies of our age. For the spirits that have been pushed out of heaven down upon the earth are chiefly spirits of falsehood who, as Spirits of Hindrance, prevent us from looking for the spiritual in our grasp of natural existence. [GA 194, 17/02/18]

* * *

The year 1841 was the critical year in respect of the onset of the modern age of materialism, for, as we have already seen, at that time a battle began in the spiritual worlds between Michael and certain Spirits of Darkness, ahrimanic spirits, belonging to the hierarchical rank of the Angels (cf. GA 178, 06/11/17). It is essential to realize, Rudolf Steiner advises us, that the current in the evolution of humanity, the materialistic view of the world, arose in the nineteenth century. In the form in which it appeared in the nineteenth century

materialism had never before manifested itself. Least of all
could it have existed in the form in which it found expression
in the nineteenth century in, let us say, the Middle Ages, or in
the centuries immediately preceding the birth of modern
thought, because in those earlier days the souls of men and
women were still open to the impulses issuing from the
spiritual world. The conception that the whole universe is no
more than a sum total of self-moving atoms in space (con-
glomerating into molecules), and that these atoms give rise to
all the phenomena of life and of the spirit, could only arise
during the nineteenth century. It was only when thinking was
taken hold of by Ahriman that such a conception could come
into being.[6]

Now as long as one had what Steiner calls a 'counterfeit
idea of materialism' (GA 254, 16/10/16), that is, an idea in
which spiritual impulses were still included, one could 'hold
on' to the fragment of spirit one still sought to find in the
phenomena of nature. It was not until Ahriman had infil-
trated our thinking in the nineteenth century that we cast out
all spirit *through* the spirit (thinking is only possible for the
spirit!). It was not until all spirit had been cast out from the
structure of the universe that the materialistic view of the
world could confront the human being in all its lifelessness.

How can we, through the spirit, transmute this view of life
so that Ahriman, the Spirit of Lies, loses his power over our
thinking? One of Rudolf Steiner's answers to this question is
this: we need to think in the sense of Michael, to think
'Michaelically'. Steiner characterizes what he means by
Michaelic thinking in the following way. When we look at
another human being what we see is that which fills the form
as mineral substance, is that which that human being unites
with him- or herself of that outer mineral world. But the
human being who does the uniting we do not see.

> You speak correctly only if you say to yourself: What confronts
> me here are the particles of matter which the human spirit shape
> stores up in itself; this makes the invisible being which stands
> here before me visible. The human being is invisible ... To cease

conceiving of the human being as a conglomerate of mineral particles which are but arranged in a certain way ... and to become conscious of the fact that we walk among invisible human beings ... this means to think Michaelically. [GA 194, 23.11.19]

In other words, we must learn to look upon ourselves as supersensible beings. To comprehend that we are not different in our essential being from the supersensible beings means to think in the spirit of Michael.

A little later in the same lecture from which we have just quoted, Steiner goes on to say that we need a condition of soul which is always conscious of the supersensible in the immediate surroundings and which does not fall victim to the delusion that human beings are real because they are visible and the spirits are unreal because they cannot be seen with the physical eye.

A profound picture of the creation of the human form is to be found in a 'Letter' Rudolf Steiner wrote in January 1925:

In order really to understand what the whole choir of the Hierarchy of the Archai accomplished when they created the human form, we must remember that there is a very great difference between this form and the physical body of the human being. The physical body is made up of the physical and chemical processes in the human being. These processes take place in the present human being within the human form. But this form itself is something that is *altogether spiritual.* It ought to fill us with solemn feelings when, on looking at the human form, we realize that with physical senses we are perceiving in the physical world something that is spiritual. For one who is able to see spirituality it is really the case that in the human form one sees a true Imagination which has descended into the physical world. If we wish to see Imaginations we must pass from the physical world to the neighbouring spiritual world, and then we realize how the human form is related to these Imaginations. [GA 26, 18/01/25]

Since the mid-nineteenth century mankind has lived in the age of materialism. All that takes place, by forces of destiny around and within us, stands 'under the banner' of materialism on the one hand and of intellectualism on the other.

These two currents in contemporary life have to be recognized and accepted. For instance, we have to accept that if one wishes to become a medical doctor today one must be willing 'to consume a goodly portion of materialism... After all, we have no alternative. Beside the fact that we are human beings pure and simple, we must be "contemporaries" of our age' (GA 237, 04/08/24). Now, Rudolf Steiner observes, those who are students of spiritual science quite naturally harbour the impulse to prove, both theoretically and practically, the falsehood of materialism. Those who do so maybe think that in this way they stand 'most thoroughly within the stream of Michael'.

> But as a rule little success is achieved... Why is this so?... *It is due to the simple fact that materialism is true.* Materialism is not wrong, it is quite right. Here lies the reason...Materialism is right, but it holds good of the outer physical body *only*... This confession must be made out of the inmost depths of our human being. I mean, the confession that materialism is right *in its own domain*—nay more, that it is the splendid achievement of our age to have discovered what is right and true in the domain of materialism. [GA 237, 04/08/24]

Steiner's observations here are as true today as they were more than 70 years ago.

On one occasion Steiner asks us to recognize that the materialistic study, the natural-scientific study, of the world around us is essential. The reason he gives is that we have to do so in order to be able to realize that, in spite of the most advanced technology, all that we 'see' is not spirit. 'In ancient times, when people beheld what is today nature, they still saw the spirit shining through it. Today we have to study nature in order to be able to say: "All that we see is *not* spirit... In order that we may be spurred towards the spirit, may receive an impulse towards the spirit, we must *learn to know* the unspiritual, the anti-spiritual."' Steiner gives us a very simple example to illustrate the point he is making. We have a minute creature before us which is imperceptible to the naked eye. By placing it under a powerful microscope it is greatly enlarged so that we can see it. 'This size is illusory. I have increased the size of the creature, and I no longer have it. I have a phantom. What I am seeing is not a reality. I have put a lie in place of the truth!' Steiner then goes on to say that it behoves us to realize 'that *natural* [author's italics] science is needed in order, from this counter-image of the truth, to receive the impulse towards the truth; then the force will be developed which can be symbolically indicated in the *overcoming of the Dragon by Michael*' (GA 223, 08/04/23).

Spiritual scientists have a twofold task. First, they need to gain a clear perception of the extent to which the ahrimanic, the materialistic, view of the world is to be opposed. And, in addition, they need to understand the materialistic world view. They need to understand it not only in its content, but also why it came about that a materialistic view of the world has entered into human evolution since the mid-1840s in such an extreme form. Rudolf Steiner treats of this twofold task in a series of lectures entitled *Materialism and the Task of Anthroposophy.*[7] A few hints as to the necessity of approaching materialism in a fruitful way and of understanding the materialist world view have been given already. To go into any further, and greater, detail is beyond the scope of this chapter, and the interested reader is therefore referred to the series of lectures just mentioned. As to why mankind had to experience the 'weight' of materialism, Rudolf Steiner gives us the following clear answer: 'In the course of the evolution of mankind, moments must needs come when human beings are, in a sense, pulled down, brought below a certain level, in order that they may later, by their own efforts, lift themselves up again.' In short, mankind had to submerge itself in Ahriman's sphere of influence. 'It would really be of no help to mankind at all if by some divine decree or the like it could be protected from having to undergo these low levels of existence. In order for human beings to attain to full use of their powers of freedom, it is absolutely necessary that they descend to the low levels in their world conception as well as in their life' (GA 204, 02/04/21).

Steiner then goes on to speak of the dangers involved in adhering to materialism.

> The danger does not lie in the fact that something like this appears at the proper time, and for theoretical materialism this was the middle of the nineteenth century. The danger consists in the fact that if something like this has happened in the course of normal evolution, people then continue to adhere to it, so that an experience that was necessary for one particular point in time is carried over into later times. If it is correct to say that in the middle of the nineteenth century materialism was, in a certain sense, a test mankind had to undergo, it is equally correct to say that the persistent adherence to materialism is bound to work terrible harm now, and that all the catastrophes befalling the world and humanity that we have to experience are due to the fact that a great majority of people still tries to cling to materialism. [Ibid.]

As we approach the twenty-first century the truth of the harm that persistent adherence to an out-and-out materialistic viewpoint has caused to the earth, the atmosphere, human health and so on, is too obvious to need further comment. What is heartening at this particular critical 'moment' in the evolution of earth and humankind is the rapidly growing number of people throughout the world who are beginning to realize the urgent need for *metanoia* (i.e. a change of heart and mind).

As was described earlier, all the tendencies towards materialism that we develop in our life of thought have their origin in the relationship between our intellect and the attacks of Ahriman. The very fact that materialistic thought is predominant today is entirely due to the confusion which Ahriman constantly strives to promote in the human intellect (cf. GA 176, 14/08/17).

8.   The Battle with the Dragon Today— The Cosmic Intelligence

One of the most important aspects which Rudolf Steiner frequently mentions in connection with Michael is his task to administer the 'Cosmic Intelligence'. Again and again he emphasizes that Michael is the one spiritual being who, with the exception of Christ Himself, is the most concerned with human beings and their destiny. Michael, the Sun Spirit and, since the Mystery of Golgotha, the Countenance of Christ, is always trying to help us in our spiritual striving without in any way interfering with our freedom.

Now when we observe the intellect as it prevails today we can but admit that it is abstract and formal, that it loads the human mind with ideas and concepts which have little to do with *living* reality. It is, indeed, unless enlivened and warmed by spirituality, cold, dry and barren.

Cold, barren and dry is how the nature of the intelligence can be described, to a very large extent, at the present time. We are living in an early period of the Michael Age, and the intelligence is still only just beginning to unfold in the general consciousness of mankind. Here we need to realize that the nature of the intelligence changes during the course of human evolution. What we consider today by the term 'intelligence' was once something altogether different. In very ancient times human beings would certainly not have said, as the materialist does today: I think with my nervous system (cf. GA 254, 16/10/15). In pre-Christian times it would not have occurred to people to believe that they were producing their own thoughts out of themselves, out of their physical brains. They did not feel that they were forming their thoughts but rather that the thoughts were *revealed* to them from the things of the world around them. They felt, Steiner states: ' "Intelligence is universal, cosmic; intelligence is contained within the things of the world; the intelligence-content, the thought-content of things is perceived just as colours are perceived; the world is full of intelligence, pervaded everywhere by intelligence. In the course of evolution the human being has acquired a drop of the intelligence that is spread over the wide universe." Such was the conception in days of old' (GA 240, 21/08/24).

Throughout the pre-Christian ages Michael had been the Regent of the Cosmic Intelligence. But after the Mystery of Golgotha something of deep significance occurred: Michael's dominion over the Cosmic Intelligence began gradually to fall away from him. By about the eighth century AD, Steiner states, the descent of the Cosmic Intelligence from the sun to the earth is accomplished (cf. GA 240, 19/07/23). In the ninth century the human being was already beginning to unfold his own, personal intelligence. The Cosmic Intelligence had streamed downwards and was to be found within the souls of human beings on earth (cf. GA 237, 28/07/24). Thenceforth the Michael-principle had to be developed through the intelligence of the human soul itself.

Michael inspires human beings with his own being in order that there may appear on the earth a spirituality consonant with the personal intelligence of human beings in order that they can be thinkers—and at the same time truly spiritual. 'For this and this alone is what Michael's dominion means' (GA 240, 19/07/24). The spiritualization of our thinking is bound up with an understanding of Michael.

However, the development of the Michael-principle through the intelligence of the human soul has met with strong resistance by Ahriman. So far we have spoken of intelligence as being a human attribute, a human faculty. But we need to remind ourselves here that Rudolf Steiner repeatedly refers to it as a spiritual substance that can be handed on from one being to another. He also says that Ahriman had his cohort spirits strive to take hold of this intelligence and make it into an intellectuality which is both universal and objective (see, e.g. Appendix Seven). This kind of intellectuality is quite impersonal—indeed, it is the same for everyone. Moreover, we are 'taught' (by Ahriman) to keep any moral sense of responsibility, for example, out of our deliberations. Such clear and cold thinking has its legitimate place when we are dealing with the 'dead' material world. For instance, no other kind of intellectuality would enable us to deal safely with nuclear energy—but what we see at work here is an intelligence bereft of spirituality.

So, summarizing, we may say: once the intelligence has entered into the human soul Ahriman sets about seizing it in an ever tighter grasp. Such, indeed, has been the 'crisis' from the beginning of the fifteenth century, when the last 'bridges' between the physical and spiritual worlds disappeared, until our day—the crisis which expresses itself as the battle between Ahriman and Michael in the midst of which we find ourselves now (GA 237, 28/07/24). Michael, though his dominion over the intelligence has fallen from him, is striving to take hold of it again on earth from the beginning of his new rulership in 1879. He would find it again at a time when an intelligence devoid of spirituality had taken root in human souls. He would find the intelligence intensely exposed to the ahrimanic forces. Since 1879 Ahriman uses all his power to challenge Michael's striving to regain dominion over the intelligence which has now become earthly. Human evolution stood at this decisive point in the last third of the nineteenth century. Ahriman strives to make the intelligence continue in the same way that began during the Rulership of Gabriel (1550–1879), making it earthly, making it an affair only of the human communities of blood (i.e. tribes, nations), of the generation, the forces of generation and inheritance (cf. GA 237, 28/07/24).

The forces of Michael are the very opposite of those of Gabriel. The latter's Rulership is characterized by the fact that his impulses enter strongly into the physical nature of human beings, whereas Michael works intensely into their spiritual being. 'You can tell this from the very fact that he is the administrator of the Cosmic Intelligence' (GA 237, 03/08/24).

Ahriman thrives on the arid intellectualism prevailing today. It is spiritual nourishment for him.

*   *   *

It is absolutely essential, Rudolf Steiner stresses, that we learn to know Ahriman and his hosts: 'The point is that in Ahriman there stands before us a cosmic being of the highest imaginable intelligence, a cosmic being who has already taken the intelligence entirely into the *individual, personal* element' (GA 237, 01/08/24). Here we can recognize a significant contrast between Ahriman and Michael, for the latter is not in the least concerned with the personal quality of intelligence, he has no wish to seize the intelligence—as Ahriman does—and make it personally his own. 'Michael only wills and has willed through the aeons to administer the pan-intelligence. And now once more, now that human beings have intelligence, it should again be administered by Michael as something belonging to all mankind—as the common and universal intelligence that benefits all human beings alike' (GA 237, 01/08/24).

However, we are constantly tempted to make our intelligence personal after the pattern of Ahriman.

We need to realize that the idea that we can have cleverness for ourselves is foolish. Steiner gives us a good example of such an absurdity:

> If we want to prove anything to another person logically, the first thing we must presume is that the same logic holds good for that person as for ourselves. And for a third party again it is the same logic. If anyone were able to have a logic of his or her own it would be absurd for us to want to prove anything to him or her by *our* logic. This after all is easy to realize but it is essential in the present age of Michael for this realization also to enter into our deepest feelings. [Ibid.]

Ahriman would render each human being a totally isolated and insulated cold entity—isolated from and insulated against all and sundry. In such a world, social life in the sense of heart-warmed feeling for and relation to another human being would be non-existent.

The contrast, or rather battle, between Michael and Ahriman was already there in the spiritual world but became of significance for human beings on earth, above all since the eighth or ninth century when the Cosmic Intelligence gradually fell away from Michael and 'descended' to earth. But it only became acute, we remind ourselves, when the consciousness soul, the spiritual soul, began to unfold in humanity at the beginning of the fifteenth century.

The point just made in regard to the ahrimanic 'isolation' and 'insulation' of the human being is illustrated by Rudolf Steiner from a quite different viewpoint in the following way. He refers to the fact that the universal thinking implicit in pre-Christian wisdom, pagan wisdom, has gradually been exhausted. In our time the human being's soul-constitution is such that this luciferic principle of unification can be of little real service to us. It has been counteracted by the fact that the God-created nature of the human being has grown ever more closely allied with, related to, the earth. Because of this the human being is less allied with the luciferic element which, as we discussed earlier, tends to draw us away from the earth.

> But woe betide if we were simply to draw from the luciferic element without putting something different in its place. That would result in nothing but evil. For then we would 'grow together' with the earth, that is to say with the particular territory on earth where we are born; and our cultural life would become completely specialized, completely differentiated... Chauvinism is more and more gaining the upper hand until it will finally lead us to split up to such an extent that a group will embrace only one single human being!... To combat this a counterweight must be created; and this counterweight can only be created if, like the old wisdom inherent in paganism, a new wisdom, *acquired by our free resolve and will* [author's italics], is infused into earthly culture. This new wisdom must again be an *initiation wisdom*. [GA 191, 15/11/19]

We may think that Rudolf Steiner is exaggerating here when he speaks of a group embracing no more than one person. However, anyone who has engaged in group work—involving, say, 15 people—may well have experienced, sooner or later, a splitting up into a number of smaller groups all assuming uncompromising, entrenched and seemingly irreconcilable positions.

If we were to make no effort towards acquiring a new wisdom—now already and in the future—then, unbeknown to us, the whole of culture, if it could then so be called, would become ahrimanic. It would be easy for the influences issuing from Ahriman's incarnation to permeate all civilization. If we allow ourselves to follow the strong inclinations inherent in us to let things just drift on and make no effort to counteract these tendencies which lead to an ahrimanic 'culture', then when Ahriman incarnates in due course in the West (cf. GA 191 and 193) the consequences would be dire. Steiner gives us a vivid—and shattering—picture of the influence Ahriman would have on humanity and, ultimately, the earth, if he is not recognized and counteracted. As soon as Ahriman incarnates he would bring to humankind all the clairvoyant knowledge which until then had been acquired only by dint of intense labour and effort. He would establish a great occult school for the practice of magic arts of the greatest grandeur. Rudolf Steiner envisages that

> lovers of ease who refuse to have anything to do with spiritual science would fall prey to his magic, for by means of his stupendous magic arts he would be able to make great numbers of human beings into seers—but in such a way that the clairvoyance of each individual would be strictly differentiated. What one person would see, a second and a third would not see. Confusion would prevail and in spite of being receptive to clairvoyant wisdom, men and women would inevitably fall into strife on account of the sheer diversity of their vision... The result would be the establishment of Ahriman's kingdom on earth and the overthrow of everything achieved hitherto by human culture. [GA 191, 15/11/19][1]

The task of Christo-centric spiritual scientists is to 'rescue' the clairvoyant wisdom of the future from the clutches of Ahriman. The issue is whether this wisdom is in the care of Christ or the clutches of Ahriman. It cannot come into the hands of Christ, Rudolf Steiner advises us, unless we fight for it. We can only fight for it by opening our souls to the Christ-impulse before the time of Ahriman's incarnation. To enable human efforts towards bringing the Christ-impulse alive within their inmost beings is the task of spiritual science (cf. GA 191, 15/11/19). It is through the reception of the Christ-principle that Ahriman will lose his power over mankind. Here we may conceive of the Christ-impulse as being the highest potency of love. Ahriman, who has a cold heart of stone, is powerless against the life-instilling heart-warmth of the Christ-impulse: 'The Christ-impulse has given the impulse by which human beings can love one another. Through humanity being Christified human love may become more and more spiritual. Love will become more psychic and more spiritual, as through this human beings will also draw along with them the lower creations, and will thus transform the earth' (GA 105, 12/08/08).

Wisdom was implanted in our predecessors on the Ancient Moon; love is to be implanted on our planet earth. The goal of our planet is to become the Planet of Love. In one of his lectures on the Gospel of St John Rudolf Steiner says: 'The mission of our earth is the cultivation of the principle of love to its highest degree by those beings who are evolving upon it. When the earth has reached the end of its evolution, love should permeate it through and through' (GA 103, 20/05/08).[2]

It is the human being's mission to battle alongside Michael against Ahriman and thus to work towards the realization of this goal. It is the human being's task to overcome the trends inspired by Ahriman to bring about a state of 'frozen rigid-ification', which, to begin with, would manifest itself in the moral sphere. 'But this can happen only if we envisage spiritually, feel inwardly and counter with our will, what would otherwise become physical reality' (GA 191, 15/11/19).

Michael, as we have seen, is the Sun Spirit who stands in a special relationship to Christ, to the Spiritual Sun and to all Sun-impulses. Michael-forces prepare the souls of those who recognize and strive to counter the deadening forces of Ahriman so that they may receive the Christ-impulse. The impulse of the Michael-forces works in a cosmopolitan sense, it works to embrace with cosmic warmth the whole of humanity—a 'gesture' which is anathema to Ahriman. These Michael-forces also work, we learn from Rudolf Steiner, in such a way as to free us from 'the narrower earthly connections of life and carry us up on to a spiritual height, where we feel the earthly connections less strongly than others do' (GA 237, 03/08/24). This does not mean that we are thus relieved of our earthly responsibilities. That would imply a luciferic victory over us. But it does mean that Ahriman has to loosen his power over those who strive, with their whole soul, in the spirit of the Michael-force.

Through the power of the Michael-force the spiritualization of the intellect can come into being.[3] Through this power the ahrimanized head-man can be transformed and become a Christified heart-man. This must happen in due course if the mission of the earth and of mankind is to be fulfilled (cf. GA 237, 28/07/24). But this will not happen unless we human beings are prepared to undertake the necessary soul and spiritual self-development and not veer away from the 'pain and suffering' inevitably entailed (cf. GA 10 and GA 13, Ch. 5) and make the effort to use the intellect in order to understand spiritual science. 'Whatever Ahriman may elect to do, he will never get hold of the intellect which human beings apply, either in the present age or in the future, to the study of spiritual science' (GA 254, 25/10/15).

On another occasion Rudolf Steiner speaks in the following vein:

It is indeed true, and initiates have always said so: 'When human beings are filled with spiritual wisdom, these are great horrors of darkness for the ahrimanic powers and a consuming fire. It feels good to the ahrimanic Angels to dwell in heads filled with ahrimanic science, but heads filled with spiritual wisdom are like a consuming fire and the horrors of darkness to them.' If we consider this in all seriousness we can feel that, filled with spiritual wisdom, we can go through the world in a way which allows us to establish the right relationship with the ahrimanic powers. Furthermore, by doing the things we do in the light of this, we can build a 'place' for the consuming fire of sacrifice for the salvation of the world, the place where the terror of darkness radiates out over the harmful ahrimanic element. [GA 177, 20/10/17]

One task of mankind during the coming phase of the evolution of civilization will be to live and work towards the time when Ahriman will incarnate, with such an alert consciousness as to his already active influence and his ultimate purpose, that this incarnation can serve, paradoxically, to promote a higher spiritual development in us. For instance, one thing we can gain through the activity of Ahriman (and this, Rudolf Steiner claims, will be far more clearly experienced after his incarnation) will be the awareness as to what can and what can *not* be achieved by physical life alone (cf. GA 193, 04/11/19).

Those who belong to the Michael-stream, who live and work with the power of the Michael-impulse, have to do battle with Ahriman. The essential fact of the matter is that in order to gain the wisdom of the future, a struggle is necessary—a struggle similar to that waged against Lucifer during pre-Christian times by the ancient initiates. What Lucifer brought to mankind, the power of thinking, was not to be allowed to remain luciferic. In the interest of the continuing evolution of mankind it had to undergo a transformation, it had to serve the coming of Christ. 'Just as it devolved upon the initiates of the primeval wisdom to wrest from Lucifer that which has become human reason, human intellect, so the insight which is to develop in the future into the inner realities of things must be wrested from the ahrimanic powers' (GA 191, 15/11/19). The wisdom of the future can only be attained here on earth. It can only be attained by those who are imbued with the Michaelic impulse through their conquest over Ahriman.

9. Anachronistic and Destructive Forces Inherent in Nationalism

The battle between Michael and the Dragon takes place, in our time, in our souls, in our consciousness. The concept that this battle continues to take place 'outside' us—in the heavens, the spiritual world, between an Archangel and his hosts on the one side and Ahriman and his followers on the other—is no longer relevant. We may indeed say, as a corollary to this statement, that every battle that takes place in the physical realm is out of step with the spirit of the age, the Michael Age. It is absolutely essential that we take hold of the Michael-impulse—take it into our being so that it becomes an active, integral element of our soul. In the present context this means that we need to recognize that every form of war-waging and nationalistic impulse is not only destructive but outdated; it also means that we need to recognize and experience that humanity is a living organism, a living totality.

A few weeks after the beginning of the First World War Rudolf Steiner spoke the following meditative verse:

> So long as thou dost feel the pain
> Which I am spared,
> The Christ unrecognized
> Is working in the World.
> For weak is still the Spirit
> While each is only capable of suffering
> Through his own body. [GA 40]

The impulse shining through these words urges us to test whether the Christ is really living in us—'the Christ who works across from our own heart into the hearts of our fellow human beings, making us one with our suffering contemporaries' (GA 157, 01/09/14). Earlier we noted that the Michael-impulse brings with it the seed of a spiritual impulse among people to live as free individual members of one 'body'.

Highly relevant to this particular aspect of the Michael-impulse are some statements Steiner made in a Christmas lecture entitled 'The Michael Path to Christ' (GA 195, 25/12/19). He is responding to the slogan rife during the First World War: 'Freedom for individual nations!' Such an idea, according to Steiner, is essentially false for, since 1879, since the onset of the present Michael period, the all-important thing is not individual nations but individual human beings. To think in terms of nations is to allow oneself to be permeated by the force of the pre-Christian time, by the Michael-force of the Old Testament, the force of the Countenance of Jehovah.

> Today it is Christ whom we must strive to find through Michael, Christ the Divine Leader of the whole human race. This means that we must seek for feelings and ideas which have nothing to do with human distinctions of any kind on the earth. Such feelings and ideas cannot be found on the surface. They must be sought where the spirit-and-soul part of the human being pulsates, i.e. along the path of spiritual science ... upon the Michael path. [GA 195, 25/12/19]

Were the Michael path to be followed, were the Michael-impulse to 'take hold' of mankind, then such injustices as, for example, the exploitation of so-called Third World countries by the advanced industrial nations would not occur; nor, to mention just one other ahrimanic trend so obvious today, would economic interests, underpinned by cut-throat competition between one nation and another, have brought about such dangerous levels of soil erosion and air and soil pollution.

In regard to wars between nations which have taken place during the past hundred years, and the fact that they are anachronistic, Rudolf Steiner gives us the following explanation: 'In the fourth post-Atlantean epoch, which began in the eighth century BC and ended in the fifteenth century AD, those conditions were developed which one can describe as a Mars-civilization (cf. GA 180, 08/01/18).

Since the beginning of the development of the consciousness soul/spiritual soul (1413, see Appendix Six), that is, since
the beginning of the fifth post-Atlantean epoch, a Mars-
civilization has been an anachronism. Nothing, Rudolf
Steiner states, can really be attained in our time through the
forces of a Mars culture, a warlike culture. 'What can make
this epoch great must be brought about from the forces of the
spiritual life.' In spite of the fact that the nineteenth and
twentieth centuries see human beings shut off from the
heavenly forces, confined in the materialistic world-
conception, it is in the fifth post-Atlantean age that they have
the greatest possibility of making themselves spiritual. 'No
age has been so favourable to spirituality as this fifth epoch.
Courage must only be found to drive the money-changers out
of the Temple. Courage must be found to confront, with the
real, abstractions and things estranged from reality, to set
against them full reality and therewith the spiritual reality'
(ibid.).

Rudolf Steiner variously characterizes every form of
nationalism as contrary to the healthy development of
mankind. For instance, in a lecture dealing with the historical
background for the forming of a judgement on the 'social
question' Steiner speaks of the fostering of nationalism as an
idea implanted in human minds by Ahriman, the Spirit of
Lies. Here he states quite categorically: 'There is nothing
more inimical to truth than nationalism.'[1] Untruth will prevail—that is, the very opposite of that which is needed in the
future—as long as nationalism prevails. Elsewhere Steiner
shows how this ahrimanic 'untruth' plays right into the hands
of Lucifer, for in nationalism we can recognize 'the shadow of
the old blood-principle. The Christian impulse towards universal humanity [is] completely overshadowed by the principle of nationalism... The antichristian impulse makes its
appearance first and foremost in the form of nationalism...
The one and only reality befitting the present age would be to
overcome nationalism, to eliminate it, and for men and
women to be stirred by the impulse of the *human universal*'
(GA 198, 03/04/20). Here we may also remind ourselves of an

earlier reference to nationalism in connection with the incarnation of Ahriman. There we saw that whatever can separate people into opposing groups, whatever can alienate them from worldwide mutual understanding, whatever drives wedges between them, strengthens Ahriman's impulse (cf. GA 191, 01/11/19; GA 222, 18/03/23).

Nationalism is an essentially false idea because in our time, in the Michael period, the all-important matter is not a division into groups of men and women, one group fighting to attain advantages over the others and maintaining its separateness from the others. No, the all-important matter, which we have just touched upon, is the growth of free individuals who, out of understanding of others, strive to maintain the health of the whole, strive to approach the all-embracing power and love of the Christ-impulse through Michael. The 'lie' of nationalism is nothing other than the endeavour to permeate each individual nation not with the new force of Michael but with the force of the pre-Christian age, with the obsolete Michael-force of the Old Testament. 'However paradoxical it may sound, there is a tendency among the so-called civilized nations at the present day to transform what was justifiable among the Hebrew people of the Old Testament into something luciferic, and to make of this the most powerful impulse in every nation' (GA 195, 25/12/19).

Rudolf Steiner also approached the matter of nationalism from the point of view of the human being's incarnation into a particular mother tongue. In the second lecture of three he gave in Oslo in 1921 he gives an illuminating account of our relationship with our individual Angel. He describes the period through which we live between death and a new birth on a number of occasions (e.g. GA 153 and GA 141), but nowhere else does he speak in such detail about certain aspects of the relationship between us and our Guardian Angel as in the Oslo lecture. There is an important moment, Steiner tells us, when, after a certain period has elapsed after physical death, our Angel has to 'hand over' to the Archangels what the Angel-world has received from us through our 'idealistic' experiences. At this important moment our soul will have a definite experience: it will either experience the warmth of acceptance or the chill of rejection on the part of the Archangels. If, during our earth-life, we have brought idealistic (spiritual) and selfless loving thoughts and feelings to our Angel we shall be able to follow consciously what takes place between the Angel and the Archangel; we shall be, as it were, in harmony with the spiritual beings and experience an embracing warmth. If, on the other hand, our consciousness during earth-life has been dedicated, more or less exclusively, to a self-centred and a materialistic, that is an ahrimanic, conception of things, then it is clear that we have had little if any contact with that spiritual being who is our Angel and, as a consequence, when the meeting takes place between our Angel and the Archangels there is little, if anything, to 'hand over' to these higher spiritual beings and we cannot, therefore, experience harmony with them at this important moment. On the contrary, Steiner says, we feel rejected and chilled (GA 209, 27/11/21).

To follow the soul's journey through the various spheres in the spiritual world after death is not our present task. Here we must content ourselves with Steiner's statement that, up to what he calls 'The Midnight Hour of Existence' (see *The Soul's Awakening*, Scene 9, GA 14; GA 226, 18/05/23), the human being has become more and more estranged from earthly existence and the soul has either been received warmly or gone through the experience of being 'rejected', chilled by the spiritual world. When the Midnight Hour of Existence has passed then the soul gradually descends again to a new life on earth. During this descent the soul once again encounters the spiritual realm of the Archangels.

Now, a great deal depends upon the nature of the two meetings with the spiritual beings in the archangelic world. Of particular relevance to our present theme of nationalism is that upon it depends to which nation, to which mother tongue, a person descends in the forthcoming earth-life.

The impulse to incarnate into a particular nation and mother tongue may have been implanted in a descending soul either deeply and inwardly, or more superficially—deeply and consciously in those who in a previous life have cultivated idealistic thoughts and warmth of love, more superficially in those who have been, to a greater or lesser degree, devoid of such tendencies and qualities and so entering, in this case, more 'automatically', more unconsciously, into what we shall have to express through our organs of speech.

Those who before their new earthly life, during their 'descent' through archangelic-angelic realms, can be permeated with a really inward love for their mother tongue will assimilate it into their very being. They thus grow into their language, and into their nation, race, as into a natural home, and their love for both is born of the soul. If, however, the urge to incarnate is implanted more superficially, then the love for the mother tongue and race, nation, arises not out of inward love but merely out of instinct and 'lower' impulses. For instance, lacking the true, inward love for either language or people (race, nation), a tendency towards aggressive patriotism manifests itself.

An inward love for language and nation expresses itself naturally and is thoroughly consistent with real and universal love, Christified love, with the Michaelic impulse. Chauvinism—a superficial and aggressive form of patriotism—finds no soil for growth in such an inwardly warm soul-attitude. A genuine feeling for internationalism or cosmopolitanism is never stultified by an inner love for language and people. When, however, the mother tongue and people (nation) are grown into more 'automatically' than 'naturally', when an over-fervid love for language and nation has its roots in instincts and ego-centred impulses, we can readily recognize false nationalism and chauvinism arising, with an exaggerated emphasis upon race and nationality.

Steiner stresses the importance of our relationship to our Angel in a lecture he gave a few years after the First World War. It becomes clear as we study this lecture, and endeavour to make its content come alive within us, that we need to be aware that in our modern civilization, submerging itself ever more deeply in materialism, our relationship to our Angel is in danger of being lost. Indeed, if the present trend of evolution persists, we face the danger of our connection with our Angel being so slight that, as a consequence, we cannot form any inner relationship to the archangelic beings, for it is through our Angel that any approach to the Archangels can be made. The Archangels, as we saw earlier on, participate in bringing the human soul back into physical life; they are particularly involved in building up the forces that bring us back into the community of a certain language and people.

But when human beings 'live inwardly unspiritually—as has been the case for centuries—the relationship of the Archangels to the human beings develops one-sidedly, and then they do not grow into their destined people with the inner soul being, but they are inscribed from outside, as it were, by means of the world order, into the people that the Archangel is assigned to guide...Those who stand within their people with soul—and this is the case with very few people today—will be unable to develop in the direction of chauvinism, of one-sided nationalism; they take up the fruitful forces within the people and develop these...They will not boast of their people in a one-sided way.' In particular, they will not exhibit an outwardly hostile attitude toward others (GA 207, 07/10/21).

'All over the earth a false attitude is being adopted to nationality, race and language' (GA 209, 27/11/21). This is surely as true today as it was when Steiner gave expression to this thought over 70 years ago and examples are all too obvious to need specific mention here (cf. also GA 332a, 30/10/19).

The Michael-impulse has entered the evolution of humanity. It is here, among us. But there are also many that will not accept this impulse but want to reject it. Among those trends that combat the Michael-impulse today are the feelings of destructive nationalism in the sense indicated above. 'By the principle of nationality many things have been ordered, or rather, disordered in the most recent times.' Again, these words are as valid today as they were when

Steiner spoke them in the 1920s. He continues: 'All this is in terrible opposition to the Michael-principle; all this contains ahrimanic forces which strive against the in-pouring and pulsing of the Michael-force into the earthly life of human-kind' (GA 233, 13/01/24).

Rudolf Steiner also spoke of nationality out of the spiritual-scientific conception of karma.

When we consider nationality in the light of reincarnation and turn our mind's eye to the human being's Higher Self, it is clear that the concept of nationality loses significance. 'For when we pass through the Gate of Death everything encompassed by the term "nationality" is among the things we cast off. And if we do in all seriousness want to be what we think people with spiritual aims should be, it is proper to remember that in passing through successive incarnations the human belongs not to one but to a number of different nationalities' (GA 157, 31/10/14).[2]

The eternal in the human being goes beyond what is national: 'The national element is a mere garment, an outer envelope' (ibid.). It is the eternal in the human being we are looking for when entering more deeply into the spirit. It is against such insight that the Spirits of Darkness fight in the human soul.

In regard to the chauvinistic feelings and passions of hatred that stir human souls, Rudolf Steiner gives us the following insight:

Here we have a soul. It needs to prepare for its reception into a spiritual world through which it will now have to pass between death and its next birth, a world which will guide it towards an incarnation that will belong to quite a different nationality from the one it is now leaving...Consider some real 'nationalist' today, someone with national feelings who directs antipathy very particularly against the members of another nation and, indeed, may be ranting and raving against this nation in his own country. [GA 157, 31/10/14]

(Steiner is speaking just a few months after the outbreak of the First World War and he is referring to the 'ranting and raving' of members of the various nations involved. However, it is clear that he is also speaking in a broader and more inclusive sense. So, for instance, we may speak with Steiner in the same vein in regard to the neo-Nazis in Germany raising their 'ranting and raving' voices and fists in the 1990s against immigrant workers and others seeking asylum in their country.)

'What,' Rudolf Steiner asks, 'is the meaning of such ranting and raving, of such antipathy?' Steiner's answer to this question can give us a great deal of food for thought, for he says: 'It signifies a premonition: my next incarnation will be into this nationality! The Higher Self has already, at a subconscious level, established links with the other nationality. This Higher Self is resisted by that part of us which is on the physical plane. *This is the human being raging against his/her Higher Self* [author's italics]' (GA 157, 31/10/14).

In the light of these statements we need to recognize that it is not primarily through the blood that one is connected with the people, the nation, into which one incarnates, but through karma. Those who are not students of spiritual science inevitably regard their blood as that which binds them to their nation. But those who take spiritual science into their soul as something both practical and living are able to give quite a different answer: 'I am connected with my nationality through my karma, for this is a part of my karma...The matter [thus] becomes spiritual' (GA 174, 07/01/17). Outwardly, those who are aware of their karma might still act in the same way as those who are not; even if they feel this more spiritual aspect. But, inwardly, they will feel spiritually; their feeling will be quite different from that of those who feel their nation purely at the blood level—we could also say at an animal level.

Those who strive to become aware of the reality of the spiritual world—in particular, in the present context, of their Angel—and who bring to their Angel the fruits of their spiritual striving, can, through the Angel, 'grow into' the Hierarchy of the Archangels, the Folk Spirits. Such people, when they incarnate again, will have an attitude towards other peoples which is imbued with Michaelic tolerant understanding. Those, on the other hand, who are overcome by Ahriman and regard the material world (blood and soil) to be the only reality will fail to 'converse' with their Angel and, as a consequence, this spiritual being is unable to lead such souls with their consciousness to the Folk Spirit. But since such souls have to be led to the spiritual sphere of the Folk Spirits, this happens unconsciously by means of the law of karma.

> Either we grow into the Folk Spirit consciously and with love, or we are forcibly led into the sphere of the Folk Spirits. When, after death, the moment is reached at which we turn to descend once more to the sense-perceptible world for a new incarnation, then it makes a great difference, as our soul is led down, whether we have consciously united in love with the Folk Spirit or whether, unaware of what is going on, this takes place forcibly, under coercion... The conflict prevailing among nations today stems from the fact that many people are born with little love for their Folk Spirit and therefore find themselves in a forced relationship to it. The *love which leads* [author's italics] us to a particular Folk Spirit can never bring about a conflict with other nations. We must do everything we can to help people regain a love-filled relationship with their Folk Spirits. This is most urgent. [GA 210, 01/02/22]

So, the nature of our relationship to the nation into which we shall be born in our next earth-life—and to those beyond the boundaries of that nation—depends, at least to some considerable extent, on whether our present life is overshadowed by the fragmenting power of Ahriman or illumined by the unifying power of the Michael-Christ impulse.

Those who strive towards an experience of 'Not I, but Christ in me', who strive to follow the path shown by Michael, will recognize that their nationality, their national 'sheath', is of secondary importance, and will join those who are pursuing a corresponding path of spiritual striving.

In a most illuminating lecture entitled 'The Spiritual Unity of Mankind through the Christ-impulse', Steiner says:

First the Gods allowed the human being to be 'split up' as the result of opposing forces [i.e. Lucifer and Ahriman] in order that, later, after the bodily nature had been thus split, the human being could, through Christ, be brought into a unity again in respect of the spiritual nature.

And this is also one of the meanings of the Mystery of Golgotha: the attainment of the unity of humankind from within outwards. *Externally*, human beings are becoming increasingly different from one another. The result will be that there is no unity but diversity over the earth, and that human beings must exert all the more force from *within* outwards in order to attain unity. There will always be setbacks to this unity of humankind over the whole earth [... Setbacks] emanate from earlier epochs that take their course in opposition to the Christ-impulse, and not with it.

Here, to be sure, we have a deep, deep meaning of this Christ-impulse. And out of a true knowledge we can say that the Christ saves humankind from splitting up into groups. [GA 165, 09/01/16; *Anthroposophical Quarterly* 13:1]

Rudolf Steiner reminds us that on the physical plane it is a fundamental law that everything must operate through antithesis, through polarity. Therefore, Christ could not descend to earth at the beginning of human evolution—

for then this antithesis of *external diversity* and *inner cohesion* [author's italics] could never have arisen. Mankind, however, is bound to live in this condition of antithesis and polarity. Then the human being approaches the Christ with true feelings, so that He can become, in ever greater measure, that Being who fills our own innermost Ego when we behold in Him the Being who saves earth humanity from division. Everywhere where we are able to comprehend this union of the whole of humanity over the earth, there is Christianity. In the future ... very much will depend upon the fact that in the Christ human beings seek spiritually the Uniter [*den Vereinheitlicher*], and that they accept the idea that external diversity will become greater and greater in the world. [Ibid.]

Rudolf Steiner makes it quite clear that it is the forces of both Lucifer and Ahriman that will wage war against a spiritual comprehension of the unity of mankind over the whole earth: 'There will be many a terrible onslaught, and for the most part the purpose of them will be to continue the luciferic-ahrimanic war against the Christ-impulse' (ibid.). It is these forces which strive to bring out what is special and peculiar in single groups of men and women to the exclusion of other groups. Of paramount importance to bring to full consciousness is the realization that, even when we belong to one or other of these groups, 'we can know that we can bear something which may express, "Not I, but the Christ in me," and that which is "the Christ in us" will not work for the forming of groups but rather to bring it about that the glory of the name of *Man* [*die Glorie des Menschennamens*] may be spread over the whole earth' (ibid.).

Rudolf Steiner, in this lecture, 'The Spiritual Unity of Mankind through the Christ-impulse', wished above all 'to make it clear that the Christ was that Spirit from the cosmos who, during the course of Earth evolution, brought, in a spiritual manner, that which was originally intended to come in external form, but which could not develop to completion in external form because in that case the human being would have become an automaton of love and human uniformity.' He concludes the lecture with the words:

> This is what I wanted to bring before your souls...It is all connected with the question concerning the meaning of our whole Earth evolution. For when spirits from other planets look down on the earth and ask, 'What is the meaning of this Earth evolution?' they realize it when they experience something of the Mystery of Golgotha. Everything that happens in the course of Earth evolution first attains its meaning through the Mystery of Golgotha. The Mystery of Golgotha streams out into cosmic space, and imparts to everything else what streams out from the earth, its meaning, its central meaning! [Ibid.]

The goal of mankind's evolution on earth is the development of the Higher Ego, the Ego in which Christ lives, the Ego that is both individuality and unity.[3]

* * *

Elsewhere Rudolf Steiner speaks of laws which are not founded on ordinary logic and which can only be explained by spiritual science. Such a law is the following: 'In the measure to which human beings ... permeate their souls with recognition of the spirit world ... so that the spiritual world can flow into their consciousness, in the same measure can the everyday life of mankind also unfold and human beings be given the possibility to reach beyond their antisocial impulses and beyond all that works against true community (GA 187, 01/01/19).

Progress towards the achievement of true community is not gained 'by the mere preaching of universal love, but by the extension of our interests further and further, so that we come to interest ourselves increasingly in souls with widely different characters, racial and national peculiarities, with widely different temperaments, and holding widely different religious and philosophical views—and approach them with understanding. Right interest, right understanding, calls forth from the soul the right moral action' (GA 155, 30/05/12).

In the light and warmth of such interest and understanding, we find Lucifer's benevolent participation and we can sense the suffering and pain of Ahriman.

It is not without reason that it has often been stated that it is certainly true that Christ was crucified on Golgotha, but that it is equally true that He is crucified again and again through the deeds of human beings, through our deeds. We, by our immoral deeds, unkindness and lack of love and understanding for our fellow human beings in everyday life, continually crucify Christ.

*   *   *

A time will come when mankind will have outgrown communities founded upon the blood. They will be founded upon the spirit, upon community of souls.

If we look at groups instead of the souls, we have family connections, connections of tribe and nation, and finally connected races. The race corresponds to a group soul. All these group connections of early humanity are what human beings outgrow and the more we advance the more the race conception loses its meaning. [GA 102, 01/06/08]

People of earlier times were born into connections. Today we are at a transitional point. Race will slowly but surely disappear and something new will take its place. We are moving towards connections and associations that will come into being out of the free will of those who form them. People will unite in groups, small and large, in which they will have similar ideas while retaining their complete freedom and individuality. Intellectual-ethical-moral aspects will form in increasing measure (beginnings are already discernible) the foundation of such associations—not racial, blood connections.

> The individuals voluntarily allow their feelings to stream together and this again causes the forming of something that goes beyond the merely emancipated human being. An emancipated human being possesses an individual soul that is never lost when it has once been attained. But when men and women find themselves together in voluntary associations they group themselves. The feelings streaming in this way to a centre once more give beings the opportunity of working as a kind of group soul, though in quite a different sense from the early group souls. All the earlier group souls were beings who made the human being unfree. These new beings, however, are compatible with the human being's complete freedom and individuality. Indeed, in a certain respect we may say that they support their existence on human harmony; it will lie in the souls of human beings themselves whether or not they give as many as possible of such higher souls the opportunity of descending into the human sphere. The more that people are divided the fewer lofty souls will descend into that sphere. The more that associations are formed where feelings of fellowship are developed with complete freedom, the more lofty beings will descend and the more rapidly the earthly planet will be spiritualized. [GA 102, 01/06/08]

Rudolf Steiner observes that this new spirit of community is needed to bring about the 'descent' of the spirit-self.[4]

It is the task of spiritual science to overcome the luciferic–ahrimanic form of community, for it belongs to the past. In a community of a luciferic-ahrimanic character there reigns a coercion of belief such as that prevailing in, for instance, the established Churches. 'Such a community will not understand true freedom of thought—least of all will it be able to rise to the level where complete individuality is associated with a social life in which brotherhood prevails... What grows up as a community of souls—this is what we develop, in its child-hood stage, in our working groups' (GA 159, 15/06/15).

10.   Spiritualism and Materialism

We could easily fall into the trap of characterizing the nine-teenth and twentieth centuries as being solely materialistic. However, the time in which we have been living since the middle of the last century cannot be said to be only materi-alistic. On the whole, Rudolf Steiner suggests, we may say that the fundamental character of our modern age is ex-tremely spiritual. Concepts and ideas more spiritual than those enunciated by today's scientists never existed before in the evolution of mankind. But these concepts are attenuated, 'thin' (*dünn*), they are abstract. They are spiritual in them-selves and also in regard to their substance, but if they are not used in the right way they cannot express anything spiritual. Natural-scientific concepts, inoculated in every branch of our present culture, are, Steiner says, like a two-edged sword. They may be used as academic scientists use them, in which case they are certainly spiritual, but are merely applied to the sense-perceptible world. Their spiritual essence is conse-quently denied. Yet these natural-scientific thoughts can also be used in such a way that they serve as material for medi-tation. Used in such a way they lead us with certainty into the spiritual world. If, Rudolf Steiner states, those who hold a natural-scientific view of the world were not too lazy to apply their thoughts in a meditative way, they would very soon come to spiritual science. The essential thing to bear in mind here is not the contents of the natural-scientific thoughts, but the way in which they are applied. The thoughts themselves are fine, but the way in which they are applied is materialistic. Ahriman, of course, encourages the laziness to which Steiner is alluding here.

The concepts, thoughts and ideas as used by those working in the field of the natural-sciences are 'thin', they are 'dis-tilled' spirit, distilled spiritual truths (*destillierter Geist*), so that it would only require a strong effort to pass over from them to spiritual science. These are the very thoughts and ideas which should enter human evolution in the present Michael Age. However, it is just these thoughts and ideas that are most of all subjected to confusion by the ahrimanic spirits which were overcome by Michael in the nineteenth century and cast out of the spiritual world onto the earth. Our thoughts and ideas are today exposed to a high degree to the confusing influence of such Spirits of Darkness (see GA 174b, 24/02/18; NSL 241).

The task of our age is to develop living concepts, perceptions and feelings, and not to invoke dead theories. The former, we learn from Steiner, are directly inspired by spiritual beings who are united with Michael (see GA 243, 18/08/24).

In one of his lectures in a series entitled *The Occult Movement in the Nineteenth Century*, Steiner shows that even among those who had some knowledge of the spiritual worlds, considerable confusion reigned. This confusion arose because Ahriman and Lucifer were continually being intermingled, that is, a clear understanding of the distinction between Ahriman and Lucifer was lacking. Now if such an intermingling prevails then one is induced to accept the materialistic picture of the world because Lucifer comes to the aid of Ahriman...

> ... and a certain *longing* [author's italics] arises in one to weave certain fallacies in the guise of truths into one's conception of the world.
>
> A remarkable trend has developed, namely, to harbour fallacies which indeed could flourish only in the age of materialism—one might say in the age of ahrimanic deception—because Lucifer helps from within. Ahriman insinuates himself into the concepts formed of outer phenomena and deceives us about them. But we would see through these wiles if Lucifer did not *incite* [author's italics] us to lend force to certain materialistic facts in our view of the world. [GA 254, 17/10/15]

And so it could happen that Lucifer had sufficient influence on entirely materialistic human beings so that they did not believe in materialism and attempted to find in materialism itself a spiritual conception of the world. 'Just think of it—the nineteenth century could produce a type of person whose head produced a thoroughly materialistic kind of thinking but whose heart was longing for the spiritual' (ibid.).

It is therefore not surprising that when the battle between Michael and the Dragon, i.e. Ahriman, began in the 1840s the practice and beliefs of 'spiritualism' entered the world-arena. Spiritualism made its appearance at a time when the ahrimanic spirits brought confusion into human thoughts in regard to the true nature of the spiritual.

In the first of the lectures in the series entitled *The Occult Movement in the Nineteenth Century* Rudolf Steiner speaks of certain groups of occultists who, in the middle of the nineteenth century, attempted to deal in some way with the materialistic tendencies of the age. They realized that it did not suffice to do no more than talk about the spirit, about the esoteric teaching, because those who immersed themselves in materialism, who had adopted the natural-scientific attitude, would need some form of visible demonstration, visible proof, if they were to take any teaching about the spiritual world seriously. The outcome of the occultists' deliberations was that mediumship was brought onto the nineteenth-century scene. It was by this means that these groups of occultists sought to convince people of the existence of a spiritual world. It was through the mediums that people were to see with physical eyes that which originates in the spiritual world. The medium produced phenomena which could be demonstrated on the physical plane (cf. GA 254, 10/10/15).

At this stage it is helpful to recapitulate some of the ground we have covered already.

Between 1840 and 1880 the battle between Michael and the Dragon, Ahriman, was reflected on earth in the powerful impulse for the development of materialism. 'Materialism could only develop in consequence of major occurrences in the spiritual world which then continued in a downward direction and gradually caused materialistic impulses to be instilled into humanity' (GA 177, 27/10/17).

When we consider how events in the spiritual world were reflected here on earth, two things are particularly evident.

The first is that the 'purely physical intellect' and a culture based thereon showed a pronounced upsurge during the four decades mentioned. 'There has never been such an upsurge in subtlety of conception, acumen and critical faculties for the adherents of materialism as during those decades. All the thinking ... that leads to technical inventions, to criticism and to brilliant definition is physical thinking and bound to the brain' (ibid.). Here we see a mirror-reflection develop in human souls of the aims certain Spirits of Darkness, ahrimanic spirits, were seeking to achieve.

The second 'reflection' was the emergence of spiritualism in the 1840s and later.

As we have just observed, certain groups of occultists sought to explore connections with the spiritual world by using mediums, that is, essentially by physical means.

Now if the Spirits of Darkness, the ahrimanic spirits, had succeeded in gaining the victory over Michael and his hosts in 1879—and we could say that such a risk certainly existed for, as Steiner indicates, it is precisely in their scientific, materialistic ideas that people are least of all in the Michael Age (cf. GA 219, 17/12/22)—then, Rudolf Steiner observes, spiritualism would have spread enormously.

> For spiritualism gets its impulses not only from the earth, but is also governed by influences coming from the other world ... The things that happened in spiritualistic circles ... certainly arose from impulses which came from the spiritual world and were often bound up with human destinies. They were, nevertheless, a mirror-reflection of the battle which had been lost in the spiritual region. This is also why spiritualism lost momentum and became so strangely corrupted after that point in time. It would have been the means by which people's attention would have been drawn to the spiritual world, and it would have been *the only means if the Spirits of Darkness had gained the victory in 1879* [author's italics]. [GA 177, 17/10/17]

So, if the ahrimanic spirits had won, the cold critical faculty and an incredibly penetrating acumen would rule in every sphere of life—callously eliminating every indication of the slightest moral impulse. This is the one aspect of what could have occurred if Ahriman had defeated Michael. The other would have manifested itself in the universal use of physical means of mediums to satisfy spiritual needs. 'So there you have what the Spirits of Darkness intended: physical acumen on the one hand, and a way of seeking connection with the spiritual world based on reduced consciousness on the other. Above all else, the Spirits of Darkness, ahrimanic spirits, wanted to prevent spiritual experiences, living experiences of the spirit, from coming down into human souls' (ibid.).[1]

In regard to states of 'reduced consciousness', dimmed wakefulness—a state to which a trance medium is reduced— we need to heed the fact that Ahriman takes full advantage of moments when, in waking life, a person falls into a twilight consciousness (cf. GA 254, 15/10/15). It is not dimmed consciousness but clarity of consciousness and therewith clarity of thought that are needed to keep Ahriman in his rightful place. The highly intelligent ahrimanic spirits have had no difficulty in recognizing this and, as has been seen already, have attached particular value, since the battle with Michael in the nineteenth century, to the 'breeding' of confusion among human beings so that they do not succeed in forming the right thoughts and ideas in regard to the human kingdom itself and to the spiritual worlds.

Rudolf Steiner gives many examples of the confusion in human thought instigated by Ahriman. For instance, to regard Darwinism as the only valid conception of the development of the human being, so that people believe that they have descended entirely from forces that also produce the animals, is to completely ignore the spiritual dimension in the process of evolution. 'The grandeur of Darwinian thought is not disputed,' says Rudolf Steiner, 'but it does not explain the integral evolution of the human being. It only sees the lower, inferior elements. So it is with all purely physical explanations which do not recognize the spiritual essence of the human being' (GA 94, 26/05/06).

In a cycle of lectures Rudolf Steiner gave to a group of

young people he speaks very graphically about the way in which human thinking has 'lost' itself in the past few centuries in the conviction that natural-scientific research into matter would give the answers regarding the nature of life. The spiritual has been relegated to the unknown, the unknowable—indeed, its very existence denied. Science conducted in such a one-sided direction can do no more than concern itself with outer manifestation, but has no inkling of the creative formative forces through which such a manifestation has come into being. Goethe characterizes this one-sided natural-scientific attitude with acute perception:

> He who would know and treat of aught alive,
> Seeks first the living spirit thence to drive:
> Then are the lifeless fragments in his hand,
> There only fails, alas! the spirit-band[2]
> [Tr. Anna Swanwick]

The kind of thinking that is circumscribed by the earth-bound bonds of materialism, which produces a lifeless picture of the world and of mankind, appears like a Dragon which threatens to devour, bit by bit, the soul life of the human being.

In the lecture to the group of young people Rudolf Steiner uses the term 'Dragon' as a synonym for Ahriman.

'Consider,' he says, 'how this devouring has taken effect. Whereas from the fifteenth century onwards natural science has been triumphantly progressing, knowledge of the human being has been more and more on the downgrade.' Previously Steiner had mentioned that the Darwinian theory of evolution had given a survey of how animals evolve from animals (the more complex from the simpler, etc.), and how the human being is to be seen as the culmination point in the ranks of the animal kingdom. But it does not give us any picture as to what we are as human beings. 'If we fill our soul with what our thinking has become through nature, there appears in the picture of the human being devouring Dragon what is the most potent factor in modern civilization.' In the last third of the nineteenth century the Dragon, Ahriman, threatened to devour the individual life of the soul. 'Those who had within them a fully developed life of soul felt how the Dragon ... had acquired fresh life in the new age through observation and experiment, but it was a life that devoured the human being.'[3] But, since the dawn of the new Michael Rulership we have the means at our disposal, if we will make the effort to avail ourselves of them, to conquer the Dragon. We can do this by making 'ourselves allies of the approaching Michael' and thus uniting ourselves with the spiritual world. We need 'to lift up our eyes to Michael who, since the last third of the nineteenth century, has been striving to enter our outworn Dragon-civilization' (GA 217, 15/10/22). In so doing we gain the ability, through our moral impulses, to implant the truth of life-giving spirituality into the false conception and consequent degeneration of humanity instigated by the Dragon, Ahriman.[4]

> For the reality of the moral world-order is what the approaching Michael can give. The old religions cannot do this; they have allowed themselves to be conquered by the Dragon. They accept the Dragon who kills the human being, and by the side of the Dragon establish some special, abstractly moral divine order. But the Dragon does not tolerate this; the Dragon must be conquered. He does not suffer human beings to found something alongside him. What we need is the force that we can gain from victory over the Dragon. [GA 217, 15/10/22]

The overall influence of Darwinism has been considerable, not only in the field of biology but also in those of philosophy, psychology, ethics, aesthetics, astronomy, geology, and so forth.[5]

What has happened in modern civilization? One of Rudolf Steiner's many answers to this question runs as follows:

> 'Well, every science has become a metamorphosis of the Dragon, all external culture too is an outcome of the Dragon. Certainly, the outer world-mechanism, which lives not only in the machine but also in our social organism, is rightly called a Dragon. But besides that, the Dragon meets us everywhere, whether modern science is telling us about the origins of life,

about the transformation of living beings, about the human soul, or even in the field of history—everywhere the result proceeds from the Dragon. [GA 217, 15/10/22]

Today the battle of Michael with the Dragon has, for the first time, become real in our own souls. Simultaneously with the culmination of Ahriman's power, there also came—at the turn of the century—Michael's impulse with which we can unite ourselves. Michael now actually penetrates from spiritual realms into our earthly realms. But as has been mentioned already, Michael does not force himself upon us, for today human beings must act out of their own free will. Ahriman, on the other hand, pushes himself forward, demanding the highest authority.

The authority of science is the most powerful that has ever been exercised in the world. Compare the authority of the Pope; it is almost as powerful... Everywhere the Dragon rears up to meet one. There is no other way than to unite ourselves with Michael, that is to say, to permeate ourselves with real knowledge of the spiritual weaving and being of the world. Only now does this picture of Michael truly stand before us; for the first time it has become our essential concern as human beings. [Ibid.]

Let us now remind ourselves of some aspects of human evolution already touched upon and place them in the present context of the discussion on spiritualism.

The conclusion of a particular process in the evolution of mankind was reached in the mid-nineteenth century. In the period from the early fifteenth century (birth of the consciousness soul) to the middle of the nineteenth century, humanity was developing a faculty that had not been present in the same way in any earlier period. The faculty in question is made up mainly of forces that make possible an intellectual grasp of the world through reason. The method of applying merely the intellect to phenomena of nature in a purely external way represents the faculty which belongs to those centuries. From that time mankind was mature enough for the gradual development of other faculties. Since that time, Rudolf Steiner states, 'it is a growing necessity for other forces to be added to those of observation and knowledge based on mere intellect,' namely, 'full conscious insight into the spiritual world' (GA 171, 23/09/16).

In answer to the question 'For what purpose have the faculties of observation and knowledge based on mere intellect appeared since they penetrate so little below the surface of things?' Steiner answers that they have appeared because only by their means could human beings go through a certain stage of their development. In earlier times human beings were still 'linked'—through an ancient heritage—with the spiritual world. Indeed, the further back we go in historical evolution the more possible it was for human beings to 'look' into the spiritual world. But this faculty was not such that they could use it in freedom; it was, to a greater or lesser extent, involuntary.

Now, in order that human beings should be able to achieve the faculty of making free decisions and developing freedom, they had to lose the forces which, in earlier times, brought them nearer the spiritual world but at the same time allowed them little freedom. 'They had to pass through a period of development in which they were shut off as by a veil or sheath from the spiritual world so that they might become free' (ibid.). This development is still far from having been brought to maturity, but a first stage was completed in the mid-nineteenth century. As noted already, it is since that time that additional forces have to join those based on mere intellect. The intellectual development has led to a conception of the world and of mankind that is materialistic. It is for the sake of freedom, Rudolf Steiner stresses on a number of occasions, that humanity has gone through such a development during the past few centuries. Were the intellectual conception of the world alone to hold sway—this is Ahriman's aim and would have been mankind's destiny if Michael had not conquered the Spirits of Darkness—we would only be able to understand the dead and lifeless; and understanding of life and the living—and of the spiritual—would be lost.

Through its one-sided development over the past five or

six centuries, thought has become 'thin', attenuated, and as a consequence also powerless to arrive at a conscious knowledge of the spiritual—for it had to stop short at the surface of things in order to free humankind from involuntary, instinctive, clairvoyance and clairaudience.

With the absence of conscious knowledge, there began, from the 1840s onwards, attempts to get in touch with the spiritual world through a subconscious knowledge and a lowering, dimming of consciousness which, we have seen, is vulnerable to Ahriman's assaults. In one of his lectures dealing with true and false paths in spiritual investigation Rudolf Steiner makes a comment which is pertinent here: 'Human beings are only in a mediumistic or somnambulistic condition when their ego and astral body are outside their physical and etheric bodies; but in this case ... their ego and astral body are possessed by an alien being' (GA 243, 20/08/24).

It was not only through spiritism, spiritualism, but also through hypnotism and various methods of suggestion that attempts began to be made to prove that spiritual activity lies behind the sense-world. All of these methods constitute endeavours to research the spirit by materialistic means.

Something quite other than that which could be expected has, in fact, come to light from even the subtlest mediumistic seances. Instead of knowledge of the spiritual world that surrounds us while we are alive, the experiences gained have emanated from spirits of the dead.

We are actually surrounded by a spiritual world just as we are by a physical one. That this should emerge is what might have been expected, but little indeed has come out concerning this... The mediumistic manifestations and revelations have always referred to the spirits of the departed. Nor, in truth, could anything else happen by this method. Why? ... Nothing has been achieved other than the knowledge of what comes to light if one expels the best qualities of the new age [e.g. the exact, objective and fully conscious scientific approach] from human consciousness and leads us back to earlier times, to subconscious conditions of soul. The remains of this subconscious condition that had carried over into the new age were now laid bare. It was this that was revealed...Nothing had been done towards developing new forces for new connections with the spiritual world. Nothing had come out but the old connections, which went in the direction of that to which they had been linked earlier. They did not unite with what was living in the contemporary environment but with death, with the lifeless. [GA 171, 23/09/16]

In answer to the question 'Why is this so?', we may say that it was inevitable because the direction of the evolution of mankind since the fifteenth century—in particular, since the mid-nineteenth century—has so determined the character of the human soul that it is particularly 'conditioned' to obtain knowledge of the dead and lifeless. Thus all these medium-istic, spiritualistic experiments did not—and do not—open up a path to the 'living' in the spiritual world, but to what is dead. It is only with what is really dead and does not there-fore live on with the living soul that one could connect one-self with the spiritual world by means of the materialistic, mediumistic pathway. 'If, through contemporary science, one reached a knowledge of the material, the lifeless, the dead, so also through this spiritual longing that had to be satisfied along materialistic paths one reached nothing but a knowl-edge of the dead, though, to be sure, it was a knowledge of the supersensible' (GA 171, 23/09/16).

Contemporary materialistic science can find only the external dead; spiritualism, an apparently spiritual but in reality materialistic procedure, can find only the super-sensible dead.[6]

However, the mediumistic seances do not even necessarily reveal communication with the supersensible dead. Rudolf Steiner reminds us on numerous occasions that we must be quite clear as to the fact that when a human being passes through the Gate of Death the human individuality is at first, for a short time, enshrouded in the astral body and the etheric body, and that the latter, after a brief period—never longer than three to three and a half days—passes out into the etheric world. The individuality, therefore, enters the spiri-tual world with the astral body only. Now, in spiritualistic seances we must ask ourselves the question: Do communications, via a medium, come from the actual individuality of the dead or only from the cast off *etheric corpse*? This corpse, we learn from Steiner, still remains in continual communication with the individuality. However, it is essential to realize that 'when one contacts the spiritual world in a roundabout way through a medium, one comes *in touch with the etheric corpse first* [author's italic], and so can never be sure of reaching in this way the actual individual' (GA 175, 06/02/17).

Rudolf Steiner gives another enlightening example of the misguidance and misinterpretation resulting from mediumistic seances in a lecture on the life of the soul in Kamaloca (which he describes as 'the place of desire') (GA 95, 24/08/06). He gives us a picture of the experiences different people have in regard to their astral bodies in Kamaloca. St Francis of Assisi, for instance, denied himself many things; he 'used' his ego to ennoble his desires and lower impulses. He gained power, control, consciously over his astral body during his life on earth. His experiences in Kamaloca cannot but be different from those of a person who, during life on earth, indulged to the full their desires and animal impulses. One can say that the human being has two parts to his astral body: one part is permeated with animal impulses, the other results from the ego-work that has been done on it. 'When one has "lived" through the necessary time in Kamaloca [i.e. for about one-third of the length of the past life on earth], one will be ready to raise the "higher" part of one's astral body, the outcome of one's own endeavours, and to leave the "lower" part behind.' With those who have made little, if any, effort to purify, transmute, their animal impulses, a large part of the lower astral body remains behind. Lower astral bodies are always hovering around us—they are 'corpses'. They 'continue to hover about in astral space ... This, too, is a body which can manifest in spiritualistic seances. It often survives for a long time, and may come to speak through a trance medium. People then begin to believe that it is the dead person speaking, when in reality it is only an astral corpse which has done so. The corpse retains its lower impulses and habits in a kind of husk; it can even answer questions and give information, and can speak with just as much sense as the "lower" aspect of the human being used to display in life on earth' (ibid.).

* * *

The nineteenth-century spiritualist phenomenon spanned approximately 40 years—from 1840 to 1880. Since the 1960s there has been a resurgence of mediumship, primarily through 'voice channellings'. Characteristic of most of these mediums is that they are not consciously participating in the process. Their spiritual self-development is not such that they can consciously cross the threshold between the physical and supersensible worlds and, as a consequence, both Lucifer and Ahriman have easy access to their souls and can therefore ensure that distorted and confused information as to the real 'life' in the spiritual world is communicated (see GA 147).

In the second lecture in the series *The Occult Movement of the Nineteenth Century*, Rudolf Steiner speaks in some detail of various Brotherhoods, Brotherhoods of the right, Brotherhoods of the left.

> The further the occultists inclined to the left, the less were they concerned to promote that which alone is justifiable, namely, the *universal-human*. In occultism people belong to the 'left' when they try to achieve some ultimate goal with the help of what they know in the way of occult teaching. People belong to the 'right' in occultism when they desire that goal purely for its own sake ... those who belong to the extreme 'left' are those who combine special aims of their own with what they promulgate as occult teaching. A person is on the 'left' to the extent to which he or she pursues special aims, leads people to the spiritual world, gives them all kinds of demonstration of it, and instils into them, in an *illicit way*, promptings that simply help to bring these special aims to fulfilment. [GA 254, 11/10/15]

In the nineteenth century a principal goal of the Brotherhoods of the left was to prevent a coherent knowledge of reincarnation from entering western culture. They used the mediums to oppose the teaching of repeated human lives (GA 254, 19/10/15).

In the twentieth century, particularly since the 1960s, the principal goal of the Brotherhoods of the left is to prevent the true cognition of the Christ-impulse and thus also the experience of Christ in the etheric.

It was particularly in the West (USA) that the 1960s witnessed a mass pseudo-initiation into the spiritual world. Many people, above all the young, glimpsed, under the influence of LSD for instance, the Guardian of the Threshold. This experience, because of the lack of proper preparation—particularly in the moral sphere—often had devastating consequences.

Richard Leviton, who has undertaken considerable research in this field, writes:

> The 1960s birthed a strange combination of LSD cults, occultism and oriental religions, a Bohemian revisioning of the dream of the earlier nineteenth-century theosophical occult revival and its espousal of spiritual evolution, expanded consciousness and liberation. Through the esoteric writings of H.P. Blavatsky, Annie Besant, Charles Leadbeater, Georges Gurdjieff, P.D. Ouspensky and Paul Brunton, among others, the outer court of the Mysteries was thrown open to the public at large. In America the sons and daughters of WASPS [White Anglo-Saxon Protestants], Catholics and Jews converted wholesale to the unusual eschatologies of Theosophy, Buddhism, and Hinduism as the Tibetan rigors of the 'great path of liberation and Nirvana' supplanted the empty pieties and metaphysical dead-ends of establishment religion.[7]

We have noted earlier that without the presence of clear, conscious cognitive forces all manner of misrepresentations in regard to the spiritual world prevail. The Brotherhoods of the left, the agents of the Ahrimanic/Soratic impulse, manipulate the channels of the twentieth century so that the spiritual worlds are construed materially. (For Sorat see pages 177–182.) Moreover, these Brotherhoods—we could also call them 'black lodges'—work to stifle conscious cognition. They would oust all activity of the consciousness soul and hold the development of the human soul firm in the phase which manifested itself in, for instance, ancient Egypt, in the phase of the sentient soul in which conscious, independent discrimination is lacking. They would also promulgate a multiplicity of gods, of false messiahs.

We have seen elsewhere that Ahriman strives to cause fragmentation. This tendency is patently obvious in the confusion of 'tongues' issuing forth from the mediumistic materials featuring, particularly in the USA, in the second half of the twentieth century. We could characterize this fragmentation by saying that the Brotherhoods of the left are instigating the erection of a second Tower of Babel. In such a creation the Whitsuntide experience of the power of the Holy Spirit which endows human beings with an all-embracing, universal voice permeated by the Creative Word, the Christ, is absent. The Christ-Logos can never emerge from such a confusion of tongues. Rudolf Steiner makes it clear that very little of any real value emerges from channelling or mediumship. In any event, we should not mistake psychism for spirituality.

We have noted that the Brotherhoods of the left work to stifle independent conscious cognition. Independent spiritual activity is anathema to the Brotherhoods of the left who strive to negate the reality of the Michael-Christ impulse. Freedom in the sphere of spiritual activity is Michael's gift to mankind. Here, as always, Michael is acting on behalf of Christ.

In the present Michaelic Age our cognitive activities need to be conducted in the full light of ego-consciousness. Clear and awake consciousness—not present in by far the greater number of mediums, channellers—is the Michaelic soul quality needed for entering into and communing with the spiritual world.

However, as Rudolf Steiner emphasizes again and again, our faculty of thinking must become sense-free, that is, independent of the objects surrounding us in the sense-perceptible world. It is along the 'path' of sense-free thinking that we approach the 'portal' into the spiritual world. Steiner also emphasizes again and again that the spiritual world must be approached with the same intellectual clarity that is required by the scientific method when investigating the sense-perceptible world. 'That is what the real method of spiritual science ought to be—to enter into the spiritual world along the same path that the human being has entered into nature during the last three or four centuries' (GA 171, 23/09/16).

The discipline of natural scientific research must be retained but the way of thinking has to be transformed. Whereas the natural-scientific method of forming thoughts is that of dismemberment, reductionist dissection, the spiritual scientist employs a completely different kind of mental process. In contrast to differentiating, dismembering, it is a creative, formative manner of thinking. It is a manner of thinking that leads us consciously—and safely—to the spiritual worlds. It has a living quality, for 'the Christ-impulse stands in the direct line of formative, creative thinking' (GA 187, 01/01/19).

To reiterate: genuine spiritual-scientific endeavour requires the clarity and exactness of wide-awake thinking and fully conscious involvement at every stage of the process. A trancelike or semi-conscious form of perception is open to illusion, in particular, today, to the distortions brought into being under the aegis of Ahriman.

Freedom, too, is fundamental to genuine spiritual science. Steiner gives us a picture of the kind of freedom meant here: 'The initiate has passed beyond all superstition, for he knows what the true form of the spirit is. *Freedom* from the preconceptions of the personality, of doubt and superstition— these are the hallmarks of one who has attained to discipleship on the path of higher knowledge' (GA 9, Ch. 4). We may enlarge the picture given here by including, in the present context, freedom from all forms of external compulsion (e.g. dogmatic instructions and guidance), also freedom from subservience to the subconscious (e.g. prejudices, biased opinions and feelings of our own) and, as already discussed, freedom from sense-bound thinking.

In the transition from sense-bound thinking to sense-free thinking the will plays an all-important role. In order that the will be active in thinking it must be free from the constraints of a subconscious dream-life and confused emotions. Moreover, it is of paramount importance that the will exerted is one's own and not that of an outsider, e.g. a guru. In a Michaelic striving for spiritual knowledge, the carrying out of guidelines for soul-spiritual development is entirely voluntary (cf. GA 12). Such development undertaken out of one's own free will is in tune with the present Michael Age. To fall back on authority, to carry out instructions simply because they are given by someone in higher authority is to regress to an earlier Age, to that of Gabriel.

In his basic work *Knowledge of the Higher Worlds. How is it Attained?* (GA 10), Steiner draws our attention to an all-important process in our self-development if we are to attain direct perception of the spiritual world and of our own spirit-being, namely, the need to develop moral qualities to a higher degree than we usually possess. This golden rule of genuine spiritual science Steiner formulates as follows: 'For every *one* step forward that you take in seeking knowledge of occult truths, take *three* steps forward in the development of your own character.' In his autobiography Steiner writes:

> Moral laws—in the form of commandments—arising from an external situation do not become a person's moral impulse by one's submission to them, even though they originally issued from the spiritual world; they do so only if as an *individual* one experiences their thought-content as a living spirituality within oneself. It is within our thinking that freedom lives. Of itself the will is not free; it is the thought that empowers the will that is free. [GA 28, Ch. 23]

We could now ask: To what extent do the paths of mediumship and channelling, manifesting themselves in the latter half of the twentieth century, meet the criteria just discussed? Do they manifest sense-free thinking in full consciousness, independent spiritual activity and freedom of will? Do they represent a true or a false path in spiritual investigation? Do they meet the present conditions of consciousness, of the consciousness soul, the spiritual soul? Are they, in short, responding to the Michael-Christ impulse? With very few exceptions the answers to these questions must be 'No.'

Here is not the place to go into any detail as to the multiplicity of phenomena in the mediumistic and channelling field which confront us today.[8] An overall guideline in every endeavour to attain initiation knowledge is indicated by Rudolf Steiner in the following few words: 'The essential point is that we must be fully conscious, in full control of experiences. The phenomena and experiences as such are not the decisive factor, but the way in which we respond to them' (GA 243, 21/08/24).

* * *

There are examples of Michaelic consciousness-soul activity grounded in the fully conscious attention and spiritual freedom of the channeller, the agent of communication. One such example came to the attention of Rudolf Steiner.

The sister of a young musician, Sigwart, who died, at the age of 30/31, of a bullet wound on the Russian front in 1915, began to receive communications from him about two months after his death.[9]

A few characteristic features of these communications and the relation between the deceased brother and his sister will have to suffice here to give us at least a partial picture of the reason why Rudolf Steiner could give them his approval.

The sister and brother had been very close to one another during his lifetime on earth. Immediately after his death he tried to communicate with her. She sensed that he was doing so, but she could not tolerate the thought of indulging in mediumistic or spiritualistic practices. However, after about two months what could be described as an inner awakening enabled her to 'build a bridge' to him in full consciousness. Describing this experience she said: 'In the seclusion and quietness of these past days I have come to recognize what Sigwart expects of me, which is not to guide my hand and influence it externally; rather, I myself must open a door in

my mind, then I shall hear the words I have to write down.'
The sister, then, is fully conscious during the exchanges with
her brother. Indeed, as she herself says, she has to exert
herself to hold her mind open to hear Sigwart's words. Permeating the relationship between brother and sister is a close
karmic bond (Sigwart makes this quite clear). She also
exhibits, in addition to selfless love, steadfast faith and a
remarkable understanding of Sigwart's journey and experiences in the spiritual world—experiences which Sigwart
describes with great objectivity. His 'letters' give factual
descriptions of life in the spiritual world. He experiences the
power and love of the Christ and speaks of the spiritual world
as being filled with the multifarious activities of the spiritual
Hierarchies. Sigwart also makes it clear that his progress in
the spiritual world is dependent on his being able to fulfil
various karmic obligations. In answer to a question he says:
'Even after death we cannot immediately see *higher* beings,
but only after one has removed all of one's sheaths.'

Sigwart emphasizes that also in the spiritual world ever-
increasing self-knowledge, undertaken out of free will, is
essential. With this growing self-knowledge also comes an
increasing sense of responsibility towards those he has left
behind on earth. *Inter alia*, he makes clear that he cannot in
any way 'interfere' with their lives. 'I cannot and dare not mix
in, because it would mean interference with your karma; I am
permitted merely to be with you, to listen in, console you, try
to comprehend, give you strength: "That I live!" But I *must
not* change anything in the path of life ... Do not ask me for
something I cannot give you.'

It seems clear that both Sigwart and his sister have shared,
during the last few years of his short life, a common spiritual-
scientific striving. Such a common endeavour has facilitated
the building of the bridge between them. Of himself, Sigwart,
in answer to another question, says: 'I am not in the so-called
"astral sphere", nor in the "Devachan sphere" at present,
but in the middle realm. I have advanced further in a shorter
time than many others because of my interest in everything
spiritual during my life on earth' (22 August. A little over two

months after his death). In the same 'letter' he says to his sister: 'I come to you today to thank you. The currents of your love that steadily flow to me are engulfing me completely. I feel every thought you are sending to me, and I hear every note you are playing for me.' He then goes on to say: 'I am happy because you all have overcome yourselves.'

It is clear from a number of Sigwart's utterances that it is not a one-sided relationship. It is not only those on earth who need the help of spiritual beings in the conduct of their lives, but also those who have crossed the threshold into the spiritual world need the loving help of those on earth. 'We too,' Sigwart says, 'need much help and must not lose heart. I thank you for all the love you have given me the past year. How rich you have made me—how much you have helped me! Thank you, and again thank you! Together we shall walk into the new life and vow to be worthy of Christ, who is our Helper.'

Rudolf Steiner's approval of the various aspects of the relationship between Sigwart and his sister, somewhat sketchily indicated here, would have been enhanced by Sigwart's awareness that his sister's participation in the exchange with him should strengthen not weaken her for her tasks in life on earth. It should help her to carry her responsibilities. 'Be never afraid I might draw you away from your duties—*no*—you should become stronger, more capable, so you can confront them as masters and not as knaves.'

Similar connections between the dead and the living were exhibited by the British theosophist Mrs Kenningdale-Cook, who wrote under the pen-name of Mabel Collins. The genuine impulse behind her work—in particular the spiritual treatise *Light on the Path*—was recognized by Rudolf Steiner (see GA 42/425).

There are also other works that may be said to illustrate a conscious connection between earthly and spiritual spheres. In the second half of the 1960s Frances Banks, a nun and educator who had died in November 1965, sent messages from the spiritual world to a close friend and co-worker,

Helen Greaves, who was clairaudient and wrote them down. They first appeared in book form under the title *Testimony of Light*.[10]

Helen Greaves was always fully conscious when she received communications from her 'dead' friend. One could describe her as being a pure, unobstructed 'channel'.

In his preface to the first edition, the then Canon of Southwark Cathedral, J.D. Pearce-Higgins, spoke of the communications from Frances Banks as coming 'through the intermediary of her friend Helen Greaves'. He then goes on to say: 'I have used the word "intermediacy" rather than "mediumship" because this book would appear to contain the ideal form of communication, namely, between two minds, which already on earth were well in tune with each other, and appear, though parted physically, to have been able to continue in "unity of the spirit" across the gap of death.'[11]

Another inspirational writer of interest is Cynthia Sandys, described by Rosamond Lehmann[12] (who, we could say, was Cynthia's amanuensis) as being 'a mental channel and recorder of exceptional purity (clairaudient, not clairvoyant). After five or ten minutes of silent preparation for listening, her spiritual hearing opens and she starts rapidly to write... There is no question of trance or automatism; her normal consciousness is, however, slightly withdrawn while she writes...'[13]

Rosamond Lehmann, in her Foreword to Part 1 of *Letters from our Daughters*, writes: 'We have agreed [...] to omit all intimate and personal references, and to concentrate chiefly on those letters containing information relating to their special interests: in Patricia's case, healing in its more diverse aspects; in Sally's case, the functions and potentials of music in extra-terrestrial planes of consciousness.'

An example from one of Sally's 'letters' runs as follows: '...I am growing in music—using every single particle of creation from which to extract sound: trees, mountains, flowers, streams and oceans—and trying to unite them in harmony... You don't know how wonderful an effect all the looking back thoughts have had, and how exciting it is to feel and see quite new forces, which the sum-total call into the earth atmosphere. And apart from that, into the aura of each one taking part in thought and prayer comes a tiny reflection which alters the whole chemical outlook of the etheric body. You may boggle at my saying chemical—but there are etheric chemistry beyond your ken but going out from your world of chemical without a break, and leading right on into the highest spheres.'

Shortly after Rosamond Lehmann had paid her first visit to Coventry Cathedral Sally 'writes': 'The music in Coventry will be something quite out of this world, because consciously or unconsciously they have attached this curiously aerial-shaped spire to the roof, and the music will escape that way to build cities in the ether. Music has such a wonderful building power.'

In one of her 'letters' Patricia writes of her many incarnations and her experiences through the ages of illness and death. In one of her lives a much loved daughter died as a child. In a later life this child was her sister. She also died young. 'When she died I gave up, something snapped inside me, and I became wild and unfeeling. I don't know what I said or did; but eventually I went to the hospitals, and I worked and worked among the dying. You must never let anyone die alone, that was my feeling. On and on I worked, feverishly, until one day I suppose I, too, dropped down, and never moved my physical body. That was why in my last life I came with the urge to heal ... So now I have gained through all the quagmire of misery a tremendous love of healing, and the sure and certain knowledge that death is no dictator. He often comes as a friend, and the pain of parting is an illusion ... It's the next fence we have to climb.'

Mention could also be made of the works of David Spangler and of the book *The Boy Who Saw True* by an anonymous author with a foreword by the British occultist and musical composer Cyril Scott (although evidence points to the book being a disguised autobiography of Scott's own childhood in diary form).[14] The boy is a natural clairvoyant

and much of what he confides to his diary and, later, his
personal tutor, supports Rudolf Steiner's indications, albeit
in a simple way. Excerpts from the author's adult diary are
included at the end of the book and contain a number of
statements contrary to Steiner's (e.g. the impulse behind
Woodrow Wilson's division of Europe), but the evidence of
an objective inspirational link during the boy's childhood is
clear, allowing spiritual truths to be imparted in a most
accessible manner.

Spiritual information, if it is imparted correctly, if it is
transmitted with love and understanding, should assist us to
deal more efficiently, and with deeper love and greater
understanding, with the various tasks which confront us in
life on earth.

Rudolf Steiner stresses the fact that genuine spiritual
experience cannot fail to lead to an enrichment of our inner
and our 'outer' life. It leads to moral impulses that bring
about a betterment in the way we conduct ourselves towards
our fellow human beings and also to planet Earth. It brings
about a 'living'—not a theoretical—relationship with the
beings active in the spiritual world.

These are some of the yardsticks by which the value and
the authenticity of channelled information and spiritual
experiences may be gauged.

*   *   *

Our materialistic age wants the spirit to descend into the
material world whereas the only true way to find connection
with those who have crossed the threshold is through inner
spiritual development—raising oneself to full consciousness
to the spiritual world.

If, Steiner says, spiritual science is to have any meaning it
must clearly recognize and emphasize 'the spiritual inward-
ness of true spirituality as compared with these materialistic
strivings after a world of spirit' (GA 175, 06/02/17).

'We stand today at the infinitely important juncture in
human evolution where, on the one hand, the spiritual world
is willing to reveal itself with great power, while, on the other,

human beings must find the strength to free themselves from their greatest entanglement in what is material and come to a new reception of spiritual revelations' (GA 193, 12/06/19).

We are still standing at the 'infinitely important juncture' Rudolf Steiner highlighted many years ago.

11.   The Revelation of John

When Adam and Eve, through the seductive power of the Serpent, Lucifer, were expelled from the Garden of Eden, they found themselves in a world that was cold, dark and breathed of death. They found themselves in Ahriman's domain. Christ, for the sake of mankind, overcame both the luciferic and the ahrimanic powers, but the battle to be won by mankind has yet to be fought. John's prophetic vision gives us a picture of the future destiny of humanity. The war that was waged in heaven is now to be fought on earth in the human soul.

When evil first appears in the Revelation of St John it is concentrated in the figure of the Dragon (Ch. 12). However, we soon learn that it rises up in the form of two beasts (Ch. 13). The seer, John, sees a monster rise out of the sea; it has ten horns and seven heads. Out of the earth he sees another beast come up. This beast has two horns, hard as steel. Evil, in John's vision, appears in its double character.

In the spiritual science of Rudolf Steiner the distinction between the two aspects of evil—the luciferic (*diabolos*) and the ahrimanic (*satanas*)—is in full accord with the pictorial wisdom of John's vision; the seven-headed, ten-horned Beast is the luciferic power; the two-horned Beast is the ahrimanic.

Through the one-sided emphasis on the physical and the consequent lack of recognition of the spiritual, we can recognize that the conception of materialism is itself the image of the two-horned beast, for it regards the human being as an animal. Men and women are thus alienated from their true being and their destiny. The conception of their animal origin and of the determination of their character through the bloodstream, through heredity, must ultimately lead to men and women losing the nobility and dignity of the human being and bearing 'in their foreheads' the mark of the Beast. In such a picture of the human being there is no place for Hamlet's vision: 'What a piece of work is a man! How noble in reason! how infinite in faculty! in form, in moving, how express and admirable! in action like an angel! in apprehension how like a god! the beauty of the world! the paragon of animals!' (Act II, Scene II).

The Michaelic battle fought in the spiritual world has yet to be won on earth. Human beings will be involved in the apocalyptic battle. A hint of this future involvement is given to us in the Old Testament. In Psalm 91 we read that the human being, in association with the Angels—'like an angel'—is to triumph over the Dragon:

> For he [the Lord] shall give his angels charge over thee,
> To keep thee in all thy ways.
> They shall bear thee up in their hands,
> Lest thou dash thy foot against a stone.
> Thou shalt tread upon the lion and the adder:
> The young lion and the dragon shalt thou trample under feet.

Those who see and hear the angelic world, the world of the spirit, who regain through Christ their connection with the angelic world, will be a match for the Dragon. Through conscious union with the power of Christ humankind will be able to encounter the adverse powers with courage. In this psalm the forces of hindrance are spoken of as being the 'stone' against which the foot may be dashed.

Let us now return to the Revelation of St John.

In the fourteenth chapter we hear an Angel pronounce a very severe judgment: 'If any man worship the Beast and his image, and receive his mark in his forehead, or in his hand, the same shall drink of the wine of the wrath of God ... the smoke of their torment ascendeth up for ever and ever, and they have no rest day nor night.' Such a picture of the Judgment should not be regarded as only referring to an event in the distant future. It is also relevant in regard to the way human beings lead their lives today. The worship of the Beast—and the image of the Beast—does not only occur where immoral thoughts, feelings and deeds manifest them-selves; for the materialistic conception of the human being is the 'image' of the Beast, since such a conception comprehends men and women *only* in so far as they are akin to the animals and completely ignores, denies their relation to the angelic worlds. It is certainly true that in some respects technology, the fruit of material science, has brought many benefits to mankind. That, for instance, a machine, a robot, can take the place of human beings and thus relieve them of the dehumanizing drudgery of the conveyor belt is certainly to be welcomed. But, in many respects, the 'curse' far outweighs the 'blessing'. The danger to the health of both nature and humankind of radioactive fallout, or of a generally polluted atmosphere and the consequent depletion of the ozone layer—to mention but two consequences of scientific and technological achievement—is becoming increasingly apparent. More and more, what was intended to be of benefit to mankind, what was intended to allow a more human life to prevail, is in fact causing us to live in mechanized conditions—we could say, subhuman conditions. For the machine is increasingly setting the life-style of mankind—indeed, 'enslaving' us. We are creating a synthetic civilization, which eventually must recoil upon us because we are beings of soul and spirit.

Indeed, this process has begun already. For instance, those who dwell in high-rise 'sterile boxes' are witnesses to this fact. Such dwellings, devoid of any aesthetic qualities, constitute an inhuman environment, a mechanized, 'cold', ahrimanic expediency. Our technical achievements have begun to recoil on us—in particular, on our nerves. When we look around us—particularly in the octopedian industrial cities—it is not difficult to find countless examples of the way in which, in large cities, a 'wasteland' of the soul and spirit prevails. In the early 1920s T.S. Eliot expressed this fact succinctly:

> Unreal city,
> Under the brown fog of a winter dawn,
> A crowd flowed over London Bridge, so many,
> I had not thought death had undone so many.
> Sighs, short and infrequent, were exhaled,
> And each man fixed his eyes before his feet.
> (*The Waste Land*)

In terms of the Revelation of St John, the all-powerful Ahriman-inspired machine-city tends to reduce the human being to the level of the Beast, to print the mark of the Beast on the human forehead. John's vision of the future also gives us the picture of human beings with the mark of the Beast having 'no rest day and night' (Rev. 14:11), and prophesies a state of affairs which shows signs of prevailing today. Rush and bustle, restlessness and nervousness are some of the main fruits of a soulless, spiritless, materialistic civilization. Every fourth or fifth person in so-called advanced countries suffers at some stage in his or her life a nervous breakdown! In an environment of machine-directed efficiency it is already becoming an exceptional achievement if one can maintain for any length of time a state of inner peace and contemplation, or, as John expresses it, 'patience of the saints ... and the faith of Jesus' (Rev. 13:10; 14:12). But it is only by cultivating inner peace in the midst of the turmoil and relentless pace of modern civilization—and by striving towards a union with the angelic worlds—that we can achieve and preserve our true humanity.

In the sixteenth chapter of the Revelation of St John we learn that the first of the seven Angels, 'having the seven last plagues', pours out his vial on the earth, 'and there fell a noisome and grievous sore upon the men which had the mark of the Beast, and upon them which worshipped his image'— that is, upon those who were under the domination of Ahriman. We can understand this to mean for us today that the physical earth and the physical human body are plagued by disease, have become a 'wasteland'. A fundamentally distorted attitude to and relationship with the earth and the human physical body seems to be an all too obvious pheno-menon to need further discussion here. A materialist view of life, at first purely theoretical, has grown more and more influential, particularly since the middle of the nineteenth century. As mentioned earlier, the picture of the human being given to us by materialism is, in terms of the Revela-tion, 'the Image of the Beast' because it can conceive of human beings only in terms of their animal nature. Human beings have gradually assumed the stamp and, as the Latin Bible expresses it, *character bestiae*, because they have submitted to a view of life which recognizes only their animal nature but is blind to their spiritual being. The inevitable consequence of such blindness is 'dis-ease'—one feels 'uncomfortable' in one's physical body. Something, one senses, is lacking. That something is the experience of the reality of the spiritual. Whether one is aware of it or not, the body of both the earth and of the human being suffers from the carcinoma of materialism.

It would take us too far to consider in any detail the meaning for us today of all seven vials of 'the wrath of God'.[1] A few comments relevant to the theme of the two faces of evil will have to suffice. We shall, therefore, take a brief look at the significance of the vials of wrath of the third, fourth, fifth and seventh Angels.

Under the influence of what the third Angel pours over them the 'rivers and fountains of water ... become blood' (Rev. 16:4), and John hears the stern judgment pronounced: 'For they have shed the blood of saints and prophets, and thou hast given them blood to drink' (Rev. 16:6). It can hardly be sufficiently emphasized that one of the conditions of a healthy personal spiritual development is that we recognize the role blood should play. It is not difficult to recognize today—in, for instance, the widespread occurrence of Aids—that the blood should cease to be the bearer of purely carnal desires and needs to be transformed into that of the ideals of morality and spirituality—needs to be 'purified'. We can see a link here between those who today seek the 'purification' of their blood and the great spiritual Christian messengers of the past, whose blood was 'purified' through compassion and selfless love.[2]

How fortunate is the child who has grown to love, say, St Francis of Assisi, who had faith in the power of the spirit and could heal lepers. But how seldom today is such a figure the object of emulation! In his place we find the rock star, the movie star, the baseball or football player and, perhaps above all, the successful businessman and entrepreneur—the man who dominates the lives of others and, in his chase for financial gain, is not above 'sacrificing' his fellow human beings, 'shedding their blood'. By and large the great torch-bearers of the spirit are ignored and those who endeavour to follow in their footsteps are regarded as being no more than ascetic sentimentalists and strangers to 'real' life and there-fore of no earthly use. Such an attitude—characteristic of modern materialistic, ahrimanic thought—'kills', spiritually sheds the blood of those in whom the Blood of Christ lived and would live again today.

What, we could now ask, does it mean that those who 'have shed the blood of saints and prophets' should be given blood to drink? In answer to this question, Emil Bock suggests: 'Whoever thinks he can grow a personality without the ideals of a higher world is turned back to his own blood, pulsed through by carnal impulses and desires.'[3] A personal inward life cannot find its way to true humanity, to the Christ in the human being, if it relies solely on a lifeless materialistic, mechanistic view of life. The level on which the personality then unfolds instead of being 'raised' is lowered to mere sensuality. So it is not then surprising that in an age in which a living spirituality is becoming weaker rather than stronger that sexuality is becoming increasingly dehumanized, is—one could almost say—running riot, and thus, in its betrayal of the divine, the spiritual in the human being, contributing to the formation of a civilization ruled by *character bestiae*. Sen-suality 'sheds the blood' of spirituality!

The fifth vial of the wrath of God does not seem, at first sight, to affect mankind at all, for it is poured upon the Beast, causing a profound darkness in its realm to come into being. However, the consequences of this darkness show themselves among men and women, too. For 'they gnawed their tongues for pain, and blasphemed the God of heaven because of their pains and their sores' (Rev. 16:10–11). The process of ahri-manic desiccation, of hardening, leading to hostility towards all that is spiritual, takes a further step towards complete alienation and develops into the utmost bitterness. The kingdom of the Beast 'was full of darkness', we learn from

John. What, we may ask, is meant by this. Its meaning is twofold. It refers, clearly, to the domain of Ahriman, but it also refers to a kind of animal kingdom—not, of course, to creatures of the third kingdom of nature (to lions, elephants, snakes, dogs and cats, etc.), of whom it would be an illusion to speak of either good or evil, but to members of the human race who have fallen below the level of their true human nature. This darkness is, in short, a kingdom peopled by those who dedicate their efforts to the Image of the Beast— peopled by those who have degenerated spiritually and sunk to a level of existence in which essential elements of the human kingdom, such as compassion, selfless love, brother- hood, sisterhood, are non-existent. The fall into the kingdom of the Beast brings with it the decline, ultimately, the death- throes, of living communion, of living and creative relation- ships between human beings.

Here we touch upon the very root of social life, the very cause of the threatening breakdown of any form of human community. Unless such human qualities as love and fellowship are nurtured, human souls will drive more and more deeply into the cold, rigidifying realm of Ahriman— into isolation, separation and extreme egoism. Fear, a quality instilled in the human soul by Ahriman, will sterilize the human soul in its coldness and, fearing for their very exis- tence, men and women will grab whatever they can reach, totally disregarding the effect on their fellow human beings. It is clear that such a soul attitude can but lead to a total impoverishment of an inner life and, ultimately, to a War of All against All, to a cold, loveless 'wasteland'.

When the awe-inspiring power of love dies, happiness and joy also die. The cold, ahrimanized human soul knows no humour either. Bitterness and depression spread their black wings over mankind.[4] Unless we learn, with John Donne, that 'No man is an Island, entire of itself; every man is a piece of the Continent, a part of the main' (*Devotions*, XVII), we shall suffer total isolation and haunting fear and be wholly sub- servient to the power of Ahriman.

When the seventh vial is poured out into the air, a voice

resounds with the Johannine words: 'It is done' (Rev. 16:18).[5] 'And there was a great earthquake' and through 'thunders and lightnings' (ibid.) a cosmic death overtakes everyone and everything. A cosmic Good Friday overshadows the earth and humankind. The city of Babylon, in which that portion of humanity dwells which has dedicated itself solely to material existence, to the realm of Ahriman, breaks into three pieces and sinks into the abyss (Rev. 16:19). Humankind is embroiled in the death-throes of civilization.

Here we come face to face with the mystery of death. If we fail to raise ourselves above the level of the material and 'animal' worlds, if we fail to recognize the reality of the spiritual world, of the spiritual cause of all material manifestation, we not only do not grasp the meaning of death but also fail to comprehend the secret of life. Wolfgang von Goethe, speaking of nature, once expressed this thought in the following words: 'Life is her finest invention, and her device for producing an abundance of life is her masterstroke—death.'[6] Through fear of death we are tempted by Ahriman to cling more and more keenly to material existence. In so doing we fail to see that we thereby surrender ourselves even more 'tightly' to the forces of death, to Ahriman.

Death, we need to realize, is the 'key' to life, to spiritual life. This is not to be understood as merely referring to the death of the physical body and, expressed briefly, the ensuing entry of the inner core of the human being into spiritual life, but also to everyday life on earth. Rudolf Steiner makes the very significant observation that no consciousness, no thought, is physiologically possible without death playing a role in the processes of the human body. Ahriman has a positive role to play here. But his role becomes negative, evil, when he tempts us to fear death—a fear which, for instance, prevents us exercising self-sacrifice, and from, as William Blake expresses it, the 'Annihilation of Selfhood'.[7] Unless we respond to a life-situation which calls for a measure of self-sacrifice, we cannot quicken true humanity in ourselves, nor give an impulse to the growth of true humanity in others.

At ever-increasing speed we are approaching a critical phase in the evolution of humankind. We can either strive towards the Pauline experience of 'Not I, but Christ in me', strive towards the selfless offering of our soul so that it gradually opens itself as Grail Chalice receptive to Divine Love, or we can selfishly submit to ahrimanic, Satanic hatred of the Light and warmth-filled spirit and thus contribute to the spread of total spiritual darkness, total lifelessness over the whole of humanity and the earth. The flow of divine Love which is poured from the seventh vial is directed towards bringing to birth in the human soul the experience of death as a friend, not as an enemy.

*   *   *

The pictures John places before us of the activity of the Angels with the seven vials lead us to that of the 'great city Babylon' (Rev. 18:10).

The consequence of the outpouring of the seventh vial is the irresistible fall of Babylon.

The great city Babylon is the antitype of the New Jerusalem. It is the embodiment of all that which binds us to the ahrimanic principle.

Usually, when the apocalyptic Babylon is mentioned, the picture of the 'scarlet woman' prevails. However, the 'Mother of Harlots' (Rev. 17:5) is also described as being a city, that is, as being a part of the human community. Conversely, Jerusalem is usually envisaged as being a city, whereas the 'Bride' is not so readily present in the symbolic picture. In the image of the city, the 'body' of a representative part of humanity is seen; in that of a women, its soul. It is Babylon's manifestation as a city we shall be concerned with here.

Following on John's vision of the Lamb, Christ, on Mount Zion surrounded by those who have his 'Father's name written on their foreheads' (Rev. 14:1), he, John, sees three Angels appear. Each has a stern message to impart. That of the second Angel concerns us here. He announces an awe-inspiring verdict: 'Babylon is fallen, is fallen, that great city, because she made all nations drink of the wine of the wrath of her fornications' (Rev. 14:14). Here the division of human souls is placed before us. Two cities appear as pictures of two sections of humankind. The New Jerusalem is built by those who assimilate spiritual nourishment from above. They so permeate themselves with divine spiritual forces that, through them, they can transform all earthly things, including, ultimately, their physical bodies. The city which falls into the abyss is called the Whore of Babylon because those who contribute to its building have defiled the spirit by the untransmuted bodily, material element. Such builders represent that section of humankind which has been 'deaf' and 'blind' to its true humanity.

'Babylon the Great, the Mother of Harlots and Abominations of the Earth' (Rev. 17:5) is described as sitting 'upon a scarlet coloured beast, full of names of blasphemy, having seven heads and ten horns' (17:3). Here we recognize the Dragon which threatened the 'Woman clothed with the sun, and the moon under her feet, and upon her head a crown of twelve stars' (Rev. 12:1), who was to give birth to a child. We then hear that the Whore is 'arrayed in purple and scarlet' (17:4). It is clear that she has been absorbed into the realm of the Dragon. Both are enveloped in grasping greed and that scarlet of dehumanizing animal passion. It is this Beast—and the Woman who sits upon it—that all 'shall worship whose names are not written in the book of the life of the Lamb' (Rev. 13:8). Babylon represents that quality which selfishly 'grabs' and demands, culminating in the taking of the 'souls of men' (Rev. 18:13). It is such a quality which plunges humankind into the abyss. Jerusalem, on the other hand, manifests quite a different quality, namely, that of giving, of the Bride who selflessly loves. Whereas the whole of Babylon seduces us into the darkness of the abyss, Jerusalem selflessly and without any element of coercion shows us— like the Archangel Michael—the way into the Light. This is beautifully expressed by Goethe in the final four lines of his *Faust*:

The Indescribable,
Here it is done:
The Woman-Soul leadeth us
Upward and on![8]

While the Mother in heaven, 'clothed with the sun' (Rev. 12:1), radiates from *within* the golden spiritual sun, the debased Babylon, abandoning herself to the earthly world, adorns herself *outwardly* with the material gold—which is no other than the materialized physical, earthly shadow of the sun.[9] Babylon is the antithesis of the heavenly Mother.

A significant clue to the antithetical relationship prevailing between the city of Babylon and the New Jerusalem is given to us in the picture of the 'pearl'.

We learn that to the New Jerusalem 'every single gate was of one pearl' (Rev. 21:21). To cross the threshold into the city of the New Jerusalem we have to go through the 'pearl-experience'. Now pearls grow through the reaction of a living organism to the intrusion of a foreign body. We could say that the oyster develops the pearl through the overcoming of pain. The pearl, then, is a symbol of pain overcome in the human soul. It is a symbol of the overcoming, through inward, spiritual effort, of forces inimical to life—of dark forces, ahrimanic forces, which battle to extinguish the inner, spiritual light.

We also hear that the Whore of Babylon is decked with pearls. But the pearls in the city of Babylon are not earned through inner effort. They are no more than outward material show.

We have the choice, now and in the future, of choosing between Light and Darkness, between striving to attain entrance to the New Jerusalem and thus realizing our Higher Self or succumbing to our lower self—to that which focuses our attention on the material world and causes us to turn our back on the spiritual world—and thus becoming slaves to the power of Ahriman manifesting itself through the city of Babylon.

At the centre of the Babylonian evil is our attitude to

matter, to material existence. Through the gifts of the Whore of Babylon 'merchants of the earth are waxed rich' (Rev. 18:3). Our attitude towards material existence has taken on an increasingly exploitative stance over the centuries, in particular since the end of the sixteenth century and beginning of the seventeenth. It was Francis Bacon (1561–1626) who was the instigator of the inquisitorial attitude which experimental science has adopted in its dealings with nature—an attitude with which Wolfgang von Goethe, for instance, was so profoundly in disagreement. For him—and for those who think like he did—the right approach to nature, indeed, to every endeavour to gain knowledge, was that which is imbued with devotion and reverence:

> Mysterious even in open day,
> Nature retains her veil, despite our clamours:
> That which she doth not willingly display
> Cannot be wrenched from her with levers, screws, and hammers.
> [*Faust*, Part I, Scene I][10]

Generally speaking, the mind of western man has assumed the Baconian stance; he has put nature on the rack (a characteristic feature of the Babylonian attitude). Nature is being subjected to inquisitorial and exploitative treatment for short-term gain and convenience. Soil erosion, air pollution, deforestation, adulteration of foodstuffs, etc., etc. are the inevitable consequences. In the tenth lecture of *The Temple Legend* (GA 93) Steiner makes the highly relevant point that what is materially around us now—mineral kingdom, plant and animal kingdom—will eventually be taken inwardly into the human being. The diseased environment will become our own inner diseased self. In this context we could also mention the matter of the release of atomic energy involving the process of nuclear fission, a process in which the 'innards' are torn out of matter, as it were. Today we are also witnessing the science and technology of genetic engineering in which certain life-processes can be, and are, manipulated (see Appendix Eleven).

It is not being suggested here that research into and use of atomic energy and genetic engineering should not take place. But what is essential is a moral evaluation, not only of the use but also of the processes involved. It is not a question of turning the clock back, but such evaluation is of vital importance if we are not to fall into the abyss with the city of Babylon, which, infused with the power of Ahriman, is completely devoid of heart-enfilled morality. Counter-measures need to be developed to balance the over-emphasized materialistic observation and understanding of the human being and nature. The source of balance, Rudolf Steiner stressed time and again, is the recognition of the living presence of Christ—the experience of the reality of His existence in the world. For from that source—in terms of power and guidance—the inspiration comes which gives us the moral strength both to live in a world in which denaturing and dehumanizing tendencies exist, and enable us to resist being drawn into the whirlpool of the civilization of Babylon.

Certainly that which we generally designate as being wicked and sinful is involved in the 'descent' to Babylon, but, as we have seen, John also gives us a vivid picture of something which is of paramount significance, namely, of our attitude to Earth evolution, to material existence in both nature and ourselves. It is this attitude, to which we have alluded already, which constitutes the core of the path leading to Babylon. In regard to the 'ascent' to the Holy City, the virtues of, say, goodness and honesty are most certainly significant contributory factors. But, again, it is our inner attitude to material existence—the great gift of the present planetary stage of existence—which is of paramount importance.

In contrast to the Babylonian stance, those who strive to cross the threshold, to go through the pearl gate into the New Jerusalem, do not approach nature as selfish 'robbers' and exploiters but as 'listeners' who, with gratitude, love and reverence, hear and perceive both the needs and the offerings of a living organism. We could characterize such a warden of the earth as being a creative sculptor who does not impose his own conception upon a block of marble but, as Michelangelo is reputed to have been able to do, sees and reveals what is dormant in it. Such an approach could be said to be that of a scientist imbued with artistic perception and selfless religious devotion.

The New Jerusalem—the Holy City of the future—is potentially already present in certain attitudes of the human soul. They need not be majestic, they can find expression in very modest ways, but they are inherent in and concerned with the selfless love of redemption and transformation of the material world.

It was Christ Himself who set the example for us. He, through the transformation of the body of Jesus, gave us a blueprint of the New Jerusalem, for after His Crucifixion He redeemed His material body and transformed it into a spiritual resurrection body, into a source of spiritual power so that no physical remains could be found. The spiritualization of matter, through the power of an all-embracing selfless love, through the experience of 'Not I, but Christ in me', is the distant future goal towards which that portion of humankind which does not fall prey to seduction by Babylon can gradually move.

The realization of such a goal lies in the future, but the challenge to achieve it is present, like a seed, now, today. The temptation to join those who will ultimately fall with the doomed city, Babylon, is also making its presence known today.

The evolution of the Earth and the future of the generations of men and women yet to incarnate depends on each preceding generation. The question before us today—and before each subsequent generation—is: Does one join those of the doomed city and the darkness of a loveless catastrophe, or does one work towards the 'building' of the New Jerusalem, the 'fruit' of cosmic transformation wrought through the struggle within the human soul to follow the path shown by Michael, the path which brings alive within the soul the experience of the Christ-impulse?

*   *   *

In answer to the question 'What power will be used to spiritualize matter?' Rudolf Steiner says: 'The power of love gained through the Christ-principle. Beings become capable of dissolving matter through taking love into their souls. The more the soul is warmed by love the more powerfully will it be able to work on matter; it will spiritualize the whole earth and transform it into an astral globe' (GA 104, 25/06/08).

And in answer to the question 'What will those have made of their body who have taken the Christ-impulse into their being?' Steiner answers:

> If we now observe the human body we find that it is not yet the expression of the soul within, but it will gradually become an expression of what the soul experiences within. Our outer body will thus become an expression of the good by our receiving the highest message [i.e. of selfless love], the highest teaching there is on this earth; and this highest teaching is the message of Christ Jesus on the earth... We must take it up thoroughly, not merely with the understanding; we must take it into our innermost being, just as one takes nourishment into the physical body... The power of love is contained in the Gospels, the whole power of love, and the seer can say nothing else than: 'In the spirit I see a time before me when that which is in the Gospel will no longer be outside in a book but when it will be devoured by human beings themselves.' [Ibid.][11]

Here it should be mentioned that Rudolf Steiner, on a number of occasions, spoke of our earth as being the Cosmos of Love. 'Prior to the earth the Old Moon was the bearer of our creation. This Old Moon was the Cosmos of Wisdom; our earth is the Cosmos of Love. It is the mission of our earth to bring human beings together in love... This power of love must flow in as the earth-mission of humanity—just as you now see the power of wisdom in your environment' (GA 104, 24/06/08).[12]

* * *

Further insight into the core of the Babylonian evil power is given when it is revealed that the 'Woman' sits on seven mountains (Rev. 17:9).

The picture of the mountain occurs on numerous occasions in both the Old and the New Testaments. For instance, it was on Mount Sinai that Moses received the Ten Commandments (Exod. 34:27–28); on Mount Horeb the Lord appeared to Moses in the burning bush (ibid. 3:2); Christ 'went up into a mountain' to deliver the great Sermon which includes the Beatitudes (Matt. 5:1–12). From these few instances (many others could be mentioned) we can see that the mountain 'points' not to an earthly but to a spiritual sphere. William Wordsworth describes his experience of the power of the spirit when he had reached and rested for a while on the top of Mount Snowdon:

> A meditation rose in me that night
> Upon the lonely Mountain when the scene
> Had pass'd away, and it appear'd to me
> The perfect image of a mighty Mind.
> (*The Prelude*, 13:66–69)

However, it is clear that there is quite another meaning attached to the picture of the mountain when it is associated with Babylon. Materialism inhibits any ascent to an experience of the reality of the spirit. One-sided reliance on physical sense-perception can be seen as being the 'mountain' which forms a barrier and thus prevents a view, an insight into the inner spiritual realm of existence. We may understand that the Seven Mountains of the Revelation of St John are spoken of as constituting a barrier, a thick veil, between the world of sense-perception and the world of the supersensible. The attraction of a glittering civilization founded on material wealth seduces the human being to such a degree that, eventually, the Seven Mountains and the seeming glory of the world 'below' blind the eye for the world 'above'. When the Revelation speaks of the Woman who 'glorified herself and lived deliciously' (18:7) sitting on the Seven Mountains, it is showing us an ahrimanic power whose intention it is to separate humankind from any experience of the spiritual world. It is in the interest of this power that we should either be convinced

that there is no such thing as a spiritual world, that it is no
other than an illusion, or, failing that, that we should submit to the dogma that it is not possible for us to have any
real knowledge of that world.

Christ Himself opposed this power when, for instance, he
vehemently denounced the scribes and Pharisees:

> Woe unto you, scribes and Pharisees, hypocrites! for ye shut up
> the kingdom of heaven against men; for you neither go in
> yourselves, neither suffer ye them that are entering to go in...
> Woe until you, scribes and Pharisees, hypocrites! for ye compass
> sea and land to make one proselyte, and he is made, ye make him
> twofold more the child of hell than yourselves. [Matt. 23:13–16]

Christ rebuked a priesthood which had reneged on its
calling. Instead of helping mankind to cross the bridge from
the physical to the spiritual world and thus acquire citizen-
ship of both worlds, the leaders of religious life were themselves the power which hindered mankind from experiencing
the spiritual world. In short, Christ is stating here that the
religious leaders deny the very meaning of what they should
be representing, religion; they themselves have become the
Babylonian power which prevents mankind from finding
communion with the spiritual world.

The 'woes' were pronounced against the misuse of power
by the priesthood.[13] What was justified during the 'childhood' of humanity (that is, before human souls had emerged
from a group-soul consciousness and begun to experience an
individual ego-consciousness), namely, the practice of
authoritative guidance, was no longer in keeping with the
development of the human soul. Once the seed of individual
egohood and individual spiritual endeavour had begun to
grow (by the time of Christ's Ministry on earth this process
had been active for some time already),[14] the authoritarian
power of the priesthood should have ceased to be active and
the ministering pastor, the shepherd, had to become the new
ideal of the priesthood.[15] Authoritarianism, verging on
dictatorial power, can but be a threat to the freedom of
human souls and individual endeavour; it constitutes a threat

to Christian spiritual life and enhances the power of the Woman who sits on the Seven Mountains.

The power of the Whore of Babylon is a threat to the spiritual life of humankind. As yet this threat is not totally overpowering, but as we go towards the future ever greater courage and spiritual alertness will be needed to counteract and overcome it. The suppressive and oppressive spectral power of Babylon will make ever greater efforts to oust the Christian principle of brotherhood and sisterhood selflessly and freely attained. William Blake, in his inimitable way, touches upon such a spectral power when, in his epic work *Jerusalem*, he cries:

> I turn my eyes to the Schools and Universities of Europe
> And there behold the Loom of Locke, whose Woof rages dire,
> Wash'd by the Water-wheels of Newton: black the cloth
> In heavy wreathes folds over every Nation: cruel Works
> Of many Wheels I view, wheel without wheel, with cogs tyrannic
> Moving by compulsion each other, not as those in Eden, which,
> Wheel within Wheel, in freedom revolve in harmony & peace.

Whenever and wherever the individual is led to blind obedience, to a dogma instead of being encouraged to attain individual experience and knowledge of the world of the spirit, it is not only the Church but also seats of learning that are threatened by the same spectral power.[16] The denial of a *free* and *conscious* personal relationship with the Spirit of Christ, the denial of a free and conscious striving towards a deeper and deeper understanding of the Mystery of Golgotha, is the hallmark of that type of leadership which was so vehemently censured by Christ.

The threat to humankind which the writer of the Revelation brings before us in the picture of the Whore of Babylon is not only relevant in regard to the errors perpetrated by those in positions of authority, for in every human soul the ahrimanic power is active which strives to prevent, hinder us from gaining knowledge of the spiritual world. To follow the path leading to the New Jerusalem requires patience, perseverance and, above all, courage. The ahrimanic power of hindrance attacks the human soul with 'arrows' of impatience and fear. The same power that 'sits' on the Seven Mountains is also within the human soul. It prompts us to find 'legitimate' excuses to follow an inner life of ease. Why bother? Are we not taught that we only have this one life to live? Let us make the most of it! Earn as much money as possible, amass material possessions! Let us enjoy ourselves now! And the Devil take the hindmost! The 'outer' life is all that really matters!

This power within us makes every effort to fetter us more and more strongly to earthly things.

In the social sphere we find this power active too. We cannot dwell at any length on this sphere of Babylonian influence. But let us glance at two great social movements of recent times.

The first led to the French Revolution. Thereafter democracy and the rights of free individuals became increasingly accepted as fundamentals of social life. In North America these principles were enshrined in the Constitution: freedom of personal opinion and its expression; equality before the Law; and private enterprise—above all in the economic sphere.

The second movement is that of Marxism, the ruling principle of which is social equality, organized from 'above' by the all-powerful State. Marxism emerged, as an abstract idea, as the consequence of indignation at conditions of life unworthy of the dignity of the human being, but it became anti-human in its practical application. Marxism has shown all the hallmarks of the age of materialism in which it came into being.

Many conceptions emanating from the USA have exercised a powerful influence, particularly to begin with, on western Europe. Among them is the idea that as psychic and social beings we are to be regarded as products of our environment. Such a conception gives birth to the view that all inner, spiritual activity in us is no more than an illusion, since we are no more than products of our environment—we are mass products.

In the sociology of the world of Communism, the individual human being as such is of no fundamental significance. Personal freedom of decision or responsibility is not recognized. According to Marxist doctrine, the individual is one of a 'mass', and anybody who dares to think otherwise is a threat to the State.

In both social movements it is apparent that the Whore of Babylon exerts her oppressive power to prevent men and women from realizing their true humanity. A Babylonian society makes every effort to make it impossible for us to assume any social and moral responsibility. A sense of individual responsibility, of bearing responsibility with and for the community, can only flourish in an atmosphere of trust in one's fellow human beings. In a Babylonian society, one in which each and every person's main concern is to 'grab' as much as possible and to give as little as possible, trust cannot exist between one human being and another. In a Babylonian, ahrimanic community (if such a term as 'community' can possibly be used in connection with Ahriman), trust is placed in statutes, regulations and instituted customs handed down from an anonymous authority.

* * *

Let us here recall that it is not only in the last book of the New Testament that Babylon plays an important role. The theme 'Babylon' is brought to our attention throughout the Old Testament. For instance, in Genesis the consequence of building the Tower of Babel is described as being the confusion of tongues. Whereas previously there had been but one language now there are many (Gen. 11:1–9).

The living word of God, which had united all mankind, is now no longer present. It is splintered, as it were, into the multiplicity of strange tongues. No longer, after the fall of the Tower, did speech emanate from above, inspired by the Divine. Speech became devoid of the living breath of God. Isolated nations began to fight one another. No longer did the name 'Babel' signify the 'Gate of God', but the confusion of nations and languages. We can see in the fall of the

Tower of Babel the seed for the yet to come 'War of All against All'.

The erection of the Tower of Babel gives us a picture of a culture that had degenerated. It was built from below upwards, in complete contrast to the New Jerusalem which descends from above to earth. Babylon builds a tower which is a clear expression of luciferic human arrogance and thus defies the Gods.

We may remind ourselves here that in pre-Christian times, of the two powers Lucifer and Ahriman, Lucifer was predominant. But particularly since the fifteenth century, it is Ahriman, active alongside Lucifer, who exerts the more powerful influence. Now pre-Christian religions were, in fact, centred on a principle which may be described as implying an 'upward' direction. All genuine religious experience in pre-Christian times was founded on ecstasy (Greek *ec* = out; *statis* = standing), that is, on a state of being 'beside', 'outside' oneself. Communion with the Gods was experienced when the soul left, rose out of the physical body. However, human nature has gone through a number of changes during the course of time. Human souls became increasingly earthbound, and stronger measures were needed to lift the soul free from the physical body and thus into a state of ecstasy. In Babylon decadent means of conjuring up this condition were practised, in particular, orgies of uncontrolled passion and intoxication. This descent into sensuality found its counterpart in the building of material monuments reaching towards the heavens. When the earlier and purer union with the Gods could no longer be experienced, it was thought that human beings could reach—and vie with—the Gods by building monuments with their tips piercing the heavens.

The Old Testament bears witness to the horror experienced by the upholders of a pure spiritual life when they learnt of the degenerate practices perpetrated in Babylon. In Jeremiah, for instance, we find this horror expressed with great vehemence. Jeremiah hears the voice of the Lord condemning Babylon:

> Look at her, the mere rump of the nations,
> a wilderness, parched and desert,
> unpeopled through he wrath of the Lord,
> nothing but a desolate waste;
> All who pass by Babylon shall be horror-struck
> and jeer in derision at the sight of her wounds.
> ...
> I am against you, O Mount of the Destroyer,
> you who destroy the whole earth,
> and I will stretch out my hand against you
> and send you tumbling from your terraces
> and make you a burnt-out mountain.[17]

Earthly sensuality and animal passion were brought into relationship with the spiritual world by means of the decadent Babylonian cults. Emil Bock speaks of this as being the beginning of the principle of 'spiritual fornication'.[18] Babylonian men and women carried earthly sensuality and passion with them in their intercourse with the world of the spirit. Spiritual impurity, resulting in ecstatic intoxication, had its origin in degenerate Babylonian cults. Such intoxicated possession is not a state of being we can simply shrug off as not being of any significance to us today. We cannot justifiably speak of it as relevant only to the long distant past. Such 'possession' exists in various forms still today. People are held in its grip when, for instance, they fall victim to the joint efforts of Lucifer and Ahriman and succumb to the use of drugs,[19] or to the betting and/or gambling mania, or to a possessive and uncontrolled lust for wealth or power. These compulsions in the life of human beings may be seen in the same light as the decadent Babylonian cults, namely, as having their roots in a misguided conception as to how something 'above' that which can be found in the routine of everyday life can be attained. This wish to escape by material means from what increasing numbers of people today experience as a purposeless and 'dead' existence can only lead, sooner or later, to an even greater entanglement with the very world above which they hope to rise.

* * *

The wrong way of reaching for the heights can only lead to a fall into the abyss of darkness. The fall of the city of Babylon is lamented by those who fall with her; they are 'the kings of the earth [who] have committed fornication with her, and the merchants of the earth [who have] waxed rich through the abundance of her delicacies' (Rev. 18:3) and 'every ship-master, and all the company of ships, and sailors, and as many as trade by sea, stood afar off, and cried when they saw the smoke of her burning, saying, What city is like unto this great city! And they cast dust on their heads, and cried, weeping and wailing, saying, Alas, also the great city, wherein were made rich all that had ships in the sea by reasons of her costliness' (Rev. 18:17–19). With the fall of Babylon the doom of the kings, merchants and those who 'trade by sea' is sealed.

In regard to the kings, we may here remind ourselves of the way in which Christ rebuked those in authority, the scribes and Pharisees. The kings should be representative of the wise leadership which encourages individual initiative and spiritual enterprise, but in the city of Babylon they have abused their power. They, like the scribes and Pharisees, have fettered individual freedom of action and thought; they have hindered, in the manner of Ahriman, all spiritual endeavour to strive towards the building of the New Jerusalem. The Whore Babylon 'sins' against the emerging Higher Self in the human being.[20]

Of both the merchants on land and those who 'trade by sea' it is characteristic that in the city of Babylon every negotiation is based on material values and greed. Ultimately, such an attitude in the economic sphere is bound to fail, for, as the commercial world has yet to learn, trade can only thrive—and be beneficial to both seller and buyer—if it is governed by trust and reciprocal service. If material gain and money-making constitute the dominant aim, Ahriman/Babylon has the upper hand.

Those who voyage on the seas are, it is true, also involved in commerce—often in partnership with the merchants on land. But this picture of the voyaging sailor also gives us another picture, namely, the journey through life—a journey which, if undertaken with spiritual alertness, perseverance, patience and courage, evolves to increasing soul-maturity. But such is not the journey undertaken by those under the dominion of the city of Babylon. Their journey is dedicated to the purely material, to living, as does the Whore of Babylon, 'deliciously' and 'seeing no sorrow' (Rev. 18:7). But, as we saw earlier, no inner, spiritual maturing development can take place without sorrow, suffering and pain.

In regard to the inner effort needed in order to advance in soul-spiritual maturity Rudolf Steiner makes an interesting observation concerning the changing relationship through the ages existing between 'development through our nature, our physical forces' and the 'transformation of the soul and spirit nature' (GA 180, 11/01/18). During the Ancient Indian Age (c. 7227–5067 BC)[21] human beings, according to Steiner, were capable of soul-spiritual development independently of any inner action or effort on their part.

> They remained so into the fifth decade of their life, and they always knew that the process of growing older was connected with a transformation of the soul and spirit nature. If today we wish to have a development of the soul and spirit nature after our twenties, we must seek for this development by our power of will. We become physically different in our twenties and in this becoming different physically there lives at the same time something that determines our progress of soul and spirit. Then the physical ceases to let us be dependent on it; then, so to speak, our physical nature hands over nothing more, and we must make any further advance through our own will-power... As regards humanity as a whole, we are living, so to say, in the twenty-seventh year, are entering the twenty-sixth, and so on. So that we are condemned to carry right through life the development we acquired in early youth through natural forces, if we do nothing of our own free will to take our further development in hand. [Ibid.][22]

Steiner's observation confirms that what we have called 'the journey through life' in modern times does not necessarily mean that we are wiser, more mature at the age of 50

than we were at the age of 20 or so. Indeed, in a world
ruled by a Christ-denying power, by the ahrimanic power
streaming through the city of Babylon, any kind of development which, after the mid-twenties, can only be achieved
through activity based on free will, is rendered impossible.
The 'journey' through life ceases early in life if Ahriman/
Babylon assumes control. Many people today do not seem
to grow beyond the age of 25 or so. They become set, rigid-
ified, in their ways and remain emotionally immature. They
become slaves to frenetic rushing from one party or event
to another, from one sensual experience to another. In all
this frantic to-ing and fro-ing, underpinned by ever-increasing fastness of transport, etc., human life ceases to be a
true 'journey'. Those who are citizens of the city of Babylon are completely lacking in respect and esteem for one
another. Moreover, the very foundations of law and justice
are non-existent; power and functional utility weigh far
more heavily than justice. The countless material gains of
the Babylonian power are offset by the loss of the true
values of human life.

*   *   *

In the spiritual world Michael gained victory over the
Dragon, 'called the Devil, and Satan' (Rev. 12:9). Through
the Mystery of Golgotha Christ has shown humankind the
path to the New Jerusalem. In order to be able to journey
along this path we, out of our own free will, have to follow the
rider on a white horse, 'whose name is called the Word of
God' (Rev. 19:13). It is we who have to make the effort to
conquer the Beast upon whom the city of Babylon is seated.
Such a conquest can no longer be left to Michael and his hosts
in the spiritual world to achieve. It is through taking the
Michael-impulse into our inmost being that we shall be able
to 'fight' as knights on white horses.

Let us pause for a while to consider the meaning of the four
apocalyptic horsemen mentioned in the sixth chapter of the
Revelation of St John. What do these four horses and their
riders represent? Here we need to remember, in the first

instance, that the horse has been a symbol, through the ages, of intelligence.[23]

In the sixth chapter the rider on the white horse is described as being crowned with a golden crown and holding a bow in his hand. He is called a conqueror. This we may see as being the apocalyptic picture of a very early stage of human thinking which is illumined by divine light. At this early stage in the process of evolution human beings did not really think; they were endowed with thoughts by the Gods. The golden crown—a symbol of the light-filled creative wisdom of the spiritual world—tells us that higher, spiritual beings are 'thinking', are active in the human being. The bow reveals how, through the power of light-filled thinking, the arrow, speeding from the eye, an organ of light, finds its goal with certainty.

The second horse is red. It is the colour of blood. The intellect is shown here as being subservient to the emotions. The second horseman wields a sword. The 'power was given to him that sat upon the red horse to take peace from the earth' (Rev. 6:4). When the voice of the blood speaks, wars are started. Here we have a picture of the fact that human beings have absorbed the power of intelligence into their individual souls, and in so doing have lost the original divine light. The 'downward' progression of intelligence from the white horse to the red horse entails the loss of the original harmony and peace. Discord arises as a consequence. Concurrent with the flaring up of strife between human beings, egotism comes into being.

The third horse is black. He who sits on it has 'a pair of balances in his hand' (Rev. 6:4). He expresses a conception of the world that relies solely on the calculable—a purely ahrimanic conception. The rider shouts words like those of a stall-holder: 'A measure of wheat for a penny, and three measures of barley for a penny' (Rev. 6:6).

In the succession of the three apocalyptic riders, from white to red and then to black, we are given a picture of the transition which first led from spirit to soul, then soul to matter. The transition from the red to the black rider illustrates the descent of thinking from the sphere of the living to that of the dead. Darkness and death rule in the sphere of the black rider. When intelligence 'sinks down' to the material plane, material concerns assume overall prominence in the human mind.

Both the red horse and its rider and the black horse and its rider conceal dangers: behind the red, luciferic desires and passions threaten; behind the black, ahrimanic cold, soulless intellectual cleverness is hidden.

The fourth horse is described as being 'sickly pale' (Rev. 6:8).[24] He who rides the horse is called Death—'and hell followed with him', that is, the underworld followed him. 'And power was given unto them ... to kill with sword, and with hunger, and with death' (ibid.). To him and to those who follow the fourth rider is allotted the baleful authority to destroy a large part of living beings on earth.

The transition from the black to the sickly pale horse expresses a deeper plunge of intelligence than witnessed hitherto. Wordsworth characterizes this state of the fallen intellect in the lines:

> Sweet is the lore which nature brings;
> Our meddling intellect
> Mid-shapes the beauteous forms of things—
> We murder to dissect.
> [From: *The Tables Turned*, 1798]

Charles Dickens gives us a most telling picture of the 'killing' power of the rider on the sickly pale horse in a chapter of *Hard Times* entitled, significantly, 'Murdering the Innocents'. The schoolmaster, Mr Thomas Gradgrind (the very name gives us a clue as to his nature), has one leg over the black horse and one over the sickly pale horse, as it were. He is 'a man of facts and calculations ... Ready to weigh and measure any parcel of human nature, and tell you exactly what it comes to. It is a mere question of figures, a case of simple arithmetic.' To Gradgrind a horse, for example, is little more than a machine that consists of so and so many parts. He declares himself completely satisfied with a lifeless definition of a horse given by one of the boys in the class. His method of teaching 'kills' the living, creative imagination in the children or, as Dickens expresses it, 'in the little pitchers before him, who were to be filled so full of facts'.

The black horse, representative of what we could call 'straightforward materialism', still has some human quality, whereas the bloodless abstractions represented by the sickly pale horse are inhuman. Indeed, the subhuman world begins to take over and enslave thinking. When this happens then our thinking begins to lead a spectral existence. In our modern world we surround ourselves with intelligence divorced from ourselves, with machines. Machines are the dead images of the fallen human intellect. They have become objective and the very threat exists that they assume spectral, demonic, dictatorial power over our lives, enslave us. Taking its start from human thinking, Death, the rider on the sickly pale horse, permeates mankind and the whole surrounding world with processes of decay. Indeed, the sickly pale horse represents the danger of the human intelligence becoming demonic. This is, in fact, indicated in the ninth chapter of John's Revelation. There we witness a sinister development of the power of the sickly pale horse. Demonic powers are shown spreading like swarms of locusts over the earth. They are described as coming out of the smoke-filled bottomless pit and as having the death-bringing power of the scorpion: 'And the shapes of the locusts were like unto horses prepared unto battle ... and their faces were as the faces of men ... and their breastplates, as it were, breastplates of iron; and the sound of their wings was as the sound of chariots of many horses running to battle. And they had tails like unto scorpions, and there were stings in their tails, and their power was to hurt men...' (Rev. 9:9).[25] And John sees: 'horses in the vision, and them that sat on them, having breastplates of fire and jacinth and brimstone ... and out of their mouths issued fire and smoke and brimstone. By these three was a third part of men killed...' (Rev. 9:17–18).

We can recognize these gruesome, machine-like beings as metamorphoses of the sickly pale horse.

Now the death-bringing activity of the sickly pale horse and the 'locusts', machine-like beings, might well tempt us to be dissuaded from employing technical science, from projecting scorpion intellect into our environment in the form of dead machines. However, it would not only be counter-productive not to avail ourselves of the inventions of the fallen intellect, but also counter to the 'stream' of the destiny of humankind. In order to be really free, we have to go through the extreme pain of the loss of 'given' guidance by the spiritual world; the 'given' light of the spiritual world is extinguished. Now, and in the future, it is out of our own free will, our own spiritual activity that we shall once again experience, fully consciously, the divine light. We are challenged to recognize our mechanized, increasingly computerized civilization as a reflection of our own human condition. To meet this challenge we also need to recognize—with ever-growing strength as we move into the future—that we can only surround ourselves by the products of ever more complex and sophisticated products of technical science and, *at the same time*, lead a life as free, creative beings if we, out of ourselves, complement the external, mechanized civilization by a cultivation and strengthening of the divine spiritual core within us if, differently expressed, we can raise ourselves out of the darkness of scorpion forces of death into the light-filled sphere of the Eagle, into the sphere portrayed in the Logos Gospel, St John's Gospel.

The descending movement of intelligence reveals its meaning and purpose only if we can ultimately regain the 'heights' by the power of the freedom which we attain in the vale of spiritual darkness. In the distant past, at the beginning of the evolution of intelligence, the divine lived in men and women, and they lived in the divine. They were imbued with the power of the white horse without any effort being called for on their part. We shall be able to ride with the white horse and rider when, out of our own free will, we undertake the upward journey out of spirit-darkness, the first step of which entails the painful process of tearing the poison of the scorpion-sting out of our very being.

The downward movement, culminating in the spiritual death-bringing poison of the scorpion, can be transmuted into an upward movement, a movement borne on the wings of the Eagle, when human beings open their inmost being to receive the Michaelic impulse into their own thinking and the creative Logos into their own words.

It is through the power of thought that we, after passing through the vale of isolation from the divine, can rise again to union with the spiritual world. In our age, deceived by and weary of predominantly abstract, sickly pale thinking, many people are tempted to throw overboard the heritage of past aeons of thought in order to lead a life based on instinctive forces of the soul. But, even though our thinking has fallen into arid intellectualism and lifeless abstraction, the white rider admonishes us not to lose faith in thinking. In the picture of the white horse whose rider is the bearer of faith and truth (cf. Rev. 19:11), John shows us the power of thinking redeemed by Christ. The white rider is described as having eyes 'as a flame of fire, and on his head were many crowns' (Rev. 19:12). Here we are shown a picture of men and women of the future whose thinking will be imbued both with the flame of inspiration and the golden light of cosmic wisdom. In such people abstract thought will have been transmuted into a living knowledge of the spirit. The rider on the white horse shows us that we can regain the wisdom of living thoughts, that we can again be at one with—participate in—the wisdom-fount of divine thoughts, but not as in the past instinctively, but fully consciously, out of our own creative spiritual activity. Thoughts will then no longer be 'spun' by us as they are now, but will come to us from the divine heights in response to such activity.

* * *

John saw in his majestic and awe-inspiring vision that the Beast with seven heads and ten horns upon which the Whore of Babylon sat would turn against her: 'The ten horns which thou sawest upon the beast, these shall hate the whore, and shall make her desolate and naked, and shall eat her flesh,

and burn her with fire' (Rev. 17:16). A civilization which has
been founded on materialism collapses eventually. Abstraction cannot nourish a living reality. Lifelessness cannot sustain a living organism.

The fall of the seven-headed, ten-horned Beast is brought
about by the power of the rider on the white horse and his
host of followers. Together with the 'false prophet' (Rev.
19:20) and those with 'the mark of the Beast' (ibid.), the
Beast who bore the city of Babylon on his back is overcome.
Here we are not witnessing the use of material weapons, but
the fiery power of Christ-imbued thought, word and action. It
is this power that will effect the fall of the bearer of the city of
Babylon. In the picture of the sword held in the mouth of the
white rider we may see the power wielded by those who
strive, with Michael before their inner eye as inspiration, to
become bearers of Christ.

After the fall of the city of Babylon and the conquest of the
seven-headed, ten-horned Beast, the other Beast, whom
John sees as having 'two horns like a lamb' (Rev. 13:11) still
remains to be deprived of its power. The two-horned Beast is
the very antithesis of the Being of Christ.

12.   Sorat—The Sun Demon

The two-horned Beast is designated by the number 666. Rudolf Steiner interprets this number as signifying the name of the Sun Demon.[1] This number, John hears, 'is the number of a man' (Rev. 13:18). Rudolf Steiner helps us to understand what this statement really means. According to him, it is not the number of all human beings, but solely of those who 'out of their own cunning free-will have become black magicians by placing spiritual forces in the service of their own egotism' (GA 104a, 21/05/09).

The two-horned Beast, Sorat, may be understood to be an intensified expression of Ahriman's satanic cunning to enlist humankind's aid in the fight against Christ.[2] In John's Revelation we hear that the two-horned Beast is the adversary of the Lamb. Steiner describes this power as being the adversary of the sun, the adversary of Christ.[3]

In order to gain some small insight into the spiritual being Sorat and his sphere of activity, we need to focus our attention on a particular period in the evolution of the earth. Rudolf Steiner shows us that in the long distant past the sun and the moon were still united with the earth.[4] Now, the forces of the moon have a powerful 'hardening' tendency, and if it had not separated itself from the earth the physical bodies of human beings would have become 'hardened' to such an extent that no souls would have been able to incarnate into them. It is these hardening forces of the moon that Sorat and his agent, the black magician, employ.

Centres of black magic arise where moon forces cooperate with spirits who have entered directly in their service—a service that makes for evil. And because many activities of this kind have been practised in recent centuries, a dangerous atmosphere has been created on the earth. This dangerous atmosphere is undeniably there and is transfused with multitudinous forces that are born of a union of human activities with moon elements and of dynamic moon forces with elementary beings in the service of illicit moon forces. It is this region that is actively opposed to all that is destined to proceed from the sun region in the Michael Age. [GA 243, 18/08/24]

Michael works from the sun. The spiritual influences emanating from the spiritual sun can also be called the influence of Michael and his followers (ibid.).

For human beings to be led into that which is merely immoral, the influence of Sorat is not needed.

Only when spiritual eminence is turned to its opposite, only when spiritual power is placed in the service of the lower 'I'-principle, can it bring humanity to the point when the Beast represented with two horns gains power over it. The misuse of spiritual forces is connected with that seductive power of the Beast with the two horns. And we call this abuse of the spiritual power black magic, in contradistinction to its right use, which is white magic... In the mystery of 666, of Sorat, is hidden the secret of black magic... Thus there appears on our horizon, so to speak, the division of humanity in the far distant future: the chosen of Christ, who finally will be the white magicians; and the adversaries, the terrible wizards, the black magicians who cannot escape from matter and whom the writer of the Apocalypse describes as those who make prostitution with matter. [GA 104, 29/06/08]

It is through the right use of spiritual forces, that is, used in complete selflessness and out of purified love for the earth and mankind, that the earth will be transformed into a sun-like state. Therewith the first step will have been taken towards the spiritualization of the earth, towards the 'building' of the New Jerusalem. The New Jerusalem will be 'produced by white magic' (ibid.). Sorat works against this transformation in that he enlists human beings to misuse spiritual forces—to use such forces for purely egoistic, power-seeking motives and intentions.

In the city of Babylon the community is made up of all those who practise black magic. There, as we have noted already, an 'unrestrained marriage between man and the forces of prostituted matter' prevails. 'And thus,' Steiner states, 'in the far future we see two powers confronting each other; on the one hand those who swell the population of the great Babylon, and on the other hand those who rise above matter, who as human beings unite with the principle represented by the Lamb' (GA 104, 29/06/08). This is what will appear in the far future, but, as Steiner points out, those who in our time are beginning in an unjustifiable way to oppose the spiritual, who oppose the Michaelic impulse and therewith Christ, are already beginning to nurture the germs of something one might call black magic. It is only when the ABC of black magic is practised that one begins to tread the path downwards into the abyss. 'The ABC consists in the pupil of a black magician being taught to destroy life quite consciously, and in doing so to cause as much pain as possible and to feel a certain satisfaction in it... The beginning in black magic is to cut and stab into living flesh... This draws the pupil closer and closer to the being described as the two-horned Beast' (ibid.).

Elsewhere Rudolf Steiner says:

> The black magician draws the most powerful forces out of the morass of sensuality. The purpose of sexual rites is to introduce such magic into these circles... In no way can one so readily assimilate destructive astral forces as by killing. Every killing of a being possessing an astral body evokes an intensification of the most brutal egotism. It signifies a growing increase of power. In schools of black magic, therefore, instruction is first given as to how one cuts into animals. [GA 93a, 17/10/05]

The black magician gains sensual pleasure in cruelty. In contrast to this, the basic principle of all white magic is that no power can be either gained or increased without selfless devotion.

Whereas, according to Rudolf Steiner, white magicians would impart to other human beings, to other souls, the spiritual life with which they themselves are imbued, black magicians have the urge to kill, that is, to create a void around themselves in the astral world, for it is in such a void that their egotistic desires can unfold themselves. A necessary step towards the creation of the void around oneself in the astral world is the acquisition of the power which results from seizing the vital forces of anything that lives, that is to say, by deliberately killing, destroying, it. That is why the first rule of black magic is: Life must be conquered (cf. GA94, 02/06/06).[5]

Any form of *egotistic* power-seeking influence upon the will of another person is also an integral part of the ABC of black magic. For instance, the *overpowering* of a human being by means of hypnotism is a form of 'killing', for it nullifies the will of the person hypnotized. White magicians, on the other hand, address themselves to the conscious faculty of thinking and never intrude upon the unconscious levels of being in another person; they never intrude upon another person's freedom.

When black magicians hypnotize other people they have the power to implant harmful instincts in the etheric body of those people. It is only permissible, Rudolf Steiner states, to work on another person's etheric body when one is certain that one's instincts have undergone catharsis. Under hypnosis it can happen that the person hypnotized 'works into the world the harmful instincts of the hypnotist'. In the case of people who are fully conscious the physical body prevents the etheric body from being 'shuttled' hither and thither. 'When, however, the physical body is in a state of lethargy, it is possible for the etheric to be worked into. If a person hypnotizes others and works harmful instincts into them, these remain with them after death' (GA 93a, 27/09/05). Many of the practices of black magicians have consisted in creating willing servants by this means.

Black and white magic are not only opposed to one another in regard to their relationship to human souls but also in regard to their role in the future evolution of the cosmos. In the long distant future the earth will be spiritualized and the condition Rudolf Steiner designates as 'Jupiter' will come into being (cf. GA 102, 24/03/08). In the New Testament this condition is spoken of as being the New Jerusalem. Those who follow the 'white path' help in the preparation of the process of spiritualization. Those who follow the 'black path' work with forces opposed to such a transformation. They are subservient, willingly, to the two-horned Beast, to the Ahriman-Sorat forces of destruction.

Our earth is the arena of the opposing forces of black and white magic. The white power strives to spiritualize the earth once again after it has reached a certain degree of physical density; the black power, on the other hand, strives to make the earth ever more dense. The earth could take on two entirely different 'expressions'. It could become the physical expression for the good powers through human beings unit-ing themselves with the spirits working for unification, with those spiritual powers who are active in the service of Michael, the Countenance of the Sun Spirit, Christ. Or it could become the physical expression for the evil powers, those who are active in the service of the Sun Demon, Sorat. The earth 'becomes the physical expression for the good powers through human beings uniting themselves with the spirits working for unification, in that they seek the ego in the community... Were we to burrow more and more deeply into ourselves, the final result would be that we should strive to separate ourselves from one another... To be a black magician means to develop more and more the spirit of separateness. There are black adepts who are on the way to acquire certain forces of the earth for themselves. Were the circle of their pupils to become so strong that this should prove possible, then the earth would be on the path leading to destruction' (GA 93a, 18/10/05).

Some three years after Rudolf Steiner gave the lecture from which I have just quoted, he gives us a further insight of profound significance. Because Christ has united Himself with the earth, because the earth is His body, Sorat has been unable to receive anything from the earth, from earthly existence. 'This being could only have got something from the earth by being able to gain the rulership at a certain moment, namely, when the Christ-principle descended to the earth. If the Christ-principle had then been "strangled" in the germ, if Christ had been overcome by the Adversary, it would have been possible for the whole earth to succumb to the Sorat-principle. This, however, did not take place, and so this Being has to be content with those human beings who have not inclined towards the Christ-principle, who have remained embedded in matter; they in the future will form his hosts' (GA 104, 30/06/08. See also GA 346).

13. The Academy of Gundeshapur

Characteristic of Sorat is his constant endeavour to degrade the human individuality, the ego, to such a degree that it is incapable of uniting itself with the spiritual power of Christ. The ego, the 'I', the essential being of the human being (cf. GA9, Ch. 1), can 'absorb' into itself the eternal life-giving power that emanates from the Being of Christ. However, if the ego unites itself with life-destructive forces, with the misuse of spirituality and esoteric knowledge, through black magic activities, it is debased and, because it is imbued with soratic forces, the human being is deprived of the possibility of progressing towards higher spiritual development. If human beings are to evolve 'normally', that is, with no intervention from Sorat, they will have to progress to spirit-self, life-spirit, spirit-man (cf. GA 9, Ch. 1).

Whereas Ahriman strives to render the earth so lifeless that no human being, no 'I', can exist upon it, and Lucifer desires to take human souls away and 'found a planet with them of his own' (GA 171, 17/09/16), it is Sorat's goal to destroy both the human 'I' and the earth. Sorat, the Adversary of the Sun Being, Christ, aims to destroy the bearer of the Christ-principle, the 'I' in the human being, as well as the earth, without the living and evolving presence of which the progress towards the realization of a person's spiritual being would be rendered impossible.

It was, in particular, in regard to the development of the consciousness soul, the spiritual soul, that Sorat could have had a devastating effect on the human being's spiritual development.

Now Rudolf Steiner states that, since the advent of Christ, Sorat's influence upon humankind would manifest itself with particular strength every 666 years. The years in question are: AD 666, 1332 and 1998—dates, however, that are to be regarded as being approximate, not exact.

The first critical point occurred, therefore, round about

666 years after the Mystery of Golgotha. According to Rudolf Steiner it was the intention of the two-horned Beast, Sorat—who had fully developed the consciousness soul, whereas human beings had reached only the 'age' of the intellectual soul (747 BC–AD 2413)—to bestow prematurely on humanity, particularly on men and women of the Western Hemisphere, all the soul-spiritual achievements unobtainable through the efforts of the intellectual soul. In short, the culture epoch of the consciousness soul (AD 1413–3573) was to come prematurely to humanity. 'An unjustified mingling of the intellectual or mind soul with the consciousness soul was the object in view' (GA 184, 11/10/18). Had Sorat achieved his goal, human beings would have become automatons in the service of the Adversary of the Sun Spirit, Christ.

> This year 666 was intended to deluge humanity with a knowledge and a culture which the primal gods had intended for human beings only during the third millennium. It cannot be conceived—and need not be conceived—into what situation the so-called civilized world would have come if it had been deluged with this wisdom in the year 666! With their lack of self-discipline people would have come utterly to grief. For go to your history books and see what they say about the human being's unbalanced mood of soul in 666, and you will get some idea of how people would then have behaved if in this way genius had come among them. [GA 184, 06/10/18]

Geniuses there would have been, particularly in the fields of science and technology. What has been achieved in the past 500 years or so by considerable effort and ingenuity would have been attained effortlessly. This effortlessness in regard to scientific and technological achievement—outdoing by far what we have achieved so far—would have been accompanied by a parallel lack of soul-spiritual self-development, for such development demands tremendous conscious effort.

That Sorat was not successful, Steiner states, was due to the fact that a state of balance was brought about through the

Mystery of Golgotha. 'Something that could have happened was prevented by an actual event' (GA 184, 11/10/18).

Steiner gives us further insight into what could have happened:

> What, then, was meant to happen from 666 on, if the Mystery of Golgotha had not occurred and the Beast of that time had been able to intervene in the evolution of mankind, what could have happened?... Mankind was hurrying on towards the fifteenth century; if the Beast had gone on stirring up mischief among human beings from 666 until the fifteenth century, he would by then have gained complete control of what was approaching. What was approaching was the grasping of the world through a ghostlike natural science and, with that, the unleashing of human instincts. Because the consciousness soul was to grasp the human being as a mere ghost, the real human being lagged behind; one did not understand oneself. And in the age of the consciousness soul one can become a true human being only by becoming conscious of what one is: otherwise one remains an animal; one lags behind in one's human evolution. [GA 184, 11/10/18]

The aim of the Beast who worked to intervene in AD 666 was to prevent human beings from directing their gaze to the spirit, from experiencing the reality and activity of the spiritual world. Indeed, the Sorat-impulse was to some extent successful in that it influenced certain decisions taken at the Eighth Ecumenical Council held at Constantinople in AD 869. Among the beliefs proclaimed by Rome was one that Rudolf Steiner frequently referred to, namely, that the human being is to be regarded as a twofold, not a threefold, being consisting of body and soul but not of body, soul *and spirit* as had been held by theologians in earlier centuries. Steiner points out that it was, from a spiritual point of view, a crucially important decision when it was proclaimed by Rome that the human being is a twofold, not a threefold, being, for it reflected the disappearance of the true knowledge of the human being from the Church, and a partial victory for those spiritual beings, 'particularly for a being of ahrimanic nature who was to lead these spirits', who planned that Sorat should appear 'even if not on the physical plane—

but he was to appear' (ibid.). It was no more than a partial victory, for the knowledge of the threefold human being—and thus a true knowledge of the human being—went underground, as it were. It resurfaced intermittently, though sometimes incompletely, in the West in such movements as the Knights Templar, the Cathars and Friends of God or among individuals such as the Grail writers, various mystics, true Rosicrucians and alchemists, and original Freemasons. In the twentieth century it has finally and completely surfaced into the open in the form of Rudolf Steiner's spiritual science.

It has been intimated already that if the Mystery of Golgotha had not taken place Sorat would have been victorious; he would have made himself God and he would have said: 'Human beings will no longer be interested in the spirit; they will turn their attention to nature and form ghostlike concepts of nature. Then I shall do something that human beings will not notice, because they will not recognize themselves as real human beings, but only as ghosts ... I shall let them go on grasping only the ghost of themselves and I shall pour all the wisdom of the consciousness soul into their intellectual or mind soul. Then I have them—then I shall have caught them' (ibid.).

Human beings were to be prevented from rising, in the future, to the spirit-self, life-spirit, spirit-man. They would have remained at the stage of the consciousness soul, 'and human beings would have been automatons [*Undinge von Wissen*] in face of the knowledge that from the sixth epoch (beginning mid-fourth millennium) onwards would have been poured into them. But then it would have been all over with them—they would have developed no further. They would have drawn this knowledge into their consciousness soul, would have placed it all *with the utmost egoism* [author's italics] at the service of the consciousness soul' (ibid.).

Such was the intention of the being who wanted to appear in AD 666—to prevent the possibility of all future human and earthly evolution. If Sorat had won more than a partial victory, if the Mystery of Golgotha had not taken place and if, moreover, the forces of Michael had not been at work, then human beings 'would have gone no further along the path on which those beings of the higher Hierarchies wished to accompany us; beings who from the beginning have taken our normal human evolution in hand' (ibid.).

In a lecture Rudolf Steiner gave on 15 June 1915,[1] he gives us a picture of some of the characteristics of the cultural epoch just alluded to, the sixth epoch. What will give to external culture in that epoch its content and character must, Steiner says, be prepared in advance, must, indeed, be prepared in our present epoch. There is a quality, largely, if not completely, lacking as yet in human society, which will be characteristic of those men and women who have either overcome or not submitted to the Soratic impulse, namely, a certain moral quality. This moral quality will, of course, not be found in those who have followed the precipitous path of black magic. For those who do so are drawn—and will be drawn—into the sphere of influence exerted by the two-horned Beast, by Sorat (cf. GA 104, 30/06/08).

The moral quality to which Steiner is drawing our attention may be characterized in the following way. Unlike conditions in our present cultural epoch (the epoch of the consciousness soul), in the sixth epoch, in the epoch during which those human beings who have pursued the path of 'normal' development will evolve the spirit-self (cf. GA 186, 07/12/18), a *common consciousness will come into being* so that those 'who stand at the peak of culture in the sixth epoch will not only feel pain such as is caused today by the sight of poverty, suffering and misery in the world, but such men and women will experience the suffering of another human being as their own suffering. Those who see a hungry fellow human being will feel the hunger right down into the physical, so acutely indeed that the hunger of the other person will be unendurable to them' (GA 159/160, 15/06/15).

Earlier we saw that it was Sorat's intention to deprive human beings of any interest in the spirit and to 'turn their attention to nature and form ghostlike concepts of nature'. Without a recognition of the reality of the spirit nothing other than ghostlike concepts of nature and of mankind, humanity, can prevail. Materialism, then, can do no other than form such ghostlike concepts. Materialism, Steiner said on more than one occasion, ' is unwittingly influenced by the Conciliar decree of 869 which abolished the spirit and declared that the human being consisted of body and soul only (GA 175, 08/05/17), the soul being seen as having a few spiritual functions.

In the lecture concerned with preparation for the sixth cultural epoch, Steiner gives us an insight into another characteristic quality which will manifest itself.

> What is known as science today with its materialistic trend will certainly not be honoured by the name of science in the sixth post-Atlantean epoch. It will be regarded as antiquated super-stition, able to pass muster only among those who have remained behind at the stage of the superseded fifth post-Atlantean epoch ... As a matter of course people will accept as science only such forms of knowledge as are based upon the spiritual, upon pneumatology. [GA 159/160, 15/06/15]

Moreover, the laboratory table will have become an altar (cf GA 118, 27/02/10).

It is the whole purpose of Christo-centric spiritual science (anthroposophy), imbued as it is with the forces of Michael, the Countenance of Christ, to prepare mankind for the sixth cultural epoch—and beyond.

We have just seen that it was—and still is—Sorat the Sun Demon's intention to turn our attention away from the spiritual and to focus our efforts and aspirations exclusively upon material concerns.

Ahrimanic–soratic powers would have cut human beings off from the path of their future destiny and claimed them for an entirely different kind of evolution. 'People of great wis-dom would have arisen, but materialistically thinking people, people entirely of the earth' (GA 184, 12/10/18). The project of these soratic beings was not fulfilled, but, nevertheless, traces of it have manifested themselves in the history of mankind. They have manifested themselves through the deeds of those human beings who, Rudolf Steiner states, act 'as agents of certain spiritual beings' (GA 182, 16/10/18). The Emperor Justinian I (AD 483–565) was such an agent.[2] It was he who, as an enemy of all that emanated from the lofty wisdom of Greece, closed the schools of philosophy in Athens in AD 529. As a consequence, all the learning of olden times that had been drawn into the Greek schools of philosophy and had found expression in, for instance, an Anaxagoras (*c.* 500–428 BC), a Heraclitus (*c.* 540–*c.* 475 BC), a Socrates (*c.* 470–399 BC), a Plato (*c.* 428–*c.* 348 BC), an Aristotle (385–322 BC), was swept away from its homeland. The last representatives of Greek scholarship were banished from Greece and fled to Persia, where they joined those Greek sages who had been driven out of Europe and Edessa to Gundeshapur by the Emperor Zeno Isaurikus (AD 426–91) in AD 489.

Thus, when AD 666 was approaching, there had gathered in the Persian Academy of Gundeshapur a peerless group of scholars 'that had come over from ancient Greek culture *and had taken no account of the Mystery of Golgotha*' (GA 182, 16/10/18).

Mention has been made of the dire consequences in regard to mankind's spiritual development—both now and in the future—if Sorat had achieved his aim, if the soratic impulse issuing from Gundeshapur had progressed unimpeded. We have also seen that it was the Mystery of Golgotha which acted as a counterforce to the Sun Demon's intentions. Rudolf Steiner also mentions on several occasions another 'counterforce'—Mohammedanism. He speaks of Mohammedanism 'blunting' the influence of the soratic wisdom promulgated by the Academy of Gundeshapur.[3]

The intention of this centre of great learning was to deluge with its diabolical wisdom not only the immediate vicinity in Persia but the whole of the then known civilized world— Europe, Asia and northern Africa.

The preliminaries for this were prepared. But the influence that

was to have gone out from Gundeshapur was deadened...
Through the appearance of Mohammed and his visionary religious teaching, there was a deadening of the influence that was
meant to go out from Gundeshapur. Above all, in those regions
where it was wished to spread the Gnostic wisdom of Gundeshapur, Mohamed took the ground from under its feet... Here
you can see the wisdom in world history; we come to know the
truth about Mohammedanism only when, in addition to other
things, we know that Mohammedanism was destined to deaden
the Gnostic wisdom of Gundeshapur, to take from it the strong
ahrimanically seductive force which would otherwise have been
exercised upon mankind. [GA 184, 12/10/18]

However, the Gnostic wisdom of Gundeshapur was not
entirely eliminated, for that which has arisen from the
blunting of the influence of the soratic wisdom is western
scientific thinking (cf. GA 184, 12/10/18). Modern science—
in its various branches—with its particular 'brain-bound'
method of thinking has not developed from anything to do
with Christianity as such.[4] It is possible to trace, from decade
to decade, how the Gnostic wisdom of Gundeshapur—in a
blunted form, it is true—was brought into Europe by the
Arabs. Scientific thinking derives, ultimately, from the
Academy of Gundeshapur. This 'blunted' Gnostic wisdom
spread over Southern Europe and Africa to Spain, to France,
to England, and then over the Continent by way of the
monasteries. 'We can trace,' Rudolf Steiner observes, 'how
the supersensible is driven out and only the sense-perceptible
retained; we can trace the tendency, as it were, the intention'
(ibid.).

Elsewhere Steiner affirms: 'Whereas Christianity brought
an impulse connected essentially with the human being's life
of soul, the greatest impulse given to the human intellect was
brought by the Arabs... There could have been no Kepler,
no Galileo, without the impulses that were brought by
Arabism into Europe' (GA 124, 13/03/11).

Thus in the evolution of western culture we have two
impulses, two streams converging in the Middle Ages—the
Christian stream and the stream flowing into Europe through

Arabism.[5]

It was characteristic of the Arab genius to be interested in a rather one-sided way in the material aspects of life. This genius was exceptionally gifted in the natural sciences—in particular in those aspects which can be mastered by the calculating intellect (in which Ahriman manifests a particularly powerful influence). The Arabians' interest was centred above all on the discoveries in the classical heritage which had been cultivated in Alexandria and which embrace mathematics, astronomy, geography, medicine, chemistry, botany and zoology.[6]

The nations of Christian Europe, on the other hand, had neglected this part of the classical heritage. The soul of the medieval Christian was directed far more towards the hereafter. Indeed, so strong was this tendency that frequently the things of the here and now, the things of this earthly world, were only experienced in a dreamlike state of consciousness.

In this connection, Rudolf Frieling makes the following observation in regard to Rudolf Steiner's statement that 'the greatest impulse given to the human intellect was brought by the Arabs':

> This 'greatest stimulus for the human intellect', originating outside the Christian world, must at first have affected Christendom merely as a terrible and devastating blow from an unexpected quarter. In the long term it had the task of leading European Christianity to complete earthly awareness of this world; only when this clear consciousness is its starting-point can Christianity move towards clearer spiritual perception of the supersensible, and above all of the true meaning of the Mystery of Golgotha. If Christianity is to carry enlightenment for future times and be inspired by the Holy Spirit, intellectual activity must be really absorbed in genuine expansion of consciousness, and human intelligence transformed into higher spiritual vision.[7]

Only through the convergence, or, rather, the union of Christianity and Mohammedanism during the period from the mid-sixth century to the thirteenth century was it possible for our modern culture to come into being. 'Thus actually six to six-and-a-half centuries after the Christ Event the ... moon-cult of the Arabs appears, expanding and spreading into Europe and, until the thirteenth century, enriching the Christian culture which had received its direct impulses by other paths' (GA 124, 13/03/11). In the monasteries of medieval Western Europe—in spite of apparent opposition to Arabism—the Arabian concepts made their way into Christian philosophy and into science. One Christian cleric who was strongly influenced by the impulse issuing from Gundeshapur was the Franciscan monk Roger Bacon (c. 1214–92).[8] Roger Bacon included natural scientific perceptions in his theological manner of thought. In 1250 a work by him appeared in which he called up a picture of the materialistic, exoteric aspect of the coming time of the consciousness soul:

> Explore nature and make experiments! Then you will be able to accomplish unprecedented things. I can imagine a vehicle coming into existence that will move with unbelievable speed over the earth without the use of a draught animal; a single man will sit in it pressing a handle, and the vehicle will speed away. I can imagine a ship that will sail the seas with much greater speed than is possible by rowing; a single man in the inner part of the ship will press a handle and, through this alone, the ship will be set into fast movement. I can imagine a human being flying through the air as a bird; he will be sitting in a structure with wings like birds, which he will set in motion with the help of an apparatus.[9]

It was, in particular, the Arabian philosopher and scientist, Ibn Rushd Averroës (1126–98), living in Cordoba, who had the most marked influence on, among others, Roger Bacon. Averroës' direct forerunner was the Persian philosopher and physician Ibn Sina Avicenna (980–1017). In these two highly gifted and influential thinkers and scientists from the Near East the impulse of Gundeshapur, though much weakened, was still working. In both the impulse of Gundeshapur emerges in the form of a theory of knowledge.

Avicenna characterizes the power of thinking in the following way:[10] The active thought-creating power which

produces human thoughts is a *universal* 'active understanding' (Aristotle: *Nous Poetikos*) which acts in every
human being in the same way. The *human* power of thinking
is itself merely a receptive one (Aristotle: *Nous Pathetikos*).
Its potentialities, similar to the animal soul, are aroused by
the inraying of the 'active understanding' and, in that way,
first 'made into' thinking. The source of its own thinking
activity does not arise in each individual human soul. The
universal active understanding, not human beings themselves, is the creator of thoughts. The productive thought
force is to be denied to the human being.

The most important representative of Arabian philosophy
was Averroës. He regarded Aristotle as the greatest of all
thinkers. According to Averroës the active intellect (*Nous
Poetikos*) is not a faculty of the human being's spiritual
individuality; it only 'speaks' in human beings during their
lifetime. The nature of the active intellect is impersonal, i.e.
beyond the personal altogether. However, by virtue of it we
partake as individuals of the eternal intellect, which mankind
as a species has in common. The passive intellect (*Nous
Pathetikos*) only can be regarded as personal—it comes into
being, arises and fades with the earthly life of the human
being. Averroës claims that the earth and the human beings
on it are *one* and endowed with *one* common earth-
understanding. Into the *one* common understanding-
potentiality of the human being—which for itself is only
passive—thoughts are radiated from outside by the one
common active understanding (*Nous Poetikos*).

The content of the active intellect is eternal in character,
but the individual function of human knowledge is transitory—as indeed, according to Avicenna and Averroës, is the
human soul itself.

These few sentences do not by any means do justice to the
theory of knowledge promulgated by Avicenna and Averroës, but from them we can see the following picture emerging. In the words of Sigismund von Gleich: 'In all the human
beings on earth there is the *one* species-like, half-animal,
merely receptive sense unable out of its own forces to rise up

to thought and to experience itself in thinking as an individual being—a dull, earth-man-animal'. However, alongside such a frightful perspective of egoless human beings, there is another conception maintained by Avicenna and Averroës which, Rudolf Steiner states, is true, namely, that thoughts flowed down to human beings out of a realm beyond the earth. With such a conception spiritual science finds no quarrel. However, whereas Rudolf Steiner recognizes the Sun Spirit light as radiating down to mankind in full clarity of consciousness, Avicenna and Averroës—and others under the influence of the Gundeshapur impulse—conceive of this downstreaming power as emanating from the sublunary sphere. Sigismund von Gleich comments here: 'From without, from the moon-ether-sphere, there shines into its [i.e. into the "dull, earth-man-animal's"] dark sense-receptiveness a bright wisdom light, the *reflection* of the Sun Spirit light. A life hovering and swaying between dreamy sense-orientating and fantastically brilliant seerlike somnambulism, a life of hopeless unfreedom...'

In a lecture given on 1 July 1924 Rudolf Steiner speaks in some detail about the theory of knowledge which, blunted though it was, streamed via such thinkers as Avicenna and Averroës, from Gundeshapur, over Western Europe. With particular reference to the power of thinking, Steiner says:

> Today, when human beings reflect upon themselves they feel themselves as the possessors of thoughts, feelings and impulses of will which lead to action. Above all, human beings ascribe to *themselves* the 'I think', the 'I feel' and the 'I will'. But in the personalities of whom I am now speaking [i.e. Avicenna, Averroës, *et al.*] the 'I think' was by no means yet accompanied by the same feeling with which we today would say 'I think'... Out of an ancient background of culture, they rather lived in the sensation 'It thinks in me' rather than 'I think'. [GA 237, 01/07/24]

They connected their egohood only with feeling and willing, not with thinking, for, as we have noted already, they experienced thoughts as something general 'outside' them.

Thought they said lived in the sublunary sphere.

'Just as we say, "We breathe in the oxygen of the air," so did these people say, not, "We breathe in the thoughts," but "We perceive the thoughts, receive them into ourselves." ' Steiner then goes on to say:

> Today, no doubt, people can also familiarize themselves with such an idea as a theoretic concept. They may even understand it with the help of anthroposophy, but as soon as it becomes a question of practical life they forget. For then at once they have this *rather strange idea that the thoughts spring forth within themselves* [author's italics]—just as though they were to think that the oxygen they receive in breathing were not received by them but sprang forth from within them. [Ibid.]

If the ideas propounded by Avicenna and Averroës—the brilliant commentators of an Aristotle that had passed through Gundeshapur—had succeeded, if they had not met with strong opposition, led, in particular, by the Dominicans, Albertus Magnus (1193–1280) and his pupil, Thomas Aquinas (1226–74),[11] then the evolution of the consciousness soul, the spiritual soul, would not have come about (cf. ibid.).

Averroës was teaching in the twelfth century. Rudolf Steiner spoke the words quoted above in the twentieth century. About 800 years too early Averroës expressed what may be asserted again only in our time when the consciousness soul, the ego-conscious personality, is developing towards its full potential. Three centuries or so before the onset of the consciousness soul, before 1413 or thereabouts, the conception 'it thinks in me' may be described as being out of harmony with, contradictory to, the time, i.e. to the age of the intellectual soul, for it could not be a conscious inner experience of the still semi-dreaming soul of the Middle Ages. In short, human souls had first to awake to a strong ego-sense, precisely in thinking, in order that in due course during the present age of the consciousness soul they might experience in the ego their own individual conscious activity of thinking[12] and only then—in this conscious activity—become increasingly aware of the ether-sphere pouring into the thoughts. So here we can recognize how the soratic impulse working through Gundeshapur strove to reveal in the first millennium to unprepared human souls what should be the experience only in the third post-Christian millennium.

The aim of the brilliant teachers inspired by the soratic impulse issuing from Gundeshapur was, Rudolf Steiner advises us, to make human beings very wise in all matters pertaining to the earth, to the material world. By instilling such wisdom, the *soul* was to be induced to partake of death 'so that when the human being had passed through the gate of death he or she would have no desire to participate in spiritual life or in future lives on earth. The intention was to prevent the human being from attaining to spirit-self, life-spirit, spirit-man' (cf. GA 9, GA 13 and also Appendix One). Death, which is foreordained for the physical body only, would in a certain respect have become the destiny of the human soul as well. *This was prevented by the Mystery of Golgotha.* 'The human being did become related to death, but through the Mystery of Golgotha a means of protection was given to the human soul against it... Through the Mystery of Golgotha the human soul was brought nearer to the spirit' (GA 182).

*   *   *

Mention was made earlier that the Franciscan monk Roger Bacon was strongly affected by the impulse of Gundeshapur.[13] All the impulses kindled by that great centre of learning were active in him. Here we shall confine ourselves to considering a few aspects of his theory of knowledge. His affinity with Avicenna and Averroës is obvious. The human soul possesses only the 'passive intellect' (*Nous Pathetikos*). Active understanding (*Nous Poetikos*) works into the soul from without. The 'active understanding' is not a part of the human soul but an essentially different and separate intellective substance from the human intellect. All knowing is achieved through the streaming in of divine illumination. Only the active thinking is immortal, and this does not belong to individual human beings but illumines them from without. The thought-active understanding can only exist as *pure*, it cannot enter into essential union with the human understanding.

This is a purely Averroës-inspired thesis. Roger Bacon, then, is the thirteenth-century European representative of the impulse of Gundeshapur in both the way he thinks and works in the realm of natural science and in that of a theory of knowledge. But it lies beyond the scope of these pages to illustrate in any further detail the soratic impulse of Gundeshapur as it manifested itself in such a personality as Roger Bacon and, much metamorphosed and modified, has continued to do right into the twentieth century.

Sufficient has been indicated to recognize two closely linked main streams. The first, based on the Arabian methods of science and the concept of the human being as 'creature' (i.e. not 'creator'), leads inevitably to the view of natural science which conceives of the human being as being a mere 'earth-man-animal'. The second, based on the sublunary-sphere thinking of Arabism* (cf. GA 237, 01/07/24), denies to human beings the productive power of thought, and thus their freedom and true immortal ego-being.

What we see here, in a diluted form, is the activity of the Sun Demon, Sorat, the Adversary of the Sun Spirit, the Christ, the 'I AM THE I AM'.[14]

To reiterate, if the Christ-principle, the Christ-impulse, had been 'strangled in the germ' by the Adversary, it would have been possible for the *whole of humankind* to succumb to the Sorat-principle. This, as has been indicated already, has not and will not happen. This powerful spiritual being will have to be content with those who remain embedded in matter, who deny the reality of the Michael-Christ spirituality, who, in the language of St John, descend with

---

*It should be noted that the term 'Arabism' refers to a particular historical, spiritual impulse—which, as we have seen with Roger Bacon, is not restricted to any one nation or culture—and is not used in a prejudicial sense against any modern-day individuals or cultures.

Babylon into the abyss.

What has succumbed to the principle of the two-horned Beast, to Sorat, 'and hence has hardened itself into the Beast with the seven heads and ten horns, is driven forth. The power by which the Sun Genius [the Sun Spirit] ... drives them down into the abyss is called the Countenance of the Sun Genius, and the Countenance of the Sun Genius is Michael, who, as the representative, so to speak, of the Sun Genius, overcomes the Beast with the two horns...' (GA 104, 29/06/08).

* * *

At the time when Charlemagne (c. AD 742–814) was ruling over a vast empire in Western Europe, Harun al-Rashid (c. 763–809) was the figurehead of a splendid civilization. He gathered around him in Baghdad a circle of men of real brilliance in the field of science. The wealth of Harun al-Rashid procured Greek manuscripts (many of which were medical) from the Roman Empire. These were then translated into Syriac and Arabic. An association had been formed with the Academy at Gundeshapur by the Abbasid court (Harun al-Rashid was Abbasid caliph of Baghdad 786–809) when it was established near Baghdad. And when Harun al-Rashid sought for scholars to aid in his mission of Hellenizing Persian and Arab subjects, he drew many from that rich centre of learning. There emerges within this spiritual culture, of which Harun al-Rashid was the soul, something that had been spreading in Asia in a continuous stream since the time of Aristotle (384–322 BC). Aristotelian philosophy and natural science had spread across into Asia and had been elaborated by oriental insight and vision. It was this Arabianized Aristotelianism which took hold of Europe.

Now, we have noted that Arabism—in particular the theory of knowledge as expounded in Europe by Avicenna and Averroës—was counteracted by, for instance, Albertus Magnus and his pupil Thomas Aquinas, but it certainly did not die out (cf. GA 235, 16/03/24). We may certainly speak of an 'outward extermination' of Arabism, but that was not the end of it. For, as Rudolf Steiner shows in several lectures he gave in 1924 (*Karmic Relationships*), the souls who were once active in Arabism, after they had passed through the gate of death, developed 'onwards' in the spiritual world and remained connected, in a sense, with their previous work on earth. This is what happened in the case of the individuality of Harun al-Rashid.

> He passes through the gate of death and develops onwards in the spiritual world. In its external form, Arabism is repulsed; Christianity implants itself into Middle and Western Europe in the exoteric form it has gradually acquired. But although it is impossible to continue to be active in the old form of Arabism, in Europe, it is very possible for the souls who once shared in this brilliant culture at the court of Harun al-Rashid ... to work on. And that is what they do.

Rudolf Steiner then goes on to reveal that Harun al-Rashid reincarnates in the personality of Francis Bacon (1561–1626) 'whose influence has affected the whole of modern scientific thinking, and therewith much that is in the minds of human beings today ... The fundamental trend and tendency of what Bacon poured into European thinking is the old Arabism in the new form. And so Arabism lives in the scientific thinking of today...' (GA 240, 16/04/24).[15]

When we bear the historic karmic connection between Harun al-Rashid and Francis Bacon in mind it is not difficult to see why the latter's writings have so little that is truly Christian about them, nor why they have such a strong Arabian overtone.[16]

Francis Bacon lived and worked in the sphere of Christian civilization. Yet, Steiner points out, there is little, if any, trace of the Christ-impulse to be found in his writings. 'Bacon of Verulam might equally well have arisen from some non-Christian civilization. What he actually says about Christianity is extremely superficial compared with the real impulse that was within him' (GA 240, 12/08/24). We may note here that Christianity was certainly known to Harun al-Rashid and the learned scholars at his court but they regarded it as primitive and elementary in comparison with their own intellectual achievements.

According to Rudolf Steiner, Harun al-Rashid and his counsellor bore with them through the gate of death a strong affinity with the individualities of Alexander the Great and Aristotle (who had, of course, preceded them into the spiritual world by many centuries) and harboured an intense longing to come into contact with them. A meeting did take place. It took place in the spiritual world precisely when, here on earth in the year AD 869, the Eighth General Ecumenical Council took place in Constantinople.

The effect of this Ecumenical Council upon the development of western civilization was profound, for Trichotomy, the definition of the human being as a threefold being, a being of body, soul and spirit, was then declared heretical. It was decreed that Christians must speak of the human being as a twofold being, consisting of body and soul, only—the soul possessing certain spiritual qualities and forces.[17] Not surprisingly, there is not a great inclination to spirituality to be discerned in the western Church today. Outside the Church, however, there are many encouraging signs that the spirit is being rediscovered, is becoming a conscious experience in ever-expanding groups of people.

The growth of the fading from consciousness of the spiritual in Christianity is described by Rudolf Steiner in an Easter lecture:

The all-embracing wisdom by means of which in the first centuries of Christendom people were still endeavouring to understand the Mystery of Golgotha, and all that pertained to it, was gradually submerged by the materialism of the West... The original eastern concept of *religion* came to be bound up with the concept of the *State* that was developing in the West. In the fourth century AD Christianity became a State religion—in other words, there crept into Christianity something that is not religion at all...

In the fusion of Christianity with the declining culture of Rome, the influence of western materialism begins to take effect... And under this influence there appeared a picture of Christ Jesus which at the beginning simply was not there, was not part of Christianity in its original form: the picture of Christ Jesus as the Crucified One, the Man of Sorrows, brought to His death by the indescribable suffering that was His lot. [Depictions of Christ on the Cross did not occur before the sixth century].

This made a breach in the whole outlook of the Christian world. For the picture which from then onwards persisted through the centuries ... is of the Christ who could no longer be comprehended in His spiritual nature but in His bodily nature only... With the concentration on this picture of the Redeemer suffering and dying on the Cross, leave was taken of a truly spiritual conception of Christianity... The attitude of mind which caused the triumphant Spirit, the Victor over death, to vanish from the picture of the grave from which the Redeemer rises—this same attitude of mind, in the year 869 at the Eighth Ecumenical Council in Constantinople, declared belief in the spirit to be heretical... [GA 203, 27/03/21]

So, as we have observed already, it was during the Eighth Ecumenical Council that Harun al-Rashid and his Counsellor met Alexander and Aristotle in the spiritual world. Over eight centuries had passed since the Mystery of Golgotha. What Alexander and Aristotle had established on earth over three hundred years before that event—the one in the field of thought, the other giving effect to a great genius for rulership—had continued to work among mankind on the earth below. They beheld, from the spiritual world, the fruits of their activities flowing on through the centuries, during one of which the Mystery of Golgotha had taken place. They saw what was being done to spread the knowledge of this Mystery; they also saw their work spreading through the activities of such individuals as Harun al-Rashid and his Counsellor.

But, Rudolf Steiner perceives, in the souls of Alexander and Aristotle themselves there was an urge for 'a new and mighty impulse whereby a particular form of Christianity would be instilled into earthly civilization—it was to the inauguration of this impulse that Alexander and Aristotle dedicated themselves ... [they] affirmed at that time that what had been established in earlier days must now be guided undeviatingly into the dominion of Michael. For it was known that Michael would again assume his Regency in the nineteenth century' (GA 240, 14/08/24).

At this point it is relevant to remind ourselves that during the course of the evolution of mankind seven Archangels alternate with each other, in a regular sequence, as Regents for a period of about three-and-a-half centuries each. At the time when Aristotelianism was borne by Alexander the Great to Asia and Africa, at the time when the spread of this culture was imbued by a cosmopolitan spirit, Michael was the ruling Archangel.

In the century when the meeting with Harun al-Rashid took place, Alexander and Aristotle turned their gaze to the Rulership of Michael under which they had lived and worked; they also turned their gaze to the Mystery of Golgotha which—as members of the Michael-community—they had experienced from the sphere of the Spiritual Sun, not from the earth, for at the time when the Mystery of Golgotha took place Michael's rule on earth had been over for some two hundred years. Michael and his community did not experience the Mystery of Golgotha from an earth-viewpoint. Nor did they witness the arrival of Christ on earth. But they had witnessed His departure from the Spiritual Sun.[18] 'But all that they experienced formed itself into the impulse which remained alive in them—the impulse to ensure that the new Michael Rulership ... would bring a Christianity not only firmly established but more inward, more profound. The new dominion of Michael was to begin in the year 1879 and last for three to four centuries' (ibid.).

Clearly, neither Harun al-Rashid nor his Counsellor—key representatives of Mohammedanism—could concur with Alexander and Aristotle, for above all else they desired that the world should be dominated by the 're-emergence, in a different form, of the Yahveh-moon religion' (GA 124, 13/03/11). They desired that the intervening Christ-impulse should be ignored and that mankind should be dominated by the impulse that had manifested itself in Arabism.[19]

The aftermath of this confrontation in the spiritual world has worked on, particularly in the western world, to this day. Two strengthened streams flowed from that meeting in the spiritual world, 'one taking its course in Arabism and one whereby, through the impulse of the Michael Rulership, Aristotelianism was to be led over into Christianity' (GA 240, 14/08/24).

'Thus in our own time,' Steiner continues, 'we have on the one side the direct, unbroken line of Christian development and, on the other, the penetration of Arabism, first and foremost in abstract science' (ibid.).

Some impulses kindled by events in the spiritual world— such as that of the meeting between Alexander, Aristotle, Harun al-Rashid and his wise counsellor—furthered the spread of true Christianity, while others were the causes of hindrances along the evolutionary path.

Alexander and Aristotle, who were members of the Michael-community in the sphere of the Spiritual Sun, may be understood as working in our time towards the formation of a Michael-community on earth. Michael, as described several times in this book, is essentially a Sun Spirit. He, the Countenance of Christ, has the task in our present age to encourage mankind to find and experience a deeper and more esoteric understanding of the truths of Christianity.

Since the Mystery of Golgotha Christ, the Sun Being, has lived in supersensible communion with mankind on earth. But before we can live with Him in such a communion, before the whole Mystery connected with Christ can reveal itself to the human soul, mankind must become sufficiently mature and the necessary deepening will to a great extent have to be achieved during the present age of Michael' (GA 240, 21/08/24).

14. The Mexican Mysteries

Reference has been made already to a passage in the twelfth lecture of the Apocalypse cycle (GA 104, 20/06/08) in which Rudolf Steiner mentions that if the Christ-principle had been 'strangled' in the germ by the Adversary, by the Antichrist, the Sun Demon, it would have been possible for the whole of humanity to succumb to the Sorat-principle. Christ battled against and weakened the power of Sorat to such an extent that this being has 'to be content with the refuse of mankind who have not inclined towards the Christ-principle ... they in future will form his [i.e. Sorat's] cohorts'. Steiner then goes on to illustrate for us how the Sorat-cohort can be recognized and thus also gives us a clue as to where the 'battle' just referred to took place in the western world. In the same lecture from which it has just been quoted we also hear—not for the first time in these pages: 'He who systematically cuts into flesh, and feels satisfaction in it, begins to follow the precipitous path of black magic. And this opens the way for him to draw closer and closer to the being described as the two-horned Beast' (ibid.).

Now, Mystery Schools, black magic Mystery Schools, in which pupils were led through progressive stages of initiation in the practice of such sadism, did not exist in Palestine during Christ's life on earth, but they did exist in Mexico. According to Rudolf Steiner many people underwent the processes of initiation in these Mystery Schools. The spirit being they worshipped and who gave them instruction and commands was named Taotl—a mighty ahrimanic being who did not descend to physical incarnation.

Rudolf Steiner speaks of these soratic Mystery Centres and practices in two lectures he gave in 1916 (GA 171, 18/09/16 and 24/09/16).[1] Here we learn that as AD 30 approached the 'greatest' black magician ever to tread the earth faced a momentous decision, namely, whether or not to become so powerful through continuous initiation in the Mysteries of

Taotl that he would come to know a certain basic secret. Knowledge of this secret would have made it possible for him 'to rigidify and mechanize all earthly life, including that of human beings, to such a degree that a specific luciferic planet ... could be founded above earthly life. The souls of human beings could then be drawn out to it, by force and pressure' (GA 171, 18/09/16).[2]

Once they had entered this luciferic sphere human souls would have no wish to incarnate in a physical body again and would thus be deprived of all future progress towards spiritualization in the light of the Christ-impulse. The goal of the soratic–ahrimanic powers was to make the whole earth a realm of death in which everything possible could be undertaken to eliminate independence and every inner soul-impulse in human beings. Here we have a clear example of the working together of the adversarial powers, Lucifer and Ahriman.

Now it was in AD 30 that, in Palestine, the most innocent and purest of human souls was united with the divine 'I' of the Christ Being. Three years later, through the Mystery of Golgotha, in the words of St John the beloved disciple, the Prince of this World was cast out (John 12:31 and 16:11). This is true in respect of the whole world, including, for instance, Mexico. In Mexico, however, it was not Christ Himself who conquered Sorat. In Mexico at that time Sorat would have proved invincible had not a man of remarkable courage and spiritual insight opposed the greatest of black magicians who was a high initiate of Taotl.

Steiner's account of this remarkable man who bore the name Uitzilopotchtli (or Vitzliputzli, as the name was transcribed in Steiner's account)[3] includes the following statement:

> Now at a certain time a being was born in Central America who set himself a definite task within this culture. The old, original inhabitants of Mexico linked the existence of this being with a definite idea or picture. They said he had entered the world as a son of a virgin who had conceived him through super-earthly powers, inasmuch as it was a feathered being from the heavens

who impregnated her.[4] When one makes researches with the occult powers at one's disposal, one finds that the being in whom the ancient Mexicans ascribed a virgin birth was born in AD 1 and lived to be 33 years old. [GA 171, 18/09/16]

It was in AD 30 that the conflict began between the super-black magician and the being to whom a virgin birth was ascribed.

The three-year conflict ended when Vitzliputzli was able to have the great magician crucified, and not only through the cruci-fixion to annihilate his body but also to place his soul under a ban, by this means rendering its activities powerless as well as its knowledge. Thus the knowledge assimilated by the great magi-cian of Taotl was killed. In this way Vitzliputzli was able to win again for earthly life all those souls who, as indicated, had already received the urge to follow Lucifer and leave the earth. Through the mighty victory he had gained over the powerful black magician, Vitzliputzli was able to imbue these human souls again with the desire for earthly existence and successive incarnations. [Ibid.]

So, after three years of struggle against the most powerful initiate of the Sorat Mysteries, Vitzliputzli, a supersensible being but in a human form, was victorious. Rudolf Steiner states that it was in AD 33 that Vitzliputzli succeeded in causing the mightiest black magician to be crucified. 'Thus, in the other hemisphere of the earth, an event parallel to the Mystery of Golgotha took place' (GA 171, 24/09/16).

Here we have a clear example of the power of the Christ-impulse. Vitzliputzli was able to gain victory over a high initiate of Taotl because, throughout his life on earth, he had placed his whole being unreservedly in the service of the Michael-Christ impulse. It is, of course, only Christ Himself who has the power to overcome Sorat, but He needs human beings to be active on His behalf. Vitzliputzli, we may say, was an agent of Christ who could overcome a powerful agent of Sorat. Clearly, Vitzliputzli was a high initiate, for Steiner describes him as 'a supersensible being but in human form ... who had appeared on the earth for this purpose' (ibid.).

Vitzliputzli's victory in AD 33 was momentous. However, Steiner draws our attention to the fact that although the ahrimanic–soratic powers did not attain their goal in the fourth post-Atlantean cultural epoch, they have prepared powerful onslaughts for our fifth post-Atlantean epoch (i.e. from c. AD 1413 to c. AD 3513, for they still mean to achieve their purpose (cf. GA 186, 18/11/17).

Sorat's goal remains today what it was 2000 years ago: the elimination of the human 'I'. Sorat, *the* Adversary of Christ, aims to destroy the bearer of the Christ-impulse, the human 'I', and to so rigidify, mechanize, life on earth that (as has been touched upon already) any future soul and spiritual development on the part of human beings would be rendered impossible.

15.   The Knights Templar

One of the critical years in the proximity of which the activity
of Sorat was enhanced was AD 1332 (i.e. 2 × 666). Rudolf
Steiner himself speaks of the annihilation of the Order of the
Knights Templar in 1314 in this context.

It was in AD 1119, in Jerusalem, that the Order of the
Knights Templar was founded. It was dedicated to Christ.
'The written and unwritten rules of the Order were such
that the Knights were to think of nothing except how they
could completely fill themselves in heart and soul with the
sacred Mystery of Golgotha' (GA 171, 25/09/16). Pierre
Morizot writes: 'The chief aim of the Templars was a deepening of the inner life...They wanted every Christian to
become a Sir Galahad, that incarnation of perfect purity
conceived by poets, whose heroic will-power is forever
striving to accomplish without faltering in his duty to his
family and his people.'[1] Their aim was the Christianization
of the whole of Europe. However, reality soon fell short of
the ideal.

The numerous duties undertaken by the Templars became
increasingly worldly. The knights had to be road builders who
looked after the highways, the people who kept bandits in
check, the bankers who lent money to kings—for they had
accumulated substantial wealth which they had brought back
to France from the East. They were also the brokers who
managed the currencies, and so on. The Order also had
several weaknesses built into its structure from the outset,
including the fact that its founders' original intent to offer a
spiritual Christianity was 'materialized' by what the Crusades
actually became and that the Order found itself having to
work with and, later, almost become part of the Roman
Catholic Church. The founder of the Cistercian Order, Bernard of Clairvaux, himself drew up the rules by which the
Order should live and operate at the Council of Troyes in
1128. Rudolf Steiner tells us that initially the impulse behind

the Crusades, led by Godfrey de Bouillon, was to form a western esoteric Christianity that was not centred on Rome.

> Then when the path indicated by the servants of the Holy Grail as a spiritual path was replaced by the physical path to the physical Jerusalem in the Orient—when the *Via Crucis* to the Grail was replaced by the Crusades to the physical Jerusalem— when Godfrey de Bouillon wished to set up an exterior kingdom in Jerusalem in opposition to Rome and sounded forth from out of his feeling the call '*Away from Rome*', then, indeed, this was less suggestive than Peter of Amien's [i.e. Peter the Hermit, a Catholic monk] call which worked like a powerful suggestion, seeking to transfer into a materialistic sphere what the servants of the Holy Grail had meant spiritually. [GA 204, 16/04/21; also *The Golden Blade* 1981]

Walter Johannes Stein has shown us that Godfrey of Bouillon (leader of the first Crusader army that captured Jerusalem and whose nine comrades in arms under Hugo de Payens founded the Templars) was linked with the Grail family connected with St Odile.[2] The Crusades had originally been a movement on behalf of the Michaelic Christ-impulse. 'Jerusalem was to be the centre and from there the secret concerning the relationship of man to the Christ should stream out all over the world. What was represented symbolically by the temple should becoming a living reality' (GA 93, 22/5/05).

At the close of the thirteenth and the beginning of the fourteenth century the Templar Order had attained great prestige and wealth through its activity throughout Western Europe. At that time Philip IV (Philip the Fair) reigned in France (1285–1314). He was harassed by successive financial crises and resolved to confiscate the gold and silver held by the Templars. In order to do so Philip brought numerous charges—including that of heresy—against the Knights Templar. The most damning charge—and one with which the French Pope, Clement V, residing not in Rome but in Avignon and generally subservient to Philip, was finally coerced to agree—was heresy.[3]

In 1307 Knights Templar throughout France were arrested. The trial, once instituted, lasted seven years and was conducted by the Inquisition, notorious for its use of torture.

According to Rudolf Steiner, Philip the Fair was a man 'equipped with an extraordinary degree of cunning and the most evil ahrimanic wisdom'. Inspired by Ahriman he had a genius for avarice. 'He felt the instinctive urge to recognize nothing else in the world but what can be paid for with gold ... He wished to bring forcibly under his control all the power that can be exercised by gold' (GA 171, 25/09/16). What Philip sought was not moral power in the service of his fellow human beings, but immoral power in the service of his personal avarice. Philip was filled with fear (induced by Ahriman) because he recognized the moral power exercised by the Knights Templar. They did not seek riches for themselves but placed the wealth of the Order in the service of spiritual activity and creative work. In short, they strove to make it possible for Christ to accomplish His mission. They aimed at a broadening and deepening of the general conception of Christ's mission on earth for the whole of humankind and the cosmos itself. To that end consciousness of the real nature of this exalted Spiritual Being and of His connection with the cosmos had to be cultivated. Admittedly, only a few knights of the Order really knew and valued esoteric Christianity by this time.[4] It was these few, however, who were feared by the soratic powers whose aim was—and still is—to oppose and eliminate the Christ-impulse. Sorat chose Philip the Fair as his tool—just as he had once chosen the great magician of Taotl as his tool, his agent.

The evil forces aroused by Philip's excessive avarice and unbridled lust for gold brought about in him intuitions comparable, according to Rudolf Steiner, to those received through the rites of Mexican Mysteries. Philip's passionate desire to possess gold, 'aroused in such a materialistic way and working so intensely, creates powerful forces in the soul. At the same time, it creates knowledge, although of an Ahrimanic order. So it was possible for a certain second-hand sort of knowledge to arise in the soul of Philip of those methods that we have seen flame up in the harshest, most horrible way in the Mexican Mysteries' (GA 171, 25/09/16).

Without perhaps being fully conscious of it Philip sensed that, through the blood of tortured men, impulses enter into history which give it an antichristian tendency. Thus he was led to order the most horrible methods of torture and to revel in the accounts he received of them. Philip had certainly learned the ABC—and more—of black magic. In regard to the horrible methods of torture Philip ordered to be applied Rudolf Steiner says: 'The torture was applied in the most cruel way so that many of the harassed Knights lost consciousness. Philip knew that the pictures of the temptations emerged when, in terrible agony on the rack, their consciousness became clouded' (ibid.).

We may remember here that ahrimanic spirits are most potent in attacks against Michael and Christ when a diminution of consciousness takes place in human beings.[5]

The Knights' answers to questions were, of course, given out of a consciousness dulled by the torture. The answers were always suggested in the way the questions were put. They would accuse themselves of the most sacrilegious behaviour, which normally lived in their subconscious as temptations. The powers opposing the good spoke through their mouths. In a lecture of 12 September 1924 Rudolf Steiner states that the tortures were so arranged that Sorat spoke his blasphemies through the mouths of the tortured Templars.[6] In relation to this, the French author Pierre Morizot, writing about the Order, refers to Steiner's statement about 'Baphomet', the idol or head that Templars were accused of worshipping, an accusation subsequently added into the charges against members of the Order. Morizot reports Steiner as saying, in reply to a question on 9 June 1920, 'Baphomet is the name of an ahrimanic entity which appeared to people who were being tortured ... and when they returned to consciousness they brought back all sorts of visions.' Baphomet was an aspect of Sorat.

In 1314 Jacques de Molay, the Grand Master of the Order,

and many of his followers were burnt at the stake in Paris. Rudolf Steiner has stated that, subsequently, the spiritual bodies of these 54 individuals have been able to inspire and assist those on earth working for the Michaelic Christ-impulse.

We may surmise that Philip had become an initiate into soratic–ahrimanic activities, and that he sensed that the Templars were initiates, but in a sphere entirely different from his own. They had occult knowledge opposed to his and capable of thwarting his ambitions. They were his most powerful opponents because their spiritual forces were 'rooted' in the Christ whereas his issued from Sorat.

After the 54 knights were burnt at the stake in Paris, action was taken against the Templars throughout Europe. Steiner, speaking of the destiny of the Templars in connection with the evolution of mankind, makes the following observations:

> Humanity was not yet ripe to receive the impulse of wisdom, beauty and strength in the way the Knights desired…The spiritual world was not to be attained in the way in which the Templars entered it. It would have been gained too quickly, which is the luciferic way. We actually behold here a most important twofold attack of the forces of Lucifer and Ahriman: Lucifer urging the Knights on, driving them into their misfortune, and Ahriman [Sorat] working actively through the inspiration of Philip the Fair. [GA 171, 25/09/16]

Humanity was not yet ripe in the thirteenth and fourteenth century to receive the impulse of wisdom in the way the Knights Templar desired. They foreshadowed the spiritual activity which needs to be nurtured and developed in our present epoch of the consciousness soul, which began about one hundred years after the martyrdom of Jacques de Molay and his companions in 1314. But, we learn from Steiner, what lived and worked in the Knights Templar could not be killed. Spiritual life cannot be eradicated. However, 'their impulses, which now, between their death and their next birth, go out to souls who have since descended, and also to souls who are still above awaiting incarnation, *must be metamorphosed from the character of the activity of the physical earthly world into spiritual activity* [author's italics]' (GA 171, 25/09/16).

What came from the souls of the murdered Knights became for many others a principle of inspiration. Powerful spiritual impulses have 'flown down' into humanity from the souls of the Knights who, before their death by burning, had to undergo the most horrifying experience a human being can suffer.

Rudolf Steiner mentions Wolfgang von Goethe (1749–1832) as being one of those souls who was inspired by the cosmic wisdom of the Knights Templar.

When we seek the most beautiful spiritualizations of this wisdom ... then we find one precisely in all that works and lives in the powerful imaginations of Goethe. Goethe knew the secret of the Templars. Not without purpose has he used gold as he has done in his *Fairy Tale of the Green Snake and the Beautiful Lily*, in which he made the snake consume the gold and then sacrifice itself. By this deed the gold is wrested from the powers with which Goethe truly knew it must not be allowed to remain. Gold—naturally everything is also meant here of which gold is a real symbol...

Through the way in which Goethe lets gold flow through this fairy-tale, he shows how he looks back into the time in which wisdom—for which gold also stands, hence, 'The Golden King of Wisdom'—was exposed to such persecution as those described... The secret of European evolution in the fifth post-Atlantean epoch lies concealed within this fairy-tale... In Goethe we have a true continuation of the life of the Knights Templar but ... in a spiritualized way. [GA 171, 25/09/16][7]

16. The Twentieth Century—The Etheric Christ and Sorat

In the fifteenth century the time had come for men and women to develop the forces of the consciousness soul, which would lead to spiritual freedom and individual responsibility. To this end they had to lose all understanding of inherited Christian wisdom in order to find it again through the strength of their own thinking, feeling and willing. The initial stage of the development of the consciousness soul brought with it the fact that attention was increasingly focused on the sense-perceptible world and—encouraged by Ahriman—the conviction has grown over the past five or six centuries that only that which could be perceived by the physical senses could be confirmed as being true and real.

One consequence of this trend can be seen in the fact that the 'Simple Man of Nazareth' has increasingly taken the place of the risen Christ, and that the image of the Cruci-fixion has taken precedence over that of the Resurrection.

From the Gospels we learn that nearly two thousand years ago, at the time of Christ's ministry in Palestine, human beings had fallen victim to two great 'errors', which may be characterized, on the one hand, by possession by demonic beings, and, on the other, by the rigid fundamentalism—fanaticism—of the scribes and Pharisees. Comparable aber-rations prevail today. For instance, on the one hand, we find the 'nervous breakdowns' and the drug addiction of ever-increasing numbers of people who, certainly in many instances, are unable to face and deal with the realities of everyday life. On the other hand, we see the global strife of religious and political groups with one another. We may think here of the 42-month-long civil war between Croats, Muslims and Bosnian Serbs in the former Yugoslavia in the 1990s, or the 25-year-long conflict between Protestants and Catholics in Northern Ireland. It has been estimated that, at the time of writing (1997), there are some 50 martial conflicts taking place in as many countries.

Seen against such a background and also bearing in mind the manias of Joseph Stalin and Adolf Hitler who, in the 1930s and 1940s, instigated the murder of millions of innocent people, we may justifiably say that since the early 1930s we have been witnesses to an age of spiritual 'darkness' similar to that of the time when Christ first appeared: 'And so Pilate, willing to content the people, released Barabbas unto them, and delivered Jesus, when he had scourged him, to be crucified' (Mark 15:15).

In a lecture dealing with the wrong and right use of esoteric knowledge Rudolf Steiner draws our attention again to the fact that the twentieth century should bring human beings into a close relationship with the Christ, that, in short, the Christ would appear to an increasing number of people in the etheric realm.[1] He then goes on to say: 'Now we know that we are living in the age of materialism, and that since the middle of the nineteenth century this materialism has reached its peak. But *in reality opposites always occur together.*' Precisely the high point of materialism is necessarily accompanied by that inward development which makes it possible for the Christ to be really seen 'in the etheric realm' (GA 178, 18/11/17).

There are Brotherhoods—Rudolf Steiner speaks of them as 'Brotherhoods of the left'—who are aware of the reality of the appearance in the twentieth century of Christ in the etheric realm but who wish to keep such knowledge to themselves, because when it is possessed by a small group it (the group) then has power over those who do not have such knowledge. These Brotherhoods do not want the knowledge of the appearance of the Etheric Christ to become the common property of humankind. There are Brotherhoods, Steiner maintains, whose members possess genuine esoteric knowledge and as a consequence are able to exert considerable influence on public opinion. Among other things they disseminate the idea that the time of materialism will soon be over, or, indeed, that it is already over. This is a view held by numerous so-called 'New Age' groups since the late 1960s and early 1970s. However, we must not forget that since the 1960s there are also groups of people who are consciously striving to experience the spiritual in the full clarity of wakefulness. We may think here of many who took part in the student riots of the Sixties. They wanted to go beyond the purely intellectual approach to the sense-perceptible world. In movements such as the Peace Movement and that of the environmentalists (Greenpeace, etc.) there are people, both young and old, who are not prepared to submit to the existing system of justice because they experience it as fundamental injustice, often linked with a few power-seeking people, or institutions, who see no further than short-term material, financial gains. Here again we should remember the network of small enterprises inspired by E.F. Schumacher. People are working in this network who have 'discovered' non-material motives within themselves. There are many enterprises to be found in which we can sense the striving towards the experience and manifestation of the reality of the spiritual world and its activity in the world of the senses. Among these enterprises we could mention here the world network of Camphill/Steiner Special Education homes and communities for both children and adults who are in need of special care. Also such an enterprise as the Findhorn Foundation in Scotland—and its many 'daughters' throughout the world—is setting an example as to how human beings can consciously strive to live as citizens of two worlds—a sense-perceptible world and a spiritual world.

In a lecture entitled 'The Deed of Christ and the Opposing Spiritual Powers' (GA 107, 22/03/09), Rudolf Steiner shows that had the Event of Golgotha not taken place human beings would have become out-and-out egoists. Brotherhood on earth, an all-embracing selfless love, would have had no prospect of manifesting itself. Inner harmony between human souls would have been rendered impossible to attain. There are signs today that, in spite of all the horrors of civil wars and genocide, a feeling of unity between north and south, east and west—of brother- and sisterhood—is growing in strength (see GA 56, 23/11/05).

Without the flowing of Christ's blood on the Cross, Lucifer's temptation and promise in the Garden of Eden that 'ye shall be as gods, knowing good and evil' would have led to nothing less than a caricature, a distortion of semblance with the Gods, namely, out-and-out egotism.

In one of his many lectures on the Mystery of Golgotha, referring to the evolution of humanity before the Advent of Christ, Rudolf Steiner says:

> Now we must clearly understand that with the human blood was connected that which produced the feeling which expressed blood-love [See Ch. 9]. This later developed into selfishness; the blood took on the character of egoism, selfishness. This blood which had become egoistic had to be overcome. The surplus egoism in human blood was sacrificed on the Cross. If it had not flowed then, selfishness would have become greater and greater. Human blood was sacrificed in order to cleanse humanity from egoism; and this cleansing of the blood from the egoistic 'I' is at the core of the Mystery of Golgotha.
>
> Those who see only the material process, who only see the man bleeding on the Cross can never understand this deeply mystic event. We only begin to understand the Mystery of Golgotha when we know that on the Cross flowed the blood which humanity had to lose in order to be set free from the bonds of egoistic selfishness. [GA 96, 01/04/07]
>
> The 'clever' people who today are promoting through so many gatherings and books and societies the idea that materialism is finished and that something of the spirit is now within reach, but without ever being able to offer people more than the word 'spirit' and little phrases of a similar kind—these people are all more or less in the service of those who have an interest in declaring what is not true: that materialism is in ruins. [GA 178, 18/11/17]

According to Steiner the materialistic outlook will continue to advance for some four or five hundred years.

Rudolf Steiner spoke in this way nearly 80 years ago. That materialism is still deeply engrained in most people's outlook on life is all too apparent, but—to reiterate—it needs also to be said that there is an increasing number of people throughout the world who are beginning to speak of and experience the reality of the beings of the spiritual world and also that of the Etheric Christ.

In regard to the experience of the Etheric Christ, Alfred Heidenreich makes a significant and illuminating point. It may well be, he says, that people who are on the fringe of spiritual science and not those who are within the Anthroposophical Movement will have the experience that Steiner predicted in the first decades of the twentieth century. 'You might find ... a hint of this in Steiner's first Mystery Play. Remember Theodora who has the vision. She moves in the circle of [the initiate] Benedictus but she obviously is not one of his disciples. She is a striking character right at the beginning of the play, the one who sees the Etheric Christ there.'[2]

Part of Theodora's speech to which reference is made here runs as follows:

THEODORA: Before my soul
                   A picture form stands wrapped in robes of light;
                   . . .
                   A human form steps from that sphere of light.
                   And speaks to me: 'Thou shalt make known to all
                   Who will give ear to thee, that thou hast seen
                   What all mankind shall soon experience:
                   Once, long ago, Christ lived upon the earth,
                   And from this life ensued the consequence
                   That in soul-substance clad He hovers o'er
                   The evolution of humanity,
                   In union with the earth's own spirit-sphere;
                   And though as yet invisible to men,
                   When in such form He manifests Himself,
                   Since now their being lacks that spirit sight,
                   Which first will show itself in future times;
                   Yet even now this future draweth nigh
                   When that new sight shall come to men on earth.
                   What once the senses saw, when Christ did live
                   Upon the earth; this shall be seen by souls
                   When soon the time shall reach its fullness due[3]
                   [*The Portal of Initiation*, 1910, GA 14]

A few months after Rudolf Steiner wrote this Mystery Play, in answer to the question 'Can Christ Jesus appear to people on earth?', he replied: 'In the way in which He appeared to St Paul, this is possible. When this happens it is a kind of initiation which can sometimes take place without previous training. From the middle of the twentieth century many people will have this experience.[4]

There *is* something, Rudolf Steiner states, that works against the endeavours of the Brotherhoods of the left, against those who would 'materialize human souls' (cf. GA 178, 18/11/17). This something is the impulse of the Mystery of Golgotha. There is no human power, no initiate, however knowledgeable, who can influence those actions of the Christ which, from the 1930s onwards, will lead to His appearance in the etheric sphere. The Brotherhoods of the left, however, want to take over the Christ's sphere of influence and hand it over to another being. 'There are western Brotherhoods who want to dispute the impulse of the Christ and to set in His place another individuality who has never appeared in the flesh—an etheric individuality, but a *strongly Ahrimanic one* [author's italics]' (ibid.). This being is the Sun Demon, Sorat, the Antichrist. In the German text of the lecture from which it has just been quoted we find that Steiner described the endeavours of these Brotherhoods of the left as being *im eminentesten Sinne antichristlich*, which in English could read 'antichristian in the profoundest sense of the term'.

*   *   *

Sorat's objective has not altered during the course of time. This spiritual being's intention is to extinguish the human 'I'. Sorat clearly opposes every effort made by free, spiritually active, individual human beings to found communities imbued with selfless love, for it is only those who have followed the path indicated by Michael and taken the love of Christ into the very core of their being, into the ego, the 'I', who will contribute towards the creation of the community of Philadelphia. Rudolf Steiner makes it clear that these followers of Michael need not be great in number:

It is, however, necessary that at the present time [the fifth post-Atlantean age, *c.* 1413–*c.* 3513] a spiritual conception of the world should gain ground, a conception which leads a small group of people to this spiritual view of the world. This group will comprise those who will lay the first foundation of the great bond of brotherhood in the Sixth Age ... not very far distant. [GA 104, 30/06/08]

To such a small group will also belong those who, since the first third of the twentieth century, have had experiences of the Etheric Christ either as near-death experiences or in fully awake consciousness. Earlier we heard Steiner saying that 'when this happens it is a kind of initiation which can sometimes take place without previous training'. There seems ample evidence to show that those who experience the Christ in the etheric sphere are steadily growing in number—small though this number may still be in comparison with the hundreds of millions of human beings now occupying the earth.

During the third and fourth decades of the present century various signs of an awareness of the Etheric Christ began to manifest themselves. For instance, T.S. Eliot in his poem *The Waste Land* (1922) gives us a powerful picture of our present civilization as an arid desert without water. But then he also speaks of a supersensible experience which might offer new life:

> Who is the third who walks always beside you?
> When I count, there are only you and I together
> But when I look ahead up the white road
> There is always another one walking beside you
> Gliding wrapt in a brown mantle, hooded
> I do not know whether a man or a woman
> —But who is that on the other side of you?

Eliot left it to the reader to make the connection with the journey to Emmaus, as told in Luke 24:13–15.

Roy Campbell had a more direct experience. In the last of his *Mithraic Emblems* (1936) to which he gave the title 'To the Sun':

Oh let your shining orb grow dim,
Of Christ the mirror and the shield.
That I may gaze through you to Him,
See half the miracle revealed.
And in your seven hues behold
The Blue Man walking on the Sea;
The Green, beneath the summer tree,
Who called the children, then the Gold,
With palms; the Orange, flaring bold
With scourges; Purple in the garden
(As Greco saw): and then the Red
Torero (Him who took the toss
And rode the black horns of the cross—
But rose snow-silver from the dead!)

Campbell recognizes the Christ as a Divine Sun Being, who descended through the seven colours of the rainbow to suffer on 'the black horns of the cross', but who 'rose snow-silver from the dead'.

In his books *Life after Life* (1975) and *Reflections on Life after Life* (1977), the psychiatrist Dr Raymond Moody gives many examples of near-death experiences. He found many common features in the experiences of those who had been near death. One of these was a sense of passing through a dark tunnel and emerging into a wonderful life which gradually took on the form of a Being, which a number of people recognized as the Christ.

In his book *Return from Tomorrow* (1978) George Ritchie describes his near-death experience. He describes very vividly how he became aware of a Being of radiant light. This Being gazed at him with compassion and complete under-standing of all faults.

Since these accounts of near-death experiences first appeared on the scene many more people have come forward with similar accounts.

It is clear from what has been said so far that 'meetings' with the Etheric Christ are not confined to near-death experiences. Indeed, Rudolf Steiner speaks in very 'down to earth' terms about such meetings. For instance, in 1911 Steiner says:

In only a few decades from now it will happen, particularly to those who are young in years ... that some people here or there have certain experiences ... they may become aware that suddenly someone has come near to help them, to make them alert to this or that. The truth is that Christ has come to them, although they believe that what they see is a physical man. They will come to realize, however, that this is a supersensible being, because it immediately vanishes. Many a human being will have this experience when sitting silently in a room, heavy-hearted and oppressed, not knowing which way to turn. The door will open, and the Etheric Christ will appear and speak words of consolation. The Christ will become a living comforter to men and women. However strange it may as yet seem, it is true nevertheless that many a time when people, even in considerable numbers, are sitting together not knowing what to do and waiting, they will see the Etheric Christ. He Himself will be there, will confer with them, will cast His word into such gatherings. We are now approaching these times... [GA 130, 01/10/11]

These times are here now.

Rudolf Steiner repeatedly indicated the years 1930–40 as the time when new supersensible faculties would begin to develop which would enable people to perceive and consciously experience the Etheric Christ. On 25 January 1910 we hear: 'The first signs of these new soul faculties will begin to appear relatively soon now in isolated souls. They will become more clear in the middle of the fourth decade of this century, sometime between 1930 and 1940. The years 1933, 1935 and 1937 will be especially significant'[5] (GA. 118).

Steiner then goes on to say:

Everything is changing, but the most significant event of our time is a deep, decisive transformation in the faculties of the human being ... It could easily happen that this event might pass by without the understanding of human beings. If, then, in the years between 1930 and 1940, the materialists were in triumph ... it would not disprove what we have said; if they were to triumph, however, and if humanity overlooked these events, it would be a great misfortune. Even if they were unable to perceive the great occurrence that can take place, it will nonetheless occur. [GA 118, 25/01/10]

The greatest Mystery of our time is the appearance to an ever-increasing number of people (over the next two thousand years or so) of the Etheric Body of Christ. 'The materialistic mind will conceive of this event as another descent of Christ into the flesh, as another physical incarnation [see e.g. the works of Alice Bailey].' There will even be a number of people who in their colossal conceit will proclaim that they are the reincarnated Christ.[6] In his Gospel Matthew recounts how Christ spoke of the appearance of false Christs (Matt. 24:24; also Mark 13:22) and warned us not to be deceived. Spiritual scientists, Rudolf Steiner states, 'should be people who will be so mature in their spiritual life that they will not confuse the second coming of Christ in a spiritual body, perceptible only to a higher vision, with such a reappearance in a physical body' (GA 118, 25/01/10).

Rudolf Steiner repeatedly warns that to conceive of Christ as reincarnating in a physical body is one of the direst temptations to beset humanity. To be so tempted, so deceived, opens the way for the power of evil to have increasingly devastating power. Steiner touches upon this dire possibility in another lecture he gave in 1910: 'Humanity is called upon to decide whether or not it shall allow itself to be led into darkness even lower than that of Kali Yuga ... or to work towards achieving what will enable them to enter the realm that is truly alluded to as Shamballa' (GA 116, 09/03/10).[7]

On one occasion Steiner spoke of the quality of the vision needed to perceive 'Christ in a spiritual body'. 'It is the wish of spiritual science to prepare for this faculty which humanity must take hold of again. Not the old instinctive vision, but a supersensible perception founded on full consciousness... And it is into this faculty of vision that a true comprehension of the Mystery of Golgotha can shine again' (GA 200, 30/10/20).

Another statement by Rudolf Steiner that is of paramount importance and touches the very foundation of the appearance of the Etheric Christ in the present century runs as follows:

Today when Christ is destined to appear again in the etheric body, when a kind of Mystery of Golgotha is to be experienced anew, evil will have a significance akin to that of birth and death for the fourth post-Atlantean epoch! In the fourth epoch the Christ-impulse was born out of the forces of death for the salvation of mankind. We can say that we owe the new impulse that permeated mankind to the event on Golgotha. Thus by a strange paradox mankind is led to a renewed experience of the Mystery of Golgotha in the fifth epoch through the forces of evil. Through the experience of evil it will be possible for the Christ to appear again, just as He appeared in the fourth post-Atlantean epoch through the experience of death. [GA 185, 25/10/18]

Elsewhere Steiner gives expression to this matter in somewhat simpler terms: 'What people in our epoch must learn is the need to wage a fully conscious fight against the evil that is making its way into human evolution.' Steiner is speaking in broad terms here and probably also has in mind that the Bolsheviks seized power in Russia no more than eleven days prior to his giving the lecture from which the last few words have been quoted. He then goes on to say: 'Just as in the fourth epoch the struggle was to come to terms with birth and death, so now we have to come to terms with evil' (GA 178, 18/11/17).

Just eight days before Rudolf Steiner gave his last lecture he said: 'Before mankind can understand Christ in the etheric in the right way, it will have to come to terms first of all with the encounter with the Beast, which will *arise in 1933*' [author's italics] (GA 346, 20/09/24). The year 1933 was when Adolf Hitler came to power! That year saw the beginning of a twelve-year period in the history of Central Europe which may well be described as having been taken out of the mainstream of civilization.

In the first of the many lectures Rudolf Steiner gave dealing with the appearance of the Etheric Christ he also specifically mentions the year 1933 as being fraught with dangers which would create confusion in the human soul (*Verwirrung der Seele*). *Inter alia* he also says: 'About the year 1933 there will be many agents of schools of black magic who will proclaim the falsehood that the Christ will appear again in a physical body.[8]

Rudolf Steiner, then, pinpoints here (and elsewhere) a clear connection between the appearance of the Etheric Christ and that which arose with particularly destructive power in the year 1933—the two-horned Beast, Sorat. This Beast (cf. Rev. 13:11–18), a supersensible being of great power, reveals itself through human agents in historical events, present, past and future. One could think here, in the 1990s, of the barbarity of the civil war of neighbour against neighbour in Bosnia-Herzegovina and the extreme callousness of so-called 'ethnic cleansing' and genocide.[9] Of similar horror was the massacre by Hutus of between 500,000 and 1,000,000 Tutsis in Rwanda during a few months in 1994. Nor should we forget—to mention just two more examples of soratic destruction of human life—the reign of terror in the 1970s in Cambodia. The Khmer Rouge leader, Pol Pot, is said to have been responsible for the deaths of more than 2,000,000 Cambodians, while over 200,000 East Timorese, more than 25 per cent of the race, have been exterminated by the Indonesian Government.

Rudolf Steiner speaks of human beings being possessed by Sorat to such a degree in the second half of the twentieth century ($3 \times 666 = 1998$) that one could have every reason to doubt whether they were really members of the human race.

The essential difference between Sorat's activity in the past and in the present century was described by Rudolf Steiner in September 1924 (GA 346). In the past Sorat used the seductive influences of both Lucifer and Ahriman to lead human beings astray in preparation for the undisguised activity of his ego-destructive powers. It is first in the twentieth century that mankind has been subjected to the experience of the Soratic principle without the luciferic and ahrimanic 'masks'. Whereas Ahriman works towards the mechanistic/materialistic rigidification of earthly life—and of the earth itself—in which no human 'I', no human ego, can live, and Lucifer strives to take the 'I' of every human being away from earth-existence and establish a 'planet' with them of his own (cf. GA 171, 17/09/16, and see Appendix Four), it is Sorat's aim to destroy both the human 'I' and the living earth itself, thus rendering any further development of the human soul and evolution of the earth impossible. As *the* Adversary of the Sun Being, of Christ, the Sun Demon, Sorat, aims to destroy both the bearer of the Christ-principle in the human being, namely, the 'I', and the earth itself which the 'I' needs for the future development of the human soul (cf. GA 9, Ch. 10).

The new phase of Sorat's activity showed signs of manifesting itself at the beginning of the twentieth century. For instance, during the First World War (1914–18) it could be said that a number of individual human beings in positions of responsibility were possessed by the Sun Demon. For example, the orders from higher command (political and military) which saw the use of poison gas at the second Battle of Ypres (22 April–2 May 1915), the massive German onslaught at Verdun (21 February–15 December 1916) and the British use of tanks at the Somme (July–October 1916)—resulting in the space of a few months in over 2,000,000 casualties—clearly show, on an unprecedented scale, the life-destructive force of the soratic power. This power also found an agent in Joseph Stalin who, during 29 years as virtual ruler of the USSR (1924–55), was responsible for the deaths of some 20,000,000 fellow citizens—often as the consequence of horrendous, dehumanizing torture. In the forced labour camps (Gulags) men and women were subjected to the most inhuman living and working conditions, in which they were treated as nameless, numbered automatons. Every effort was made to deprive human beings of their identity.

We have noted already that Rudolf Steiner himself refers to the year 1933 as being that of the appearance of a particularly vitriolic attack against humanity by the Sun Demon. It was on 30 January 1933 that Adolf Hitler came to power in Germany. During the twelve horrendous years of a totalitarian regime, instead of the Bible it was *Mein Kampf* which was placed on the altar, as it were; instead of the Cross, the black swastika was revered. Indeed, Hitler could be described as being an incarnation of the power of the Demon from the abyss. Physical power and material strength were the be all and end all; there was no space in the Third Reich for spiritual activity. Freedom of thought was 'outlawed', the consciousness of millions was channelled along prescribed lines; the individual ego was 'diluted', swamped by a decadent group soul amorphousness. The concept of the sanctity of human life was only applicable in Nazi Germany to the 'chosen', the master race, the Nordic race of the original Caucasian stock with no mixture of Semitic. Inevitably Hitler and his cohorts attempted racial extermination, especially of the Jews, of whom about 6,000,000 died in concentration camps, where atrocities were perpetrated against human beings on a vast scale. In the end, even the sanctity of life of men and women of the 'pure' Nordic race no longer prevailed, for shortly before the Russians took Berlin (2 May 1945) and a few days before Adolf Hitler committed suicide, he gave the order that Berlin had to be defended to the last drop of blood; Hitler decreed, in short, that the German people should commit themselves to a suicidal defence of a city in ruins...[10]

* * *

In the latter part of the twentieth century there are other phenomena which suggest the influence of Sorat. Here we shall look, very briefly, at two phenomena: the new disease Aids, spreading particularly since the 1980s; and the increasing use of drugs since the 1960s.

In regard to Aids the reader is referred to *Aids the Deadly Seed* by Klaus Dumke (1991). All we shall do here is paraphrase one or two passages from Dumke's seminal work.

In a person who is suffering from Aids the 'I' becomes incapable of distinguishing its own existence from alien matter. The power of immunological recognition of such matter dwindles away.

The immune system breaks down in the Aids sufferer and as a consequence the physical body is 'open' to various infections which ultimately lead to death. Dumke suggests that the experience of fading immunological resistance can be compared with walking in a marsh. The 'I' has lost the supporting ground under its feet, as it were.

In respect of the effect on the human being of the use of drugs, the reader is referred to a very recent work by the psychologist Ron Dunselman entitled *In Place of the Self: How Drugs Work* (1996), also to an essay by him in a book published in 1987 entitled *Rock Bottom: Beyond Drug Addiction.* Here again we shall confine ourselves to a very general statement. Summarizing Dunselman's observations regarding the various different drugs and their effects, we may say: A regular use of drugs 'mineralizes' the physical body, and exhausts the etheric body. 'The soul functions of thinking, feeling and willing become paralysed, and the ego loses its impulse for development and its sense of purpose because it is forced out. The human being dies in body and soul; spiritual development comes to a halt' (*Rock Bottom*, p. 54).

We are reminded here of a couple of statements Rudolf Steiner made in regard to the god Mammon and the Michael event of 1879: 'Already today a dark godhead has taken up rulership at the same time as Michael—the god Mammon. For occultism Mammon is not only the god of money; he is also the leader of all low, dark forces; and his army attacks not only the human soul but also the physical bodies of human beings to corrupt and destroy them.'[11]

Elsewhere, again referring to the battle between the hosts of Michael and those of the god Mammon, Steiner says: 'Mammon is, on the one hand, the god of hindrances, who places destructive, hindering things in the path of progress. On the other hand, one sees in this god Mammon the creator of quite definite forms which work disturbingly in human life just *in the sphere of infectious illnesses* [author's italics]. Certain infectious illnesses, unknown in earlier times, are brought about by the god Mammon' (GA 93a, 03/11/05). Aids is certainly an infectious illness unknown in earlier times.

It is, perhaps, symptomatic of our time that out of a

primary school class of 29 eleven-year-olds, 21 could answer their headmaster's question 'Do you know how and where to obtain drugs?' in the affirmative! The headmaster wondered whether the other eight were being quite honest!

* * *

Spiritual darkness manifestly exists in our time—materialism, civil wars, genocide, the abuse of human rights, Neo-Naziism and other political extremists, the 'knife culture', Aids, the drug culture, and so forth. But there are also very clear rays of light, spiritual light, penetrating this density of darkness. Above all there is the gradually all-permeating experience of a growing number of people of the Etheric Christ. Those who experience the Etheric Christ may be said to take the power of Christ into themselves. 'When this power has permeated the soul, it drives away the soul's darkness' (GA 118, 27/01/10). The human 'I', purified by the power of Christ, is immune to the ego-destructive forces emanating from Sorat.

In the closing lines of the Foundation Stone Meditation, Rudolf Steiner calls upon Christ to be with us so that thinking, feeling and willing can be active in good deeds:

> O Light Divine!
> O Sun of Christ!
> Warm Thou our hearts,
> Enlighten Thou our heads,
> That good may become
> What from our hearts we would found
> And from our heads direct
> With single vision.

* * *

The battle against the two-horned Beast is laid in the human heart, 'decisive indeed will be what human hearts do with this Michael-impulse in the world in the course of the twentieth century; when the first century after the end of Kali Yuga [i.e. 1899] has elapsed, humanity will either stand at the grave of all civilization—or at the beginning of that Age when in the souls of human beings who in their hearts ally intelligence with spirituality, Michael's battle will be fought out to victory' (GA 240, 19/07/24).

We need not, it would seem, hold too dogmatically to the year 1998 mentioned by Rudolf Steiner as being a point in time at which Sorat is particularly powerful in his assaults on struggling humanity. Speaking about quite a different date in quite a different context—3101 BC—Rudolf Steiner observes: 'This date is not to be taken as an absolute but as an approximate date' (GA 118, 10/05/10). Elsewhere, referring to the quoted date AD 333 (see GA 182, 16/10/18 and GA 184, 13/10/18), Steiner states quite clearly: 'It does not matter whether something occurs a few decades earlier or later. In outer physical reality, which takes on the form of the "great illusion", things are sometimes misplaced' (GA 171, 17/09/16). Ahriman—we could also say here the ahrimanic-soratic impulse—does everything in his power to hinder us from inwardly contemplating, inwardly 'digesting', happenings in the world. His tendency is to rush us through events, to give us no time for conscious spiritual enlightenment as to their real meaning. Events in Russia and Germany in the 1930s and 1940s could, perhaps, be regarded as preempting to a major extent the year 1998. We could, perhaps, say that mankind has been experiencing 1998 over a period of many decades. These decades of darkness also reveal shafts of light not seen and experienced in earlier times. These 'shafts of light' may be experienced by no more than a small group of people, but, as we have heard Steiner expound already (see p. 220), such a small group will have the power to 'lay the first foundation of the great bond of brotherhood in the Sixth Age'.

It is as though in spite of, or perhaps because of, the premature breaking-in of the soratic impulse a space has been created in which men and women of good will, warmth of heart and clarity of thought can work towards the goal of being true fighters in the spirit of Michael.

Is it not such men and women who have heeded the words Christopher Fry has Meadows speak in *A Sleep of Prisoners*?

The human heart can go to the lengths of God.
Dark and cold we may be, but this
Is no winter now. The frozen misery
Of centuries breaks, cracks, begins to move;
The thunder is the thunder of the floes,
The thaw, the flood, the upstart Spring.
Thank God our time is now when wrong
Comes up to face us everywhere,
Never to leave us till we take
The longest stride of soul men ever took.
Affairs are now soul size.
The enterprise
Is exploration into God.
Where are you making for? It takes
So many thousand years to wake,
But will you wake for pity's sake.

17. Ahriman's Purpose in Incarnating

Rudolf Steiner speaks with great earnestness about the future of humankind. We have already seen, in Chapter 5, that we are approaching the time when the one great adversary of Christ, Ahriman, will incarnate on earth. In one of his lectures on the influences of Lucifer and Ahriman, Steiner points to the fact that we either receive spiritual knowledge consciously or 'consume' the spirit unconsciously and thereby deliver it into the 'hands' of Lucifer. There is much to suggest that many, not all, of the so-called New Age groups of people are afloat in this stream of 'spirit-and-soul-consumption'. It is a stream strongly sponsored by Ahriman because, by means of it, he can lull human beings into greater and greater spiritual drowsiness, so that when he incarnates he will be able to ensnare them in his web of extremely cunning intellectuality. This he will certainly be able to do if we do not confront him consciously.

There are many people today who foster a spiritual life, but it is purely intellectual with little, or no, connection with the spiritual world. Since the fifteenth century this purely intellectual life has become increasingly widespread. At first it took effect mainly in science, but today it has taken hold of the human mind in virtually every sphere of life—religious, social, artistic.

In answer to the question 'What is the essential characteristic of this intellectual life?' Steiner replies: 'This intellectual life has very little to do with the true interests of men and women!' He then asks us to face a question which is as pertinent today as it was at the beginning of the twentieth century. 'I ask you: how many teachers do you not see today, passing in and out of higher and lower educational institutions *without bringing any inner enthusiasm to their science but pursuing it merely as a means of livelihood*? [author's italics]. In such cases the interest of the soul is not directly linked with what is being done...Everything that is developing as intellectual life without being suffused by warmth of soul, without being quickened by enthusiasm, directly furthers the incarnation of Ahriman' (GA 193, 04/11/ 19).

Let us now consider some aspects of his incarnation.

In the West, in North America, perhaps even as early as the twenty-first century, a human being will be born into whom Ahriman, at the right moment, will incarnate. In short, Steiner does not suggest that a woman will give birth to this spiritual being. As soon as Ahriman incarnates, we learn from Steiner, he will found a great occult school. In this school magic arts of the greatest grandeur will be practised, and what otherwise can be acquired only by strenuous effort will be poured out over humanity (GA 191, 15/11/19). He can instil supersensible knowledge into his pupils. They will be able to absorb it without the necessity of undertaking, in full consciousness, the transformation of their thinking. It is, and will continue to be, Ahriman's aim to lead humankind to an ever-intensifying form of brain-bound, earth-bound, materialistic thinking.

Steiner warns us not to imagine that Ahriman will appear as a kind of trickster.

No, indeed! Lovers of ease who refuse to have anything to do with spiritual science would fall prey to his magic, for by means of these stupendous magic arts he would be able to make great numbers of human beings into seers—but in such a way that the clairvoyance of each individual would be strictly differentiated. What one person would see, a second and a third would not see. Confusion would prevail and in spite of being receptive to clairvoyant wisdom, people would inevitably fall into strife on account of the sheer diversity of their visions. [GA 191, 15/11/19]

For some decades now the number of people manifesting clairvoyant faculties has been on the increase in a natural way. These faculties can open the way to experiences of the Etheric Christ. However, they can also be taken advantage of by Ahriman. The only forces which can hold Ahriman in check have been given to us, to the whole of humankind, by the spiritual world through the unique spiritual event of the Mystery of Golgotha.

We may say that since the mid-1930s we have been standing in the early dawn of a new consciousness.[1] If this new consciousness were able to develop freely and unhindered, then a new, more spiritual culture could come to fruition in a not too distant future. In the final lecture of a series with the overall title of *The New Spirituality and the Christ Experience of the Twentieth Century*, Rudolf Steiner speaks in some detail of this new consciousness. *Inter alia*, he mentions that through this new consciousness human beings are able to recognize that they are not merely earth-beings but also cosmic, super-earthly beings. We may ask ourselves here: Who can decipher for us our nature as cosmic beings? Everything that we can gain in the way of knowledge from the natural sciences accounts for us only as earth-beings and leaves the true being of man as an unsolved riddle. It is Christ alone who can give an answer to this riddle. 'Just as the physical Christ appeared at the time of the Mystery of Golgotha so the spiritual Christ will appear to humanity.' Steiner said this about 15 years before the onset of the appearance of the Etheric Christ. 'He alone can give the answer because He is not in some indefinite place but must be recognized as a Being from beyond the earth who has united Himself with earthly humanity. People will have to understand that the question of cosmic man can be answered only if He who unites Himself with the earth from out of the cosmos comes to their aid' (GA 200, 31/10/20).

The riddle of being an earth-being *and*, with far greater reality, a cosmic being brings with it an experience of being 'weighed down'. As just stated, it is Christ alone who can answer the riddle and thus 'lift off' the 'weight'.[2]

There are, of course, two alternative ways by which the experience of being 'weighed down' can be overcome. As free human beings we can go the way of Lucifer and 'float' in the enjoyment of cosmic experiences, or we can follow Ahriman and experience ourselves to the full in our earthly human nature. Both alternatives lead to the loss of our true being. But the forces of attraction to the physical earth, particularly in the West, will be far more powerful than those of Lucifer the nearer we approach the incarnation of Ahriman. Already now Ahriman is making every effort to render the Second Coming of Christ in the etheric ineffective. Such efforts will be far more powerful once he has found incarnation in an earthly body. Ahriman sees far more clearly than we what tremendous possibilities the appearance of Christ in the etheric can have for the spiritualization of human thinking, feeling and willing. Ever since the fifteenth and sixteenth centuries he has striven to prevent the breakthrough of humanity to the spirit under the guidance of Christ in the etheric world, in whose service Michael stands. Ahriman seeks to achieve this by the conservation of that kind of thinking which cuts human beings off from the spirit. He seeks, in short, to bring about a 'hardening' of all human soul faculties, particularly that of thinking. Were he to be successful materialism would be 'solidified' on earth.

Now it is Ahriman's aim to counteract in every possible way the spiritualization of human thinking. He does everything to conserve the materialistic knowledge and thinking of today, so why, we could ask, does he, when he incarnates, make men and women clairvoyant.

It is clear that Ahriman, a powerful spiritual being, has a clear insight into everything that is in process of becoming in the evolutionary process through which humankind is, or should be, progressing. He knows, therefore, that clairvoyance is appearing in human beings as a natural development in the course of evolution. He sees that clairvoyant capacities are manifesting themselves more and more widely and strongly. With this the great Calculator has to reckon. A time is coming, Steiner states, when everything will pass over into the spiritual. Ahriman's aim is to influence this process. He would do this most efficiently by enabling people to become clairvoyant without having to make any effort to transform themselves. In so doing he would divert them from experiencing the appearance of the Etheric Christ. He was successful in achieving his aim to a large degree during the years

1933–45 (see Chapter 12). What form would the ahrimanic clairvoyance take? If human beings were to remain as they are, if, in short, they did not have to transform, spiritualize, their present intellectual thinking, nor their life of feeling, nor the life of instincts, then Ahriman could seize, in particular, all the unconscious capacities, the life of instincts and urges. He could then transform them into clairvoyant imaginations. Human beings would then experience everything in their life of instincts as imaginations. Their world of instincts presents itself to them as imaginations, as an imaginative world.

Now since each human being has different instincts and urges, each one lives within his or her own encapsulated being. What is experienced is the individual, his or her life of instincts, not the true spiritual world. It is true that we should become conscious of our instincts and urges—which are of the nature of will—but they need to be 'seen', experienced, with clear, objective spiritual thoughts, otherwise they rise up like a cloying fog and can readily overwhelm attempts at conscious spiritual striving.

'Our concern,' Steiner says, 'is that the wisdom of the future—a clairvoyant wisdom—shall be rescued from the clutches of Ahriman. [...] there is only *one* book of wisdom, not two kinds of wisdom. The issue is whether this wisdom is in the hands of Ahriman or Christ. It cannot come into the hands of Christ unless we fight for it. And we can only fight for it by telling ourselves that *by our own efforts* we must assimilate the content of spiritual science before the time of Ahriman's appearance on earth. That,' Steiner continues, 'is the cosmic task of spiritual science.' (Ibid.)

Without such efforts on our part the result would be the establishment of Ahriman's kingdom on earth and the abolition of everything achieved by human culture.

In another lecture on the influences of Lucifer and Ahriman, Steiner speaks of the incarnation of Lucifer in the East at the beginning of the third millennium BC.[3] Humanity, according to Steiner, was completely unconscious of Lucifer's incarnation. Only in the Mysteries of the East was something known of Lucifer's existence in a human being on earth. We may also say here that the incarnation of Christ passed by with little awareness on the part of humanity (GA 193, 04/11/19). Such unawareness must not under any circumstances take place in regard to Ahriman's incarnation, for we are now living in the time of the consciousness soul, the spiritual soul. Nothing of significance for humankind should take place in our time without our being as conscious as possible of its activity—and the meaning of that activity.

It is clear that Ahriman is not—and will not be—at pains to make us particularly spiritual 'but rather to *kill in us the consciousness of our own spirituality*' (GA 182, 09/10/18).[4]

To 'kill', to darken in us, the consciousness that we are an image of the Godhead is what Ahriman aims to achieve by subtle—and less subtle—scientific means in our age of the conscious soul (spiritual soul). He is the teacher *par excellence* of materialistic Darwinism (ibid.).

Ahriman would attain his various goals—many of which we have not touched upon here—if he could pursue them unhindered. How much he will attain in reality will depend upon those men and women who have consciously and full-heartedly placed themselves at the service of Michael, through whom the experience of the Etheric Christ becomes a reality.

One of our missions during the present phase of civilization (this cannot be repeated and emphasized too often) 'will be to live towards the incarnation of Ahriman with such alert consciousness that this incarnation can actually serve to promote a higher, spiritual development' (GA 193, 04/11/19).

How can this be understood?

Earlier we heard Steiner speak of the wisdom of the future, of the *one* book of wisdom. It is imperative that this new wisdom is in the 'hands' of Christ and not of Ahriman. As we have seen already it can only come into Christ's 'hands' if, having recognized and absorbed the Michaelic spirit, human beings fight for it.

Now just as during the pre-Christian times in which Lucifer worked, in which he transmitted thinking to humankind, a constant battle had to be fought by the ancient initiates to prevent Lucifer enticing mankind away from the earth (to achieve this they had to wrest from Lucifer that which has become human reason, human intellect), so today a battle must be fought against Ahriman. He aims to reveal to humanity the kind of future he would like to have, the kind of future which human beings can simply take over from him without any effort. But in the present consciousness soul (spiritual soul) stage of the spiritual development of mankind (this is particularly relevant to the West), nothing of real spiritual value can be gained without conscious effort. Ahriman, now and in the future, is the catalyst, as it were, which acts, can act, as a spur to prevent us failing to attain the wisdom of the future. Indeed, we could say that we can only attain this wisdom in battle with Ahriman.

It is especially in the West that the hardest battles will be fought. It is there Ahriman is strongest. It is there he will incarnate. Bearing this in mind, it is extremely interesting to hear Rudolf Steiner speak of a 'hidden' anthroposophy in America that manifests, expresses, itself in a natural way. This natural tendency, however, becomes wooden through materialism.

> We in Europe build [*bilden*] anthroposophy out of the spirit. Over there they build something which is somewhat like a wooden doll of anthroposophy—a caricature of anthroposophy. Everything becomes materialistic.
>
> But for those who are not fanatics, American culture has something which is similar to what anthroposophical knowledge is in Europe, only everything is wooden. It is not yet alive. In Europe we can make it alive from out of the spirit; over there they bring it up out of the instincts. [GA 349, 03/03/23][5]

Steiner then goes on to say:

> Materialism in America is growing like weeds [*grassiert*], but is actually on the way to the spirit, whereas if someone in Europe becomes a materialist, then he or she dies as a human being. Actually all children are materialists at first, but then they grow out of it into something that is not materialism. Thus the crass

American materialism will [eventually] grow into something spiritual. [Ibid.]

*   *   *

In the light of this last statement by Steiner it is illuminating to consider, briefly, an expression of the 'new' spirituality emanating from North America at the end of the twentieth century. James Redfield, an American, is the author of *The Celestine Prophecy** (reprinted in Great Britain alone 22 times during the short period of 1994–97) and *The Tenth Insight, Holding the Vision*† (reprinted five times in this country since its first edition in 1996). Both novels are concerned to describe the process involved in becoming conscious of a higher, a spiritual reality, behind a purely empirically perceived reality—the physical world.

In his introductory note to *The Tenth Insight* Redfield describes it as an adventure parable, 'an attempt to illustrate the ongoing spiritual transformation that is occurring in our time'. Indeed, *The Tenth Insight* shows some very clear spiritual understanding. The basic motif running through the novel is the idea of a pre-life vision. On one occasion, Wil, the teacher figure whom we first meet in *The Celestine Prophecy* (his role is similar to that of Benedictus in Rudolf Steiner's Mystery Plays), explains the significance of the pre-life vision: 'Before we are born, each one of us experiences a vision of what our life can be, complete with reflections on our parents and on our tendencies to engage in particular control dramas, even how we might work through these dramas with these parents and go on to be prepared for what we want to accomplish.' However, there is no question here of pre-ordination for, in relation to life on earth, pre-life vision is more ideal than what actually happens. Wil comments here:

> The vision apparently is an ideal guide for what our highest self intends to happen in life, the best-case scenario, so to speak, if all of us were following our intuitions perfectly. What actually occurs is an approximation of this vision, the best everyone can

*Bantam Books, London 1994.
†Bantam Books, London 1996.

do under the actual circumstances... When we have an intuition, a mental image, of a possible future, we're actually getting flashes of memory of our Birth Vision, what we wanted to be doing with our lives at that particular point on our journey. It may not be exact, because people have free will, but when something happens that is close to our original vision, we feel inspired because we recognize that we are on a path of destiny that we intended all along.

The idea of reincarnation—lacking in the earlier book—is self-evident here, and is made clear on a number of occasions. For instance, in an after-death retrospective tableau we become aware of what our goal in the earth-life just past actually was. The pain we experience when we are thus confronted with all that we have neglected to do gives rise in us the decision to reincarnate in order to do better next time.

There are many other aspects of Redfield's narrations that show similarities with Steiner's spiritual science, including, to mention a few: a clear understanding of the evolution of consciousness; the central significance of the incarnation of Christ; the role of the established Church vis-à-vis individual striving towards experiences of the activity and reality of the Christ within.

It is relevant to mention that Redfield himself does not wish to be regarded as a guru. He has no intention to exert any kind of power over others. In the Preface to his second book, *The Celestine Prophecy: An Experiential Guide,** co-authored with Carol Adrienne,[6] he writes: 'The Paradigm shift that is occurring in our time is best thought of as a new common sense... I firmly believe that this level of experience is humanity's destiny, but it is not real for any of us until we discover it individually and map it out on our own terms... We [i.e. J.R. and C.A.] could in essence elaborate on the ideas set forth in *The Celestine Prophecy* ... by providing more information, but encouraging the reader to investigate these elaborations in self-directed ways.'

Redfield does not suggest that those who read and study

*Bantam Books, London 1995.

his works should practise exercises which are incomprehensible to 'new common sense'. As a fundamental exercise in meditation, for instance, he suggests immersing oneself in the life of nature around one. Particularly interesting are his recommendations to contemplate the history of one's life and to become conscious of nodal events and characteristic tendencies to think, feel and act in this or that way. Much of what he recommends can also be found in anthroposophically orientated Biography Work.

One of the most significant methods of 'awakening' to a higher level of consciousness consists for Redfield in the spiritual perception of those with whom one comes into contact. In *The Tenth Insight* he describes how people can be helped to broaden and extend their consciousness by deepening their experience of and feeling for the facial characteristics of those before them so as to be able to perceive in them the perceptible expression of the real, the higher, Self: 'If we look closely at another's face, we can cut through any facades, or ego defences, that may be present, and find the individual's authentic expression, his or her *real* self... When we focus in love, love energy is sent to this higher-self aspect of the person, and the person will seem to change before our eyes as his or her greater capabilities shift into place.' Such an exercise—and others Redfield describes—bring to mind some of Steiner's indications for our spiritual development.

Unlike many other esoteric streams Redfield's 'insights' do not appeal to egotism or our aspirations for personal, selfish happiness. Nor is there any suggestion that the ego should be overcome. On the contrary, enhancement, not abrogation of the individuality is essential. As with Steiner, Redfield makes it quite plain that the task of humankind can only be consummated by individuals on the earth.

Towards the end of *The Tenth Insight* Wil says: 'We are all souls in growth; we all have an original intention that is positive... Our responsibility is to hold that idea for everyone we meet. That's the true Interpersonal Ethic; that's how we uplift, that's the contagion of the new awareness that is encircling the planet. We either fear that human culture is falling apart, or we can *hold the Vision* that we are *awaken-ing.*'[7]

However, in his books so far unclarities remain in Red-field's presentation of the spiritual world. On the one hand we find allusions to, for instance, undefined spiritual 'ener-gies', on the other hand, he writes in concrete terms about human souls in the spiritual world. However, *The Tenth Insight* ends with Wil saying: 'I think we are supposed to understand the Angels next.' Redfield is currently engaged in writing a book on the theme of Angels, so perhaps he will speak with greater clarity in regard to spiritual beings in his new work.

Nevertheless, from a spiritual–scientific viewpoint there are a few difficulties regarding his spiritual world view. For instance, in his first book, *The Celestine Prophecy*, he has adopted a seemingly materialistic interpretation of the non-sense-perceptible world. Spiritual power is rendered by the word 'energy' and spiritual forces represented by 'vibrations'. He also appears to advocate the materialistic models of evolution in the world of nature. Finally, Redfield recognizes the spiritual greatness of Christ, but nowhere (as yet) does he say anything about the divine Cosmic Being whose sacrifice gave humankind the possibility of a spiritual awakening.

Nevertheless, it is clear that Redfield is representative of those who, mindful of 'western' spirituality, are part of and active in a positive advance in the evolution of conscious-ness.[9]

* * *

There is a perceptible hunger in the human soul, manifesting itself in many different ways, particularly in the West, to receive the spiritual world. We are standing at the Threshold. Rudolf Steiner emphasizes time and again that the con-sequences of crossing this Threshold are dire—catastrophic, in fact—if the soul is not rightly prepared before doing so.

In the cycle of lectures *The Occult Movement in the Nineteenth Century* (GA 254), Steiner speaks of two dangers we all meet, to a greater or lesser degree, when we reach this Threshold. One of these dangers is inherent in any approach we make towards the Threshold out of a materialistic conception of the world. Such an approach has two consequences. On the one hand, one's life of thought is taken over by ahrimanic powers, and, on the other hand, this analytical, cold, heartless thinking is accompanied by an overwhelming, uncontrolled sensuality and sexuality.

The second danger with which we are confronted if we approach the Threshold into the spiritual world without being properly prepared—as outlined, for instance, by Rudolf Steiner in *Knowledge of the Higher Worlds* (GA 10); *Stages of Higher Knowledge* (GA 12); and *The Threshold of the Spiritual World* (GA 17)—manifests itself in our life of will. There is today, among an increasing number of people, particularly among the young, a fervent wish to believe in the reality of a spiritual world. However, without adequate inner preparation such fervour can but lead to the 'arms' of Lucifer, to feelings of ecstasy and 'floating' mystical experiences. Here the human soul is exposed to self-delusion and surrender to an illusory spiritual world.

In an article entitled 'Some Thoughts on Waco',[10] Antoinette Reynolds writes:

> A culture steeped in materialism, in which human beings are born who have a genuine need for a spiritual dimension to their lives, is an excellent breeding ground for religious cults. No wonder there are so many of them. In this deeply materialistic society morality is by and large either not nurtured at all or is merely being paid lip service to, with laws and conventional behaviour patterns. Thus human beings are not inwardly armed for the combat with these negative spiritual powers and the false messiahs are created, together with their gullible followers.

One such false messiah was the leader of the Branch Davidian sect David Koresh in Waco, Texas. It seems clear that both he and his followers in the fortified compound—stormed by the FBI on 19 April 1993, with tragic consequences—were exposed to both dangers just mentioned.

To go into further detail here is unnecessary. What may be added, however, is that the activities of the David Koreshs of this world, proclaiming themselves to be in possession of messianic powers and exerting dictatorial power, are inspired by adversary forces.

In contrast, James Redfield is deeply concerned to help his fellow human beings to find a safe path to clear and fully conscious experiences of spiritual reality. He does not set himself up as a guru, but leaves those who heed his 'insights' free in their thinking and will.

18.   Thinking and Michael's Activity

We need to be clear about the fact that when our thinking merely reflects external events and processes we are developing thoughts which are purely ahrimanic. This does not mean that they are necessarily wrong or incorrect, but they are nevertheless ahrimanic. As Rudolf Steiner stresses time and again, the ahrimanic element must of necessity exist. The whole content of natural science as it is pursued today is ahrimanic, and will only lose its ahrimanic nature when it becomes imbued with life. This will take place when our thinking ceases to do no more than mirror external phenomena in a mechanical way. Thinking must become creative, it must become saturated with spiritual content; it must become creative when we are confronted with life-situations, life-processes. To rely solely on the ahrimanic element is to drive life out, to deal with nothing other than a corpse. In his *Faust*, Goethe gives us this picture:

> He who would study organic existence
> First drives out the soul with rigid persistence;
> Then the parts in his hand he may hold and class
> But the spiritual link is lost, alas! [Tr. Bayard Taylor]

> (*Wer will was Lebendiges erkennen und beschreiben,*
> *Sucht erst den Geist heraus zu treiben,*
> *Dann hat er die Teile in seiner Hand,*
> *Fehlt leider! nur das geistige Band*)

When ahrimanic forces are active in spheres where they do not legitimately belong they become destructive. 'Creative thinking is only attained when we are inspired—even unconsciously—from the spiritual world' (GA 176, 31/07/17).

* * *

In his basic book *Knowledge of the Higher Worlds. How is it achieved?* Steiner makes it clear that if we seek to deepen our knowledge of life, to go beyond the kind of thinking which merely reflects external events and processes, we have to recognize and 'obey'—out of our own free will—the golden rule of genuine spiritual science: 'For every *one* step forward that you take in seeking knowledge of spiritual scientific truths, take *three* steps forward in the improvement of your character' (GA 10).[1] Elsewhere we learn from Steiner: 'Interest in the spiritual world must take hold of us if morality is to develop to the same extent as intellectuality has done.' However, such a development is by no means easy. Indeed, it can prove 'uncomfortable'.

> There are many reasons why this is highly uncomfortable for modern men and women. For example, when people embark upon developing their thinking, in ways I have often described, their thinking becomes capable of functioning in the spiritual world. This leads them of necessity to develop something else which has declined during our materialistic age, namely, an inner feeling of responsibility. [GA 176, 25/09/17]

We are called upon to feel responsible not only towards our fellow human beings but also towards concepts and ideas. Such a sense of responsibility does not come into being if one lives exclusively in materialistic concepts and ideas (cf. GA 127, 06/03/11, and GA 4).

*   *   *

The generally held ideal of what thinking should be today is that it should be 'objective'. In short, it should be, as Steiner expresses it, 'a motionless reflection of the outer world'. Such thinking contains 'no force; no impulse of feeling and of will arise from it' (GA 307, 08/08/23). This kind of thinking is 'dead'. Dead thinking is entirely closed to the Michael-Christ impulse. It is a form of thinking which is devoid of the creative power of the 'I'.

The fundamental idea which runs through Rudolf Steiner's book *The Philosophy of Freedom* (GA 4) is expressed by him on several occasions. For instance, in a lecture to young people he says:

In what I have named Anthroposophy, in fact in the Foreword to my *Philosophy of Freedom*, you will meet with something which you will not be able to comprehend if you only give yourself up to that passive thinking so specially loved today, to that popular godforsaken thinking of even a previous incarnation. You will only understand if you develop in freedom the inner impulse to bring activity into your thinking. You will never get on with spiritual science if that spark, that lightning, through which activity in thinking is awakened does not flash up. Through this activity we must reconquer the divine nature of thinking. [GA 217, 10/10/22]

Elsewhere Steiner advises us: 'The "I" must stream into the dead thoughts and bring them to life... This bringing to life of our dead thoughts is the aim of everything I have presented in my book *Knowledge of the Higher Worlds* [GA 10, and see Appendix One]. It is intended to help us let our will burst forth into our soul life so that we can wake up' (GA 221, 03/02/23).

That which we carry within us as dead thought-pictures was something quite different in antiquity. In those times thoughts 'were not shadowy as they are today, nor were they merely living; they were full of soul and spirit. But this means that human beings did not only *think* their thoughts; they had as an experience the perception of concrete spiritual beings' (GA 26, 12/10/24).

The gradual separation of the material–earthly from the spiritual during the course of earth-evolution brought with it a gradually increasing loss of an experience of the spiritual world.

In the evolution of humankind consciousness descends on the ladder of unfolding thought. There was the earliest stage in consciousness when human beings experienced the thoughts in the ego—experienced them as real beings, imbued with spirit, soul and life. At a second stage human beings experienced the thoughts in the astral body; henceforth they appeared only as the images of spirit-beings—images, however, still imbued with soul and life. At a third stage human beings experienced the thoughts in the etheric body; here they manifest only an inner stirring, like an echo of the quality of soul. At the fourth, which is the present stage, human beings experience the thoughts in the physical body, where they appear as the dead shadows of the spiritual. [Ibid.]

The process by means of which we become conscious of dead thought-pictures is described by Steiner: 'If we call up before our mind's eye the essential feature of everyday thinking we can say: It rests on our thinking in the etheric body, and on what is thus thought, sinking into the nervous system of the brain; there it makes impressions which do not, however, go very deep but rebound. In this way the thinking is reflected and thus enters our consciousness' (GA 161, 01/05/15). In *Anthroposophical Leading Thoughts* we find Rudolf Steiner saying: 'The thoughts of the human being have their true seat in the etheric body. There, however, they are forces of real life and being. They imprint themselves upon the physical body, and as such "imprinted thoughts" they have the shadowy character in which the everyday consciousness knows them' (GA 26, 05/10/24).

Michael's mission is to imbue human etheric bodies with those forces through which the thought-shadows may again acquire *life*. 'Then the souls and spirits in the supersensible worlds will incline themselves towards the enlivened thoughts, and the liberated human being will be able to live with them' (GA 26, 12/10/24).

The resurrection of thoughts from the 'shadowy character' prevailing today—thoughts which are only able to grasp the sense-perceptible—is brought about by the activity of the awakened ego. The will, 'bursting forth' into the sphere of 'dead' thoughts, raises them to a new level of life. The process, according to Rudolf Steiner, 'consists in our removing our thinking—it is no longer thinking, only the activity of thinking—from the etheric body to the astral body, thus transferring to the more volatile etheric body the task of retaining the traces which formerly the physical body had assumed. This is the essential feature of the first stage in initiation' (GA 161, 01/05/15).

As the process of initiation continues a stage is reached at which spiritual beings, in their various forms, are inwardly experienced. As soon as we develop the thinking that is free of the physical body, of the physical brain, 'every thought becomes like a husk, and into this husk there slips an elemental being.'

> The thought is no longer under our restrictive control. We let it go out, like a feeler, into the world, and into it slips an elemental being. Our thoughts are thus filled out, as it were, by elemental beings... So that it may be said: When we 'send out' the soul-spiritual part of our head into the spiritual world (we have it outside only because we are within the physical head), when in this way we project it into the spiritual world, we no longer experience thoughts such as we do in the physical world, for it is the life of being that we experience. [GA 161, 27/03/15]

Rudolf Steiner continues: 'It is like this, in reality, right up to the highest of the Hierarchies. If we wish to experience Angels, Archangels, Archai (Spirits of Personality), this has to be in such a way that we project our thoughts, live in the spiritual beings, just as I have described... There is no need to be afraid of having the thoughts of the Hierarchies instead of those which are earth-bound' (ibid.).

Now Rudolf Steiner makes it quite clear that human beings cannot attain the experience of spiritual beings as just outlined without the presence of Michael's activity. A lecture he gave in Dornach in 1922 can help us understand why Michael's active presence is necessary. The lecture, published in *Man and the World of the Stars*, is entitled 'Spiritualization of the Knowledge of Space. The Mission of Michael' (GA 219, 17/12/22), and here Rudolf Steiner speaks in some detail of the difference between beings in the spiritual world and human beings on earth in relation to the experience of time and space.

The conception of space is an entirely human conception. The spiritual beings with whom human beings live together between death and a new birth have a vivid conception of time, but no conception of space. Human beings enter into space first when they descend from the spiritual world into physical incarnation on the earth. Since the fifteenth and sixteenth centuries,[2] the conception of space has become engrained in the human being in ever-increasing measure. It has been since that time that human beings have emancipated their thoughts from the divine world. Hence human thinking has become less and less intelligible to the Gods, to beings in the spiritual world.

With all this in mind, let us turn our attention now to that event which took place in the last third of the nineteenth century, namely, the beginning of the Rulership of Michael.

What, we could ask, does it actually mean in the whole cosmic setting that Michael is now the Spirit of the Age. 'It means,' answers Steiner, 'that of all the beings who spiritually guide humanity, Michael is the spirit who is the first to draw near to what human beings here on earth are doing as the result of the emancipation of knowledge since the first third of the fifteenth century' (GA 219, 17/12/22). Here we need to remind ourselves that since the eighth or ninth century the Cosmic Intelligence has passed from Michael into the 'hands' of human beings. However, this does not mean that Michael is inactive, for, in contrast to his predecessor, Gabriel, who is a being orientated more to the passive qualities of human beings, Michael is the being who 'as it were, pulses through our breath, our veins, our nerves, to the end that we may actively develop all that belongs to our full humanity in connection with the cosmos' (ibid.). Michael challenges us to be active in our very thoughts. He leaves us free, but he 'can at least instil his activity into such thoughts of human beings as can be impulses for their free deeds. Michael can work into free, pure thinking which must be the true impulse for the individual will of the human being acting in freedom in the new age. And with the human deeds which spring from the impulse of love, Michael has his own particular relationship' (ibid.).

Michael, then, can form a bridge, as it were, between mankind on earth and the spiritual world. Hence, Rudolf Steiner states, he is the messenger whom 'the Gods have sent down so that he may receive what is now being led over from knowledge emancipated from the spirit into spiritual knowledge' (ibid.). It is the task of spiritual science, of anthroposophy, to spiritualize spatial, earth-thinking, and to lift it again into the supersensible.

> This spiritual science works from below upwards to grasp the hands of Michael stretching down from above. It is then that the bridge can be created between human beings and the Gods. Michael has become the Regent of this Age because he is to receive what the Gods wish to receive from what human beings can add to the time concept through the space concept—for this augments the knowledge possessed by the Gods. [Ibid.]

Michael directs his gaze down towards the earth and humanity. He is able, by entering into connection with what human beings develop in pure thought and objectify in pure will, to take cognizance of what human beings acquire as the fruit of thinking in terms of space, and to carry it up into the spiritual worlds to the Gods.

If human beings do no more than develop space knowledge and fail to spiritualize it then Michael can do no other than bring to the Gods the message that mankind desires to separate itself from the spiritual world. If, however, efforts are made by human beings to bring time and the supersensible again into the spatial, if they are not content to remain immersed in materialism (only accepting that as real which has material, spatial form), then they 'can be regarded as having linked their lives directly to the life of the Gods' (ibid.).

Thinking which is solely concerned with the spatial world has become despiritualized. 'In the present age very much is at stake; it is a matter of whether we shall or shall not sow the seed for true communion in the future with the divine-spiritual world' (ibid.).

The direction towards which we apply our thinking is clearly of paramount importance. Do we direct it exclusively towards earthly things, or do we also, in freedom, dedicate our efforts towards the spiritual? If the former is the case then we fail to hold the Dragon, Ahriman, under our feet.

On one occasion Rudolf Steiner speaks specifically about the relationship of mankind to the Spirits of Personality, the Archai. He does not actually mention Michael in this particular lecture, but what he says can serve to enhance our understanding of our relationship to this spiritual being, for since 1897 Michael has advanced from the Hierarchy of the Archangels to that of the Archai or Time Spirits (cf. GA 121, 12/06/10).

After mentioning the fact that human beings go through the process of evolution during their lives on earth, Rudolf Steiner states:

> The individual Spirits of Personality look down upon us, asking continually: Will you give us something, too, that we can use for our development? The more human beings develop their thought content, their treasure of thought, the more they try to refine their aesthetic judgement and carry out their duty beyond the requirements of karma, the more nourishment there is for the Spirits of Personality; the more substantial these Spirits of Personality become. [GA 107, 17/06/09]

Rudolf Steiner also makes it clear that human beings have to make an active contribution towards Michael's regency (cf. GA 218, 19/11/22). We need to progress in our spiritual development to the point where we have the ideal:

> When I think, I do not do so for my own satisfaction but in order to create nourishment for the Spirits of Personality. I lay upon the altar of the Spirits of Personality my highest and most beautiful thoughts, and what I feel is not prompted by egoism. I feel it because it is to be nourishment for the Spirits of Personality; and what I can practise in the way of virtue, I do not practise for the sake of gaining influence for myself but in order to bring it as a sacrifice to provide food for the Spirits of Personality. [GA 107, 17/06/09]

* * *

Michael's sword is the image of creative will, its blade of light subduing the Dragon on earth. If human beings want to be free and conquer, or, we could say, transmute, the death-bringing Spirits of Darkness, they must forge the sword of the free, self-reliant will in full, light-filled consciousness.

Michael accepts the spiritual thoughts human beings offer him. It is, indeed, the task of Michael 'to lead human beings back again, *on paths of will* [author's italics], whence they came down, when with their earthly consciousness they descended on the paths of thought from the living experience of the supersensible to the experience of the world of sense' (GA 26, 12/10/24).

Rudolf Steiner frequently reminds us that there are two ways to form thoughts. One is the dismembering, differentiating way, that is, the way of Ahriman. It is the way of forming thoughts which William Wordsworth had in mind when he wrote:

> Our meddling intellect
> Mis-shapes the beauteous form of things
> We murder to dissect

This is the prevailing scientific method and is perfectly justified when dealing with the inorganic world. 'This manner of thinking is a mask used with particular astuteness by the spirits who ... would like to tear us apart' (GA 187, 01/01/19).

The second way of thinking is a totally different kind of mental process. It is a formative (*gestaltende*) way of thinking—a Goethean way of thinking (cf. GA 1). It has quite a definite quality; it does not ignore the minutiae but is, above all else, concerned with processes, with life. When we dissect with our thinking we are thinking in just the same way as spirits of the ahrimanic world think and we thus make it possible for them to enter our souls. If, on the other hand, we exercise creative, formative thinking, in which both the power of will and the warmth of heart are engaged, then we place ourselves at the service of Michael, the Countenance of Christ. Indeed, Rudolf Steiner states quite clearly that 'the Christ-impulse stands in the direct line of formative thinking' (ibid.). It stands in the direct line of the creative Logos. Ahriman can do no harm to those who exercise the formative, creative—we could also say the spiritual-scientific—mode of thinking. Steiner encapsulates this realization in the following words: 'Only the spiritual beings connected with the normal evolution of mankind can work creatively, sculpturally, as a human being works within himself or herself with formative thinking. This is the amazing thing about it. You can never go astray on a wrong path if through spiritual science you engage in formative thinking' (ibid.).

In his Letter of 23 November 1924 to the members of the Anthroposophical Society ('The World-Thoughts in the Working of Michael and in the Working of Ahriman'), Steiner give us a very clear picture of the contrast between Michael's and Ahriman's administration of the intellect. A cold and frosty, heartless, cynical, soulless cosmic impulse is the power of the intellect as it issues from Ahriman. Those who are in the clutches of this impulse manifest chains of reasoning which, in merciless and heartless fashion, are devoid of any inward connection of heart and soul with what is being thought, said and done.[3] Michael, on the other hand, wields the intellectual force in such a way that it shows itself to be capable of being made an expression of the heart and soul as well as of the hand and mind. Nothing of deadly frost or soullessness is conveyed by Michael into the reasoning of the intellect.

In the same Letter of 23 November 1924 Steiner writes:

When human beings seek freedom without inclining towards egoism—when freedom becomes for them pure love for the action which is to be performed—then it is possible for them to approach Michael. But if they desire to act freely and at the same time develop egoism—if freedom becomes for them the proud feeling of manifesting *themselves* in the action—then they are in danger of falling into Ahriman's sphere.

In this Letter we also read:

When one feels oneself as a free being in proximity to Michael one is on the way to carry the intellectual power into one's 'whole being'; one thinks indeed with one's head, but one feels the brightness of the thought or its shade; *the will radiates forth the essential being of oneself* [author's italics] by allowing thoughts to stream into it as intentions and aims. One becomes more and more a human being by becoming the expression of the world; one finds oneself, not by *seeking* oneself, but by uniting oneself voluntarily with the world. [GA 26, 23/11/24]

But if, striving towards the attainment of freedom, one succumbs to Ahriman's temptation, it follows that one is drawn into cold intellectuality as if into a spiritual automatic process in which one is no more than a cog. One is no longer oneself.

All one's thinking becomes an experience of the head; but this separates it from the experience of one's own heart and the life of one's own will, and blots out one's own being. One loses more and more of the true inner human expression by becoming the expression of one's own separate existence; one loses oneself by *seeking* oneself, one withdraws oneself from the world which one refuses to love. It is only when one loves the world that one truly experiences oneself. [Ibid.]

In an earlier Letter to the members it is stated very clearly—as also in a number of other instances—that since 1879 Michael has taken over the spiritual guidance of human affairs, but that he performs what he has to do in such a way that he does not yield any direct influence upon human beings: 'But they may follow him in freedom in order, with the Christ-power, to find the way out of that sphere of Ahriman which [since the fifteenth century] they were obliged to enter' (GA 26, 19/10/24).

The fact that Michael is now entering the soul and spiritual life of mankind has its 'visible' counterpart, for an ever-growing number of people are beginning to realize that we, as human beings, are livingly and constantly connected not only with the earth through our physical bodies but also, through the presence and activity of soul and spirit within us, with the spiritual world.

There is a gradual, consistent growth into conscious spiritual knowledge. This is the one aspect of the leadership of

Michael, but there is also another. To be sincerely, honestly imbued with spiritual knowledge also affects the human heart, the very core of the human soul. The more the light of Christo-centric spiritual science spreads into human deeds, the less will it remain more theory; it will flow out and into human feeing, and will be present in the form of Christ-imbued human love in ever-widening circles.

We could clearly ask at this juncture: What, in effect, is the relation of the human being to all the scholarship and information accumulated during the past few centuries? It 'sits'—can it be said to live?—as knowledge in the human head; it does not permeate the whole human being, for it fails to flow from the head into the human being as a whole. Knowledge of this sort becomes a kind of tumour in the soul (cf. GA 218, 19/11/22). It lacks the life-giving warmth of the forces of the heart and gradually hardens. This is what happens, Rudolf Steiner remarks, 'when we merely grow more clever in our head, and the appropriate feelings, springing from the rest of our being, no longer permeate our increasing cleverness. A kind of cancerous growth becomes established in our soul and spiritual life. The head itself cannot truly thrive if the whole human being is not living in the world with heartfelt love, and also willing what is loved (GA 218, 19/11/22).

We saw earlier that the Archai, the Spirits of Personality—of which Hierarchy Michael is now a member—look to mankind for spiritual nourishment (cf. GA 107, 17/06/09). This is borne out by Steiner many years after he had spoken in such a way about our relationship to the Hierarchy of the Archai: 'Human beings will never understand what the leadership of Michael intends unless they go out to meet it with their own *active contribution* [author's italics]—unless they open out their mind to spiritual enlightenment' (GA 218, 19/11/22).

We recollect that in Old Testament times Michael was the minister of Yahveh. In our fifth post-Atlantean epoch Michael is 'destined' to become in increasing measure the ministering being of the Christ.

Thus, when we say that Michael's leadership now begins to help regulate the historic destinies of mankind, it also signifies that the Word shall presently come true: the leadership of Christ will spread over the earth. It is as though Michael goes before, bearing the light of spiritual knowledge, while after him there comes the Christ, calling humankind to universal, all-embracing love. [Ibid.]

From the few observations we have made hitherto, it is clear that Michael is indeed the Guide to Christ, who, out of selfless love for mankind, went through the experience of death on the Cross. Michael himself goes with selfless love through the world. Those who follow him 'cultivate love in *relation to the outer world*' (GA 26, 23/11/24).

What stands before us as a challenge of Michael is that we become active in our very thoughts. We only belong to the Michael Age when, with selfless love, we co-operate actively in what the world and our fellow human beings offer us in the way of experience. Michael can find a sphere in which to be active in what Rudolf Steiner calls 'free, pure thinking', that which must be the true impulse for the individual will of the human being acting in freedom. And Michael can also 'work' with the deeds of human beings that spring from the impulse of selfless love, with which, as we have seen, Michael has his own close relationship.

*   *   *

As a brief aside—and without any suggestion of condemnation and/or evaluation—one can ask oneself here: How many of the so-called New Age groupings in the worldwide New Age movement attempt to strive towards the donning of the spiritual garb of a co-worker in the Michaelic stream, the Michael-Christ stream? Is it not often the case that pre-Christian Mysteries and pagan traditions and so forth are being placed in the centre of the attention of many of these New Age endeavours while Christ—and with Him Michael— are regarded as being irrelevant, 'out-dated'?

*   *   *

We have just seen that Michael does not exert any direct influence upon human beings. To do so would be to counteract the 'healthy' development of the consciousness soul. We have to be able to follow Michael in freedom in order to free ourselves from the sphere of Ahriman. Let us now look a little more closely at what Rudolf Steiner means by freedom in the present context.

In a lecture entitled in English 'The Path to Freedom and Love and their Significance in World Events' (GA 202, 19/12/ 20) Rudolf Steiner observes:

> Now, it is possible to attain complete freedom in our inner life if we increasingly efface and exclude the actual thought-content, in so far as this comes from outside [i.e. the external world], and kindle into greater activity the element of will which streams through our thoughts when we form judgements, draw conclusions and the like. Thereby, however, our thinking becomes what I have called in my *Philosophy of Spiritual Activity: pure* thinking... But pure thinking may equally be called pure *will.* Thus from the realm of thinking we reach the realm of will, when we become inwardly free; our thinking attains such maturity that it is entirely irradiated by will; it no longer takes anything in from outside, but its very life is of the nature of will. By progressive strengthening of the impulse of will in our thinking we prepare ourselves for what I have called in the *Philosophy of Spiritual Activity* 'Moral Imagination'. Moral Imagination rises to the Moral Intuitions which then pervade and illumine our will that has now become thought, or our thinking that has now become will. In this way we raise ourselves above the sway of the 'necessity' prevailing in the material world [cf. GA 166], permeate ourselves with the force that is inherently our own, and prepare for Moral Intuition. And everything that can stream into the human being from the spiritual world has its foundation, primarily, in these Moral Intuitions. There *freedom* dawns when we enable the will to become an ever mightier and mightier force in our thinking. [GA 202, 19/12/20]

It is through the inner, will-permeated work we activate in our thoughts that we become more spiritual. 'This,' says Steiner, 'is why meditation, too, consists in not indulging in haphazard thoughts but in holding certain easily envisaged thoughts in the very centre of our consciousness, drawing them there with a strong effort of will. And the greater the strength and intensity of this inner radiation of will into the sphere of thinking, the more spiritual we become' (ibid.).

In the same lecture Rudolf Steiner gives us an answer to the question: How do we achieve greater perfection in our actions? It can be achieved by enhancing in ourselves devotion to the world in which we live. The more such devotion grows and intensifies, the more the external world stirs us to action.

> But it is just through unfolding devotion to the outer world that we succeed in permeating our actions with thoughts. What, in reality, *is* devotion to the outer world? ... [It] is nothing else than *love.*
>
> Just as we attain freedom by irradiating the life of thought with will, so do we attain love by permeating the life of will with thoughts... And because, as human beings, we are a unified whole, when we reach the point where we find freedom in the life of thought and love in the life of will, there will be freedom in our actions and love in our thinking... Thus you see how in the human being two great ideals, freedom and love, grow together. Freedom and love are also that which the human being ... can bring to realization in himself in such a way that, through him, the one unites with the other for the good of the world. [Ibid.]

*   *   *

Since 1879, Michael has sought a metamorphosis of his task. Whereas formerly he allowed thoughts to stream from the spiritual 'outer' world into the souls of human beings, he now wishes to live in the human souls in which the thoughts are formed. Whereas in earlier times those human beings who were 'related' to Michael saw him unfold his activity in the spiritual world, they now realize that they need to let Michael dwell in their hearts; 'they now dedicate to him their spiritual life which is based upon thought; they now, in their free and individual life of thought, allow themselves to be instructed by Michael as to which are the right paths of the soul' (GA 26, 17/08/24).

Also, since 1879, those who in their former earth life had looked upon Michael as the inspirer of their thoughts now need to turn to him out of their own free will and seek his guidance in forming higher, spirit-enfilled thoughts. For, as Steiner succinctly expressed it on one occasion, Michael 'liberates thought from the sphere of the head; he clears the way for it to the heart; he enkindles enthusiasm in the feelings, so that the human mind can be filled with devotion for all that can be experienced in the *light* of thought' (ibid.). Those who are thus enspirited by the power of Michael form, with him, a Christ-imbued force against which the two-horned Beast, Sorat, is powerless.

> Hearts are beginning to have thoughts; spiritual fervour is now proceeding not merely from mystical obscurity but from souls clarified by thought. To understand this means to receive Michael into the heart. Thoughts which at the present time strive to grasp the spiritual must originate in hearts which beat for Michael as the fiery Prince of Thought in the universe. [Ibid.]

We need to pause for a while to consider what is meant by 'heart', for it is not the physical heart Rudolf Steiner is referring to here. He is speaking of a heart which is, as it were, a spiritual mirroring, reflection, of the physical organ— a heart which comes into being as something quite new when the human being goes through the first stage of initiation (i.e. living in imaginative knowledge, cf. GA 78, 2/9/21; GA 227, 19/8/23; GA 218, 14/10/22).

When we begin to develop Imaginative knowledge, then—

> we grow etherically out of ourselves and the strange thing is that, while we are doing so, something develops out of our body which I would call a kind of *etheric heart* [author's italics]...A kind of spiritual heart develops outside our physical body, parallel to the phenomena I have described in *Knowledge of the Higher Worlds. How is it achieved?* [cf. the chapter 'The Stages of Initiation'], just as the blood-system develops and has its centre in the heart. This blood-system

goes outside the body and there, outside the body, we feel ourselves in our heart united with, bound up with [*herzlich verbunden*], what we know in the way of spiritual science. We must not seek to enter into knowledge of spiritual science with the physical heart but with the heart outside the physical body, the etheric heart. [GA 161, 01/05/15]

It is 'upwards' to the etheric heart that Michael leads our thoughts when we selflessly strive to grasp the spiritual. Whereas before 1879 those human beings who were 'related' to Michael saw him develop his activity in the spiritual sphere, the spiritual world, they now know that they ought to let Michael dwell in their hearts. Moreover, 'they now dedicate to him their spiritual life which is based upon thought' (GA 26, 17/08/24).

Michael would live in the hearts of human beings, in the hearts which feel 'the brightness of the thought or its shade' (GA 26, 23/11/24). When this occurs morality, unhindered, presents itself in thinking; thinking is permeated with love; the frigidity of intellectuality is overcome; the gulf between head and heart no longer prevails.

In order to enable Michael to perform such an activity we need to develop—alongside the permeation of our thinking with will—another quality in our thinking. We need to imbue our thinking with our life of feeling.

In ancient Greece it was known that all human enquiry must proceed from the quality of *wonder* if it were to reach reality. This insight is as valid today as it was then. 'In actual fact,' Steiner says, 'in the soul that wants to penetrate the truth, this condition must first be present: the soul must "stand" before the universe in a mood of wonder and marvelling' (GA 134, 27/12/11). All true thinking must ensue from the mood of wonder. In addition to wonder, another soul-condition must manifest itself, namely, the quality of *reverence*—'reverence for all that to which thought brings us' (ibid.). According to Rudolf Steiner—and one does not need to be spiritually far advanced to sense this—any thinking that is devoid of reverence will not be able to penetrate to reality.

'Thinking must never, so to say, go dancing through the world in a careless, light-footed way. It must, when it has passed the moment of wonder, take firm root in the feeling of reverence for the universe' (ibid.).

In addition to these two requisites—wonder and reverence—on the path towards spiritual insight and knowledge, Rudolf Steiner speaks of two more qualities with which the soul must be permeated. Briefly stated, Steiner describes these two further qualities of soul as *'feeling oneself in wisdom-filled harmony with the laws of the world'* and *'devotion or self-surrender'*.[4]

So, 'wonder, reverence, wisdom-filled harmony with the phenomena of the world, surrender (devotion) to the course of the world—these are the stages through which we have to pass and which must always run parallel with thinking, never deserting it; otherwise thinking arrives at what is merely correct and not at what is true' (ibid.).

These soul-qualities form the feeling-background for ego-willed, spiritualized thinking. They open the door, prepare the path, as it were, to a heart in which Michael can live and fulfil his mission.

The apparently deadest of soul-activities—thinking (and it is 'dead' when it is brain-bound) becomes 'substance' for new life when irradiated by the will and permeated by the four soul-qualities just mentioned.

In his *Philosophy of Spiritual Activity* Rudolf Steiner writes:

No other activity of the human soul is so easily misunderstood as thinking. Will and feeling still fill the soul with warmth even when we live through the original event again in retrospect. Thinking all too readily leaves us cold in recollection; it is as if the life of the soul has dried out. Yet this is really nothing but the strongly marked shadow of its real nature—warm, luminous, and penetrating deeply into the phenomena of the world. This penetration is brought about by a power flowing through the activity of thinking itself—the power of love in its spiritual form. There are no grounds here for the objection that to discern love in the activity of thinking is to project into thinking a feeling, namely, love. For in truth this objection is but a confirmation of what we have been saying. If we turn towards thinking *in its essence*, we find in it both feeling and will, and these in the depths of their reality. [GA 4, Ch. 8; Steiner's addition, 1918]

*   *   *

Rudolf Steiner gives us a remarkable picture as to what it means to think Michaelically.

Let us consider a man in regard to his external form. That which *constitutes* his external shape you do not really see with your physical eyes, for it is filled with more than 90 per cent fluid... That which fills the form as mineral substance is what you see. That which the man unites with himself of this outer mineral substance is what you see; the human being who does the uniting you do not see. You speak correctly only if you say to yourself: what confronts me here are the particles of matter which the human spirit stores up in itself; this makes the invisible being visible. The *human being* is invisible, really invisible ... supersensible. To say this to oneself with full consciousness ... constitutes the Michaelic mode of thinking ... to become conscious of the fact that we walk among invisible human beings ... this means to think Michaelically... *To comprehend that we are not different in our essential being from the supersensible beings* [author's italics]... This means to think in the spirit of Michael. [GA 194, 23/11/19. See also p. 94]

*   *   *

Let us quote again a passage from one of Rudolf Steiner's Letters to members:

The Age of Michael has dawned. Hearts are beginning to have thoughts; spiritual fervour is now proceeding, not merely from mystical obscurity but from souls clarified by thought. To understand this means to receive Michael into the heart. Thoughts which at the present time strive to grasp the spiritual must originate in hearts which beat for Michael as the fiery Prince of Thought in the universe. [GA 12/08/24]

*   *   *

Finally, in the last speech of Rudolf Steiner's fourth Mystery Play, *The Soul's Awakening* (GA 14), it is indicated that by learning to distinguish clearly which thoughts are ahrimanic the spiritual scientist redeems Ahriman.

Epilogue—Fighters for Michael

What stands before us as a challenge of Michael is that we become active in our very thoughts. We only truly belong to the Michael Age when we do not adopt inactivity and passively wait for enlightenment to come to us (cf. GA 219, 17/12/22).

Michael concerns himself most of all with that which human beings create out of the spirit. He lives with the consequences of that which human beings have created. He lives with the consequences when the other spirits live more with the causes; they kindle in us the impulses for that which we shall do. From Michael, the true spiritual 'hero' of freedom, no impulses come—at least not to begin with—for it is characteristic of his present period of rulership that deeds should come into being out of human freedom (cf. GA 233, 13/01/24).

The battle against the Spirits of Darkness, against the ahrimanic spirits—which are led, we may say, by Sorat, the two-horned Beast, the Sun Demon—is laid in the human heart. It is there, in the human heart, that the battle has been fought since the last third of the nineteenth century. What human hearts do with the Michaelic Christ-impulse now and during the remaining two hundred years or so of Michael's present Regency will be decisive. On one occasion Rudolf Steiner gave expression to the urgency of the end of the present century in the following laconic statement: 'When the first century after the end of Kali Yuga [1899] has elapsed, humanity will either stand at the grave of civilization—or at the beginning of that Age when, in the souls of men and women who in their hearts ally intelligence with spirituality, Michael's battle will be fought out to victory' (GA 240, 19/07/24).

Quite clearly these sombre words spoken by Rudolf Steiner during the last year of his life have to be taken very seriously. We could, perhaps, place alongside them the picture that deep shadows are an indication of the more brilliant light that is dawning. In an earlier chapter we learnt that it is during this century that the experience of the Etheric Christ is to become a reality; we have seen that such an experience has, indeed, been and is—and will continue to be—a reality for a growing number of people.

Here we may remember Rudolf Steiner's statement that Sorat's intention in AD 666 was to cut off the possibility of all future evolution (both of the earth and of humankind), but that this mighty dark power was not successful owing to the fact that a state of balance was brought about through the Mystery of Golgotha. 'Something that could have happened was prevented by an actual event' (cf. GA 184, 11/10/18). (See p. 184.) Now, in view of this fact, it seems justified to suggest that the quickening appearance and experience of the Etheric Christ, or rather that the very presence of such a cosmic spiritual Being, the Christ Being, has the power to meet the soratic impulse 'head on' and thus mitigate against its efficacy. As a consequence it would appear that we are given further space and time to ally within ourselves intelligence with spirituality; we are given a further opportunity to really belong, to strive to belong, to the Michael Age, and to contribute to the light that is dawning in a time of threatening spiritual darkness ruled over by the two-horned Beast.

In regard to the process of allying intelligence with spirituality within ourselves, we may also bear in mind that Rudolf Steiner speaks of another happening that will take place at the end of the twentieth century which is of vital, profound significance for the future evolution of humankind. Steiner speaks of this 'other happening' on 20 July 1924 (i.e. the day after he had spoken of the real danger of humanity standing 'at the grave of civilization'). In this lecture of 20 July Rudolf Steiner speaks of a supersensible School, a Michael School which, since AD 1500, prepared human souls so that they could participate in the new Sun Mysteries. From the fifteenth into the eighteenth century supersensible tuition took place under the direct leadership of Michael. All those who 'studied' under Michael have been coming to the earth during the last few decades of the present century and will continue to come to the earth during the first decades of the twenty-first century. Included among those incarnating during these decades are the great teachers of Chartres and all those who went to the schools of Plato as well as those who came under Aristotle's tuition (cf. GA 240, 20/07/24, and GA 238, 12/09/24; and see Appendix Ten). Together these streams are already building and will continue to build new forces to strengthen certain qualities of soul that are anathema to Ahriman–Sorat; they are qualities that Ahriman–Sorat can do no other than shrink from. In particular, it is the power of selfless (we could say, Christified) love and the power of Michaelic light which overcome Ahriman–Sorat.

If we are to be members of Michael's host we find that we are called upon to seek for the light-forces in our thinking, and to enter with the fullness of our heart into the sorrow and compassion of the world in our feelings. Both these challenges can only be met and answered out of selfless freedom of will, a will imbued with the iron-strength of Michael's sword.

It is, above all, when Christ truly lives in us, when He works across from our heart into the hearts of our fellow human beings, that an all-embracing compassion begins to speak and work in us. We may say that such compassion—or, at least, what we could call a 'bud' of such compassion—has to live in us before we can move *consciously* towards an experience of the Etheric Christ (see also pp. 218–19).

It is the Etheric Christ who creates seed soul-forces with which we may enter into battle with the ahrimanic-soratic forces under the gaze, the 'banner', of Michael. For those hearts that, warmed by compassion, beat for Michael there is clearly nothing totally devastating in the world. There is, and would be, nothing totally devastating in the world if we gradually gain the capacity to think Michaelically.

We may supplement what was previously brought forward as an example of such thinking (see Chapter 18) with another picture Steiner has given us. In one of his lectures on the mission of Michael he says:

We must rise to the conception of the real eternity of the human soul. This is what may be called Michael culture. If we move through the world with the consciousness that with every look we direct outward, with every tone we hear, something spiritual, something of the nature of the soul, streams into us, and that, at the same time, we let our soul element stream out into the world, we have gained the consciousness which humankind needs for the future ... To permeate oneself with this consciousness means to permit the Michael culture to enter. [GA 194, 20/11/19]

In such a culture Michael will work as a real power among human beings. 'They will be free and yet proceed along their spiritual path of life through the cosmos in intimate companionship with Christ' (GA 26, 16/10/24).

*   *   *

In his last address to members of the Anthroposophical Society on 28 September 1924, Rudolf Steiner spoke of certain spiritual work that needed to be done; he spoke of 'the work that shall be accomplished at the end of the century, and that shall lead mankind past the great crisis in which it is involved'.

Now, whether or not sufficient work will have been accomplished by the end of the present century perhaps only the future will be able to tell, but it seems justifiable to assume that the work Rudolf Steiner was referring to should continue into the future:

The work is this: to let the Michael power and the Michael will penetrate the whole of life. *The Michael power and the Michael will are none other than the Christ will and the Christ power*, going before in order to implant in the right way into the earth the power of the Christ. If this Michael power is able verily to overcome all that is of the Demon and the Dragon (and you well know what that is), if you all, who have in this way received the Michael thought, have indeed received it with true and faithful heart and with tender love, and will endeavour to go forward from the Michael mood of this year, until not only is the Michael thought *revealed* in your soul but you are able also to make the Michael thought *live* in your *deeds* in all its strength and all its power—if this is so, then will you be true servants of the Michael thought.

MICHAEL-IMAGINATION

Sun-all-mighty offspring,
Luminous, world-endowing
Spirit powers, to be Michael's garment of rays,
You are predestined by the thought of the gods.

He, the Christ proclaimer, makes manifest in you—
Mankind-sustainers—holy cosmic will;
You, the bright world-ether beings,
Bear the Christ's word to men.

So Christ's heralder appears
To longing, thirsting souls;
To them your word of light streams forth
In the cosmic era of spirit-man.

You, the pupils of spirit knowledge,
Take Michael's wise, directing glance,
Take the World-Will's loving Word
Into your soul's high purpose, actively.*

---

* Rudolf Steiner, *Truth-Wrought-Words* (Anthroposophic Press, New York, 1979). Translated from the German by Arvia MacKaye Ege.

APPENDICES

Appendix One
The Ego; the 'I'

Human beings have the sentient or astral body in common with the animal, just as they have the etheric or life body in common with the plants, and the physical body in common with the mineral. Over and above these three 'bodies' the human being has an 'I', an ego. The 'I' is the essential in us; the 'I' thinks and feels; the 'I' wills and acts.

Our 'I' expresses itself for us in our thinking, feeling and willing, i.e. in our soul-life. The 'I' dwelling in each one of us perceives the external world through the impressions of the senses, and reacts to these impressions through feeling; it responds from within to the impressions of the world without. That is the most primitive expression of the 'I', the ego, in the human being, and in spiritual science is designated by the term 'sentient soul'.[1]

The 'I' can also so function that it reflects upon that which is brought to it of the external world. This expression of the 'I' is called the 'intellectual soul'.

Furthermore, the 'I' can also be conscious of its spiritual nature and can 'give itself up' to the world of the spirit, just as in the sentient soul it 'gives itself' to the world perceived by the senses. This expression, this activity, of the 'I' is called the consciousness or spiritual soul.

The human soul, then, consists of three 'members'—the sentient soul, the intellectual soul (also known as the mind soul), and the consciousness or spiritual soul.

Our soul-being as it is today is made up of these three. However, as Steiner repeatedly states, the human being has not yet completed his soul-spiritual development. We still have much work to do. This work consists therein that the 'I' must become more conscious of its spirituality. Its whole thinking, feeling and willing must be interpenetrated with this consciousness. The 'I' must become a fully conscious ruler in and over the astral, etheric and physical bodies.

The ego must more and more 'move upward, working out the Beast',[2] and in so doing it transforms the astral body into the spirit-self. The spirit-self becomes manifest in proportion as the 'I' rules over the life of passions and desires, purifies and refines them and thus transforms them into spiritual powers. In other words, the astral body is spiritualized.[3]

The 'I' also works on the etheric body to transform it into life-spirit and on the physical body into spirit-man.[4] The transformations of these two bodies are far more difficult to attain than that of the astral body. Indeed, the spiritualization of the physical body will only take place in the distant future. That of the etheric body, however, can be worked on by the 'I' to some extent in our time. It is a far more difficult task than transforming the desires and passions of the astral body into spirit-self, for it involves changing one's temperament, deep-seated habits and character traits such as forgetfulness, tardiness and indecision.

Beredene Jocelyn writes in this connection:

> It will take many earth-lives, in co-operation with the Christ-impulse, to achieve this transmutation until one's life-spirit in some small measure partakes of the exceedingly exalted nature of the life-spirit of the Christ, but earnest effort should be made. How is this accomplished? The best aids are art and religion. True art harmonizes and uplifts. Religion, in its outreach, forgives, maintaining an undisturbed harmonious relationship with others. In its upreach, it uplifts through prayer, meditation, reverence for the divine, repeated ritual, devotion to truth and comprehension of the Christ Mystery.[5]

Appendix Two
The Two Jesus Children

The Gospels of St Luke and St Matthew, the only canonical records of the birth of Jesus, quite clearly refer to two different children.

Briefly, the nativity story of St Luke is as follows. The Jesus-child is born in a manger in Bethlehem—the family actually live in Nazareth—and is visited by shepherds. Joseph was the son of Heli. This Jesus stays in Nazareth, with the exception of an annual visit to Jerusalem. The lineage of this child is traced back by Luke to the priest Nathan, at which point it joins with that of David. This child is the 'Nathan Jesus'.

In the Matthew account the child is also born in Bethelem, where Joseph and Mary lived. He is born in a house. There is no mention of a manger. Joseph was the son of Jacob. This Jesus-child is visited by Magi and afterwards, in order to escape the Massacre of the Innocents, is taken by his parents to Egypt. After the death of Herod they return to Nazareth, not to their earlier home, Bethlehem. The lineage of this child is traced by Matthew back through a quite different scion to Solomon, at which point the genealogy merges with that of David. This child is the 'Solomon Jesus'.

The two Jesus-children were not born at the same time. The Gospels make this quite clear. The Luke Jesus, the Nathan Jesus, was born when Joseph and Mary went to Bethlehem to be taxed— 'And this taxing was first made when Cyrenius was governor of Syria' (Luke 2:2). The Matthew Jesus, the Solomon Jesus, on the other hand, was born 'in the days of Herod the king' (Matt. 2:1). By the time that Cyrenius became governor of Syria, Herod was already dead.[1]

In some of the apocryphal literature the idea of two Jesus-children is quite explicit. For instance, in the Gnostic Book *Pistis Sophia* (third century AD) there is a moving account of a meeting between the two Jesus boys:[2]

> When thou wert little, before the spirit had come upon thee, whilst thou wert in a vineyard with Joseph, the spirit came out of the height and came to me in my house, like unto thee; and I had not known him, but I thought that thou wast he. And the spirit said unto me: 'Where is Jesus,

my brother, that I meet with him?' And when he said this unto me, I was at a loss and thought it was a phantom to try me. So I seized him and bound him to the foot of the bed in my house until I went forth to you, to thee and Joseph in the field [...] It came to pass, therefore, when thou didst hear me speak the word unto Joseph, that thou didst understand the word, wert joyful and saidest: 'Where is he, that I may see him; else I await him in this place.' [...] And we went down together, entered the house and found the spirit bound to the bed. And we looked on thee and him and found thee like unto him. And he who was bound to the bed was unloosed; and he took thee in his arms and kissed thee, and thou also didst kiss him. Ye became one.

The significant difference in the ages between the two Jesus-children already referred to is frequently indicated in those paintings and sculptures which depict them.[3]

Rudolf Steiner was able to give many indications as to the significance of the incarnation of the two Jesus-children in his lectures on the four Gospels and elsewhere.[4]

Appendix Three
The Paradise Legend and the Grail Legend

The Paradise Legend
The gist of this legend is as follows. In the Garden of Eden, where God had placed Adam and Eve, He had planted 'the Tree of the Knowledge of Good and Evil', and He warned Adam on penalty of death not to eat the fruit of this tree. But the serpent (Lucifer), 'more subtle than any beast of the field', came to Eve and tempted her to eat of the fruit of the tree, telling her that if she did so her eyes would be opened and she would be like the gods, knowing good and evil (Gen. 3:1ff.). Being tempted, Eve ate the forbidden fruit and gave some also to Adam. 'And the eyes of them both were opened, and they knew that they were naked...' (Gen. 3:7).

Because Adam and Eve had disobeyed His command, and seeing that they might also eat of the fruit of the Tree of Life that grew in the Garden of Eden and become as gods, the Lord laid certain punishments upon them both and banished them from the Garden of Eden. Because of the sin of Eve, He decreed that thereafter all women should bear their children in pain and should be subject to their husband. Because Adam had likewise sinned, God decreed that henceforth man should earn his bread by the sweat of his brow. And He said to Adam: '... dust thou art, and unto dust shall thou return' (Gen. 3:19).[1]

The Grail Legend
According to some versions of the legend,[2] the Grail is the vessel, the chalice, from which Jesus Christ drank at the Last Supper, and in which Joseph of Arimathaea gathered some of the blood that flowed from His wounds on the Cross. This chalice was cut from a particularly precious stone from Lucifer's crown when it was struck by Michael's sword of light during the battle waged in the spiritual world between Lucifer and Michael.[3]

One legend speaks of Joseph of Arimathaea travelling to England. He is said to have landed on the island of Avalon (where Glastonbury stands today). In later times the tomb of King Arthur and his wife Guinevere is said to have been found there.

There is, indeed, a close link between the Grail-stream and that which was represented by King Arthur and his Round Table.

In this connection it is relevant to note that Rudolf Steiner distinguishes three phases in the unfolding of Grail-Christianity. The first is characterized by King Arthur and his knights, the second by the Holy Grail, and the third by Parzival.

The Knights of the Round Table are Knights of the Sword.[4] They fight against the dark powers of the soul or, as many stories relate, against dragons and evil knights. According to W.J. Stein: 'We must picture Arthur to ourselves as a being of light. He and his knights are guardians of what is noble and just ... Wherever Arthur and his knights appeared, wherever the Round Table was set up, there the sinister forms who hate the light were compelled to withdraw from their presence.[5]

The Knights of the Grail are Knights of the Word.[6]

In this connection, Steiner writes that the Grail Knights 'know that there is only one truth and they want to serve it. But the one truth has many aspects; there is only one Christ but He shows the comprehensive nature of His being in many ways in different religions. The one *harmonizing* element in the many is the "Holy Spirit", the "spirit of truth". The disciples spoke in *many tongues* when the Holy Spirit alighted upon them at Whitsun, but they spoke of the *same being*. Lucifer, who caused the confusion of tongues in Babylon, [opposes] the Grail. The *one word*, the cosmic Word, the Logos, stands in contrast to the *many languages*.'[7]

The Knights of the Grail serve the Logos in an inner way; they draw their spiritual strength from the contemplation of the Grail in which the blood of Christ becomes life-giving substance as the Holy Spirit descends upon it. But the King of the Grail, Amfortas, suffers torment at the sight of the Sacred Vessel. He has been wounded by the Holy Spear (the spear with which Longinus pierced Christ's side) and the wound does not heal. Amfortas had taken the Spear into battle against the black magician, Klingsor, and lost it to his arch-enemy. It was Klingsor, wielding the Spear, who inflicted the wound upon Amfortas.

Amfortas will not be healed until Parzival, 'pure in heart', regains the Spear from Klingsor and touches the wound with it. It is Parzival's destiny to overcome Klingsor.[8]

In the three phases of development mentioned above, Rudolf Steiner shows that the path of the evolving human soul can be recognized. In the battles fought by the Knights of the Round

Table the process of development of the sentient soul is reflected. The attacks against them are experienced as coming from 'outside'. The Knights of the Grail represent the struggle within the intellectual soul, the mind soul. This struggle is clearly of a more inner nature. Parzival's path—leading through many trials and tribulations—is that of the consciousness soul, of the awakening 'I'. It is the path along which a cognitive awareness of the being of Christ arises. Parzival gains spiritual insight through compassion.[9]

Why, we may ask, does the King of the Grail, Amfortas,[10] suffer excruciating pain at the very sight of the Grail. It is because he has succumbed to the temptations of the flesh. In so falling, he has received a wound at the hands of the black magician Klingsor that never heals.

In a broader—and deeper—sense we may say that this wound is very much with us today. It is symptomatic of a modern cultural problem. We can recognize many consequences of the lack of control, of sovereignty, of the ego-filled soul over certain aspects of the physical and etheric bodies. For instance, we can frequently witness a growing lack of sound, healthy common sense in our fellow human beings (and in ourselves), states of depression are ubiquitous, affecting a healthy life of feeling and mind, and weaknesses in the life of will—misuse of alcohol, drugs and sexuality—are all too familiar today to need further comment. There is also, Steiner warns, a very real danger of the de-egofication' (*Entichung*) of the human being, that is, of the human being possessed and enslaved by the Spirits of Darkness.[11]

It is in such conditions of the human soul that we can discern the joint influence of Lucifer and Ahriman, of (in terms of the Grail legend) the union between the Queen of Sicily, Iblis, the daughter of Eblis,[12] and the black magician Klingsor, imbued with the darkest of ahrimanic forces. Rudolf Steiner spoke of this union in the following terms: 'Among all evil unions which have taken place within the Earth's evolution between beings in whose souls there were occult forces, the one known to occultists as the worst of all was between Kingsor and Iblis' (GA 144, 07/02/13).

In a medieval work entitled 'Saengerkrieg auf der Wartburg' ('A song contest on the Wartburg') we learn that Klingsor had studied alchemy and astrology in Baghdad and Babylon. In short, we find that he is a representative—we could say, a tool—of the Arabian stream, that is of the Anti-Grail stream, of the ahrimanic-soratic forces.[13]

Klingsor is possessed by a strong desire to become a Knight of the Brotherhood of the Grail. But he is quite incapable of achieving self-purification (i.e. of sublimating desires of the flesh) and he is barred forever from crossing the threshold to the Castle of the Grail. In the words of Wagner's opera *Parsifal*, 'no other / save pure in heart, as brother / may enter, to those who work the will of Heaven / the Grail's most wondrous might is given.[14]

'No other / save pure in heart, as brother / may enter', may become a Knight of the Grail. We are reminded here of Rudolf Steiner's golden rule in regard to spiritual development: 'For every *one* step forward that you take in seeking knowledge of occult truths, take *three* steps forward in the improvement of your own character' (GA 10). Steiner supplements this statement by two others which are relevant to quote here: 'Throughout their training, the would-be initiates must continually enhance their moral strength and their inner purity' (ibid. slightly adapted). And: 'In all occult science there is a fundamental principle which cannot be transgressed if any goal is to be reached [...] *All the knowledge that you pursue merely for the enrichment of your own learning and to accumulate treasure of your own leads you away from your path; but all knowledge you pursue in order to grow more mature on the path of human ennoblement and world-progress brings you a step forward*' (ibid.).

It is clear from what has been said in regard to Klingsor that he did not meet any of the requirements Steiner postulates.

It must be said that Amfortas, too, fails to 'enhance his moral strength and his purity', for he falls victim to the allurement of beautiful maidens in Klingsor's enchanted garden.[15] Amfortas, we learn, sets out to vanquish the stronghold of the Anti-Grail.

Klingsor has succeeded in corrupting many Knights of the Grail when they have entered his stronghold of the Anti-Grail. It is Amfortas' intention to bring about Klingsor's downfall and thus save further Knights from falling victim to the powers of darkness. But, as Winkler[16] points out, Amfortas fails to recognize that Klingsor's success is possible only because the Knights of the Grail are weakening in their spiritual dedication. Instead of fighting against evil in his own domain, Amfortas takes up arms to destroy *the* principal representative of evil on earth. But the decisive battle against evil cannot be won by such means. Moreover, Amfortas compounds his error by taking into battle the Holy Spear itself and subsequently losing it to Klingsor. Here we may note that after

Parzival, 'pure in heart', has regained it from Klingsor, the Spear is never again used in battle.

In Amfortas' misuse of the Holy Spear we can recognize one of the tragic errors so often repeated in human history. 'This error occurs whenever spiritual leaders, in defence of their cause, good as it may be, rely on divine help without being pure enough to deserve it.'[17]

Amfortas is well prepared to confront the darkness of ahrimanic forces, but finds himself defenceless against Lucifer, against the lure of eternal Eve. His suppressed but not fully sublimated life of desires renders him an easy victim of temptation (in Klingsor's enchanted garden). No less a sinner than those Knights of the Grail he had presumed to redeem, Amfortas betrays his sacred mission as King of the Grail. The Holy Spear falls into the hands of Klingsor.

Klingsor's victory over Amfortas signifies more than the weakness of the spiritual power of the Knights of the Grail; it is symptomatic of a radical change in the consciousness of humankind. Head-knowledge, knowledge focused solely on the material world, which recognizes as real only that which is perceptible to the physical senses—knowledge, in other words, which is ruled by Ahriman—is completely devoid of the soul-qualities, the heart-qualities, of compassion, wonder and reverence.[18] It is such qualities which can transform the intellect into an instrument in the service of true human progress. Through them 'the spiritual eyes of the human being are opened'.[19] It is these qualities which Parzival develops to a high degree.

Applied in a merely intellectual, cold, analytical, materialistic fashion, knowledge becomes the conquering tool in the hands of Klingsor, an agent most powerful of ahrimanic forces—of what, in his Book of Revelation, John speaks of as the two-horned Beast, Sorat.

Amfortas' misdeed resulted not only in his wound, which would not heal, but also in a lifeless region all round the Castle of the Grail. Nature is suffering under, sharing in, the wound of Amfortas.

T.S. Eliot, in his poem *The Waste Land*,[20] gives us a vivid picture of a wasteland that is without a living spiritual life:

> ... each man fixed his eyes before his feet.
> Flowed up the hill and down King William Street,
> To where Saint Mary Woolnoth kept the hours
> With a dead sound on the final stroke of nine.[21]

Eliot here characterizes people whose eyes are fixed upon the ground before them. They are more asleep than awake and show no interest in the world around them. Their lives are dictated to by earth-bound time.

Parzival, too, on his first visit to the Castle of the Grail, is more asleep than awake. In this connection Steiner makes the following observation: 'At first Parzival is not sufficiently awake inwardly to ask in full self-consciousness the question: What is the purpose of the Grail? What does it demand? It demands of the Fisher King [i.e. the King of the Grail] that he should eradicate his personal interest and enlarge his interest to embrace the interest of all humankind after the fashion of Christ Jesus. In the case of Parzival it is necessary that he should raise his interest above that of a mere spectator' (GA 145, 26/03/13).

Amfortas manifests too much self-centred interest, too much personality. Parzival, on the other hand, on his first visit, shows too little interest in what is happening around him. He is too naïve, too unresponsive to what is going on around him. What is required of a true Knight of the Grail is that the idea of universal humanity is realized. This, Rudolf Steiner reminds us, 'is attained when these words become true: "Where two or three are gathered together in my name, there am I in the midst of them"' (Matt. 18:20).

Parzival does not remain naïve and unaware of life around him. Indeed, when he enters the Castle of the Grail the second time it may be said that Christ truly lives in him: 'The Christ who works across from our heart into the hearts of our fellows, making us one with our suffering fellow human beings' (GA 40).

A turning in Parzival's spiritual development takes place in Klingsor's enchanted garden where the maidens, led by the most beautiful of them all, Kundry, set about to seduce him. It was here, we recollect, that Amfortas betrayed his true mission. Parzival, however, resists all temptation to fall victim to sexual desire. He had witnessed the agony of the Fisher King—and remained silent. But the seed of compassion had been planted deep in his heart and it is at the corresponding moment of the downfall of Amfortas that, in Parzival, the Christlike quality of compassion breaks through the narrow confines of self-centredness. He now feels the suffering of another human being as his own. He experiences what Steiner has placed before us as a goal to be attained:

> So long as thou dost feel the pain
> Which I am spared,
> The Christ unrecognized
> Is working in the world. [GA 40]

Parzival is not spared the pain of another. He experiences in his heart the intense, crippling pain of Amfortas' spear-wound. Nowhere else is the agony of Amfortas portrayed in such depth as in Wagner's *Parsifal*. This agony becomes Parzival's own, and he cries out:

> Amfortas!
> The Spear-wound—the Spear-wound—
> It burns here in my heart!
> Oh! Torment! Torment!
> The cry of anguish pierces my heart

After a time Parzival is imbued with an inner calm and, as though gazing into the spiritual world, he says:

> This gaze is fixed now on the Holy Cup—
> the sacred blood now glows:
> redemption's rapture, sweet and mild,
> to every heart brings all its healing:
> but here—in this heart will the pain not lessen.
> The Saviour's cry is stealing through me,
> lamenting, ah, lamenting
> for the profaned sanctuary:
> 'Redeem me, rescue me
> from hands defiled and guilty'
> Thus rang His lamentation,
> fearful loud, loud to my spirit.
> And I, a fool, a coward,
> to childish deeds of daring fled away!
> (*on his knees Parsifal cries out*)
> Redeemer! Saviour! Lord of grace!
> Can I my sinful crime efface?[22]

In an attempt to wound and destroy Parzival, Klingsor hurls the Sacred Spear at him. But this Spear is symbolic not only of divine wisdom but also of deep compassion (Longinus pierced Christ's side so that He would have died before the soldiers came to break His legs and thus suffer even greater agony) and cannot wound those who have experienced the living Christ in their hearts—as Parzival has clearly done. It hovers over Parzival's head. After he has taken hold of the Spear and swinging it in the sight of the Cross, Parzival directs the following commanding words to the black magician:

> So with this Spear I vanquish your enchantment:
> and the wound shall be healed now
> by the Spear that wounded.
> To darkness and ruin
> falls your deceiving display![23]

The power of the Grail triumphs over that of the Anti-Grail.

One of the lessons we can learn today from the Grail legend is this: we can either, through lack of reverence, awe and wonder, turn the world around us into a wasteland and therewith also neglect the soul and spiritual needs of our fellow human beings or we can nurture love and compassion in our hearts in full consciousness and thereby work towards the redemption of 'fallen' humankind and the earth on which we live.

All depends on the source from which we draw inspiration: Grail or Anti-Grail.

Appendix Four
The Eighth Sphere

'The stream of cosmic evolution flows through seven phases which are described by Steiner in *Occult Science. An Outline* (GA 13) and named by him the Saturn, Sun, Moon, Earth, Jupiter, Venus and Vulcan phase.[1] By the activities of luciferic and ahrimanic spirits, evolution can be diverted from its normal course. They resist such an evolution. And in so far as this resistance is successful, another 'sphere' is formed in the cosmos, not belonging to the seven spheres of normal evolution. It represents a sphere of its own, existing 'outside' the seven spheres, phases, of the normal stream of evolution. Hence it is called, in occult science, the *Eighth Sphere.*

Steiner opens a lecture dealing with the Eighth Sphere with the words: 'It is very difficult indeed to speak about the so-called "Eighth Sphere"' (GA 254, 18/10/15). A little later, in the same lecture, he gives the reason why this is the case. First of all, we need to understand that the Eighth Sphere must be described as a realm in which we are living all the time. We also need to understand that what is around us as this Sphere is accessible to imaginative-visionary clairvoyance. 'The reason why it is so difficult to speak of matters such as the Eighth Sphere is because *really clear and discriminative clairvoyance is possible by so very few*' (author's italics).

The properties of the 'substance of the Eighth Sphere' are quite different from those characteristic of the earth (the Fourth Sphere). The physical matter with which we are familiar here on earth is spiritual 'substance' solidifying or, as Steiner says on one occasion, 'Matter is a heap of ruins of the spirit. Matter is, in reality, spirit, but shattered spirit' (GA 134, 20/12/11). Now besides organic and inorganic matter, substance, there is the possibility of a third kind of substance. Valentin Tomberg explains this unfamiliar concept in the following terms: 'Besides life (which is organic substance) and death (which is inorganic substance) there is also the possibility of the spectre. The substance of the spectre is neither alive nor dead; it can best be compared with electromagnetic "substance". A spectre does not live, neither is it dead; rather is it formed of electricity endowed with sensation and consciousness.'[2]

Behind our world there is a further world of spectres created by

Lucifer and Ahriman. The spectre-like content of the Eighth Sphere is present everywhere, and 'can therefore be perceived just as actual spectres are perceived. All earthly being and existence are involved here. Lucifer and Ahriman strive unceasingly to draw from the earth's substance whatever they can snatch, in order to form the Eighth Sphere which then, when it is sufficiently advanced, will be detached from the earth and go its own way in the cosmos together with Lucifer and Ahriman. Needless to say, the earth would then pass over to Jupiter [the Fifth Sphere] as a torso' (GA 254, 18/10/15).

We, as human beings on earth, are 'mineralized through and through'. We are permeated by the mineralizing process and Lucifer and Ahriman are continually wresting 'morsels' from it. 'Therefore we ourselves are involved in the battle [against this 'robbery']. Lucifer and Ahriman battle against the Spirits of Form,[3] with the aim of wresting mineral substance from us everywhere' (ibid.).

The most perfect of our organs is that of thinking—the brain and the skull. It is there that the 'battle' is the most vehement; it is there that Lucifer and Ahriman have been most successful in wresting mineral substance from us. 'Physical substance there is more spiritualized than anywhere else [i.e. in our physical body]. Hence it is precisely through the head that we can emancipate ourselves from our organism to the greatest extent. We can soar upwards in thoughts, we can distinguish between the good and the evil. And for that very reason, Lucifer and Ahriman have been the most successful in wresting away substantiality ... This *alchemy* [author's italics] by which mineral substance is sent over into the Eighth Sphere is taking place all the time behind the scenes of our existence' (ibid.).

It was the intention, Steiner emphasizes, of Lucifer and Ahriman from the beginning of the evolution of the Fourth Sphere (the earth) to let the whole of this evolution disappear into the Eighth Sphere. It was therefore necessary that a 'counterweight' should be created. A measure had to be taken so that everything in us proceeding from the head should not fall prey to the power of Lucifer and Ahriman. A counterweight should be created in the domain of earthly life so that not everything should depend upon head-activity and the activity of the 'outward-turned senses', that there should be in the human being something completely independent of the head. 'And this was achieved through the work of the good

Spirits of Form, who implanted the principle of *love* into the principle of heredity on earth. That is to say, there is now operative in the human race something that is independent of the head, that passes from generation to generation and has its deepest foundation in the physical nature of the human being' (ibid.).

Everything in the human being that is connected with propagation and heredity, everything that is independent of human beings in the sense that they cannot penetrate it with their thinking—that, Steiner says, 'is what has proceeded from the principle of love permeating the process of propagation and heredity ... Lucifer and Ahriman want to force on us the exclusive sovereignty of the head, and they launch their attacks by way of the head against everything that is purely natural affinity. *For what is hereditary substance on the earth cannot be wrested away by them*' (author's italics).

Both Lucifer and Ahriman are rendered powerless when confronted by the principle of love.[4]

Earlier it was mentioned that we, as human beings, on earth, are, in Steiner's words, 'mineralized through and through'. In the same lecture (GA 254, 18/10/15) he asks us to remember what is said in his book *Occult Science* about the evolution of humankind prior to the coming into being of the earth (the Fourth Sphere). He reminds us that in the pre-earth stages of evolution there can be no question of *freedom*.

> In those other stages humankind is enclosed in a web of *necessity*. In order that human beings might be ripe for freedom, the mineral nature had to be incorporated into them; they had to become beings permeated with the mineral element. Hence men and women can be educated for freedom only within the earthly-material world. [...] The earth is the begetter of freedom precisely because it is the earth that impregnates the human being with the physical-mineral element. [...] What stems from the free will must be kept within the *realm of earth*.

But we are perpetually exposed to the danger of having our free will wrested from us by Lucifer and Ahriman and 'dragged' by them into the Eighth Sphere.

This happens, we learn from Steiner, if, for example, free will is transformed into visionary clairvoyance as distinct from 'clear and discriminative clairvoyance'. 'The moment the free will is transformed into visionary clairvoyance, what unfolds in the human being becomes the booty of Lucifer and Ahriman ... through the shackling of free will, the spectres of the Eighth Sphere are created.' When clairvoyance of a visionary kind develops in naïve, credulous people, it often follows that their free will has been sacrificed. Such people may imagine that they have had, for example, an experience of immortality, whereas the truth is that, in their visionary state, they see a part—or a product—of their souls being 'dragged' away to the Eighth Sphere. This occurs in mediumistic seances. The medium believes that the dead are speaking to, or through, him or her, but the clear and discriminative clairvoyant/clairaudient knows that, instead of a link being formed with the dead, with the Eternal, the medium is testifying to what is/ was continually disappearing into the Eighth Sphere.

'It would be a great victory for Lucifer and Ahriman if they could ever claim that countless numbers of the dead had been absorbed into their Sphere.' Such souls, according to Steiner, would be lost from Earth evolution. There is a way this could be achieved. Lucifer and Ahriman know that human beings seek to know something about the life between death and a new birth. So, 'they may say: [...] if we tell them that they are learning something from the dead, they will be satisfied and will direct their feelings towards the realm from which announcements are made to them as coming from the dead. If therefore we desire that the hearts and minds of men and women shall be guided towards the Eighth Sphere, let us say to them: we are telling you something that comes from the dead. We shall capture [the souls of men and women] by alleging that the dead are in our domain' (ibid.).

They could succeed if 'counterweights', particularly that of love in the sense mentioned earlier, were not active.

Steiner makes an interesting interpolation here: 'It is through knowledge alone that an approach can be made to these things ... Therefore when we began the periodical *Lucifer-Gnosis*, the first article[5] was ... on the subject of Lucifer, in order that he should be rightly understood, in order that it should be realized that inasmuch as he brings about head activity, he is a benefactor of humankind. But the counterweight must also be there: *love* must be there as the counterweight.'

Steiner then takes up the themes of clairvoyance and free will again. He urges us not to allow ourselves to be duped by what leads to the Eighth Sphere. Particular caution needs to be exercised in the domain of visionary clairvoyance. Validity should be ascribed only to that form of clairvoyance which, as much as possible, is both clear and discriminative. For it alone, in our striving to gain knowledge of the spiritual world, excludes the influence of Lucifer and Ahriman. 'If the tendency to shackle the free will and remain in the domain of visionary clairvoyance comes into evidence time and again, this is a sign that opposition is being put in the way of the clear-cut endeavour of our [spiritual scientific] movement, owing to the propensity to fetter the free will in visionary clairvoyance' (ibid.).

Steiner deplores the fact that even in this Movement 'announcements of visionary clairvoyants are greeted with rapturous wonder!' Such an attitude is 'an expression of perverse love for the Eighth Sphere'.

With regard to the exercise of the free will, Steiner makes an observation which needs to be taken to heart:

> When one or another person has insisted, 'Dr Steiner has said that such and such ought to be done,' then this means that such and such a person wants to deliver up the free will to foreign influence, to let this will be determined, not by himself, but by someone else; he wants to make someone else responsible for instilling into the physical world a willingness to allow the free will to be fettered. Whenever people give way to fatalism instead of making decisions through their own power of judgement, they show their inclination to the Eighth Sphere. And everything that passes in this way into the Eighth Sphere disappears from Earth evolution, does not go forward in the right way with Earth evolution.[6]

Appendix Five
Imagination, Inspiration, Intuition

Through the pursuit of a path of spiritual development (concentration, contemplation and meditation) as given by Rudolf Steiner (cf. GA 10, GA 12, GA 13) three higher forms of knowledge can be attained: Imagination, Inspiration and Intuition. These are three states of consciousness which lie '*above*' normal waking consciousness (cf. GA 202, 17/12/20).

F.W. Zeylmans van Emmichoven, in *The Reality in Which We Live*, gives us a fair idea of what we may understand by these three terms in the sense in which Rudolf Steiner uses them.

By means of a continued meditative path, thinking is developed as an independent power, and is thereby freed from its bondage to sense-perception. This freed thinking is a universal power, in which creative world thoughts are active. Now we come to the experience that in meditative thinking the same forces are active: in our own organism and in the world around us, forces which we [call] life forces, formative forces or life-ether forces. They reveal themselves to meditative thinking in pictorial form as imaginations.

Our dream life also gives us pictures, but they occur unconsciously, without our permission... In imaginative consciousness, however, the soul does not live in a lowered but in a heightened, strengthened state of consciousness. We may consider the imaginations as spiritual perceptions, yet they are of a subjective nature. This means that the thinking soul still determines to a large extent how the pictures come into being; spiritual realities are made conscious in the soul by means of images. When, through constant practice, the soul is able to banish these pictures from its consciousness, which means not to see them ... an empty consciousness arises during which in normal circumstances a person would be asleep. By means of exercises,[1] however, it is possible to develop a power which enables one to remain awake during this stage of empty consciousness. Spiritual reality streams into this emptiness; the soul breathes it in, as it were, and thereby attains the second stage of supersensible consciousness, namely, that of Inspiration.

In order to acquire a pure form of objective perception and judgement, it is essential that the feeling life especially should have become balanced and harmonious. Feelings of sympathy and antipathy can act as a clouded glass through which the soul sees the world around it impurely. By means of special exercises, however, the feelings can be transformed into organs of the soul through which [the presence and activity of spiritual] world-powers are revealed to us ... The soul 'sees' or rather 'hears' through inspirational consciousness, although perceptions in this sphere cannot be directly compared with the physical sensory functions of seeing and hearing. Perhaps it would be preferable to speak of a higher, perceptive faculty which embraces both seeing and hearing.

The third stage, that of intuitive consciousness, is attained by overcoming every trace of egoism in the soul. Love must now be able to make way for a complete surrender to the deepest will-power, to the divine world-will. Rudolf Steiner expressed it as follows: 'In Intuition one gives oneself up as nourishment for the Gods.' By means of this, however, the possibility exists of experiencing the spiritual world in its most essential nature, which means to come to know spiritual beings who live there.

*   *   *

In an essay entitled 'The Trinity in Man and Nature', Canon A.P. Shepherd[2] sheds further light on Rudolf Steiner's exposition of how the three stages of higher knowledge (Imagination, Inspiration and Intuition) are reached:

The first stage, 'Imagination', is reached by directing concentrated meditation upon a spiritual reality of whose existence we are aware— but which is not manifest to our sense-experience, as, for example, the growth-forces of a plant. If the meditation is successful, the spiritual reality makes an impression on us, through our developed soul-organ of perception, in form and colour. This is an 'Imagination'. It is, as it were, a spiritual sense-impression giving an awareness of a spirit-object impressing this pattern of form and colour upon us. But as yet we do not know the nature of that object itself, but only its effect upon ourselves. For us to know it, it must itself establish a direct relationship with us which will reveal its own being.

We have, therefore, to dismiss from our attention the 'Imagination'— that is, the effect which the object made upon ourselves from without— and wait until we receive from the spirit-reality a communication of the relationship which links it to ourselves. We wait in pure thought-meditation, directing our relationship-discovering faculty of thought towards the object, until, as Spinoza[3] put it, 'spirit comes to meet us'. This is the stage of 'Inspiration', the stage of the discovery of spirit-reality itself in revealed relationships, and the discovery that in those relationships not only the spirit-reality, but we ourselves, consist.

Then, when relationship is fully taken up into being, we reach the final stage of 'Intuition', where living in relationship passes into a mutual interpenetration of being, an experience of oneself in the other, and the other in oneself.

* * *

Arnold Freeman approaches the matter of these three higher modes of cognition in readily comprehensible terms in his book *Meditation under the Guidance of Rudolf Steiner*:[4]

We are nowadays for the most part content ... with knowledge ultimately dependent upon the use of the physical sense-organs. There are four distinct elements in the acquisition of such knowledge:

1) An *Object* making an impression upon our senses.
2) The *Image* of it we make for ourselves. (This picture remains in memory after we have turned away from the object.)
3) The *Concept* we form in order to come to an understanding of the object. (Seeing the object in its relationships; as a member of a group.)
4) Our *Ego* which, by preserving images, makes possible for us inner continuity and self-identification; which by forming concepts and relating them to one another, makes it practicable for us to comprehend the world.

Neither in ordinary life nor in prevalent scientific practice do we rise above a cognition dependent upon these four elements. Dr Steiner urges that other higher stages of knowledge are within our power.[5]

1) It is practicable, Dr Steiner says, to gain knowledge having its origin not in physical objects but in images that mediate higher worlds. He calls such knowledge 'Imagination'. He says it is a sort of seeing...
2) It is possible to lift ourselves above the world of images into the world of concepts...We are in a state of consciousness in which stone and plant and animal utter their being to us. We hear all things as super-earthly music. This second 'enlargement' of consciousness Dr Steiner calls 'Inspiration'...
3) In everyday experience we find ourselves able to say 'I' only to our own self. It is practicable, says Dr Steiner, to reach a very high stage of cognition in which we are able also to say 'I' to every object in the world; to stand no longer outside things but inside them... This state of knowledge Dr Steiner calls 'Intuition'.

In an earlier section of his book, Arnold Freeman (referring to GA 10, GA 12 and GA 13) discusses in some detail the attainment of 'Imaginative consciousness'.

We can get some comprehension of what is required of us if we think of what we do when we remember. We look at a tree; we turn away from it; but we retain an image of it in our soul; we can summon up this image again; we can dwell upon it. Now if instead of occupying ourselves with the image of a thing perceived by the senses we deliberately place in the centre of consciousness an image freely chosen by ourselves and concentrate upon it, we are doing an exercise in 'Imagination'.

In great detail Dr Steiner presents us with an example of such 'Imagination'. He tells us how we can build up in our mind and heart the symbol of a black cross having seven red roses at the place where the beams of the cross intersect (cf. GA 13, Ch. 5). 'Such a symbol [says Steiner] represents no external object in outer nature and for this very reason possesses an awakening power upon our inner faculties... Many symbols of this kind are used in occult training.' Steiner says that 'certain sentences, formulae, single words' may be used; and, again, that meditation may be based upon certain feelings, e.g. joy in the idea of kindness of heart... But he urges that in every case the object in view is to detach the soul from sense-impressions and to encourage it to a sense-free activity—to an activity wherein it is unfolding its own essential forces... The all-important thing is not the subject-matter of the exercise but the amount of pure soul-force we exert in practising it...

To reach 'Inspiration' we must be able to go beyond concentrating upon an image; we must become able to hold in mind the soul-activity we employ in such a process. To reach 'Intuition' we must become able, further, to obliterate even this soul-activity—and yet not sink into a void.

Appendix Six
Sentient Soul, Intellectual Soul, Consciousness Soul

The following extracts from two of Rudolf Steiner's lectures and from the works of two experienced students of Steiner's spiritual science are given here to help those not familiar with these terms to come to some understanding of their meaning.

In a lecture of 22 March 1910, Rudolf Steiner gives one answer to the question: What are the differences between the sentient soul, the intellectual soul or mind soul and the consciousness soul or spiritual soul? His answer runs as follows:

> The sentient soul operates when we are merely gazing at the things of the external world. If we withdraw our attention for a time from the impressions of this outer world and work over them inwardly, then we are given over to the mind soul, the intellectual soul. But if we now take what has been worked over in thought, turn again to the outer world and relate ourselves to it by passing over to deeds, then we are given over to the consciousness soul, the spiritual soul. For example: as long as I am simply looking at these flowers in front of me and my feelings are moved by the pure whiteness of the roses, I am given up to my sentient soul. If, however, I avert my gaze and no longer see the flowers but only think about them, then I am given over to my intellectual or mind soul. I am working in thought upon the impressions I have received. If I now say to myself that because the flowers gave me pleasure I will gladden someone else by presenting them to him or her and then pick them up in order to hand them over, I am performing a *deed*; I am passing out of the realm of the mind soul into that of the consciousness soul and relating myself again to the outer world. [GA 119, 02/03/10]

* * *

In a lecture entitled 'The Present Crisis in Man's Development' Steiner considers the nature of the consciousness soul from quite a different aspect from that outlined above:

> We have entered into the heritage of the preceding epoch [i.e. 747 BC–AD 1413] during which most of us passed through one or more earthly lives, partly as the result of physical heredity, but especially because we bear the same souls that were incarnated in the fourth over into the fifth post-

Atlantean epoch. This heritage of the previous epoch is living in everything that constitutes civilization today. We have worked the intellect and the power of thinking into the consciousness soul and this is very significant. The consciousness soul, through which we acquire a real grasp of our ego, took possession, as it were, of thinking, of the conceptual life, of the intellect at the beginning of the fifth epoch. Humanity has become clever and astute, but clever within the limits of the consciousness soul. This means the development of egotism to its highest intensity and degree of subtlety. We should not merely revile this age of egotism or do nothing but criticize it. Although it brings so many temptations in its train, and subjects us to such great dangers both outwardly and in the soul, we must recognize it to be the period during which ego-consciousness emerges in particular strength. This makes it possible for us to develop a true feeling of freedom. We have not all known this feeling of freedom in our earlier incarnations. It was necessary for us to experience egotism with all its temptations in order that a longing for freedom such as is possessed only by modern humanity might arise.

It is one of the most important principles of anthroposophical knowledge to realize that in order to reach a significant stage of evolution, we must pass through the stage which leads to the *development of freedom.* But we must realize that this stage, with all its many dangers and temptations, is connected with humanity both in respect of the life of soul-and-spirit and also of the body. Anthroposophical knowledge must make it possible for us to receive to the full the impulse and feeling of freedom, but at the same time to ennoble it, to permeate it once again with spiritual insight, which in spite of the present mature sense of egohood and ego-consciousness spurs humankind to fulfil tasks that are not merely based on egotism but connected with the whole process of human evolution—indeed of Earth evolution itself. [GA 203, 17/02/21, in *Anthroposophical Quarterly*, Vol. 13, No. 3, 1968]

*   *   *

Bernhard Lievegoed gives us further insight into the different qualities of the three soul-members being discussed here.

The sentient soul, developed in the Egypto–Babylonian evolutionary phase, had the task of awakening human beings to the sensory world and of teaching them to distinguish between semblance and reality... Here Lucifer was the counterforce that presented the beautiful semblance of reality. It was the task of the sacred art of the temples to bring to consciousness the reality behind the beautiful semblance.

The intellectual soul, developed from the Graeco-Roman times through the Middle Ages, had the task of developing independent, logical thinking. The human being had to learn to distinguish between truth and untruth in thinking. Philosophy was the school. It developed from the first Greek philosophers up to the summit of Scholasticism. Truth revealed life, untruth brought death. In the striving for truth, life conquered death. Here, Ahriman was the counterforce. He is the spirit of the lie, of the negation of the spiritual, who, with unprecedented intelligence, develops the human intellect by which each assertion can be proved logically. The struggle for truth has been the history of the Christian Churches and the Christian esoteric streams.

The consciousness soul development, in which *we* have stood since the fifteenth century, has the task of learning to do the good after the encounter with true evil. For this, forces of courage must be developed along with inner certainty in acting and doing. With good or evil it is not a question of *knowing* the right, but *doing* the good, which comes from the development of intuition. It is this force that is called up at the end of the Foundation Stone Meditation in the words: '... That good may become/What from our hearts we would found/And from our heads direct/With single purpose.' [Lievegoed, B.C.J., *Mystery Streams in Europe and New Mysteries*, p. 72ff.]

*   *   *

In her seminal work, *Citizens of the Cosmos*, Beredene Jocelyn sheds further light on the meaning of the terms sentient soul, intellectual soul and consciousness soul. In regard to the sentient soul she says, *inter alia*:

Persons in the sentient soul stage tend to live in the present moment, oblivious of the past and the future. They are motivated largely by the sensations connected with their feelings—their desires, likes and dislikes, sympathies and antipathies, pleasures and aversions, urges and passions.

When the sentient soul responds to an event with anger, this might bode either good or ill. On the one hand, if it is an outburst of rage arising from egotism, it poisons the soul, weakens the ego, and isolates one from the world. On the other hand, when anger flares up as a reaction to injustice, it can be an educator of the sentient soul still untempered by the intellectual soul and the consciousness soul which develops later. Such 'noble anger' indicates that one is not an indifferent spectator; it is a mark of independence, and of opposition to wrong in the outer world. As one matures and conquers anger, it is transformed into love. [See R. Steiner, 'The Mission of Anger' in GA 58, 05/12/09] [...]

As the name indicates, the intellectual soul—also called the rational or mind soul—is concerned with understanding, with knowledge, with finding the meaning of things...The intellectual soul seeks understanding in the light of thinking. It enables us to reflect on external impressions, to ponder over them, and to combine them in the mind, thus leading to greater independence from the influence of the outer world. Instead of taking in impressions rather passively, the intellectual soul actively thinks on them and on sense-free ideas. Aspiring to truth, it produces concepts and ideas that are sharply defined and formulates judgements.

[...]

The less developed a human being is, the less he or she exercises thought and reason. At first thought serves only the sentient soul, making possible the gratification of the desires and needs [cf. GA 9, Part 2, Ch. 1]. In its higher expression, the activity of the ego in the intellectual soul strives to cultivate a sense of truth. In order that the ego may experience truth in the intellectual soul, the sentient soul must first be cleansed, else passions and desires may intervene and either cloud or distort the truth. When the intellectual soul permeates feeling with the inner light of thought, the ego purifies and refines the soul so that it masters and guides the feelings, thoughts and volitions, giving clarity of thought and directing thought to sense-free understanding.

[...]

The ego that was still only dimly brooding in the sentient soul, and that attained greater clarity and shone forth in the intellectual soul, develops its fullest clarity and an even higher, richer life in the consciousness soul... To be a human being in the fullest sense of the consciousness soul, the ego must continually enrich itself, be creative, and radiate from its centre what will, in turn, enrich the world. This can be achieved if one progresses beyond self-awareness and beyond self-knowledge of 'I am an I' to clear self-consciousness of the spiritual nature of the 'I'.

[...]

Through the activity of the consciousness soul one disentangles oneself from personal likes and dislikes, espouses truth apart from sympathy, and genuine goodness apart from personal advantage or disadvantage. Educators of the consciousness soul are: a sound sense of the ego, full self-possession, love and devotion (not weak submissiveness, but the ego active in the will), response to duty, and willing self-sacrifice. Instead of relying on outer directives, one follows one's own intuitions which derive from spiritual sources. [Cf. GA 4.]

[...]

The task of the Egypto–Chaldean civilization, from 2907 to 747 BC, still under divine guidance, was to develop the sentient soul, and that of the Graeco-Roman civilization, 747 BC to AD 1413, the intellectual soul. In 1413 our modern age began and will continue until about AD 3573... In the Intellectual Soul Age, human beings still felt themselves to be members of the universe, whereas in our age we have become conscious of our *freedom* and our own power of resolve and action.

[...]

If the consciousness soul is to function constructively in our era, it is ... essential that we assume individual responsibility for the present and the future, contributing to world evolution through our own effort, and working to our utmost capacity. Having become ego-conscious beings, we must take our development consciously in hand.

Appendix Seven
Ahrimanic, Asuric Powers

We have seen that Lucifer desires to draw us away from earth existence, and as a consequence make us into 'immature Angels'; we have also seen that Ahriman aims to draw us away from any connection with the spiritual world. A classical example of the influence of ahrimanic inspiration is manifested by the freethinker Robert Ingersoll who insisted that all talk of the spirit was meaningless, and that *ideas were nothing but foodstuffs*—as were works of genius like the plays of Shakespeare.[1] Ahriman's goal is to make a highly intellectualized earth-bound race of his own, but of the *Asuras*, who are even more powerful and evil than the other two adversaries, Steiner has spoken little. We do learn, however, that they attack the human ego, leading us to think it to be a product of the physical body. They intend, little by little, to deprive us of the ego entirely.

The goal of these asuric spirits is that what has been attacked by them, the consciousness soul together with the ego, the 'I', should unite with earthly materiality. 'Fragment after fragment will be torn out of the "I", and in the same measure in which the asuric spirits establish themselves in the consciousness soul, the human must leave parts of his existence behind on the earth. What thus becomes the prey of the asuric powers will be irretrievably lost. Not that the whole human being need become their victim—but part of the human spirit will be torn away' (GA 107, 01/01/09). In seeking to destroy the ego—the very 'focus' and 'promise' of the individual human being's immortality—the Asuras would sever us from the sphere of the eternal in which our true being has its origin (ibid.).

The formation of the Eighth Sphere (see Appendix Four) is an asuric activity. The asuras would compress, solidify matter to such a degree that it will no longer be possible for it to be spiritualized in the distant future. They strive to prevent human beings from evolving towards their goal—union with Christ.[2]

These 'ahrimanic, asuric powers' (GA 130, 01/10/11) express their influence in the current overt tendency for human beings to live wholly in the sense-perceptual world and to be *oblivious* of the reality of spiritual beings and spiritual worlds. A powerful 'tool' being used by these powers is the dissolute, sensuous life of passions which is becoming increasingly prevalent among men and women in modern society—such an illusory mode of being, of living, certainly contributes greatly to spiritual 'blindness'.

It is such 'blindness' which forms the foundation for the teaching that the highest moral ideas of humanity are, in fact, nothing other than the sublimations of animal impulses—that, indeed, the human being is not only akin to, but has descended from, the animal.

> Human beings do not as yet *entirely* [author's italics] base their lives on the principle that their true being descends from the animal. But this view of existence will inevitably arise, with the result that they will also live like animals, will sink into animal impulses, animal passions. And in many things that need not be further characterized here, many things that in the great cities come to expression in orgies of dissolute sensuality, we can already perceive the lurid, hellish glare of the spirits we call the Asuras. [Ibid.][3]

It is surely no exaggeration to claim that today, nearly 90 years after Rudolf Steiner uttered these words of warning, the symptoms of the pernicious, ego-destroying influence of these powerful ahrimanic, asuric forces are manifesting themselves with ever-increasing intensity.

In the lecture Steiner gave on 1 October 1911 entitled *The Etherization of the Blood* [GA 130) we are given a clue as to a power which is greater than that of the Asuras—that of the Christ, of the 'Not I, but the Christ in me'.

'For most people,' Steiner says, 'the Pauline maxim holds good that the spirit is willing but the flesh is weak. This is to be changed, because moral fire will stream from the form of Christ. Through this people will recognize the necessity for morality and its impulses more and more. They will transform the earth to the extent that they feel increasingly that morality belongs to it. In the future, only those will be able to be amoral who are led to be so by evil demons, or who are possessed by demons, by ahrimanic, asuric powers, and who aspire to such possession.'

Only the experience within of the Christ—who, in our time, is active through the mediation of Michael—can help us to withstand and overcome the power of the asuric forces. [4]

Appendix Eight
The Double

In a lecture of 16 November 1917 Rudolf Steiner speaks in some detail about the ahrimanic and luciferic 'Doubles'. It is the ahrimanic Double which is of particular significance during the present stage of the evolution of human consciousness, i.e. the development of the consciousness soul (see Appendix Six).

Steiner states that an ahrimanic elemental being links up with the human being a short time before birth. This ahrimanic spiritual being has a close connection with the sub-natural forces of electricity and magnetism. Through such elemental beings Ahriman aims to permeate us with his cold intelligence and inspire a technological world in which everything is controlled mechanically and electronically.

These beings possess an incredibly sharp intellect and a very strong will, but they are devoid of both feeling and morality. They are heartless beings.

In the same lecture Steiner also said that these beings would inspire an impersonal, electronic world. Now, 80 years later, we find how true his claim was, for we are surrounded by such a world.[1]

It is in the West, in America in particular, that these ahrimanic elementals exert their strongest influence. The outstanding technological achievements can be seen against this background.

Luciferic Doubles also exert a powerful influence. We have already alluded to this in the chapter on Lucifer. They aim to draw us away from our 'down to earth' responsibilities and inspire us to 'float away' in search of personal, egotistic liberation. They are the forces which would lead us to 'lose' our ego through, for instance, the use of LSD, cannabis, cocaine, alcohol and so forth. It is they, too, which would have us submit ourselves to the authority of a guru. To do so is to ally oneself with forces that oppose the development of ego-consciousness, of the consciousness soul. In a lecture held in Dornach on 19 November 1917 Steiner emphasizes the fact that 'the impulse for freedom must penetrate all the dominating tendencies ... for it is precisely this freedom of the human mind that is opposed by ... the Double who accompanies us from shortly before birth until just before death.' Those who are under the direct influence of the Double may 'bring about all sorts of things which can appear in this epoch [of the consciousness soul] but are not in harmony with it'. It will then not be possible for them to fulfil their task of fighting against evil in such a way that to a certain extent the evil is changed into good.

In an earlier lecture dealing with the Double (GA 158, 20/11/14) Rudolf Steiner makes the point that in due course many people will ask: 'Why is it that I feel as if my being were divided, as if a second being were standing by my side?'

In the education of children, Steiner maintains, it behoves both parent and teacher to pay attention to this experience of division for it will become increasingly common in children as time progresses. Adults may hear from children many things which must not be pooh-poohed but must be understood as being 'connected with deep secrets of evolution'.

Steiner continues: 'We shall hear the children saying: "I have seen a being who ... told me what to do." The materialist, of course, will tell such a child that this is all nonsense, that no such being exists. But students of spiritual science will have to understand the significance of the phenomenon.' We need to understand that what the child experiences is a real meeting with the ahrimanic Double—and has nothing whatever to do with any form of schizophrenia.

In this lecture of 20 November 1914 Steiner also speaks of the effect the prejudices and limitations of materialist thinking has on the human ether-body, life-body. It is coarsened and dried up. The ahrimanic powers are strengthened by the presence of such an ether-body. In an ether-body that has been parched by materialism the ahrimanic Double finds a ready dwelling. Accompanied by this second being, a person will feel the urge to think materialistic thoughts—to think 'not through his or her being, but through that of the second being', the ahrimanic Double.

The prophylaxis is indicated in this lecture: '... it is our duty to educate children in the future—be it by way of Eurythmy or the development of a spiritual–scientific outlook—in such a way that they will be competent to understand the spiritual world. The ether body must be quickened in order that the human being may be able to be ... fully cognizant of the nature of the being who stands at his side.'

Elsewhere Rudolf Steiner speaks of the human soul as having

many conflicting tendencies which it cannot control. They exist deep down within it, beyond the ken of our ordinary, everyday consciousness. All human beings have elements in their souls beyond their conscious control—elements to which they are emotionally attached.

Ahriman becomes particularly active towards these especially intense attachments. The soul contains portions that can be pried loose from its entirety, and because we do not fully control these components Ahriman pounces on them. Through Ahriman's unjustified activity, overstepping his proper domain, a tendency arises for those parts of man's etheric and astral [soul] being that are inclined to separate from the rest of the soul's life, and become independent, to be formed by Ahriman and even given human shape. [GA 147, 30/08/13]

When Ahriman grasps the chance to make these parts of the human independent and give them human shape they appear to us, in the elemental world, as our Double.

'This encounter with the Double is in the nature of an elemental phenomenon. It can happen as a result of subconscious soul impressions and impulses even to a person who is not clairvoyant.' Steiner then goes on to give a concrete example.

The following can occur. Somebody or other may be an *intrigant* and thereby have done harm to other people. He may have gone out and set another intrigue in motion. On returning home, he may enter his study, where papers are lying on his desk, papers that may contain things he made use of in his intrigues. Now what may happen, despite the cynical cast of his ordinary consciousness, is that his subconscious may be seized by these impulses to make intrigues. He comes in, looks at his desk—and what does he see? He sees himself sitting there. [GA 147, 30/08/13]

* * *

In one of his Mystery Plays, *The Soul's Probation*, Rudolf Steiner gives us another insight into the nature of the Double. One of the characters, Johannes, has become more dependent on the physical presence of a woman (Maria) wiser than himself, than on her spiritual guidance. This unrecognized sensuality leads him to an inner awakening. He meets with a 'reflection' of his lower self, his Double.

In her *Introduction to the Mystery Plays of Rudolf Steiner*, Eileen Hutchins[2] comments: 'As man becomes clairvoyant he is able to recognize his own being in the spiritual world; but when he lives in illusions, Lucifer and Ahriman are able to draw near. Ahriman then has the power to step beyond his rightful position in the physical world and give form and shape in the elemental world to what should remain an inner experience.'

An awareness of this has been illustrated in literature on a number of occasions. Probably the best known is Robert Louis Stevenson's *Dr Jekyll and Mr Hyde*. Hutchins also mentions *The Man who Found Himself* by Osbert Sitwell, where a young and penniless artist 'meets with himself as he will appear when he is an elderly man who has deserted his principles in order to win success. He is filled with hate and indignation. Then in later years, bored and disillusioned, he confronts his own being as a young man. The shock causes his death.'

Johannes does not die when he hears his Double give expression to the sensual love which in reality he harbours for Maria, but he is shattered.

Wolfram von Eschenbach's *Parzival* gives us further insight into the nature and meaning of the Double. At the point where Parzival has been accepted by King Arthur as a Knight of the Round Table a strange intruder rides into the circle, an extremely ugly woman, Kundry, who cries out that Parzival has been unjustly honoured. He is unworthy because he is under the curse of not having asked the right question when he was at the Castle of the Grail.

Here Kundry is—in Jungian terms—the anima who is at the same time the Double. That this is so becomes clear at the end of *Parzival*. When, after many trials, Parzival becomes the King of the Grail, Kundry comes to meet him—but now she has become a beautiful shining figure.

*　*　*

In fairy-tales we find sometimes, more or less deeply hidden, the motif of the Double. Grimm's tale of Rumpelstiltskin may serve as a good illustration.

A poor miller boasts to the king that his beautiful daughter could 'spin straw into gold'. The king said he would put her to the test. He took her into a room which was full of straw and told her to spin it into gold. It was a hopeless task and the girl began to cry. At that moment a manikin entered the room and said he would do it for her, if she would give him something in return. She gave him her necklace and by morning the little man had spun all the straw into gold.

The king was delighted and had the daughter taken into a much larger room full of straw and gave her the same task. Again the little man came into the room and, after receiving the ring from the girl's finger, span all the straw into gold.

The greedy king was delighted but wanted still more gold and took the girl into an even larger room full of straw. 'You must spin this, too, in the course of the night. If you succeed, you shall be my wife.'

When the girl was alone the little man came again and asked: 'What will you give me if I spin all this straw into gold?' 'I have nothing left to give, answered the girl. 'Then promise me, if you should become queen, to give me your first child.' 'Who knows whether that will ever happen?' thought the miller's daughter and gave her promise, whereat the manikin span all the straw into gold.

The king married the miller's pretty daughter. A year after she gave birth to a beautiful child but gave no thought to the manikin. When he suddenly returned and demanded she fulfil her promise she was horror-struck and began to lament and cry. The little man took pity on her and said he would give her three days' grace. 'If by that time you find out my name, then you shall keep the child.' For two days a messenger travelled all over the country seeking unusual names which the queen repeated when the manikin came to her, but they were all wrong. On the third day the messenger came across 'a ridiculous little man', hopping on one leg and jumping round a fire shouting:

> Today I bake, tomorrow brew,
> The next I'll have the young queen's child.
> Ha! Glad am I that no one knew
> That Rumpelstiltskin I am styled.

Delighted the queen called the little man by his name when he questioned her on the third day. Thereupon he cried out, 'The devil has told you that! The devil has told you that!' And in his anger he plunged his right foot so deep into the earth that his whole leg went in; and then in rage he pulled at his left leg so hard with both hands that he tore himself in two.

From this tale we can learn several things about our relationship to the ahrimanic Double. This being gains power over the young girl because she makes a promise without being fully aware of the possible consequences (she assumes an improbability, namely, that she would not become queen). However, when, fearing the loss of her child, she 'wakes up' and becomes fully conscious of the consequence of her promise, the manikin finds himself offering a possible solution. Both Ahriman and Lucifer have greater power over us when our consciousness is diminished; their power is diminished when we act—and think—consciously. Furthermore, to recognize, to name the adversarial powers is a major step toward overcoming them.

Now, we hear that the little man hops on one foot. Why? Because he is unable to use both feet as one of them is a club-foot— he has a *Rumpelstelz*. In the lecture of 20 November 1914 from which we quoted earlier, Rudolf Steiner draws our attention to the fact that Ahriman, the ahrimanic Double, can insinuate himself into the 'dried up human ether-body'. He then goes on to say that Ahriman will assume the form which indicates a lack of power in the ether-body, the life-body. 'There is good reason ... for portraying Mephistopheles [Ahriman] with the feet of a goat. Myths and legends are full of meaning. Mephistopheles is very often depicted with horses' hoofs; his feet have dried up and become hoofs.'

Rumpelstiltskin reveals himself to be an ahrimanic Double through his club-foot.[3]

Appendix Nine
Sexuality and Love

It was through the original luciferic temptation that human beings were given the prospect of freedom and therewith the possibility of choosing between good and evil; *inter alia*, this also meant that we could also succumb to the passions and desires of our lower nature.

Rudolf Steiner speaks of Lucifer 'creeping' into the human astral body. Had Lucifer not done so, we would have remained in a paradisiacal state, in a state of innocence and purity in our astral body (GA 107, 01/01/09).

Prior to the 'descent' to earth-existence, the physical body—with the exception of the head—'was purely elemental, "airy" by nature' (GA 177, 08/10/17). It is entirely due to Lucifer, Steiner states, that the elemental 'airy' body condensed to become flesh.

'Something very strange has arisen as a result ... What has happened is that the human being has become the image of the Gods in the very organs which are normally called the organs of his lower nature ... Our lower nature, which is due to Lucifer's influence, was actually destined to be our higher nature' (ibid.).

Elsewhere Steiner says:

We can form an idea about how Lucifer can get at human beings in this way by considering ... the phenomenon of love in the widest sense of the word, the foundation of a true moral life in the world order of humanity. Concerning love in its widest sense, the following has to be said: when love appears in the physical sense world and has its effect on human life, it is absolutely protected from every unlawful luciferic attack if the love is for another person and for that person's own sake. When we are met by another human being ... that being meets us with certain qualities. If we are freely receptive to these qualities, if we are capable of being moved by them, they then command our love ... We are moved by the other being to love it. Where the cause of love lies not in the one who loves but in the object of love, this form and kind of love in the sense-world is *absolute proof against every luciferic influence* [author's italics]. But now if you observe human life, you will soon see that another kind of love is playing its part, in which a person loves because he himself has certain qualities that feel satisfied, or charmed, or delighted when he can love this or that being. Here he loves for his own sake ... [GA 147, 25/08/13][1]

Lucifer's influence is apparent in this form of egoistic love. This form of love must also exist, however. Love for the spiritual, longing to comprehend the beings of the spiritual world, 'must—not *may* but *must*—come about necessarily for our own sake.'

We are beings who have our roots in the spiritual world. It is our duty, Steiner states, to make ourselves as perfect, as spiritualized as possible. 'For our own sake we must love the spiritual world in order to draw as many forces as possible out of it into our own being. In spiritual love a personal, individual element—we can call it egoistic—is fully justified' (ibid.)[2] Now Lucifer has the tendency to interchange the two worlds—the physical and the spiritual—with each other. Whenever a person loves in the physical sense-world for himself with an element of egoism, 'it occurs because Lucifer wants to make physical love similar to spiritual love. He can then root it out of the physical sense-world and lead it into his own special kingdom' (ibid). Steiner then draws our attention to a fact which is just as relevant at the end of the twentieth century as it was near its beginning: '... in this modern materialistic culture there is every reason to point out these luciferic allurements in regard to love, for a great part of our present-day outlook and literature, especially that of medicine, is permeated by the luciferic conception of love' (ibid.). Steiner then goes on to say that the luciferic element in love is actually encouraged by a large section of medical science; men are repeatedly advised—for it is the male who is pandered to—that they must cultivate a certain kind, a certain sphere of love as necessary for *their* health, i.e. necessary for *their* sake.

A little later in the same lecture Steiner makes the following significant observation:

> Materialistic minds believe that the spiritual world is not there; they do not see it ... Nevertheless, in the depths of their souls, the craving for the spiritual world does not cease to exist merely because they deaden themselves and deny its reality ... there is a law that something repressed and deadened at one point will break out at another. The consequence of the repression of the egoistic impulse towards the spiritual world is that it thrusts itself into the sensual desires. The kind of love due to the spiritual worlds hurls itself away from there into the sensual impulses, passions and desires, and these impulses become perverse. [Ibid.]

We could ask ourselves: What was the catalyst that occasioned Rudolf Steiner to speak in such emphatic terms regarding the

prevailing scientific literature which was devoted to connecting
sexuality with love? It was, no doubt, primarily the work of
Sigmund Freud (1856–1939), the Austrian psychologist, whose
neurosis theory or sexual theory was being widely put into practice.

It was first in September 1915 that Steiner mentioned Freud by
name in public. In that month he gave four lectures dealing with
various aspects of Freudian psychoanalysis (GA 253, 13–16/09/15).
In the first of these lectures Steiner discusses the methods and
rationale of Freudian psychoanalysis. We are reminded that psychoanalysis aims to lift up into consciousness certain 'islands' in the
unconscious psyche. It assumes that the majority of these so-called
'islands' are sexual in nature. The Freudian theory maintains that
healing is brought about by lifting hidden sexual complexes up
from the depths of the subconscious and making the analysand
aware of them again. '[The] psychoanalyst's thinking is often
coloured by an underlying sexuality, and this is taken to extremes
when psychoanalysis is applied to any and all possible phenomena
of human life.' For instance, the Freudians are convinced that a
child's relationship to his or her father and mother is a sexual one
from the moment of birth. So if the child is a boy, he must be
unconsciously in love with his mother and thus unconsciously
jealous of his father. Steiner emphasizes that 'it really is extremely
important to regard certain processes in children's lives as simply
natural without having to see them in terms of sexuality right away'
(ibid.).

Towards the end of this lecture Steiner states that he is fully
justified in saying that 'psychoanalysis as a whole is positively
dripping with this psycho-sexual stuff, as its professional literature
reveals'.

Before referring to the second lecture Steiner gave in September
on Freudian psychoanalysis, 'Sexuality and Modern Clairvoyance',
let it be clear that he certainly did not deny the existence of an
erotic nature in a child of, say, 13, 14 or 15. In a lecture given to a
group of teachers at the first Waldorf/Steiner school in Stuttgart,
Germany, he discusses education for adolescence.

One of the important points he makes is this. If a child prior to
puberty has not had the feeling for beauty awakened in him or her,
has not been educated to view the world from an aesthetic point of
view, then, on reaching sexual maturity, that boy or girl will tend to
become sensual, perhaps even erotic. There is no better way of
restraining eroticism than by a healthy development of the

aesthetic sense. To awaken and cultivate such a sense does far more for maturing children 'than if you were to give them the sex instruction which it has now become customary to give children in their tenderest youth, and which is often carried to quite absurd lengths' (GA 302, 16/06/21). Steiner could be addressing parents and teachers of today! He goes on to say: 'As a child learns to perceive the world in all its beauty, he/she learns also to stand as a free being over against his/her own body; he/she is not oppressed by it. And that is what eroticism is—to be oppressed and tormented by one's own body. Nor is it less important that before [the age of puberty] children shall have developed something of moral and religious feeling. Such feelings have always a strengthening effect upon astral body and ego' (ibid.).[3]

In the lecture entitled 'Sexuality and Modern Clairvoyance', Steiner gives us an insight into the nature of the clairvoyance which manifested itself in the scientist and mystical thinker, Emmanuel Swedenborg (1688–1772). Here Steiner explains that under certain—and rarely occurring—circumstances, sexual energy can lead to clairvoyance. Swedenborg recognized real spiritual beings, but he could not understand them. 'He recognized them by means of some ability he should not have had because he was lacking the necessary consciousness—ordinary powers of consciousness on the physical plane are inadequate to explain what he was seeing.' But in that case we ask: How was Swedenborg actually seeing? In answer to this question, Steiner begins by making a very significant point: 'Swedenborg had spent his life not only as a great scholar but also as *a very pure person* [author's italics], and so a certain energy was transformed within him' (GA 253, 14/09/15).

What was the energy that enabled Swedenborg to see spiritual beings? '[He] was seeing by means of a force that perceives outer appearances without touching them in any way and without making use of the eyes. What kind of force is that? ... on the physical plane, it is the force that comes to expression in sexual activity, the mysterious force that pulls people together in earthly love, a force different from all other powers of perception. Swedenborg had stored up this force, and when he reached a certain age it was transformed in him, although it remained sexual energy in some respects. He used this sexual energy to see spiritual worlds' (ibid.).

The lesson to be learnt from such a case as that of Swedenborg is that clairvoyance connected with the force of sexuality is completely inadequate, for although one can see spiritual beings in the spiritual world one is quite unable to comprehend what it is one is seeing. 'These higher planes require that we work towards a new mode of perception applicable to the spiritual world,[4] a mode of perception that has nothing to do with sexual energy, since that is physical and exists only for the physical plane' (ibid.).

The two spheres, the physical/sexual on the one hand and the spiritual on the other, must not be mixed with one another.

Rudolf Steiner concludes the lecture of 14 September 1915 by referring to a case 'of the worst possible mingling of spheres, a case in which sexual drives were at work but were interpreted as something quite different.'[5]

'Our only recognition of the very great dignity and solemnity of spiritual life can guard against egotism in spiritual activity. Once egotistical mysticism enters, nothing can save us from mixing the two above-mentioned spheres in the worst possible way.'

In the third of the four lectures dealing with Freudian psycho-analysis (15 September 1915) entitled 'The Concept of Love as it Relates to Mysticism', Steiner states that when materialists attempt to formulate a concept of mysticism they are led to conclude that what mystics 'dream of' can only be found in the emotion of love in the sense-world; that is, 'everything spiritual is dragged down into a refined version of eroticism'. The stance that such men and women adopt is that 'even in our thinking, we have to replace our relationship to the spiritual world with the eroticism throbbing in our souls—a more or less refined eroticism, depending on the character of the individual in question' (ibid.).

A prime example of an individual who manifested a far from refined eroticism can be seen in Aleister Crowley (1875–1947), the self-styled Great Beast 666. In his recently published book, *At the Heart of Darkness*, John Parker gives us a vivid and well-researched exposition of witchcraft, black magic and Satanism today,[6] and he has much to say about Crowley's brand of occultism, about the man who said: 'I want blasphemy, murder, rape, revolution, anything bad...'

During his adolescence Crowley turned against Christianity so completely that he eventually sought to destroy it: 'One day his mother plucked up the courage to inform her son that he had become the Great Beast of Revelation, an identity which he was more than happy to accept' (Parker).

In adulthood Crowley threw himself into his antichristian mission with manic fervour, 'marching backwards to the Dark Ages of cruelty, superstition and diabolism. This quest was further enhanced in 1912 when he became head of a German group specializing in erotic sex magic, known as the Ordo Templi Orientis' (ibid.). He made this society his own and today, according to Parker, it is the largest of all the secret societies operating throughout the world.[7]

Without going into any detail, it shall be simply stated here that sex was always to be the most powerful element in Crowley's form of black magic.

For a number of years he had harboured the idea of owning a temple of black magic where he could practise his rites undisturbed. His dream came true in March 1920, when he located an isolated villa, hidden among olive groves near the fishing village of Cefalu, on the northern coast of Sicily.

'To study Crowley, his work and his life is to realize what is possible within the world of the occult and what is passed off as being essential for esoteric knowledge when in truth it is a whole range of sexually based ideas that can hardly be put in the context of normal life' (Parker).

It is significant that Crowley, who thought of himself as the Great Beast 666, should have chosen the island of Sicily on which to practise his perverted form of esotericism. On one occasion Rudolf Steiner speaks of how the powerful life-forces, etheric forces, emanating in Sicily were misused in the past. Even today, according to Steiner, if we tread Sicilian soil and have occult sight, we can still perceive the evil after-effects of Klingsor, the king of the realm of the Anti-Grail, for he had deepened his antagonism towards the Christ-impulse by allying himself with those enemies of the Grail who occupied the stronghold known in occultism and legend as Kalot Bobot (Kalta Bellota, and similar variations) in Sicily (GA 144, 07/02/13).[8]

*   *   *

Sexuality, eroticism, will eventually no longer exert the power it has today. On more than one occasion Steiner speaks of our planet earth as being the planet of love. 'The development of this, the first instilling of love, had to be in its lowest form ... the development of love in its lowest form began through the separation of the sexes. All further development consists in the continual refinement, the spiritualizing of this love-principle' (GA 105, 12/08/08).

Selfless love, true compassion, is immune to any interference by

both luciferic and ahrimanic forces. In this connection Rudolf
Steiner pointed out on one occasion that in an ambiance engulfed
by materialistic concepts

> ... it is exceedingly difficult to maintain in true and right perspective this
> concept of compassion and love ... [It] is distorted, in that materialism
> associates the concept of 'love' so closely with that of 'sexuality' with
> which, fundamentally, it has nothing whatever to do ... The fact that
> under certain circumstances the element of sexuality may be associated
> with love between man and woman is no argument for bringing so
> closely together the all-embracing nature of love or compassion, and the
> entirely specific character of sexuality ... to associate the concept of, say,
> a 'railway engine' with that of a man being 'run over', because engines
> do sometimes run over people, would be just about as intelligent as it is
> to connect the concept of love so closely with that of sexuality—simply
> because under certain circumstances there is an outward association.
> [GA 133, 14/05/1912]

Speaking on the same theme a few days earlier, Steiner did not
mince his words: 'Sexuality and love have nothing whatever to do
with each other. Sexuality is something quite different from and
has no connection with pure, original love. Science has brought
things to a shameful point by means of an extensive literature
devoted to connecting these two things which are simply not connected' (GA 143, 08/05/12).[9]

One day all who take into themselves the reality of 'Not I, but
Christ in me' will be imbued with spiritualized love.

In the first chapter of *The Philosophy of Freedom*,[10] Steiner
makes reference to two forms of love. The distinction is made
between *instinctive love*, i.e. sexual desire, and what he calls *human
love*. Whenever love is not merely the expression of instinct it
depends on the mental picture (*Vorstellung*) we form of the loved
one—'And the more idealistic these mental pictures are, just so
much the more blessed is our love.'

In our ordinary, everyday life it is true to say that, in general, our
feelings of love are closely linked with our instincts, to our life of
desires. But it is possible to free love from the physical body.
Whereas in our 'normal' life the original impetus for love comes
from 'within us', it is possible to develop this love through being
immersed in outer objects, things and people, so that we are able to
forget ourselves and become one with that which is 'outside' us. If
we perform an action in such a way that it does not arise out of the
impulses which have their origin in our desires and instincts, but

out of love for what is around us, then we have the kind of love which is at the same time the power of human freedom. That is why Steiner says in *The Philosophy of Freedom* that, in a higher sense, the saying 'love makes us blind' is not true, but on the contrary 'love makes us see'. Those who live and act through love make themselves free for they free themselves from the instincts and sexual desires which otherwise so easily enslave them. They can act as free human beings in the sense that they do what they know should be done and not what they would be led to do under the dictate of their instincts and desires.[11]

Human love is called forth not by *physical* perception but by the forming of thoughts about the spiritual, inner, invisible qualities of a person. These thoughts kindle our love. In this form of love we are confronted with feelings which do not rise up without our active and conscious participation, from our instinctive life, but are born of our thinking—without which they would not come into being. In contrast to this we can say that when love is based on instincts—when, in short, we merely wish to satisfy cravings arising from desires—thinking is all but non-existent. This kind of 'love' is an expression of egoism in one of its basic forms. Indeed, as we saw earlier, is not 'real' love at all.

In the eighth chapter of *The Philosophy of Freedom*, entitled 'The Factors of Life', Steiner speaks of a third, a higher form of love—the capacity of thinking to penetrate into the depths of phenomena. This power of thinking is a 'seeing' of ideas. Steiner calls it *intuition*. This power, which he also calls *spiritual love*, may penetrate into lesser or greater depths of the phenomena. It may, for instance, 'see' only as much of the idea of a thing as is actually revealed by its physical aspect; on the other hand, it may penetrate the physical veil and 'see' what 'creates' the object under observation—as Wolfgang von Goethe (1749–1832) did when he 'saw' the archetypal plant, i.e. the Idea which underlies and 'creates' all plants.[12]

Steiner brings this line of thought to a culmination in the following words in *The Philosophy of Freedom*: 'In thinking we have the element given us which welds our separate individuality into one whole with the cosmos. In so far as we sense and feel (and also perceive), we are single beings; in so far as we think, we are the All-One Being that pervades everything.'[13] In other words: in so far as we think, or rather, when we attain and 'exercise' the power of intuition, of *spiritual love*, then we and God are one. When we attain the *reality* of thinking within ourselves we realize the Divine within ourselves.[14]

In our present context we can understand the nature of spiritual love in the following way. Though my feelings for a person are on a higher level than mere sexual attraction because I admire some spiritual qualities in that person—and my feelings can therefore be described as being human love—they may nevertheless still be limited by my personality. That is to say, they depend on what *I* consider worthy of admiration and love. But if I am able to assess the other person solely for his or her sake (irrespective of whether he or she pleases or displeases me), if I am able to understand the other person completely and identify myself with him or her, then the love that now awakens in me is spiritual. Such love is no longer bound to my personality—with my sympathies and antipathies, likes and dislikes, and so forth. My thinking, my knowledge of and feeling for the person are concerned solely with the other person, not with myself. We could say that my feelings now partake of the spiritual nature of thinking. I live now not in my personal ego, my personal 'I', but in the 'I' which is one with the 'World-I'. We can also say now that the power within thinking which enables us to penetrate into the depths of the phenomena—the power which Steiner calls spiritual love—is the divine, love-filled power of Christ.

In one of his lectures on the theosophy of the Rosicrucians, Steiner gives us an insight into one aspect of the kind of education the spiritual scientist must be prepared to undertake. For instance, he or she must educate himself/herself to see in every stone, every plant, every flower, the outer expression of the spirit dwelling in the earth. Everything transitory has to be seen, experienced as a 'semblance' of an Eternal, expressing itself through it.[15]

Looking into the distant future Steiner then gives us the following imagination:

> Behold the flower chalice which receives the ray of the sun; the sun calls forth the pure productive forces which slumber in the plant and hence the sun's ray was called the 'holy lance of love'. Look now at man; he stands higher than the plant, he has the same organs within him, but all that the plant harbours in itself, perfectly chaste and pure, is in him steeped in lust and impure desire. The future of human evolution consists in this: human beings will again be chaste and pure, and speak forth their likeness into the world through another organ which will be the transformed organ of generation. The human generative organ will be chaste and pure without desire, without passion; and as the calyx of the

blossom turns upward to the holy love lance, it will turn to the spiritual ray of wisdom, and fructified by this will bring forth its own image. *This organ is the larynx* [author's italics]. [GA 99, 06/06/07]

We introduced the theme of sexuality and love with the statement that it was through the original luciferic temptation that mankind could—and would—succumb to the passions and desires of our lower nature. We may recognize, therefore, that when, in the distant future, 'the human generative organ will be chaste and pure without desire' the time for *Lucifer's redemption* will have arrived.

*   *   *

In Chapter 10 of his book *Cosmic Memory*, Rudolf Steiner gives us a remarkable insight into the affinity sexual forces have with high, 'noble spiritual forces':

> The higher, more noble divine forces have an affinity with the— *apparently*—lower forces of human nature. The word 'apparently' must here be understood in its full significance. For it would be a complete misconception of occult truths if one were to see something base in the forces of reproduction as such.
>
> It is only when these forces are misused, when they merely serve to satisfy passions and instincts, that there is something pernicious in them.[16] But this is not the case when we '*ennoble*' them through the insight that a divine spirit lies in them ... Spiritual science teaches that this whole sphere is to be ennobled, is to be placed under divine laws, but is not to be mortified.

The Asuras (see Appendix Seven) have become powerfully active in the present, the fifth post-Atlantean epoch. They are highly destructive adversarial powers and principally active in the sexual sphere, in the physical body, of the human being. The many sexual aberrations we can witness today are to be traced back to these Spirits of Darkness. (See GA 266/1, *Aus den Inhalten der esoterischen Stunden I*, p. 137.)

*   *   *

In 1996 a book by an Anglican parish priest, Charles Pickstone, was published under the title *For the Fear of Angels—How sex has usurped religion*. A short quote from the Introduction ('Landscape of Desire') gives the reader a good idea of the line Pickstone has chosen to follow:

In this book I am going to suggest that there is an underlying common thread; namely that sex has taken on many of the functions once performed by religion. In particular, sex has become a path to an encounter with primordial mystery. It is this encounter which is the subject of this book.

But more than that, in our present condition sex is not only one possible route to the encounter with mystery, it is also the most popular. This is the primary reason why sex is so important and why it is invested with such extraordinary power: it is one of the main modes of access, for those of us who are not nuclear scientists, astrophysicists or cell biologists, to the mystery of life itself; access that can be found almost nowhere else in this world, given the general lack of interest in religion, the traditional path to the mystery of life. From this point of view, sex has become the religion of the western world, the bearer of most people's hopes of encountering something truly 'other'.

Truly alarming statements to come from an Anglican parish priest!

Appendix 10
Chartres and the Platonic–Aristotelian Streams

For two hundred years during the eleventh and twelfth centuries Platonic thinking had been nurtured at Chartres. For a Platonist the sense-perceptible world is a reflection of the Ideas that 'live' in the spiritual world. It is these Ideas which are the reality. According to Platonism it is our task, setting out from the sense-world, to rise, step by step, to the *Idea* itself. For example, in our gardens we have many different species of plant. All have come into being from the Idea 'plant' in the spiritual world. Each one of them is, to a greater or lesser degree, a perfect expression in the sense-world of the Idea 'plant'. Only the Idea contains the full perfection of 'plantness'.[1]

For the Platonists at Chartres the Idea, the spirit, was a creative and imaginative artist constantly transforming matter, the sense-perceptible world. The world of Ideas is creative and mobile, not static. It is in the spiritual world that human beings have their true home. Plato's way of thinking was spiritual, it was imaginative, 'mobile'.

Aristotle, a pupil at Plato's Academy in Athens, transformed his Master's type of thinking into a more logical approach to the world of Ideas. The relationship between these two men and their modes of thinking about the material and spiritual world found expression again in history by the Platonic Cistercians in Chartres and the Aristotelian Dominicans in Paris.[2]

Now, both these two streams had been affected by the Mystery of Golgotha. Platonism was Christianized by the great teachers in the School of Chartres,[3] and the same happened later to Aristotelianism in Paris through the Dominicans and the teaching, in particular, of Thomas Aquinas.[4]

These two streams often seem to be opposing one another, but in reality there is a close interweaving with one another. On one occasion Rudolf Steiner throws the following light on this relationship. While the Platonic School of Chartres was working on the earth for some two hundred years, the Aristotelians were unable to work on earth. The conditions, Steiner states, were not yet there.

> But instead, they were preparing for the Michael stream in the super-sensible world, maintaining a continuous connection with those who were working on earth in the same direction and who then found their way to Chartres. The School of Chartres was in full flower from the end of the eleventh and throughout the twelfth century, and then a kind of supersensible exchange of ideas took place between the Platonic souls from the School of Chartres who were now coming up into the spiritual world through death and the Aristotelian souls who had remained above. It was an exchange of ideas which took place in the Middle Ages at the turn of the twelfth and thirteenth century, as to the manner of working in the future.[5] The outcome of this exchange of ideas—since different conditions now prevailed in the spiritual life of European humanity—was that the Platonists who had been so active in Chartres and were now coming up into the supersensible world, passed on their mission to the Aristotelians. And these Aristotelian souls now descended into the physical world in order to carry forward, in the way that conditions allowed, what I will call the *cosmic service of Michael*. [GA 238, 12/09/24]

Those souls who had 'conferred' with initiates in the School of Chartres before descending to a new earth-existence and who later wore the robe of the Dominicans had the task of spreading Aristotelianism with its intellectuality and of preparing the epoch of the consciousness soul (or spiritual soul). 'In the Anthroposophical Society,' Rudolf Steiner states in a lecture he gave in 1924, 'we have Aristotelianism working on, but in a spiritualized form, and awaiting its further spiritualization.' He then goes on to say: 'Then, at the end of the century many of those who are here today will return, but they will be united, then, with those who were the teachers in the School of Chartres. The aim of the Anthroposophical Society is to unite the two elements' (GA 240, 18/07/24).

Steiner characterizes the relationship of the Platonic stream to that of the Aristotelian most succinctly in a footnote to a passage in Goethe's *Geschichte der Farbenlehre* (History of the Theory of Colour). Aristotle's conception of the world does not stand in opposition to that of Plato:

> The difference lies more in the way in which the interests of the two are concentrated on different sides of reality (the world of ideas and that of the senses). For Plato the sense-world is merely a preliminary stage for

reaching the world of ideas; the former has meaning only in so far as it helps us to reach the latter. The opposite is the case with Aristotle. He wants to explain the sense-world, and seeks the explanation in the ideas. *We can say that substantially the two philosophers are of the same view, only their* interest *is centred on the two opposing sides.*[6]

René Querido concludes his book *The Golden Age of Chartres* with a quotation from a lecture Rudolf Steiner gave on the social question on 24 September 1919:

Seek real practical life, but seek in such a way that the spirit which dwells within it is not deadened for you. Seek the spirit, but not with supersensible lust, not out of supersensible egoism, but seek it so that you can apply it selflessly in practical life in the material world. Apply the ancient words 'Spirit is never without matter, matter never without spirit' in such a way that you say to yourselves: we will do all things in the material world in the light of the spirit and so seek the light of the spirit that it may enkindle warmth for our practical deeds.[7]

These words were addressed to the general public and not only to members of the Anthroposophical Society. They suggest, therefore, that it is not by any means only those in the Anthroposophical Movement in whom the two streams, the Platonic and the Aristotelian, should, in the Michael Age in which we all live and have our being, work with one another in balanced harmony.

At the beginning of the thirteenth century there took place one of the most important exchanges of ideas between those who carried up the old Platonism, inspired by spiritual vision, from the School of Chartres into the supersensible world and those on the other hand who were preparing to carry Aristotelianism down to earth—as the great transition to bring about a new spirituality that was to flow into the evolution of mankind in the future. [GA 237, 13/07/24]

Today, the Platonists who were working in the School of Chartres in the eleventh and twelfth centuries and the Aristotelians who were united with them in the spiritual world at the beginning of the thirteenth century are working together again. 'They are working together now, intending a new spiritual epoch in earthly evolution' (GA 237, 13/07/24). Their joint purpose is to cultivate spirituality once more within the civilization which, according to Steiner, 'apart from this, is sailing on into destruction and disintegration' (ibid.).

In the three lectures published in English under the title *The*

Redemption of Thinking, Rudolf Steiner relates spiritual science (anthroposophy) to the philosophical approach to spirit-reality and the problems of human thinking, and shows that its principles follow directly from the stream of philosophical thought that culminated in the Scholastic philosophy of Thomas Aquinas.

Those in whose souls the Michael-impulse was still echoing on from the previous Age of Michael (at the time of Alexander the Great) found their way, above all, into the Dominican Order. From that Order issued that Scholasticism which strove to master the true nature and *modus operandi* of the intelligence within the human mind. It was the Realists of the Dominican Order who maintained that ideas and thoughts are spiritual realities contained within the phenomena of the world, they were not merely nominal, which was the position assumed by the Nominalists. The Nominalists maintained that concepts and ideas are no more than names. They were strongly influenced by Ahriman, for we may say that their aim was to prevent Michael's dominion from prevailing among human beings on the earth. At that time, Steiner says: 'Ahrimanic spirits whispered to those who would lend their ear: The Cosmic Intelligence has fallen away from Michael and is here, on the earth. We will not allow Michael to resume his rulership over the Intelligence!... But in that heavenly conference—and precisely here lies its significance—Platonists and Aristotelians together formed a plan for the furtherance of the Michael-impulse' (GA 240, 19/07/24).

We learn from Steiner that one of the greatest of the Chartres masters, Alanus ab Insulis (*c.* 1128–*c.* 1203) spoke to a narrow circle of his initiate pupils of the need to come to an understanding with the Aristotelians who bring to humanity the intellect. It is this intellect which must be spiritualized so that 'in the twentieth century it may shine forth in a new and spiritual form among human beings' (GA 240, 18/07/24).

Through the thirteenth, fourteenth and fifteenth centuries it was as though the Aristotelians, in the physical world, and the Platonists, in the spiritual world, were working together. In due course many of those who had descended to earth in order to introduce Aristotelianism into Europe were in the spiritual world again with the Platonists who had been in the School of Chartres.

Then, in the first half of the nineteenth century, it was in the nature of things that the first to incarnate again were those who had previously worked, to a greater or lesser degree, as Aristotelians;

for, as Steiner explains, under the influence of intellectualism the time for a new deepening of spirituality—through the activity of the Platonists on earth—had not yet come. But, if civilization is not to fall into utter decadence, both streams will have to begin working together on the earth from the end of the twentieth century and into the future (GA 240, 18/07/24).

> What today shines in, as it were, through many tiny windows must in the future become a unity through that connection between the leaders of the School of Chartres and the leading spirits of Scholasticism, when the spiritual revival whereby *intellectualism itself is lifted to the spirit* [author's italics] sets in at the end of the twentieth century. [Iibid.]

The respiritualization of culture will only be possible if we, out of our own free will and out of selfless love for the earth and the destiny of humankind, take into our souls the Michael-impulse. For it will demand Michaelic courage to meet and combat the mighty spiritual being Ahriman, who, Steiner states, will 'incarnate' during the third millennium (perhaps even within the very near future). Any effort made towards the realization of a process of spiritualization is anathema to the cold and 'cutting' ahrimanic intellect (see Chapter 17).

Appendix Eleven
Cloning

On 5 July 1996, Dolly the lamb was born. Dolly is a clone. She was created not from the union of a sperm and an egg but out of the genetic material from an udder cell of a six-year-old sheep. The embryologist Ian Wilmut, of the Roslin Institute in Roslin, Scotland, fused the udder cell with an egg from another sheep, after removing all genetic material from the egg. The udder cell's genes 'direct' the egg to grow and develop. The result is Dolly, the identical twin of the original six-year-old sheep!

In her well researched book, *Clones: The Road to Dolly and the Path Ahead*, Gina Kolata, science correspondent to *The New York Times*, shows that the cloning of human beings is now theoretically possible. She quotes Wilmut as saying that human beings could clone themselves, using the same method he had used to clone Dolly.

Kolata raises awesome and profound questions. She highlights the pragmatic approach many scientists have towards the future possibilities of genetic engineering. She rightly points out that our era is said to be devoted to the self, with psychologists and philosophers battling over who can best probe the nature of our identities. 'But cloning pares the questions down to their essence, forcing us to think about what we mean by the self, whether we are genes or not, or, if not, what makes us *us*.'

It is now within the realm of the imaginable to think that, in the not too distant future, 'you could clone yourself and make tens, dozens, hundreds of genetically identical twins'. Such an idea destroys the very notion of the self, of individuality. Is it possible, as the molecular biologist Gunther Stendt suggested in the early 1970s, that 'a human clone would not consist of real persons but merely of Cartesian automata in human shape?' ('Molecular Biology and Metaphysics', *Nature*, 26 April 1974, p. 781).

'Automata in human shape'—egoless beings! Here we see the asuric spirits exerting their power and influence in a very tangible way (see Appendix Seven).

Notes

Key to Abbreviations:
AP   Anthroposophic Press (New York)
RSP Rudolf Steiner Press (London)
GA   *Gesamtausgabe*, the collected edition of Rudolf Steiner's work in the original German.

Note to Prologue (pages 1 to 3)

1. In his book *Rudolf Steiner: Herald of a New Epoch* (AP 1980), Stewart Easton observes that 'when Steiner speaks of the "Mystery of Golgotha" he usually refers to the entire sequence of events from the Baptism to the Ascension of Christ Jesus, though sometimes also he appears to mean only the events from the betrayal at Gethsemane to the Ascension' (p. 89).

Notes to Chapter 1 (pages 4 to 16)

1. See his work *The Celestial Hierarchies*, published by the Shrine of Wisdom (Surrey, 1953). Also contained in C.E. Rolf, *Dionysius the Areopagite on the Divine Names and the Mystical Theology* (SPCK, London 1957).
2. See the collection of lectures by Rudolf Steiner published under the title *The Reappearance of Christ in the Etheric* (AP 1983); also Harald Giersch (Ed.), *Rudolf Steiner über die Wiederkunft Christi* (Verlag am Goetheanum 1991).
3. See *The Mystery of Golgotha* (GA 214) (RSP 1940).
4. See Ita Wegman, 'On the Work of Michael', in *Anthroposophy. A Quarterly Review of Spiritual Science*, Vol. 5, No. 3, 1930.

Notes to Chapter 2 (pages 17 to 21)

1. In *Occult Science—An Outline* and elsewhere, Rudolf Steiner describes the earth-planet as we know it today as being the re-embodiment of an earlier planet, and that this earlier planet had been preceded by two further stages in the evolutionary process. Between each embodiment an intermediary spiritual condition prevailed. According to Steiner, therefore, this earth of ours has already 'worked through' three former

planetary conditions. The first planetary embodiment Steiner calls Old Saturn, the second is described as Old Sun, the third as Old Moon. These designations have nothing directly to do with the planets of our present solar system which are so named.

2. See *The Inner Realities of Evolution* (GA 132, 14/11/11).

Notes to Chapter 3 (pages 22–29)

1. It is interesting to read the First Letter of Peter (5:8) in relation to this.

2. In the same lecture from which it has just been quoted Rudolf Steiner describes how, during the Ancient Sun-evolution, instead of the external visible twelve signs of the zodiac, twelve great beings were present who let their 'words', creative forces, 'ring forth from the depths of the darkness—outer space being, of course, not then filled with light'. In answer to the question 'What kind of words were these?' Steiner answers: 'They were words—the word 'word' is only a makeshift to indicate what is meant here—they were words that told of primeval times, of times that even then were in a remote and ancient past. The twelve were twelve World-initiators. Today we behold standing in the directions of these twelve World-initiators the twelve signs of the zodiac, but from them resounds, for the soul that is open to the whole world, the original being of the Unspoken Word of Worlds, which would take form in the twelve Voices. And while Lucifer alone—I must now begin to speak more in pictures; human words do not in the least suffice—while Lucifer had the impulse to let stream out upon all things the light that was present in him and therewith come to a knowledge of all things, the Christ, on the other hand, gave Himself up to the impression of this Word of the Worlds, received it in its fullness and entirety into Himself, so that this Christ Soul was now the Being that united in Himself all the great secrets of the world that sounded into Him through the inexpressible Word. Such is the contrast that presents itself—the Christ who receives the Word of the Worlds, and the proud Lucifer, the Spirit of Venus, who rejects the Word of the Worlds and wants to found and establish everything with his own light' (GA 137, 12/06/12).

'All subsequent evolution,' Rudolf Steiner says, 'is a direct outcome of what Lucifer and Christ were at that time' (ibid.).

So, whereas Christ received into Himself the all-embracing

World Word, Lucifer, in contrast, was only concerned with knowing and irradiating everything around him with the brilliant light existing, in heroic pride, in his own being.

3. Re. Positivism, see Rudolf Steiner, *The Riddles of Philosophy*, Ch. 5 (GA 18).
4. See also *The World of the Senses and the World of the Spirit* (GA 134).

Notes to Chapter 4 (pages 30 to 46)
1. Cf. *The Spiritual Beings in the Heavenly Bodies* (GA 136, 13/04/12), *The Pre-Earthly Deeds of Christ* (GA 152, 07/03/14), *Christ and the Spiritual World. The Search for the Holy Grail* (GA 149, 30/12/13), *The Four Sacrifices of Christ* (GA 152, 01/06/14).
2. Walter Johannes Stein, *The Ninth Century. World History in the Light of the Holy Grail* (Temple Lodge, London, 1991), p. 267, cf. R. Steiner, GA 149.
3. In a footnote to p. 120 in the 1922 English edition of GA 113 (i.e. *The East in the Light of the West*), we find the following observation: 'It is easy to see how, conformably with the use of the ordinary word "Lucifer", ill will or ignorance may throw calumny on what has been said here; that however cannot prevent those things being stated. Anyone who understands by Lucifer what is meant here must necessarily have other conceptions.'

Notes to Chapter 5 (pages 47 to 75)
1. Steiner goes on to say: 'The luciferic tendency shows itself in everyone who begins to brood over experiences of his/her inner life, and it is extremely powerful in present-day humanity.
2. See Mees, L.F.C., *Drugs, A Danger for Human Evolution?* (Regency Press, London 1973); Berg, Aalt van den, *et al.*, *Rock Bottom* (Hawthorn Press 1990); Dunselmann, R., *In Place of the Self. How Drugs Work* (Hawthorn Press 1996).
3. Speaking in 1919 Steiner states: 'In recent times the tendencies of some artists have been more luciferic—they are the Expressionists; the tendencies of the others have been more ahrimanic—they are the Impressionists' (GA 191, 02/11/19).
4. Cf. O'Neil, George & Gisela, *The Human Life* (Mercury Press 1990).
5. See Emmichoven, F.W., Zeylmans v., *The Reality in Which We Live* (New Knowledge Books 1964), Ch. 3.

6. In his Mystery Plays (GA 14), Steiner has pictured this redemption from several different angles.

7. See *The Guardian of the Threshold*, Scene 8 (GA 14).

8. See also Collison, H., *A Commentary on Rudolf Steiner's Four Mystery Plays* (RSP 1949), p. 96ff. Also Hutchins, Eileen, *Introduction to the Mystery Plays of Rudolf Steiner* (RSP 1984), p. 90ff.

9. See also GA 137, 06/06/12, and GA 254, 23/10/15.

10. Cf. GA 237, 03/08/24, pp. 135 and 146; also GA 240, 20/07/24, p. 173; and GA 176, 04/09/17, p. 97ff.

11. See also *Polarities in the Evolution of Mankind*, GA 197, 25/07/20, p. 73ff.

12. If Lucifer and Ahriman were to be successful then, Rudolf Steiner states, 'the earth could not pass over to the Jupiter existence' (GA 208, 23/10/21).

13. The Dutch painter Hieronymus Bosch (*c.* 1460–1516) has given us a revealing picture of these two kinds of thinking in the middle panel of his triptych *The Temptations of St Anthony*.

14. Typescript. Extract. In: *Anthroposophical News Sheet*, 09/06/40. See also Unger, Georg, *Spiritual Science and the New Nature Forces* (Steiner Book Centre, North Vancouver, n.d.); also Georg Unger, 'The New Forces in Nature and How to Control Them', in *The Anthroposophical Review*, Vol. 2, No. 2, 1980.

15. See also Wilson, M., 'Rudolf Steiner's Last Message', in *Anthroposophical Quarterly*, Vol. 17, No. 2, 1972.

Notes to Chapter 7 (pages 83 to 97)

1. President of the USA, 1913–21. Stewart Easton gives us some idea as to why Steiner was so consistently critical of Woodrow Wilson. See Easton's *Man and World in the Light of Anthroposophy* (AP 1975), pp. 325–31.

2. See Nesfield-Cookson, B.J., *Rudolf Steiner's Vision of Love* (RSP 1994), Ch. 14.

3. On one occasion Steiner also includes the eighteenth century. See GA 194, 17/02/18.

4. One may think here of the wars in Bosnia-Herzegovina and Chechnya.

5. Rudolf Steiner has treated of these matters in his basic work *Knowledge of the Higher Worlds. How is it Achieved?* (GA 10).

6. Steiner reminds us: 'Without thinking one could not possibly

arrive even at a materialistic view of the world. After all, one
has thought out such a view, only one has forgotten to practise
this one particle of self-knowledge: You yourself *think*, and the
atoms cannot think! If only this one particle of self-knowledge
is practised, there is something to hold to; and by holding to it
one will always find that it is not compatible with materialism'
(GA 254, 16/10/16).
7. GA 204. A series of 17 lectures given in Dornach, 2 April–5
June 1921.

Notes to Chapter 8 (pages 98 to 106)
1. Steiner goes on to say: 'A good way of playing into Ahriman's
hands is to exclude everything of the nature of knowledge from
denominational religion and to insist that simple faith is
enough. If one clings to this simple faith, one condemns one's
soul to stagnation and then the wisdom that must be rescued
from Ahriman cannot find entry' (GA 193, 15/11/19).
2. See also GA 133, 14/05/12.
3. In a lecture Steiner gave with the title 'The Michael Path to
Christ', he observes: 'The objective fact is simply this, that in
November 1879, beyond the sphere of the sense-world, in the
supersensible world, that event took place which may be
described as follows. Michael has gained for himself the
power, when human beings come to meet him with all the
living content of their souls, so to permeate them with his
power that they are able to transform their old materialistic
intellectual power—which by that time had become strong in
humanity—into spiritual intellectual power, into spiritual
power of understanding. That is objective fact; it has taken
place. We may say concerning it that since November 1879
Michael has entered into another relationship with humankind than that in which he formerly stood. But it is required
of us that we shall become the servants of Michael' (GA 195,
25/12/19).

Notes to Chapter 9 (pages 107 to 121)
1. GA 185a, 15/11/18. Typescript R 41.
2. However, exceptions are possible; see the second lecture (17/
01/15) in GA 157.
3. Cf. GA 13 (1979), pp. 311–12.
4. 'In our epoch it is the consciousness or spiritual soul that has

developed in us through our ordinary civilization and culture ... In the sixth epoch, however, it is the spirit-self that must
be developed with the souls of men and women ... The nature
of spirit-self is that it must presuppose the existence in human
souls of three characteristics: social life in which brotherliness
prevails, freedom of thought, and pneumatology' (GA 159, 15/
06/15).

Notes to Chapter 10 (pages 122 to 145)
1. 'The kind of spiritual experience that is utilized in the spiritual
   science of anthroposophy would have been impossible if the
   Spirits of Darkness had been victorious, for they would then
   have kept this life and activity in the spiritual regions. It is only
   because of their fall that instead of merely critical, physical
   intelligence and the mediumistic approach, it has been and will
   increasingly be possible to gain direct experience in the spiritual world. It is not for nothing that I recently told you how the
   present age is dependent on spiritual influences to a far greater
   extent than people believe. Our age may be materialistic and
   want to become even more materialistic, but the spiritual
   worlds reveal themselves to human beings in many more places
   than one would think. Spiritual influences can be felt everywhere, though at the present time they are not always good
   ones' (GA 177, 27/10/17, p. 198).
2.   *Wer will was Lebendiges erkennen und beschreiben,*
        Sucht erst den Geist heraus zu treiben,
        Dann hat er die Teile in seiner Hand,
        Fehlt leider! nur das geistige Band.
3. 'What stands before us as a challenge of Michael is that we
   become active in our very thoughts, working out our view of the
   world through our own inner activity. We only belong to the
   Michael Age when we do not sit down inactively and desire to let
   enlightenment from within and from without come to us, but
   when we co-operate actively in what the world offers us in the
   way of experiences and opportunities for observation. If a man
   carries out some experiment, it does not fundamentally involve
   activity; there is not necessarily any activity on his part; it is just
   an event like any other event in nature, except that it is directed
   by human intelligence ... How is man's mental life nowadays
   affected by experiments? There is no active participation, for he
   simply looks on and tries to eliminate activity as much as

possible; he wants to let the experiment tell him everything and regards as fanciful anything that is the outcome of his own inner activity. It is precisely in their scientific ideas that people are least of all in the Michael Age' (GA 219, 17/12/22).

4. Cf. GA 194, 15/12/19, p. 49.
5. Cf. GA 18, Part II, Chapters 2 and 3.
6. 'The term "materialistically-minded spiritualists" may sound odd, but it is a fact that large numbers of spiritualists are much more materialistically-minded than ordinary materialists. The latter say, "There's no such thing as spirit," and they call matter "matter". But a lot of spiritualists are intent upon perceiving spirits materially, either as apparitions of light, as material substance, or through the sense of touch. Such are the nuances of their encounters with spirits, a materializing of the entire spirit world. We must acquire the ability to look for deeper reality than that transmitted by the senses. There is even something quite absurd in the materialistic spiritualist's seeking to see the dead with physical eyes after his own death. To see a dead person, we have to try to see him or her as though we were ourselves dead, that is, of course, without physical eyes' (GA 163, 06/09/15).
7. See Leviton, R., *The Imagination of Pentecost: Rudolf Steiner and Contemporary Spirituality* (AP 1994), Ch. 1 and p. 169.
8. Ibid. In particular Ch. 6.
9. Recorded in *The Bridge over the River*. See Bibliography.
10. First published by The Fellowship Publishing Press Ltd in 1969. Later published by Neville Spearman, Essex.
11. In his preface Canon Pearce-Higgins makes some extremely interesting observations regarding reincarnation. He writes: 'I have been asked to comment on the fact that Frances occasionally refers to reincarnation, since such references may be a stumbling-block to Christian readers, few of whom, unless they are scholars, probably are aware that there was a 500-year tradition of such belief within the early Church itself, mainly in the Alexandrian school, including such names as Clement, Justin Martyr, St Gregory of Nyssa and, most notable of all, Origen, who had a well worked out reincarnational system of belief, which certainly makes sense, and avoids many of the objectionable features of oriental versions. Further, it is far from clear that the Church ever officially rejected such belief, however little the medieval

mind was able to contain it. The Council of Constantinople in AD 353, at which it seems that a corrupt form of Origen's teaching was anathematized, is held by many historians to have been imperfectly constituted—the Pope himself refused to be present—and even Roman Catholics contest its validity as a General Council.

'The Church today has got to face the fact that in our shrunken world, with the eastern cultures on our doorstep, reincarnation is again a life issue ... *Rudolf Steiner, one of the most powerful scientific intellects and spiritual geniuses of our race, in his entirely Christo-centric 'anthroposophy', has reincarnation as central also to his teaching* [author's emphasis] ... We note also that reincarnation was in the air in New Testament times—how could it have been otherwise in the Graeco–Roman culture, heir of the Pythagorean–Platonic tradition, of three thousand years of Egyptian religion, and increasingly making contact with the East? Some of the words attributed to Jesus, notably in connection with John the Baptist, give evidence of the currency of the idea.'

12. The well-known author of highly praised novels—of deep content—such as, for example, *The Echoing Grove* and *The Swan in the Evening. Fragments of an Inner Life.*

13. From Rosamond Lehmann's Foreword to *Letters from our Daughters*, Part 1: 'Sally'. C.P.S. Paper I, published by the College of Psychic Science, n.d.

   The daughters are: Cynthia Sandys's daughter, Patricia, who died suddenly in January 1957, and Rosamond Lehmann's daughter, Sally, who died in Java on Midsummer Eve, 1958.

   In *Letters from our Daughters*, Part 1, the 'letters' are from both daughters, in Part 2 they are from Patricia only.

   A more comprehensive series of letters and 'talks' was published for the first time in 1978 under the title *The Awakening Letters* (Neville Spearman, Jersey). Later an enlarged edition, in two volumes, was published by C.W. Daniels, Saffron Walden.

14. Published by C.W. Daniels, Saffron Walden.

Notes to Chapter 11 (pages 146 to 176)

1. The interested reader is referred to Emil Bock's illuminating book *The Apocalypse of St John* (Christian Community Press 1957).

2. It is instructive to view the contrast between Amfortas and Parzival in Wagner's rendering of the Quest for the Grail in the light of the significance of 'impure' and 'pure' blood. The same applies to Wolfram von Eschenbach's depiction of these two men in his epic *Parzival.*

3. Emil Bock, op. cit. p. 137.

4. Cf. William Blake, text and Plate 6 in *Jerusalem: The Emanation of the Giant Albion.* See also Nesfield-Cookson, B.J., *William Blake. Prophet of Universal Brotherhood* (Aquarian Press 1987).

5. See also St John's Gospel (19:30).

6. From a fragment entitled 'Die Natur'. Translated by Bertha Mueller (*Goethe's Botanical Writings*, University of Hawaii Press 1952). The original runs: 'Ihr Schauspiel ist immer neu, weil sie immer neue Zuschauer schafft. Leben ist ihre schönste Erfindung, und der Tod ist ihr Kunstgriff, viel Leben zu haben.'

7. See Damon S. Foster, *A Blake Dictionary* (Thames & Hudson 1979), p. 363.

8. Barnard Taylor's translation. The original is: '*Das Unbeschreibliche,/Hier ist es gethan;/Das Ewig-Weibliche/Zieht uns hinan.*'

9. See Pelikan, Wilhelm, *The Secrets of Metals* (AP 1973), Ch. 2.

10. Barnard Taylor's translation. The German runs:
   Geheimnisvoll am lichten Tag
   Lässt sich Natur des Schleiers nicht berauben,
   Und was sie deinem Geist nicht offenbaren mag,
   Das zwingst du ihr nicht ab mit Hebeln und mit Schrauben
                                                    [Part I, Scene I]

11. See also Rev. 10:10.

12. As an example of this wisdom Steiner draws our attention, on this occasion, to the wonderful construction of the human thigh bone.

13. In the Gospel of St Luke, Christ's rebuke is even more strongly formulated than in that of St Matthew. Addressing the scribes and Pharisees, Christ says: 'Woe unto you, lawyers! for ye have taken away the key of knowledge: ye entered not in yourselves, and them that were entering in ye hindered' (Luke 11:52). Here those leaders of humankind, including the priesthood, are reprimanded for representing the doctrine that there can be no direct knowledge of the spiritual world and have therefore not

only made no effort to gain such knowledge themselves but have also prevented others from doing so. This reprimand can also be understood to apply to those who hold the key to knowledge of the spiritual world but keep it to themselves, and treat those they lead as though they were too immature to receive such knowledge. To share such knowledge would also mean that the leaders, in this case the priesthood, would no longer have the power over others they previously had had—a Babylonian power. (See also Rudolf Steiner, GA 254, in particular Lecture 1, 10/10/15.)

14. See GA 116, in particular Lecture 6; also Hiebel, F., *The Gospel of Hellas* (AP 1949), pp. 28–31.

15. See John 10:11.

16. See GA 326, 28/12/22, and GA 126, 01/01/11.

17. Extracts from Jeremiah (The New English Bible) 50: 12–13 and 51:25.

18. Emil Bock, op cit., Ch. 10, p. 154.

19. According to the first continent-wide survey by the European Union (reported in *The Times*, 09/10/96), a third of 15- and 16-year-olds in Britain are using drugs. 'The most popular drug by far is cannabis, with 30 per cent of British mid-teenagers saying they use it. LSD was used by 12 per cent ... Less than 1 per cent in Britain have used heroin.'

20. Emil Bock, op. cit., Ch. 10, p. 160.

21. *The Ancient Indian Epoch.* Steiner speaks of humankind going through distinctive evolutionary epochs in what he calls the post-Atlantean period, i.e. the period which came into being after the Flood. In numerical order the epochs described in some detail in *Occult Science* and in numerous lectures are: 1) the Ancient Indian, 2) the Ancient Persian, 3) the old Egyptian-Chaldean, 4) the Graeco-Roman, and 5) the present.

22. 'This becoming younger of humanity is shown in external symptoms ... it is shown by the fact that in Greece, let us say, a man had still to be of a definite age before he could take any part in public affairs. Today we see the claim made by great circles of mankind to reduce this age as much as possible, since people think that they already know in the twenties everything that is to be attained. More and more demands will be made in this direction, and unless an insight arises to paralyse them there will be demands that not only in the beginnings of his twenties a man is clever enough to take part in any kind of parliamentary business in the world, but the 19-year-olds and

18-year-olds will believe that they contain in themselves all that a man can compass.

'This kind of growing younger is at the same time a challenge to mankind to draw for themselves from the spirit what is no longer given by nature' (GA 180, 11/01/18).

23. Even today the term 'horse sense' is used to describe practical, common sense.

24. 'Sickly pale' is the description used in The New English Bible. The word used in the Greek text is *chloros.* Translated literally *chloros* = yellow-greenish, like sulphur. The powerful mephitic odour that sulphur emits when burning is traditionally associated with hell fire.

25. The scorpion is one of the symbols of evil. The sting of its tail is poisonous and causes considerable pain to a person who is stung. Because of the treachery of its bite, the scorpion became a symbol for Judas Iscariot. As a symbol of death through treachery the scorpion often appears in art on the clothes worn by the soldiers (also the banners and shields held by them) who assisted at the Crucifixion of Christ. Fine examples of the 'use' of the scorpion in art can be seen on two of the silver casket panels painted by Fra Angelico (in the Museum of San Marco, Florence).

Notes to Chapter 12 (pages 177 to 182)

1. Cf. GA 104, 29/06/08, and GA 104a, 19/05/09. Also GA 346, *Apokalypse and Priesterwirken* (Dornach 1995). English edition due 1998 (RSP).

2. Cf. GA 346.

3. See also Emil Bock, *The Apocalypse of St John*, Ch. 7; also A. Heidenrich, *The Book of Revelation*, Ch. 6.

4. Cf. Steiner, R., GA 11, *Cosmic Memory. Atlantis and Lemuria*, Chs. 8 and 9; also GA 13, Ch. 4.

Here it is appropriate to note that a powerful 'tool' at the disposal of the black magician is the inverted pentacle. Whereas in the upright position the pentacle is representative of the divine nature of human beings, the microcosm, the inverted pentacle is a sign of the reversal of their true nature. Steiner points out in this connection that 'all evil influences enter the human body through the feet. The black magician makes use of this' (GA 42/245, 14/11/06).

A poignant representation of the inverted pentacle can be seen in the monastery at Hohenberg (Odilienberg) in the

Vosges mountains (Alsace) where there is a series of medieval frescoes depicting the life of John the Baptist. This includes the banquet of Herod, the dance of his step-daughter, Salome, the beheading of John the Baptist, and Salome presenting the head of John to her mother Herodias (Mark 6:21–28). (The author's attention was drawn to the Odilienberg frescoes by Athys Floride—see Bibliography.)

In the fresco depicting Salome dancing before her step-father (whose birthday is being celebrated), her mother, and their guests, Salome is shown—as in other examples of medieval art—performing an acrobatic hand-stand with her head close to, if not on, the ground. She is portrayed in this instance fully draped though in fact she would have been naked (see James Hall, *Dictionary of Subjects and Symbols in Art*).

Salome's dance had a powerful effect on Herod. The Odilienberg fresco shows him with his right arm and hand outstretched towards the space between Salome's legs. The nature of the urges aroused in him could hardly be more clearly indicated.

Now, Salome would have danced before Herod on earlier occasions and Herodias would have observed the effect it had on her husband. On the occasion of his birthday Herod promised Salome 'with an oath' that if she danced before him and his guests he would give her whatsoever she would ask. 'And she, being before instructed of her mother, said, Give me here John Baptist's head in a charger. And the king was sorry: nevertheless for the oath's sake ... he commanded it be given her. And he sent, and beheaded John in the prison. And his head was brought in a charger, and given to the damsel; and she brought it to her mother' (Matt. 14:6–11). See also Mark 6.

To go into detail in regard to Herodias' request that John the Baptist's head should be brought to her on a charger is beyond the scope of these pages. Here it must suffice to mention that she was in possession of black magic forces that had come down to her from her former incarnation as Jezebel, the wife of Ahab. Ahab followed in his father Omri's (ninth century BC) footsteps and adopted the Baal cults from the neighbouring kingdom of the Phoenicians of Tyre and Sidon. Jezebel herself 'played a fanatically active part in the context of the Baal and Astarte cults' (Emil Bock, *King and Prophets*, 'The Genius of Elijah'). The prophet Elijah challenged the nation to decide

either for Baal or Yahveh, for paganism or Judaism. The Baal
priesthood, imbued with vehement hatred against Elijah, and
under the protection of Jezebel, persecuted with great cruelty
all those faithful to Yahveh.

Now, we know from Rudolf Steiner—and this is also clearly
indicated in the New Testament (e.g. Matt. 16:14; 17:10; Mark
6:15; 9:12–13) and in the Old Testament (e.g. Mal. 4:5) that
John the Baptist was the reincarnation of Elijah (see, *inter alia*,
GA 149, 31/12/13). Like Elijah, John was confronted by two
powerful armies; in the New Testament the place of Ahab and
Jezebel is taken by Herod and Herodias. Again, the hate-filled
sorceress was the driving force. (See Emil Bock, *Kings and
Prophets*, Chs. 16 and 17.)

5. 'For the same reason,' Rudolf Steiner says, 'in certain schools of
black magic the followers are taught the horrible and diabolical
practice of gashing living animals with a knife at the precise part
of the body which will generate this or that force in the wielder
of the knife. From the purely external aspect, there are certain
points in common between black magic and vivisection. On
account of its materialism, modern science has need of vivisection. The anti-vivisection movements are inspired by deeply
moral motives. But it will not be possible to abolish vivisection
in science *until clairvoyance has been returned to medicine.* It is
only because clairvoyance has been lost that medicine has had to
resort to vivisection' (GA 94, 02/06/06).

Notes to Chapter 13 (pages 183 to 203)
1. Published under the title *Preparing for the Sixth Epoch* (AP,
1976).
2. See Steiner's lecture of 16/10/18 (GA 182) published in English
with the title 'How do I find the Christ?' in *Anthroposophical
Quarterly*, Vol. 15, No. 2, 1970; Maas, Wilhelm, *Arabismus,
Islam, Christentum: Konflikte und Konvergenzen* (Stuttgart
1991).
3. See Frieling, R., *Christianity and Islam* (Edinburgh, 1978).
4. 'In contrast to Christianity, the spiritual life connected with the
name of Mohammed expresses itself more in abstractions. In
Christianity there are many more descriptions of the spiritual
world than there are in Mohammedanism... Anyone who
observes the spiritual life of Europe will realize, for example,
that our modern way of thinking—the materialistic spirit on

the one side and science with its clear-cut, arabesque-like logic on the other—would not have developed had Arabism not found its way through Europe.' Potent 'influences have had their effect upon European thinking, have moulded it into forms it would not have assumed had Christianity alone been at work. In our modern science there is, indeed, more Arabism than Christianity' (GA 239), *Karmic Relationships*, Vol. 5, 31/03/24, pp. 44–45).

5. The civilization which came into being in, for instance, Córdoba through Arabism from the middle of the eighth century, was incomparably superior to the contemporary civilization of Christian Europe. Cf. Hunke, S., *Allahs Sonne über dem Abendland—Unser arabisches Erbe* (Deutsche Verlags-Anstalt, Stuttgart 1960).

6. Alexandria was founded by Alexander III in 331 BC.

7. See Frieling, R., *Christianity and Islam* (Floris Books, Edinburgh 1979), pp. 101–2.

8. See von Gleich, Sigismund, 'Manifestations of the Jundi Shapur Impulse in the Middle Ages', in *Anthroposophical Quarterly*, Vol. 13, No. 2, 1968; also Steiner, R., *Materialism and the Task of Anthroposophy* (GA 204, 05/06/21).

9. Quoted by B.C.J. Lievegoed in *Mystery Streams in Europe and the New Mysteries* (AP 1982).

10. For the short discussion of the theory of knowledge emanating from Gundeshapur the present author has borrowed heavily from Sigismund von Gleich's work *Geisteswissenschaftliche Entwicklungslinien im Hinblick auf den Impuls von Gundi-Schapur* (J. Ch. Mellinger Verlag, Stuttgart 1966), of which the third chapter has appeared in English (see Note 8 above).

11. See GA 74, *The Redemption of Thinking. A Study in the Philosophy of Thomas Aquinas* (Hodder & Stoughton 1956); also GA 237, 01/07/24. And St Thomas Aquinas, *On the Unity of the Intellect against the Averroists* (Marquette University Press 1968).

12. The full possibility of freedom first appears in the evolutionary process when human beings no longer live—in a semi-dreamlike state—in thoughts 'suggested' to them by outside influences, but realize that they themselves 'construct' and have the experience: 'I think'. It is through this realization that human beings first grasp, in full consciousness, something of their inmost being.

13. See Note 10 above.
14. Cf. GA 103, 25/05/08.
15. 'We see the soul of Harun al Rashid after death moving across from Asia and then, from the West, influencing the later civilization of Europe, doing much to lay the foundations of modern materialism' (GA 239, 31/03/24).
16. Cf. GA 235, 16/03/24; also GA 239, 12/06/24; GA 240, 19/07/24 and 14/08/24. And GA 170, 03/09/16.
17. See Riemeck, Renate, *Glaube. Dogma. Macht. Geschichte der Konzilien* (Stuttgart 1985), Ch. 4.

    In *The Reality in Which We Live* (New Knowledge Books 1964), Zeylmans van Emmichoven writes: 'Originally Christianity had always distinguished between the psychic and the pneumatic being of man so that a clear threefoldness of body, soul and spirit existed. In the text of the Council of AD 869 the pneumatic being of man is not even mentioned and it therefore implies that man merely consists of a body and a soul. Further, if we consider that St Augustine (AD 354–430) speaks of this soul as ever newly created before birth, one readily understands that as a result of the Council of AD 869 the spiritual man was gradually doomed to fade from consciousness' (p. 221).
18. Cf. Krause-Zimmer, Hella, *Erdenkind und Weltenlicht* (Stuttgart 1979), pp. 95–99.
19. Rudolf Steiner speaks of Arabism for the first time in a lecture he gave in Stuttgart in 1908. Among other things he makes the point that if Christ had appeared on earth a few centuries later than He did He would have come too late, as it were, for humanity would have descended too deeply into abstract thought by then. Christ had to come before this impulse had been assimilated by humankind; He had to come when the religious stream could still be saved as a stream leading to belief in the spiritual. It was first after the descent of Christ into the physical world that the impulse issuing from Arabism could be given to Europe. In its passage over to Europe Arabism gave the final impulse to logical thought. Logic, Rudolf Steiner stresses on a number of occasions, can be applied directly to the things of the external sense-world. 'Of itself logical thought can never comprehend, for instance, reincarnation' (GA 105, 16/08/08). The development of logical thought runs parallel with the loss of ancient clairvoyant vision. It was achieved at the cost of this loss. The task before humankind today and in

the future is to regain clairvoyant vision, without, however, losing logical thought. In due course Imagination will be achieved, but logical thought will be retained.

Rudolf Steiner sees modern science arising 'in the sharp contact of Arabism with Europeanism [*Europäertum*] which had already accepted Christianity' (ibid.). Through the Mystery of Golgotha that which is spiritual has been saved, but scientific thought has been gripped by materialism. For example, the reason why Copernicus presented his solar system in a materialistic form, rendering it a dead mechanical rotation, is, according to Steiner, because the Arabian mentality drew it down, as it were, into materialism.

In one of his lectures on the background to the Gospel of St Mark, Rudolf Steiner speaks of the Moon-religion of Yahveh and its reflection in Arabism. 'Taking the moon, contrasted with the sun, as the symbol representing the Yahveh-religion, we may expect that a similar form of belief, by-passing, as it were, the Christ-impulse, would emerge later as a kind of moon-religion. And this is what actually happened. The old Yahveh-religion emerges again after the Christ Event, in the religion of the Crescent, carrying earlier impulses into post-Christian times' (GA 124, 13/03/11).

Beginning in the sixth century AD the religion brought by the Arabians via Africa over into Spain 'represents a re-emergence, in a different form, of the Yahveh-moon religion. The intervening Christ-impulse has been ignored.' What prevailed in Arabism, Rudolf Steiner states, is a kind of synthesis of the wisdom-teachings of the priests of Ancient Egypt and Chaldea and the Yahveh-moon religion of the ancient Hebrews. However, in respect of the teachings of the priests of ancient Egypt and Chaldea, everything connected with clairvoyant perception was discarded and human beings were to rely entirely upon reason and intellectual thinking. 'Old concepts that had been current among the Egyptians and Chaldeans were denuded of their visionary, pictorial content and recast into abstract forms' (ibid.).

Notes to Chapter 14 (pages 204 to 207)
1. In these lectures on the Mexican Mysteries Steiner does not use the term 'Sorat'. That he did not do so may have various reasons; for instance, his main concern is to highlight the

twofold attack of the forces of Lucifer and Ahriman (cf. GA 171, 25/09/16). Moreover, he was not speaking in apocalyptic terms, nor historically in relation to the number 666; hence Steiner uses such an expression as 'ahrimanic in the fullest sense' when describing the revolting practices pertaining in the Mexican Mystery Schools. We may also recall here that elsewhere Steiner speaks of Sorat as 'a being of ahrimanic nature' (GA 184, 11/10/18, p. 77). Another expression Steiner uses, referring to the year AD 666, runs: 'when the ahrimanic powers in all their strength would have brought to a climax the whole pride of materialism' (ibid.). Clearly an attack by Sorat is meant here.

2. See also GA 203, 11/03/21.
3. See Frederic Kozlik's Introduction to the English translation of GA 171.
4. In the lecture of 24 September 1916 Steiner uses the term 'bird'.

Notes to Chapter 15 (pages 208 to 213)

1. *The Templars* (AP, 1960).
2. See Walter Johannes Stein, *The Ninth Century in the Light of the Holy Grail* (Temple Lodge 1991), Ch. 7 'The Grail Lineage'.
3. Pierre Morizot writes in respect of this point: 'The Templars were never guilty of intentional or conscious heresy, but it may be surmised that, owing to the influence of oriental habits of thought (for nearly two centuries the Templars had had close relations with the peoples of the East), they gradually introduced a measure of freedom in the ritual they adopted, a kind of syncretism, though on the practical rather than the philosophical plane. Strict ritual observance meant less to them than access to supersensible reality' (ibid.).
4. A modern historian of the Order reports that, at the time of the trial, 'It was common talk among the older members that the Order had fallen from its purposes since men of learning had entered it.' Edward J. Martin, *The Trial of the Templars* (Allen & Unwin, London 1928), p. 76.
5. Cf. GA 240, 20/7/24.
6. See GA 346.
7. See also GA 22, *Goethe's Standard of the Soul*; also GA 200, 24/10/20.

Notes to Chapter 16 (pages 214 to 231)

1. From 1910 onwards Rudolf Steiner spoke on many occasions of the appearance of the Etheric Christ. For earlier indications see Harald Giersch, *Rudolf Steiner über die Wiederkunft Christi* (Dornach 1991).
2. See Alfred Heidenreich, *The Risen Christ and the Etheric Christ* (RSP 1969).
3. Translation by H. Collison, S.M.K. Gandell and R.T. Gladstone. More recent translations by A. Bittleston (1982) and by Ruth and Hans Pusch (1973).
4. GA 124, 18/12/10.
5. In *Ere the Century Closes*, Tradowsky comments: 'Human beings must have reached a degree of maturity through their repeated earthly lives which enables them to have such an encounter and render it fruitful. It becomes apparent that in the continuous flow of mankind's evolution new soul forces arise which do not stem from the conscious participation of the individual human being. It is an essential characteristic of these new soul forces that they manifest themselves as natural capacities of the human being and no longer can the meeting with Christ proceed out of the personal intention of the individual, but as an act of grace resulting from a decision for this particular individual. Therefore, it might be a tempting thought to assume that conscious esoteric training and practice need play no part in this; but even though these new capacities evolved hidden from mankind, now that they begin to enter consciousness all further development does indeed depend on the conscious participation of the human being. On one occasion Rudolf Steiner expressed this in the following way: "These ... faculties develop in the outer evolution of mankind, but our individualities have to grow into these faculties. The human egos have to learn to understand what it actually is that develops." '

The lecture by Steiner from which Tradowsky quotes is entitled 'Das Wiedererscheinen des Christus im Aetherischen', GA 118, 06/02/10. Not translated.

In a booklet entitled *Flying Saucers: Physical and Spiritual Aspects* (New Knowledge Books 1958), Georg Unger devotes a chapter to the theme of 'meetings' with the Etheric Christ. He relates an example of such a 'meeting' told to him by a friend: 'He was talking to a man who was obviously in a state of great bewilderment. This man had spent a night of prayer beside the bed of his wife, who was dangerously ill. Suddenly a radiant figure entered the room. He knew it was Christ. Next morning he was sure that his wife would recover. "But why should this happen to me ... to me above all men?" he kept asking my friend. "To me, a non-believer?"

'The answer to his question is that not only did Christ come for the sake of all mankind, but from our time onward He will be met in such encounters by more and more people when they are most despondent.'

6. Cf. Damian Thompson, *The End of Time* (Sinclair-Stevenson 1996), in particular his judicious study of the role Vernon Howell (alias David Koresh) played as leader of a fundamentalist sect called the Branch Davidians, established at Mount Carmel outside Waco during the late 1980s and early 1990s.

7. Steiner uses the oriental designation 'Shamballa' to denote the special supersensible realm in which the Etheric Christ will be visible to mankind.

8. See Giersch, H. (Ed.), *Rudolf Steiner über die Wiederkunft Christi*, pp. 107ff.

9. During this three-and-a-half-year civil war some 200,000 people were killed—including 32,000 children. About 2,000,000 people were 'displaced'.

10. In regard to the policy of ethnic cleansing we should not forget that in 1945, after the end of the Second World War, ethnic cleansing took place on a massive scale—it was known by a more euphemistic phrase, 'population transfer'. The victims were Germans. They lived in Silesia which had been German territory before the war, but in 1945 Great Britain and Russia—Churchill and Stalin—agreed that it should be handed over to Poland. Nine million Germans had to leave their land and homes. Two and a half million lost their lives through cold, starvation, epidemics and murder. Many of those who suffered death were women, children and the elderly...

11. Quoted by Peter Tradowsky in *Ere the Century Closes* (Camphill Books 1995).

Notes to Chapter 17 (pages 232 to 244)

1. See Chapter 16.

2. In the lecture of 31/10/20 Steiner points to the profound significance this new experience of the Christ has in regard to

social problems: 'No social question will be solved that is not thought out in connection with [the] spiritual-scientific endeavour that enables the human being to appear in truth once again as a super-earthly being. The solutions to our social problems will be found to the degree in which human beings are able to feel the Christ-impulse in their souls. All other solutions will lead only to destruction, to chaos. For all other solutions are based on the conception of man as an earthly being. The new experience of the Christ will arise out of the attunement [*Gestimmtheit*] of human souls and out of their need.

'*But awareness must all the more be directed towards everything that hinders the approach of this new Christ-experience.*'

3. In a significant Mystery Centre in the east of Asia a special boy was brought up. When he was about 40 years old an important change took place in him. He began to grasp through the faculty of the intellect what previously had been revealed in the Mysteries only through revelation. 'He was the first to make use of the organs of human intellect, but still in association with the Mysteries.' In him Lucifer himself was incarnated. 'We must say: through Lucifer humankind has acquired the faculty of using the organs of his intellect, of his power of intellectual discernment' (GA 193, 04/11/19).

4. *The Work of the Angels in Man's Astral Body.*

5. *Vom Leben des Menschen auf der Erde. Über das Wesen des Christentums* (GA 349). Not yet translated. See also: Stegmann, Carl, *The Other America* (Rudolf Steiner College Press 1997).

6. Carol Adrienne is an intuitive counsellor, writer and lecturer in the field of self-development. Her practice focuses on helping people discover their life-direction.

7. Cf. Meadows's last major speech in Christopher Fry's *A Sleep of Prisoners.*

8. In a lecture Rudolf Steiner gave to members of the Theosophical Society he makes the following pertinent observation in regard to the use of language when speaking or writing about spiritual matters: 'Real materialism prevails even in theosophy itself (e.g. when one describes the etheric or life-body). Whereas one should exert oneself to come to a grasp of the spirit, one mostly describes it as if it were a finer matter, and the astral body also. One starts as a rule from the physical

body, goes further to the etheric or life-body, and says: That is built after the pattern of the physical body, only finer—thus one progresses to Nirvana. Here one finds descriptions which take their images from nothing else than the physical. I have already experienced that when one wanted to express the good feeling present in a room among those present, one did not do so directly, but one said: Fine vibrations are existing in this room. One did not heed that one materializes what exists spiritually in a mood if one thinks the space filled with a kind of thin cloud, permeated with vibrations. That is what I would call the most material way of thinking possible. Materialism has even got by the neck those who want to think spiritually ... As soon ... as one begins to develop spiritual perception ... to speak of things in this way ceases to have any meaning' (GA 117, 04/12/09).

9. I am indebted to Jens Heisterkamp for some of the material to be found in his article 'Remembering what we have known' in a recent issue of the Christian Community Journal, *Perspectives*, Vol. 65, No. 2, 1997.

10. In *News Sheet for Members* of the Anthroposophical Society of Great Britain, Vol. 70, No. 3, 1993.

Notes to Chapter 18 (pages 245 to 264)

1. See p. 70 in the 1969 edition (RSP). In the Foreword to this edition Cecil Harwood writes: 'More than 50 years ago Rudolf Steiner foretold that during the course of the century there would arise in mankind a great need for forms of experience other than and beyond those given by the intellectual logical mind. Our progenitors from the time of Descartes and Bacon, Locke and Newton, believed that they had at last discovered a form of cognition which would release them from the limitations of the past and lead to a full and true knowledge of man and the universe. Today more and more people are experiencing this form of cognition not as a release but a barrier. Side by side with the explorations of outer space there has arisen a longing for spiritual exploration based on the release of deeper powers of the mind and soul. It is true that this exploration often takes facile and even grotesque forms, but the fact that it is so widely present separates the second half of our century from the first perhaps more deeply than all the technical achievements which (on the date of writing this introduction)

have placed the first men on the moon...For two reasons [*Knowledge of the Higher Worlds*] is a sure guide for modern man's spiritual exploration. Firstly, it is based on the clarity of thinking which we owe to the very forms of thought which have separated us from all direct perception of the spiritual beings behind the physical framework, or skeleton, of the universe. The aim of Steiner's method is not to deny but to extend that clear thinking beyond its present limitations. Secondly, it recognizes—as all genuine disciplines have always recognized—that the path to spiritual worlds is an arduous and dangerous one, calling for the utmost self-control in thought and word and deed. Man is a unity, and he cannot develop himself in his life of knowledge without a corresponding, and even greater, development in his life of feeling and will.

'... Many people today ... have some kind of spiritual experience. But they remain mere perceptions. It is only when a person takes the clarity of thinking and judgement which he can win from the proper use of modern consciousness into his direct perception of spiritual forces and beings, that he can evaluate his perceptions, can relate them to each other, and know what he perceives.

2. One may think here of Copernicus, Galileo and Giordano Bruno in science, or Masaccio, Brunelleschi and Donatello in art and architecture.
3. See GA 191, 01/11/19, where Steiner speaks of 'preserving jars', that is, 'libraries and institutions where the various sciences pursued by men and women without really stirring their interest are preserved; these sciences are not really alive in them but are simply preserved in the books on the shelves of libraries.'
4. Steiner discusses these two conditions in some detail in the first lecture of GA 134, i.e. on 27 December 1911.

Notes to Appendix One (pages 273 to 274)
1. See Appendix Six.
2. Alfred Tennyson, *In Memoriam*, cxviii.
3. The spirit-self is identical with what is called, in connection with oriental wisdom, 'manas'.
4. In oriental wisdom called 'budhi' and 'atma', respectively.
5. *Citizens of the Cosmos. Life's Unfolding from Conception through Death to Rebirth* (The Continuum Publishing Com-

pany, New York, 1981), Ch. 9. See also GA 13, Ch. 2, and GA 9, Ch. 1.

Notes to Appendix Two (pages 275 to 276)
1. On literary and astronomical grounds, Ormond Edwards places the Solomon child about twelve months before the Nathan Child. See *The Time of Christ. A Chronology of the Incarnation* (Floris Books 1986).
2. Translated by G.R.S. Mead (University Books, New Jersey, 1974), Ch. 61.
3. See Fred Gettings, *The Hidden Art* (A Studio Vista Book published by Cassell Ltd., London, 1978), Ch. 2. And, in particular, the remarkable work by Hella Krause-Zimmer entitled *Die zwei Jesusknaben in der bildenden Kunst* (Verlag Freies Geistesleben, Stuttgart, 1986).
4. See also Emil Bock, *The Childhood of Jesus* (Floris Books 1997).

Notes to Appendix Three (pages 277 to 284)
1. Text according to the Authorized King James Version. See also Rudolf Steiner, *Genesis. Secrets of the Bible Story of Creation* (GA 122, 17–26/08/10); also Emil Bock, *Genesis. Creation and the Patriarchs* (Floris Books 1983).
2. See Bibliography in *The Grail Seeker's Companion* by John Matthews & Marian Green (The Aquarian Press, Wellingborough, 1980).
   Here, for the most part, reference will be made to Wagner's rendering of the Quest of the Holy Grail as portrayed in his opera *Parsifal*.
3. According to another legend, the Holy Grail is the dish that held the paschal lamb of which Christ and the apostles were partaking at the Last Supper.
4. See Walter Johannes Stein, *The Death of Merlin* (Floris Books 1989), Ch. 7.
5. Ibid.
6. See Note 3, Ch. 13.
7. Ibid.
8. See Elin, L.G., 'The Wound of Amfortas', in *Anthroposophical Quarterly*, Vol. 2, No. 4, 1957 and Vol. 3, No. 1, 1958.
9. See Appendix Six regarding sentient soul, intellectual soul and consciousness (spiritual) soul. Also GA 144, 07/02/13.

10. Amfortas means 'robbed of strength'. See Querido, R., *The Mystery of the Holy Grail* (Rudolf Steiner College Publications 1991), p. 11. See also Wolfgang Greiner, *Gralsgeheimnis*, Ch. 2, 'Die Wunde des Amfortas' (Philosophisch-Anthroposophischer Verlag, Dornach/Switzerland, 1993).
11. GA 107, 01/01/09.
12. In Mohammedan tradition Eblis is the figure we know as Lucifer.
13. See Ch. 12, 'Sorat—the Sun Demon'.
14. Translation from German (Wagner's *Parsifal*) by Andrew Porter.
15. Significantly, Wagner clearly states that the garden and the costumes worn by the maidens should be set in Arabian style.
16. Winkler, Franz E., *For Freedom Destined. Mysteries of Man's Evolution in the Mythology of Wagner's Ring Operas and Parsifal* (Waldorf Press, New York, 1974).
17. Ibid.
18. See GA 10, Ch. 'How is Knowledge of the Higher Worlds Achieved?' Sub-section 'Conditions'.
19. Ibid.
20. Introducing his notes on this work Eliot writes: 'Not only the title, but the plan and a good deal of the symbolism of the poem were suggested by Miss Jessie L. Weston's book on the Grail legend, *From Ritual to Romance.*'
21. There are clearly many different glimpses, from many different standpoints, one can have of the disastrous consequences deeds can have which have been performed either out of misguided impulses or in direct opposition to the Christ/Grail-impulse. Clearly Hitler's thoughts and actions, to mention but one example, can readily be recognized as being in such opposition.

    Shakespeare, ushering in the epoch of the consciousness soul, the spiritual soul, gives a very clear picture of the consequences of a deed performed under the banner of the Anti-Grail in Act II, Scene IV in *Macbeth*. See the conversation between Ross and the Old Man.
22. See Note 13. Walter Johannes Stein in his book on the Holy Grail throws an insightful light on Parzival's failure, on his first visit to the Grail Castle, to ask the vital question of Amfortas, 'What ails thee?' Stein writes: 'What the human being sees when he enters the Grail Castle is himself. It is precisely the question for him when his own being confronts him and asks:

"Brother, what is wrong with thee?" No one else can answer this question—only he himself can do it. For the answer to this Parzival-question is: 'I myself have caused all this suffering that I see here..." Parzival must learn that Amfortas suffers because he, Parzival, has not recognized himself to be the cause of his suffering' (p. 137).

23. As previous Note.

NB For numerous statements by Rudolf Steiner regarding the legend of the Holy Grail and its significance, see *The Holy Grail. From the Works of Rudolf Steiner*, compiled by Steven Roboz (Steiner Book Centre, North Vancouver, Canada, 1979).

Notes to Appendix Four (pages 285 to 289)

1. Rudolf Steiner speaks of seven 'embodiments', seven planetary forms of our earth. The first planetary embodiment is called the Old Saturn, the second is described as the Old Sun, the third as the Old Moon, and the fourth as our earth. These designations have nothing directly to do with the planets of our present solar system. Saturn, Sun, Moon are simply names for the past forms of evolution which our earth has gone through. The earth, in other words, goes through a process of evolution of cosmic proportions. The next embodiment of the earth is called in anthroposophical spiritual science the Jupiter stage. This is further followed by the Venus stage, and, finally, by the Vulcan stage.

2. Valentin Tomberg, *Anthroposophical Studies of the Old Testament* (Candeur Manuscripts, Spring Valley, NY, 1985).

3. To go into further detail in regard to the Spirits of Form (Exusiai) would lead beyond the scope of this study. See GA 13, 1979 edition, pp. 174–81.

4. A further 'counterweight' is represented by the moon. In regard to this complex matter, see GA 254, 17–18/10/15. Also the extensive footnote by the translator of the text from German into English of GA 254 at the end of the fifth lecture. In regard to the role of the moon, see also C.G. Harrison, *The Transcendental Universe* (Temple Lodge 1993), Lecture 5.

5. The first issue of the periodical *Lucifer-Gnosis* brought out by Steiner was at the end of May 1903.

6. Steiner's criticism of A.P. Sinnett's statements about the Eighth Sphere in his book *Esoteric Buddhism*, and of H.P. Blavatsky's conception of that Sphere expressed in *The Secret*

Doctrine, has been omitted here. Those interested to follow up this matter are referred to, in particular, the fourth and fifth lectures in GA 254, and also to GA 172, 27/11/16.

Notes to Appendix Five (pages 290 to 293)
1. See, for instance, GA 10, GA 12, GA 13.
2. The essay was first published in *The Golden Blade*, 1960. A.P. Shepherd (1885–1968) was Archdeacon of Dudley, Canon of Worcester.
3. Baruch Spinoza (1632–77), Dutch philosopher.
4. Published by the Sheffield Educational Settlement, 1957.
5. See GA 10, GA 12, GA 13.

Notes to Appendix Seven (pages 299 to 300)
1. Stewart C. Easton, *Rudolf Steiner: Herald of a New Epoch* (AP 1980), p. 111.
2. See GA 266/1, p. 205.
3. In adulthood the anonymous author of the diary *The Boy Who Saw True*, journeying along the south coast of France and into Monaco, records some of his inner experiences which underline and confirm Steiner's statement in respect of 'dissolute sensuality'. The diarist writes: 'Lovely scenery spoilt by horrid psychic atmosphere. They must have practised a lot of black magic along this coast at one time. Most unpleasant thought-forms left over. Impossible to dissipate them with mediation; might as well light a joss-stick over a cesspool. Came through Marseilles yesterday. A sink of depravity.' The writer then goes on to say: 'Made an interesting observation. There are some altruistic *devas* on the hills behind the place. They absorb all the filthy psychic miasma from the town into themselves, then throw it out again all purified.'
   Of Monte Carlo the diarist comments: 'What a place. Paradise and hell combined! ... The *devas* on these hills are different from those at Marseilles: they sort of shrink from the whole business.'
4. See also Sergei O. Prokofieff, *Prophecy of the Russian Epic* (Temple Lodge 1993), p. 13. Also Nick Thomas, 'Rudolf Steiner's Comments on Energy', in *The Anthroposophical Review*, Vol. 2, No. 2, 1980.

Notes to Appendix Eight (pages 301 to 306)
1. With reference to Steiner's lecture of 16 November 1917, Bernhard Lievegoed, in his book *Man at the Threshold*, writes: 'One meets the ahrimanic Double on the way inward. It works in the unconscious organic processes, particularly in the nerve-senses system, and calls up an excessive will aimed at intelligent control and exploitation of natural forces... The luciferic Double one meets on the way outward, in the temptation of ecstasy.
2. Hutchins, E., *Parzival, An Introduction* (Temple Lodge 1979).
3. In *Occult Science, An Outline*, Steiner writes in some detail of the connection between the Double and the Guardian of the Threshold. See also Frank Linde, 'Der Hüter der Schwelle in der *Geheimwissenschaft im Umriss*', in *Flensburger Hefte* No. 45 (1994). In the same publication see the interview with Werner Barford by Wolfgang Weirauch entitled 'Am Abgrund'.

Notes to Appendix Nine (pages 307 to 317)
1. See also GA 17, Ch. 11.
2. See also Nesfield-Cookson, B.J., *Rudolf Steiner's Vision of Love* (RSP 1994).
3. See Salewski, Wilhelm, *Die Psychoanalyse Sigmund Freud's* (Verlag der Christengemeinschaft 1931).
4. In this connection see, in particular, Rudolf Steiner's fundamental work *How to Know Higher Worlds, A Modern Path of Initiation* (GA 10) (AP).
5. See the Addresses by Rudolf Steiner on 21 and 22 August 1915 (GA 253).
6. Published by Sidgwick & Jackson, London, 1993.
7. The Order had been founded in 1904 by a German Master, Karl Kellner. See Nicholas Goodrick-Clarke, *The Occult Roots of Nazism* (I.B. Tauris 1992).
   It should be noted that, according to John Parker, 'many, if not most of the lodges, secret societies and Orders that followed in Crowley's wake are no more harmful to society than the average Friday night Masonic Lodge meeting.'
8. See also Francke, S., & Cawthorne, T., *The Tree of Life and the Holy Grail* (Temple Lodge 1996), Ch. 18.
9. In *Anthroposophical Quarterly*, Vol. 18, No. 1, 1973.
10. The translation consulted here is by Michael Wilson. The 7th

English edition, 2nd impression (1970). A paperback edition—with identical pagination—was published in 1979.

11. See Rudolf Steiner, *Methods of Spiritual Research* (Multimedia Publishing Corp., New York, 1971), pp. 79–80.

12. See, for instance, Rudolf Magnus, *Goethe as a Scientist* (Collier Books, New York 1961, etc.); Ernst Lehrs, *Man or Matter* (RSP 1986), Ch. 5, 'The Adventure of Reason').

13. p. 70.

14. See GA 232 (1973), p. 12.

15. See Chorus Mysticus at the end of Goethe's *Faust*, Part II.

16. The Asuras (see Appendix Seven) have become powerfully active in the present, the fifth post-Atlantean epoch. They are highly destructive adversarial powers and principally active in the sexual sphere, in the physical body, of the human being. The many sexual aberrations we can witness today are to be traced back to these Spirits of Darkness. See GA 266/1, *Aus Inhalten der esoterischen Stunden* I (Rudolf Steiner Verlag 1995), p. 137.

Notes to Appendix Ten (pages 318 to 322)

1. A good example to illustrate this is Goethe's conception of the Archetypal Plant. *Goethe as a Scientist* by Rudolf Magnus (Henry Schuman 1949) offers a good introduction to Goethe's scientific thinking. See also GA 1 and GA 6.

2. The Cistercian Order was founded in 1098 at Citeaux in Burgundy; the Dominican Order was founded by St Dominic *c.* 1212. It has promulgated the teaching of St Thomas Aquinas. See GA 74.

3. Bernardus Sylvestris, Alanus ab Insulis, John of Salisbury.

4. See GA 74, 22–24/05/20.

5. Rudolf Steiner comments here: 'Earthly terms have to be used for these things, although naturally they are not really in keeping and can easily make one appear ridiculous.'

6. Translation by René Querido in his book *The Golden Age of Chartres* (Floris Books 1987). My italics.

7. Translation by Querido of a passage from a lecture by Rudolf Steiner entitled 'Übersinnliche Erkenntnis und sozialpädagogische Lebenskraft', published in *Die Menschenschule* 1936, Vol. 10. No. 1.

Bibliography

Works by Rudolf Steiner
The GA number identifies the volume of the German collected
edition (*Gesamtausgabe*) containing the original text of Rudolf
Steiner's writings and lectures.
NB Not all English published translations are complete versions of
the original 'GA' volume.

Key to Abbreviations:
AP   Anthroposophic Press (New York)
APC   Anthroposophical Publishing Co. (London)
RSP   Rudolf Steiner Press (London)
RSPC   Rudolf Steiner Publishing Co. (London)
RSPNY   Rudolf Steiner Publications (New York)
SBC   Steiner Book Centre (N. Vancouver)
SGP   St George Publications (New York)
SBNY   Steiner Books (New York)
ANS   *Anthroposophical News Sheet*
AQ   *Anthroposophical Quarterly*
Q   *Anthroposophy. A Quarterly Review of Spiritual Science*

GA	Title
1	*Goethe the Scientist* (AP 1950)
4	*The Philosophy of Freedom* (RSP 1988)
	Also published under the title *The Philosophy of Spiritual Activity* (AP 1986)
6	*Goethe's Conception of the World* (APC and AP 1928)
9	*Theosophy* (RSP 1989)
10	*Knowledge of the Higher Worlds. How is it achieved?* (RSP 1976)
	Also published under the title *How to Know Higher Worlds* (AP 1994)
11	*Cosmic Memory. Atlantis and Lemuria.* (RSPNY 1971)
12	*The Stages of Higher Knowledge* (AP 1974)
13	*Occult Science. An Outline* (RSP 1969)
14	*The Portal of Initiation* (APC 1925)
	The Soul's Awakening (APC 1925)

Various translations of both Mystery Plays have been published since 1925

17   *The Threshold of the Spiritual World* (APC 1956)
18   *The Riddles of Philosophy* (AP 1973)
22   *Goethe's Standard of the Soul* (APC 1925)
26   *Anthroposophical Leading Thoughts* (RSP 1985)
28   *Rudolf Steiner: An Autobiography* (SBNY 1980)
      Previously published under the titles *The Story of my Life* (APC 1925); *The Course of my Life* (AP 1951)
40   *Truth-Wrought-Words and other Verses* (AP 1979)
42/245 *Guidance in Esoteric Training* (RSP and AP 1994)
56   *Brotherhood and the Struggle for Existence* (Mercury Press, NY 1980)
58   *Metamorphoses of the Soul*, Vol. 1 (RSP 1983)
60/61 *Turning Points in Spiritual History* (Garber Communications, Inc, Blauvelt, NY 1987)
74   *The Redemption of Thinking. A Study of the Philosophy of Thomas Aquinas* (Hodder & Stoughton 1956)
78   *Fruits of Anthroposophy* (RSP and AP 1986)
93a   *Foundations of Esotericism* (RSP 1982)
94   *An Esoteric Cosmology* (SGP 1978)
95   *At the Gates of Spiritual Science* (RSP 1979)
99   *Theosophy of the Rosicrucian* (RSP 1966)
102   *The Influence of Spiritual Beings upon Man* (AP 1961)
103   *The Gospel of St John (Hamburg)* (AP 1962)
104   *The Apocalypse of St John* (RSP and AP 1977)
104a *Reading the Pictures of the Apocalypse* (AP 1993)
105   *Universe, Earth and Man* (RSP 1955)
107   *The Deed of Christ and the Opposing Spiritual Powers* (RSP 1954)
      'Evolution, Involution and Creation out of Nothingness' (AQ, Vol. 16, No. 1, 1971)
110   *The Spiritual Hierarchies and their Reflection in the Physical World* (AP 1970)
112   *The Gospel of St John and its Relation to the Other Gospels* (AP 1982)
113   *The East in the Light of the West* (RSP and AP 1940). Quoted from 1922 edition
114   *The Gospel of St Luke* (RSP 1975)
116   *The Christ Impulse and the Development of Ego Consciousness* (AP 1976)

117   *The Ego. The God Within and the God of External Revelation* (RSPC and AP n.d.)

118   *The Reappearance of Christ in the Etheric* (AP 1983). Cf. also GA 130.

119   *Macrocosm and Microcosm* (RSP 1968)

120   *Manifestations of Karma* (RSP 1976)

121   *The Mission of Individual Folk Souls in Relation to Teutonic Mythology* (RSP 1970)

122   *Genesis. Secrets of the Biblical Story of Creation* (APC 1959)

124   *Background to the Gospel of St Mark* (RSP and AP 1985). Quoted from the 1968 edition

126   *Occult History* (RSP 1982)

127   *The Significance of Spiritual Science for Moral Action* (SBC 1978)

129   *Wonders of the World, Ordeals of the Soul, Revelations of the Spirit* (RSP 1963)

130   *The Reappearance of the Christ in the Etheric* (AP 1983). Cf. also GA 118

132   *The Inner Realities of Evolution* (RSP 1953)

133   *Earthly and Cosmic Man* (RSP 1948)

134   *The World of the Senses and the World of the Spirit* (RSP 1947)

136   *Spiritual Beings in the Heavenly Bodies and in the Kingdoms of Nature* (AP 1992)

137   *Man in the Light of Occultism, Theosophy and Philosophy* (RSP 1964)

138   *Initiation, Eternity and the Passing Moment* (AP 1980)

141   *Between Death and Rebirth* (RSP 1975)

143   'Ancient Wisdom and the Heralding of the Christ Impulse' (AQ, Vol. 18, No. 1, 1973)

144   *The Mysteries of the East and of Christianity* (RSP 1972)

145   *The Effects of Spiritual Development* (RSP 1978)

147   *The Secrets of the Threshold* (RSP and AP 1987)

149   *Christ and the Spiritual World and the Search for the Grail* (RSP 1963)

152   *Michaelmas. The Festivals and their Meaning*, Vol. 4 (RSP 1981)

        Occult Science and Occult Development. Christ in the Twentieth Century (RSP 1978)

153   *The Inner Nature of Man and the Life between Death and a New Birth* (APC 1959)

154   *The Presence of the Dead on the Spiritual Path* (AP 1990)

155   *The Spiritual Foundation of Morality. Francis of Assisi and the Mission of Love* (AP 1996). Previously entitled *Anthroposophical Ethics.*

157   *The Destinies of Individuals and of Nations* (RSP and AP 1987)

157a   *The Forming of Destiny and Life after Death* (APC 1927)

159   *How Anthroposophical Groups Prepare for the Sixth Epoch* (AP 1976)

161   'Meditation and Thought Training' (Typescript Z 346, 27/03/15 and 01/05/15). See *Bibliographical Reference List of Rudolf Steiner's Works in English Translation*, Vol. 2, compiled by Craig Giddens (RSP 1979)

165   'The Spiritual Unity of Mankind through the Christ Impulse', 09/01/16 (AQ, Vol. 13, No. 1, 1968)

166   *Necessity and Freedom* (AP 1988)

170   *The Riddle of Humanity* (RSP 1990)

171   *Inner Impulses of Evolution. The Mexican Mysteries. The Knights Templar* (AP 1985)

172   *The Karma of Human Vocation* (AP and RSPC 1944)

174   *The Karma of Untruthfulness*, Vol. 2 (RSP 1992)

174b   'Michael, the Spirit of the Times', 23/02/18 (ANS, Vol. 8, Nos. 43–48, 1940)

175   *Cosmic and Human Metamorphoses* (APC 1926)

176   *The Karma of Materialism* (AP 1985)

177   *The Fall of the Spirits of Darkness* (RSP 1993)

178   *Behind the Scenes of External Happenings* (RSP and AP 1947)
        The Wrong and the Right Use of Esoteric Knowledge (RSP 1966)

180   *Ancient Myths: Their Meaning and Connection with Evolution* (SBC 1971)

182   'How do I Find the Christ?' 16/10/18 (AQ, Vol. 15, No. 2, 1970)

184   *Three Streams in the Evolution of Mankind* (RSP 1965)

185a   'An Historical Foundation for the Formation of Judgement on the Social Question', 15/11/18 (Typescript R 41). See Note to GA 161 above

186	*In the Changed Conditions of the Times* (RSP and AP 1941). Also published under the title: *The Challenge of the Times* (APC 1957)
	'Individual Spirit Beings and the Undivided Foundation of the World', in: *The Reappearance of the Christ in the Etheric* (AP 1983)
187	*How Can Mankind Find the Christ Again?* (AP 1984)
191/193	*The Influences of Lucifer and Ahriman* (RSP 1954)
193	*Some Characteristics of Today* (RSP 1943)
194/196	*Ideas for a New Europe* (RSP 1992)
194	*The Mission of the Archangel Michael* (AP 1961). Also in: *The Archangel Michael. His Mission and Ours* (AP 1940)
195	'The Michael Path to Christ', 25/12/19, in: *Michaelmas. The Festivals and their Meaning*, Vol. 4 (APC 1957)
197	*Polarities in the Evolution of Mankind* (RSP 1987)
198	'The Blood-relationships and the Christ-relationships', in: *Easter. The Festivals and their Meaning*, Vol. 2 (APC 1956)
200	*The New Spirituality and the Christ Experience of the Twentieth Century* (RSP and AP 1988)
201	*Man—Hieroglyph of the Universe* (RSP 1972)
202	*The Bridge Between Universal Spirituality and the Physical Constitution of Man, Freedom and Love* (AP 1958)
203	*The Responsibility of Man for World Evolution through his Spiritual Connection with the Planet Earth and the World of Stars*, third lecture 11/03/21 (Typescript R 62)
	'Spirit Triumphant', in: *Easter. The Festivals and their Meaning*, Vol. 2 (APC 1956)
204	*Materialism and the Task of Anthroposophy* (AP 1987)
207	*Cosmosophy*, Vol. 1 (AP 1985)
208	'On the Development of Consciousness from the Graeco–Latin Epoch to our Time and the Intervention of Supersensible Beings', 23/10/21 (Q, Vol. 6, No. 4, 1931)
209	*Cosmic Forces in Man* (APC 1948)
210	*Old and New Methods of Initiation* (RSP 1991)
211	*Knowledge and Initiation* (RSP 1936)
214	*The Mystery of Golgotha* (RSP 1940)
217	*The Younger Generation* (AP 1976)
218	*Man's Life on Earth and in the Spiritual Worlds* (APC 1952)

219   *Man and the World of the Stars. The Spiritual Com-*
       munion of Mankind (AP 1963)
220   'Concerning Electricity' (Typescript ANS 09/06/40)
221   *Earthly Knowledge and Heavenly Wisdom* (AP 1991)
222   *The Driving Force of Spiritual Powers in World History*
       (SBC 1972)
223   *The Cycle of the Year* (AP 1984)
       Anthroposophy and the Human Gemüt (AP 1946.
       Republished with the title *Michaelmas and the Soul
       Forces of Man* (AP 1982)
226   *Man's Being, His Destiny and World Evolution* (AP 1966)
227   *The Evolution of Consciousness* (RSP 1966)
232   *Mystery Knowledge and Mystery Centres* (RSP 1973)
233   *World History in the Light of Anthroposophy* (RSP
       1977)
233a   'A Michael Lecture', 13/01/24, in: *Michaelmas. The
       Festivals and their Meaning*, Vol. 4 (APC 1957)
235   *Karmic Relationships*, Vol. II (RSP 1974)
237   *Karmic Relationships*, Vol. III (RSP 1977)
238   *Karmic Relationships*, Vol. IV (RSP 1983)
       The Last Address (RSP 1967)
239   *Karmic Relationships*, Vol. V (RSP 1984)
240   *Karmic Relationships*, Vol. VI (RSP 1971)
       Karmic Relationships, Vol. VIII (RSP 1975)
243   *True and False Paths of Spiritual Investigation* (RSP and
       AP 1985)
253   *Community Life. Inner Development. Sexuality and the
       Spiritual Teacher* (AP 1991)
254   *The Occult Movement in the Nineteenth Century* (RSP
       1973)
266/1 *Aus den Inhalten der esoterischen Stunden* (Rudolf
       Steiner Verlag 1995)
275   *Art as Seen in the Light of Mystery Wisdom* (RSP
       1984)
305   *The Spiritual Ground of Education* (APC 1947)
307   *A Modern Art of Education* (RSP 1972)
322   *The Boundaries of Natural Science* (AP 1983)
326   *The Origins of Natural Science* (RSP and AP 1983)
332a   *The Social Future* (AP 1972)
346   *Apokalypse und Priesterwirken* (Rudolf Steiner Verlag,
       Dornach, 1995). English edition due 1998 (RSP).

Methods of Spiritual Research (Multimedia Publishing Corp., New York, 1971)

Other Authors

Key to further Abbreviations
CCP   Christian Community Press
DKF   Die Kommenden, Freiburg i. Br.
FB   Floris Books, Edinburgh
FHV   Flensburger Hefte Verlag, Flensburg
GWA   *Das Goetheanum Wochenschrift für Anthroposophie*, Dornach
HP   Hawthorn Press, Stroud, Glos.
MP   Mercury Press, New York
SGP   St George Publications, New York
TL   Temple Lodge Publishing, London
VG   Verlag am Goetheanum, Dornach
VU   Verlag Urachhaus, Stuttgart

Alexander, J., *Mephistopheles' Anvil. Forging a More Human Future* (Rose Harmony Publications, Spring Valley, New York, 1996)

Anon (introduced by Cyril Scott), *The Boy who Saw True* (C.W. Daniel, 11th impression, 1994)

Aquinas, Thomas, *On the Unity of the Intellect against the Averroists* (Marquette University Press 1968)

Arenson, A., *Lucifer* (MP 1992)

Barfield, O., 'Israel and the Michael Impulse' (AQ, Vol. 1, No. 1, 1956)

Beckh, H. 'Die zweite Runde des Sonnen-Rhythmus: Neue Stufe des Johannes-Opfers', in *Der kosmische Rhythmus im Markus-Evangelium* (VU 1997)

Ben-Aharon, J., *The Spiritual Event of the Twentieth Century* (TL 1996)

Benesch, F., *Apokalypse* (VU 1981)

Bennell, M., 'What is truth?' (AQ, Vol. 11, No. 3, 1966)

Berg, A. den, *et al.*, *Rock Bottom* (HP 1990)

Betti, M., *The Sophia Mystery in our Time* (TL 1994)

Black, D., *The Computer and the Incarnation of Ahriman* (SGP 1981)

Blavatsky, H.P., *Isis Unveiled* (Theosophical University Press, Pasadena, California, 1972)

—*The Secret Doctrine* (Theosophical University Press, Pasadena, California, 1974)

Bloom, H., *Omens of Millennium* (Fourth Estate 1996)

Bock, E., *The Apocalypse of St John* (CCP 1957)

—*Genesis. Creation and the Patriachs* (FB 1983)

—'Michael and Man' (Q, Vol. I, No. 3, 1926)

Boogert, A., 'Facing Michael', in *The Threshing Floor*, Oct/Nov. 1990

Bos, L., *Anthroposophie, Mystik und New Age—Metamorphosen der Wahrheit* (VG 1996)

Buddemeier, H., *Illusion and Manipulation* (VU 1987)

—'Zwischen virtueller Realität und sozialer Wirklichkeit. "Das Medium"' (GWA, Vol. 75, No. 24, 1996)

—'Zwischen virtueller Realität und sozialer Wirklichkeit. Eine Geschichte der medialen Verführung' (GWA, Vol. 75, No. 25, 1996)

Capel, E.F., *The Reappearing of Christ* (FB 1983)

—*Pictures from the Apocalypse* (TL 1989)

Carlgren, Fr., 'Symptome der kommenden Inkarnation Ahrimans' (GWA, Vol. 75, No. 27, 1996)

Collins, M., *Light on the Path.* First published by the Theosophical Society in the 1880s

—*The Wheel of Eternity* (Neville Spearman, London, 1974)

Collison, H., *A Commentary on Rudolf Steiner's Four Mystery Plays* (RSP 1949)

Debus, M., Wolfgang Weirauch *et al., Moderne Spiritualität* (VU 1997)

Derry, E.F., 'A Study on *The Michael Mystery*' (AQ, Vol. 2, No. 3, 1957)

Derry, E. & S., 'The Meaning of Freedom' (AQ, Vol. 4, No. 3, 1959)

Deverell, D., *Light Beyond the Darkness* (TL 1996)

Dieckmann, R., 'Michaels Wirken im Denken' (FHV, Vol. 26, 1989)

Dumke, K., *AIDS the Deadly Seed* (RSP 1991)

Dunselmann, R., *In Place of the Self. How Drugs Work* (HP 1996)

Easton, S.C., *Man and World in the Light of Anthroposophy* (AP 1975)

—*And Another Strong Angel* (Rudolf Steiner Institute, USA, 1979)

—*Rudolf Steiner. Herald of a New Epoch* (AP 1980)

—*The Evolution of Human Thinking* (Rudolf Steiner Institute, USA, 1984)

Edwards, O., *The Time of Christ. A Chronology of the Incarnation* (FB 1986)

Elin, L.G., 'The Wound of Amfortas' (AQ, Vol. 2, No. 4, 1957, and Vol. 3, No. 1, 1958)

Emberson, P., *From Gondishapur to Silicon Valley. Spiritual Forces in the Development of Computers and the Future of Technology* (Etheric Dimensions Press 1997)

Emmichoven, R.W. Zeylmans van, 'Rudolf Steiner and Community among Men in the Future' (AQ, Vol. 6, No. 4, 1961)

—*The Reality in Which We Live* (New Knowledge Books 1964)

Floride, A., *Der Weg zu den Hierarchien. Das Ziel der Entwicklung: Die vierte Hierarchie* (VG 1996)

Foster, D.S., *A Blake Dictionary* (Thames & Hudson, 1979)

Francke, S., and Cawthorne, T., *The Tree of Life and the Holy Grail* (TL 1996)

Franzen, O., 'Ein Sieg über den Sorat', in *Mitteilungen aus der Anthroposophischen Arbeit in Deutschland*, Vol. 4, No. 162, 1987

Frieling, R., *Christianity and Islam* (FB 1978)

—*Old Testament Studies* (FB 1987)

—*New Testament Studies* (FB 1994)

Gaedeke, W., *Anthroposophie und die Forderung der Religion* (FHV 1990)

Gettings, F., *The Hidden Art* (Cassel, London, 1978)

Giersch, H., *Rudolf Steiner über die Wiederkunft Christi* (VG 1991)

Gleich, S. Von, *Geisteswissenschaftliche Entwicklungslinien im Hinblick auf den Impuls von Gondischapur* (J. Ch. Mellinger Verlag 1966)

—'Manifestation of the Jundi Sabur Impulse in the Middle Ages' (AQ, Vol. 13, No. 2, 1968)

—*The Sources of Inspiration of Anthroposophy* (TL 1997)

Goodrich-Clarke, N., *The Occult Roots of Nazism* (I.B. Tauris, London, 1992)

Greaves, H., *Testimony of Light* (The World Fellowship Press 1969)

—*The Wheel of Eternity* (Neville Spearman, London, 1974)

Greiner, W., *Gralsgeheimnis* (Philosophisch-Anthroposophischer Verlag, Dornach, 1993)

Gulbekian, S., *At the Grave of Civilization?* (TL 1996)

Gunning, J., 'Deliver us from the Evil One' (AQ, Vol. 13, No. 4, 1968)

—'The Occult Movement in the Nineteenth Century' (AQ, Vol. 19, No. 1, 1974)

Harrison, C.G., *The Transcendental Universe* (TL 1993)

Haub, H.-W., '*Liebt das Böse—Gut*' (VG 1996)

Heaf, D., 'The Cloning of Dolly the Sheep', in *New View*, 3rd Quarter, 1997

Heidenreich, A., *The Book of Revelation* (FB 1977)

—*The Risen Christ and the Etheric Christ* (RSP 1969)

Heisterkamp, J., 'Remembering What we have Known', in *Perspectives, The Christian Community Journal*, Vol. 65, No. 22, 1997

Heyer, K., *Wesen und Wollen des Nationalsozialismus* (Perseus Verlag, Basel, 1991)

—*Rudolf Steiner über den Nationalismus* (PVB 1993)

Hillringhaus, F.H., *Das Ende unseres Jahrhunderts und die Aufgaben der Rosenkreuzer* (DKF 1969)

—*Die Heutigen Forderungen Michaels an den Menschen* (DKF 1970)

—*Die Neugestaltung Anthropos. Arbeitszusammanhänge im Hinblick auf ihre michaelische Zukunftsaufgabe* (DKF 1971)

—*Der Sturz der Geister der Finsternis und das Michael–Christus–Mysterium* (DKF 1976)

Ho, Mae-Wan, *Genetic Engineering. Dream or Nightmare?* (Gateway Books, Bath, 1998)

Hutchins, E., 'The Appearance of the Etheric Christ in our Time', in *Anthroposophical Review*, Vol. 6, No. 2, 1984.

—'The Michael Age before Christ and Today' (AQ, Vol. 18, Nos. 3 and 4, 1973)

—*Introduction to the Mystery Plays of Rudolf Steiner* (RSP 1984)

Jocelyn, B., *Citizens of the Cosmos* (The Continuum Publishing Co., New York, 1981)

Kniebe, W., *Michael* (Geering Verlag 1984)

Kolata, G., *Clones. The Road to Dolly and the Path Ahead* (Allen Lane 1997)

Krause-Zimmer, H., *Erdenkind und Weltenlicht* (Verlag Freies Geistesleben, Stuttgart, 1979)

—*Die Zwei Jesusknaben in der bildenden Kunst* (VFG 1986)

Krück von Poturzyn, M.J., *Der Prozess gegen die Templar* (Verlag Freies Geistesleben 1963)

Lees, J., 'Psychoanalysis and Spiritual Psychology', in *Anthroposophy Today*, No. 22, Summer 1994

Lehmond, R., & Cynthia Lady Sandys, *Letters from our Daughters*, Parts I and II (The College of Psychic Science, London, n.d.)

Lehrs, E., *Man or Matter* (RSP 1986)

Leviton, R., *The Imagination of Pentecost. Rudolf Steiner and Contemporary Spirituality* (AP 1994)

Lievegoed, B.J., *Man at the Threshold* (HP 1960)

—*Towards the 21st century—Doing the Good* (SBC 1972)

—*Mystery Streams in Europe and the New Mysteries* (AP 1982)

Linde, F., 'Die Hüter der Schwelle in der Geheimwissenschaft im Umriss' (*Flensburger Hefte*, No. 45, 1994)

Lindholm, D., *Encounters with Angels* (FB 1993)

Lloyd, D., 'The Battle Against Spiritual Powers of Hindrance', in *Anthroposophy Today*, No. 17, 1992

Maas, W., *Arabismus, Islam, Christentum* (VU 1991)

Magnus, R., *Goethe as a Scientist* (Collier Books, NY, 1961)

Manen, H.P. van, *Twin Roads to the New Millennium* (RSP 1988)

—'Die Verkörperung der Gegenmächte in der Sicht Rudolf Steiners' (GWA, Vol. 74, Nos. 46 and 47, 1996)

Masters, B., *The Evil that Men Do* (Transworld Publishers, London, 1997)

Mead, G.R.S. (tr.), *Pistis Sophia* (University Books, New Jersey, 1974)

Mees, L.F.C., *Drugs. A Danger for Human Evolution?* (Regency Press, London, 1973)

Moody, R., *Life after Life* (Mockingbird Books, NY, 1975)

—*Reflections on Life after Life* (Mockingbird Books, NY, 1977)

Nelson, J.B., & Longfellow, S.P., *Sexuality and the Sacred. Sources for Theological Reflection* (Mowbray, London, 1994)

Nesfield-Cookson, B.J., *William Blake. Prophet of Universal Brotherhood* (Thorsons 1987)

—*Rudolf Steiner's Vision of Love* (RSP 1994)

Nordmeyer, B., *Ein Bild der künftigen Erde: Gedanken zur Apokalypse* (VU 1985)

O'Neil, G. & G., *The Human Life* (MP 1990)

Oulton, R., *Some Thoughts about the Confluence of Two Streams at the End of the 20th Century. The Platonist and the Aristotelian* (unpublished manuscript)

Parker, J., *At the Heart of Darkness* (Sidgwick & Jackson, London, 1993)

Pelikan, W., *The Secrets of Metals* (AP 1975)

Perkins, D., 'Robert Owen—Servant of Michael', in *The Christian Community Journal*, No. 3, 1971

Pickstone, C., *For the Fear of Angels—How Sex has Usurped Religion* (Hodder & Stoughton 1997)

Pfeiffer, E.E., *The Spiritual Leadership of Mankind* (MP 1985)
—*The Task of the Archangel Michael* (MP 1985)

Poppelbaum, H., *The Battle for a New Consciousness* (MP 1993)

Prokofieff, S.O., *The Twelve Holy Nights and the Spiritual Hierarchies* (TL 1988)
—*Prophecy of the Russian Epic* (TL 1993)
—*The Heavenly Sophia and the Being Anthroposophia* (TL 1996)

Querido, R.M., *The Golden Age of Chartres* (FB and AP 1987)
—*The Mystery of the Holy Grail* (Rudolf Steiner College Publications, USA 1991)

Reuveni, A., 'Hinter der Maske des Patriotismus. Widersacher Mitteleuropas im 20. Jahrhundert' (GWA, Vol. 72, Nos. 31/32, 1993)
—'Anthroposophie versus Ariosophie' (GWA, Vol. 74, No. 22, 1995)
—*In the Name of the 'New World Order'* (TL 1996)

Reynolds, A., 'Some Thoughts on Waco', in *News Sheet for Members of the Anthroposophical Society in Great Britain*, Vol. 70, No. 3, 1993

Riemeck, R., *Glaube, Dogma, Macht. Geschichte der Konzilien* (VU 1985)

Ritchie, G., *Return from Tomorrow* (Fleming H. Revell, USA, 1978)

Roboz, S. (compiler), *The Holy Grail. From the Works of Rudolf Steiner* (SBC 1979)

Rodger, I., 'Freedom from Sexuality', in *Anthroposophy Today*, No. 2, 1986

Roszell, C., *The Near-Death Experience* (AP 1992)

Roth, P., 'The Duality of Evil' (AQ, Vol. 12, No. 3, 1967)

Salewski, W., *Die Psychoanalyse Sigmund Freuds* (Verlag der Christengemeinschaft 1931)

Schmidt-Brabant, M., *Michael-Gedanken und Drachen-Kräfte* (VG 1992)

Schneider, J.W., *Michael* (Rudolf Geering-Verlag 1981)

Schoeffler, H.H., *The Academy of Gondishapur* (MP 1995)

Schroeder, H.W., *Der Mensch und das Böse* (VU 1984)

Schroff, L., *The Archangel Michael* (Newlight Books, Virginia, USA, 1990)

Schultz, F., *Zeichen der Zeit* (VG 1996)

Schütze, A., *The Enigma of Evil* (FB 1978)

Seddon, R. (Comp. and Ed.), *The End of the Millennium and Beyond. From the Work of Rudolf Steiner* (TL 1993)

Shepherd, A.P., 'The Incarnation' (AQ, Vol. 4, No. 4, 1959)

—'The Trinity in Man and Nature', in *The Golden Blade* 1960

—'The Battle for the Spirit. The Council of Constantinople', in *The Golden Blade* 1963

The above articles have been republished under the title *The Battle for the Spirit. The Church and Rudolf Steiner* (Anastasi 1994)

Smit, J., *How to Transform Thinking, Feeling and Willing* (HP 1989)

Spangler, D., *Channelling in the New Age* (Mornington Press, Issaquah, 1988)

Stegmann, C., *Das andere America* (VG 1991). Published in English under the title *The Other America* (Rudolf Steiner College Press, Fair Oaks, California 1997)

Stein, W.J., *The Death of Merlin* (FB 1989)

—*The Ninth Century. World History in the Light of the Holy Grail* (TL 1991)

Talbott, S.L., *The Future does not Compute. Transcending the Machines in our Midst* (O'Reilly & Associates, Sebastopol, USA, 1995)

Tautz, J., *Der Eingriff des Widersachers, Fragen zum Okkulten Aspekt des Nationalsozialismus* (DKF 1976)

—*Menschheit an der Schwelle: Die apokalyptische Sprache des Jahrhunderts* (VU 1980)

Thomas, N., *The Battle for the Etheric Realm* (TL 1995)

—Rudolf Steiner's Comments on Energy', in *The Anthroposophical Review*, Vol. 2, No. 2, 1980)

Thompson, D., *The End of Time* (Sinclair-Steveson, London, 1996)

Tomberg, V., *Anthroposophical Studies of the Old Testament* (Candeur Manuscripts, Spring Valley, New York, 1985)

Tradowsky, P., *Ere the Century Closes* (Camphill Books 1995)

—*Kaspar Hauser: The Struggle for the Spirit* (TL 1997)

—*Christ and Antichrist* (TL 1998)

Trine, R.W., *In Tune with the Infinite* (George Bell & Sons, London, 1899)

Unger, G., *Flying Saucers: Physical and Spiritual Aspects* (New Knowledge Books 1958)

—*Spiritual Science and the New Nature Forces* (SBC n.d.)

—'The New Forces in Nature and How to Control Them', in *The Anthroposophical Review*, Vol. 2, No. 2, 1980

Usher, S.E., *Geistesforschung und New Age. Über ein bemerkenswertes Buch* (GWA, Vol. 74, No. 5, 1995)

Wachsmuth, G., *Bilder und Beiträge zur Mysterien- und Geistesgeschichte der Menschheit* (Verlag Emil Weises Buchhandlung, Dresden, 1938)

Wagner, A., *Nationalokkultismus*, Part 1 (FH, No. 40, FHV 1993)

—*Nationalokkultismus*, Part 2 (FH, No. 41, FHV 1993)

Waterman, J., 'Bacon and Modern Science', in *The Golden Blade*, 1962

Wegman, I., 'On the Work of Michael' (Q, Vol. 5, No. 3, 1930)

Weirauch, W., 'Michael im Kampf mit dem Bösen' (FH, No. 41, FHV 1989)

—'Über Mediumismus und Spiritismus' (FH, No. 13, FHV 1992)

—'Über die Menschenrassen in der Darstellung Rudolf Steiners' (FH, No. 41, FHV 1993)

—'Schwarze und weisse Magie' (FH, Sonderheft, No. 12, GHV, 1993)

Welburn, A., 'Learning from Islam' (*The Threshing Floor*, Oct./Nov. 1990)

Wetzl, J. (tr.), *The Bridge over the River. After Death Communications of a Young Artist who Died in World War I* (AP 1995)

Wilson, M., 'Rudolf Steiner's Last Message' (AQ, Vol. 17, No. 2, 1972)

—'The Cosmic Intelligence and the School of Michael' (AQ, Vol. 23, No. 2, 1978)

Winkler, F.E., 'About Marijuana' (AQ, Vol. 15, No. 3, 1970)

—*For Freedom Destined. Mysteries of Man's Evolution in the Mythology of Wagner's Ring Operas and Parsifal* (Waldorf Press, New York, 1974)

Zaehner, R.C., *Zen, Drugs and Mysticism* (University Press of America 1989)